THE BRITISH
Diaspora, Culture

Of Related Interest

International Diplomacy and Colonial Retreat
edited by Kent Fedorowich and Martin Thomas

The Statecraft of British Imperialism
Essays in Honour of Wm. Roger Louis
edited by Robert D. King and Robin W. Kilson

Managing the Business of Empire
Essays in Honour of David Fieldhouse
edited by Peter Burroughs and A.J. Stockwell

Emergencies and Disorder in the European Empires after 1945
edited by Robert Holland

Margery Perham and British Rule in Africa
edited by Alison Smith and Mary Bull

Empire Building and Empire Builders
Edward Ingram

Industrialisation and the British Colonial State
West Africa 1939–1951
Lawrence J. Butler

Cecil Rhodes and the Cape Afrikaners
The Imperial Colossus and the Colonial Parish Pump
M. Tamarkin

Ethnic Labour and British Imperial Trade
A History of Ethnic Seafarers in the UK
Diane Frost

Imperialism, Academe and Nationalism
British and University Education for Africans
Apollos O. Nwauwa

THE BRITISH WORLD:
Diaspora, Culture and Identity

Editors
CARL BRIDGE
King's College London

and
KENT FEDOROWICH
University of the West of England

Routledge
Taylor & Francis Group

LONDON AND NEW YORK

First published in 2003 in Great Britain by
Routledge
2 Park Square, Milton Park, Abingdon, Oxon, OX14 4RN
270 Madison Ave, New York NY 10016

Transferred to Digital Printing 2010

Website: www.routledge.com

British Library Cataloguing in Publication Data

The British world: diaspora, culture and identity
  1. National characteristics, British 2. Great Britain –
  Colonies – Social life and customs 3. Great Britain –
  Colonies – History 4. Great Britain – Colonies – Social
  Conditions 5. Great Britain – Emigration and
  immigration I. Bridge, Carl II. Fedorowich, Kent, 1959–
  III. The journal of imperial and commonwealth history
  305.8′20171241

ISBN 0 7146 5472 8 (cloth)
ISBN 0 7146 8377 9 (paper)

Library of Congress Cataloging-in-Publication Data

The British world: diaspora, culture, and identity / editors Carl Bridge and Kent Fedorowich.
  p. cm.
"This group of studies first appeared in a Special Issue on 'The British World:
Diaspora, Culture and Identity' of The Journal of Imperial and Commonwealth
History (ISSN 0308-6534) 31/2 (May 2003) published by Routledge" – T.p. verso.
Includes bibliographical references and index.
  ISBN 0-7146-5472-8 (cloth) – ISBN 0-7146-8377-9 (pbk.)
  1. Great Britain – Colonies – History. 2. Great Britain – Colonies
– Emigration and immigration – History. 4. Group identity – Great
Britain – Colonies – History. 5. Commonwealth countries – Civilization.
6. National characteristics, British. 7. Great Britain – Civilization.
I. Bridge, Carl. II. Fedorowich, Kent, 1959– III. Journal of Imperial
and Commonwealth History. IV. Title
  DA16.B697 2003
  909′.0971241 – dc21

2003006468

This group of studies first appeared as a special issue of *The Journal of Imperial and
Commonwealth History* (ISSN 0308-6534), Vol.31, No.2, May 2003,
published by Routledge.

Publisher's Note
The publisher has gone to great lengths to ensure the quality of this reprint
but points out that some imperfections in the original may be apparent.

Contents

Mapping the British World

CARL BRIDGE and KENT FEDOROWICH

Father, Mother, and Me,
Sister and Auntie say,
All the people like us are 'We',
And every one else is 'They'.

Rudyard Kipling, 'We and They' (1926).[1]

For two generations the major thrust of imperial historians has been to develop an understanding of the processes behind the acquisition, administration and exploitation of the non-white empire and its subsequent decolonisation. This is reflected in the balance of the new five-volume *Oxford History of the British Empire*, where the colonies of white settlement are given a supporting rather than a central role.[2] There have been three monumental documentary series over the last 35 years – *The Transfer of Power in India* and *Burma* and the *British Documents on the End of Empire Project* – but there is none on the changing relations with the old Dominions.[3] Of the 30-odd monographs of the 'Cambridge Commonwealth Series' only a quarter concentrate specifically on the new Britains of Canada, Australia, New Zealand and South Africa, while in the 50-plus volumes of John M. MacKenzie's 'Studies in Imperialism' series only a handful do so. This was not always the case. The nine-volume *Cambridge History of the British Empire*, first conceived in the 1920s, was dedicated overwhelmingly to the 'white' Dominions, as was the now much ignored *Survey of British Commonwealth Affairs* series whose five volumes appeared between 1937 and 1974.[4] Before that, they were the theme of the great nineteenth-century foundation works of imperial history written by Sir Charles Dilke and Sir John Seeley, which were concerned with 'Greater Britain' and the 'Expansion of England'.[5]

The dominant explanatory concepts of the Robinson and Gallagher school – 'informal empire', the 'official mind' and 'collaboration' – are of limited use when applied to the colonies of white settlement, particularly once they had become self-governing Dominions and ultimately constitutional co-equals.[6] Even the useful concepts of 'metropole' and 'periphery', first broached by David Fieldhouse, failed to comprehend adequately the dynamic that there was a multiplicity of metropoles and peripheries in the core British world. Think of the emerging importance of cities such as Melbourne, Auckland and Toronto, which barely rate a mention in his work.[7] Next was the concept of 'gentlemanly capitalism', introduced in 1980 by P.J. Cain and A.G. Hopkins, which had the virtue of acknowledging the importance of the settler colonies. However, it was narrowly elitist in focus and economically deterministic. It also downplayed the crucial human dimension of empire.[8] These were errors to which the once very fashionable Marxist historians of the empire were also prone. In his Ford Lectures of 1974 an older and wiser Gallagher called for a broadening of the analytical field to include domestic, colonial and international dimensions in all their complexity.[9] A similar note was echoed by Fieldhouse ten years later when he lamented that imperial history was threatened with fragmentation as a result of the popularity of area studies which was driving the discipline into distinct but constricting national and regional foci.[10] Similarly, a more reflective Hopkins has sounded the tocsin warning us that we must look 'back to the future' and re-integrate the imperial dimension into national histories.[11] Recent Saidian social approaches[12] exploiting the notion of the colonial 'other' have virtually nothing to say about the encounters millions of British migrants had with earlier generations of people who were curiously very much like themselves but also quite different. These were James Belich's 'neo-Britons' – those the Toronto *Globe* in 1901 called 'the Britons of Greater Britain'.[13] The gauntlet is being picked up by a wider international community of scholars from various traditions who have convened at two conferences on 'The British World: Diaspora, Culture and Identity' in London and Cape Town in 1998 and 2002, some of the fruits of which are gathered in this volume.[14]

For too long imperial historians have lived in a self-imposed ghetto into which many influences from outside have barely penetrated. On the other hand, for their part British historians have remained too England-centric and have not properly taken up J.G.A. Pocock's 1974 challenge to integrate the rest of the peoples of the home islands and of the British overseas into their accounts.[15] The intense debate sparked by domestic British historians such as Linda Colley on what it is to be 'British'[16] may have caused a wry smile on the faces of Australian and Canadian 'national' historians who have been dealing in the history of identity formation for decades. But it was a wake-up call both to historians of Britain and to historians of the empire. The delineation of Britishness as understood across the old Dominions is a relatively new avenue of enquiry. The adjective 'British', however, seems first to have gained popular currency in eighteenth-century North America where colonists of mixed English, Welsh, Scottish and Irish origin needed a common term to describe their heritage,[17] the central symbol of which was their common allegiance to the British Crown. Despite these straws in the wind, the idea of examining the British Empire as a phenomenon of British migration and mass settlement – as a key·element in the development of 'Britishness' – has yet to be properly taken up. In 1999 Pocock could still beseech us to remember that, 'There was a British world, both European and oceanic, in the nineteenth and twentieth centuries: it had a history', which remained to be written.[18]

The writing is now in progress. The British world was a phenomenon of mass migration from the British Isles. Its core was the 'neo-Britains' where migrants found they could transfer into societies with familiar cultural values. As trans-oceanic and trans-continental travel and communications improved, so this world became more intricately inter-connected and self-defining, reaching its apogee in the period from the 1880s to the 1950s. Membership of this world did not preclude, indeed it encouraged, economic competition, political conflict and contested identities, which in turn attempted to forge an overarching consensus. In other words, being British anywhere meant exercising full civil rights within a liberal, pluralistic polity, or at least aspiring to that status. 'Whiteness' was a dominant element. Nevertheless, this world was not exclusively white. People from many ethnic backgrounds (both white and non-white) eagerly adopted British identity and were accepted to varying degrees as part of the British world, within the white Dominions, elsewhere in the empire, and to some extent even outside it. It was characteristic of this complex entity that it contained within itself the means of its own disintegration even as it continued to evolve. Arguably, the commonality of values is still present. Historians of the British world are beginning to map its contours, using among other means, the three key vectors of diaspora, culture and identity. A new, but strangely familiar, face of empire is emerging.

What is needed then, to begin with, is a fresh look at the British 'diaspora', or more accurately in most cases the British 'dispersal', for most migrants were not cast out from Britain but left voluntarily in order to better their lots.[19] This included the Irish. In a stimulating re-examination of Irish migration to the British Empire, Andy Bielenberg argues that the Irish were eager participants in British colonial expansion overseas. For example, between 1630 and 1775 the net migration from Ireland to British North America and the West Indies was an estimated 165,000 souls; 40,000 of whom comprised the largest flow of white migration to the West Indies between the mid-seventeenth and early eighteenth centuries.[20] The reintegration of the Irish into the 'British' imperial project is as interesting as it is controversial, for clearly the Irish were not always passive victims in this colonising process.[21]

With the loss of the 13 American colonies in 1783 and the birth of the second British Empire, migration from the United Kingdom remained crucial in buttressing a scattered and beleaguered British community in what remained of Britain's North American possessions. It is estimated that 22.6 million people left the British Isles between 1815 and 1914. This flood of mostly voluntary British migrants dwarfs the estimated 1.4 million Europeans who migrated to the New World between 1500 and 1783.[22] True, the United States remained the main beneficiary of this flow of settlers from all parts of the British Isles throughout the nineteenth century – estimated at 62 per cent.[23] Nonetheless, there are some interesting trends that demonstrate how important British migration was in reinforcing the sense of Britishness in the colonies of white settlement. Half a million Irish (mostly Protestant) moved to British North America between 1815 and 1845, to be followed by a third of a million more after the Great Famine. In fact, between 1815 and 1865 Irish emigrants outnumbered the combined total of English, Scottish and Welsh arrivals.[24] When New Zealand was opened up to largely English migrants between 1839 and 1850, access to information about the new colony was crucial to prospective emigrants. Eager to make an informed judgement, information flows concerning the availability of land, climatic conditions and job prospects helped to sustain the growing tide of migrants to imperial destinations throughout the nineteenth and twentieth centuries.[25]

Canada remained the favoured destination for British migrants until about 1870. The termination of transportation to the eastern Australian colonies in the 1840s and 1850s helped to reduce some of the negative publicity previously associated with free migration there. Gold strikes in the Antipodes in the 1850s and 1860s were a huge positive stimulus to increased voluntary migration. But it was the opening of the Suez Canal in 1869, combined with bigger steam-propelled ships, which shortened journey times and allowed these far-flung communities to compete for more British migrants. These changes, coupled with aggressive state-subsidised migration programmes sponsored particularly by New Zealand, Queensland and South Australia in the 1870s and 1880s, gave an increasing number of adventurous Britons from the home islands the opportunity to migrate further afield but yet remain within the British world. Emboldened by self-government and growing in political and economic confidence, Australia, Canada and New Zealand at the turn of the twentieth century were more assertive in attracting growing numbers from Britain's 'surplus' population. For the decade 1900–09 an estimated 1,670,198 migrants left Britain. In 1913 alone, the staggering number of 389,394 British migrants headed overseas, an increasing proportion for destinations within the British Empire.[26]

These trends, which continued after 1918 and were strengthened by the Empire Settlement Act of 1922, saw 1,811,553 Britons migrate overseas during the decade 1920–29. The 'constructive' imperialism in the 1920s, the bedrock of which was a state-assisted migration policy involving Britain and three of its Dominions (the exception was South Africa), confounds the myth that it was only the introduction of strict immigration quotas by the United States that made the Dominions more attractive to British migrants. As Stephen Constantine has so ably demonstrated, there were more explicit reasons for the material rise in the proportions choosing imperial destinations, 'a lift from barely one-third in the later nineteenth century to around four-fifths' by 1949.[27] Between 1946 and 1963 this proportion rose to five-sixths and some 1,034,000 migrated to the old Dominions.[28] Thus the British 'diaspora' or 'dispersal' focused primarily on the United States prior to 1900, but then shifted ever more decisively to the 'white' Dominions providing the foundation of a 'Third British Empire' as the twentieth century progressed.

In the neo-Britains these migrants helped to construct a wider British identity and culture – a broader Britishness some of which was exported back 'Home'. Examples can be found readily in political culture. Peter Marshall has called for a study of the ideas about the ordering of society, which were developed in the empire and beamed back to Britain, to complement existing work on the projection of political and administrative models onto the empire.[29] Nowadays forgotten or never known, these were in fact many and significant. In the 1840s, Canada, not Britain, was first to define responsible government. By the 1850s, five of the six Australian colonies had developed the secret ballot, more than ten years before it was introduced in the United Kingdom. In 1893, New Zealand women were the first in the empire to gain the vote, a generation before their sisters in Britain. The schools in the Australian colony of Victoria were 'secular, compulsory and free' well before their counterparts back home. Universal manhood suffrage was established in Australia and New Zealand 50 years before it was in the United Kingdom. These new Britannias, or better Britains, had no established church, they controlled migration and wage policies, resorted to state intervention for the provision of utilities, and adopted simplified land title arrangements. The colonies of settlement often put into practice what the reformers in Britain itself merely talked about. Even imperial preferences (the Fielding Tariff of 1897) and Empire Day (1899) were Canadian innovations. Many of the central principles of modern British democracy were experimented with in the colonies of settlement and shipped back to the United Kingdom. The 'unofficial mind' of the British Canadians, British Australians and British New Zealanders was what counted in this process, not the thinking of increasingly marginalised British officials. As a result, the 'rights of freeborn Englishmen' attained higher levels of democratic development in the neo-Britains than in their country of origin.

The rise of colonial national identities did not contradict or undermine imperial Britishness. One person might have a number of concurrent identities. Just as in Britain one could be a Liverpudlian, Lancastrian, Englishman and Briton, so in New Zealand one might be an Aucklander, North Islander, New Zealander and Briton.[30] Beyond the core of the ethnic British diaspora there was the possibility of adopted Britishness. For instance, Aboriginal peoples, Afrikaners, French Canadians, Jews, Cape Coloureds, Hong Kong and Singapore Chinese, and West Indians all laid claim to British values and institutions.[31] Some did so with unseemly haste, such as the Transvaal lawyers Daniel Oosthuizen and A.L. Reitz who described themselves as 'British' in the roll of the Southern Mounted Rifles as early as 1911.[32] Even those who contested the established order, such as Irish Catholics, did so using British means and methods: trade unions, law courts, free press and speech, and the political process.[33] In principle, the system was colour and class blind, and often, though by no means always, it was in practice. For instance, Australia's first native-born governor-general, Sir Isaac Isaacs (1931–36), was a Jew, as was its first Army commander in the Great War, Sir John Monash. The great exception, of course, was the restriction of non-white immigration into the Dominions by such means as language or dictation tests (the 'Natal formula'), quotas, capitation taxes, and health and sanitation regulations.[34]

The cultural glue which held together this British world consisted not only of sentiment and shared institutional values but also of a plethora of networks. These ranged from the obvious family and community connections to business, religious, educational, scientific and professional associations, to trades unions, and to itinerant workers of all kinds – transported convicts, miners, seamen, indentured labourers, domestic servants, travelling players, soldiers and administrators. The extent and influence of these networks – globalisation from below, or at least from lower down than the commanding heights – has barely been explored let alone mapped.[35] A promising start has been made, however, with humanitarian and administrative networks between the 1820s and 1840s;[36] with scientists in South Africa in the early twentieth century;[37] with elements of the professional middle class such as engineers, civil servants and accountants;[38] with philanthropic agencies, such as the Red Cross;[39] and with women's organisations such as the Victoria League, the Guild of Loyal Women of South Africa, and the Canadian Imperial Order Daughters of the Empire.[40] Press barons, railway and shipping magnates, captains of industry – 'ungentlemanly capitalists' to a man, such as the Canadians, Sir Samuel

Cunard and Lord Beaverbrook, and the Australian Essington Lewis (chairman of Broken Hill Proprietary) – were local Rhodeses born in the empire. They made careers which to one extent or another spanned it and depended on it. No 'prefabricated' white colonist 'collaborators' these, they were principal participants in the British world. Robinsonian collaboration is irrelevant not only for the Rhodeses, but also for almost everybody else in the British world. Collaboration is about 'us' and 'them', but the British world was emphatically about 'we'.

We need to understand what our generation sees as a paradox, that this British world was bound more tightly together even as it threatened to come apart. Steam navigation, rail and eventually air travel made connections easier.[41] Trans-oceanic cables, overland telegraph and then telephone and wireless technology rendered communications more efficient.[42] The empire of the airwaves brought London ever closer as an imperial metropole and, if only occasionally, brought overseas imperial cities (in themselves regional metropoles) closer to London.[43] The potential strength inherent in these connections was not lost on Lord Burnham, owner of the London *Daily Telegraph*, when he declared in 1920 that 'The British world is a world of its own, and it is a world of many homes.'[44]

The crises of war and depression brought the British world together even as they sowed the seeds of its eventual unravelling. There is more than a little truth in G.K. Chesterton's observation that the countries of the empire (by which he meant essentially the Dominions) were like passengers on a London omnibus. They did not talk to each other unless there was an accident (such as the Great War) but then they pulled together in the common cause.[45] At the beginning of the twentieth century, in a dress rehearsal for what was to come, Australia, Canada and New Zealand raised 31,500 men for the imperial forces fighting the Boers in South Africa.[46] In the First World War the old Dominions provided 1.3 million troops and India 953,000 to Britain's 6.1 million; in the second, the respective figures were 2.5 million, 2 million and about 6 million. Moreover, it is insufficiently realised that in the Second World War the British Commonwealth had more men in the fighting line than the Americans at all stages before the summer of 1944. Further, Britain would have starved but for the great dominion granaries in both wars.[47] The significance of the British world's contribution is indisputable, but in what ways it variously contributed and on what terms would reward further research. Also what should we make of the remark made by a 'prominent American' with regard to the old Commonwealth family members that 'they all write home to mother often enough, but not to one another'?[48] To answer these questions we need to know much more about the networks that bound together the British world beyond the mother country.

It is important to understand that though there is, and was, much overlap between them, the British world is a broader and more fluid concept than the British Empire or British Commonwealth, and that it casts a longer shadow. Britishness outside Britain persists well beyond the demise of the British Empire. Also, Charles Dilke, Winston Churchill and others included the United States in their Greater Britain (or English-speaking union of peoples) and certainly, in terms of shared values and aims, the Americans at some crucial or convenient junctures have identified themselves as honorary 'Britons', as in the two world wars.[49] Other places not painted red on the map had their British communities, most noticeably in South America, but also in places like Shanghai.[50] The British world was a consensual association that included much of the formal and informal empire. The much more familiar empire of compulsion and subordination had limited relevance in this context.

Co-operation, equality and autonomy rather than coercion became the watchwords in Anglo-Dominion relations after 1918. Granted, some Dominions pursued these goals and asserted their claims with greater alacrity than others. Canada, South Africa and the Irish Free State, the fifth and newest Dominion (created in December 1921) were quicker off the mark than their seemingly more contented Antipodean cousins.[51] Despite resistance from some of the more reactionary sections of the British political establishment (like Lord Curzon who tried unsuccessfully to orchestrate a common imperial foreign policy) these elements were forced begrudgingly to accept the Dominions' quest for full nationhood. Still, at exactly this time, as John Darwin has correctly argued, the concept emerged of a new world-system – a Third British Empire – which focused almost exclusively on Britain's relations with its 'old' Dominions. This also involved a parallel awakening of a 'Britannic' identity, which proved increasingly attractive to a growing number of politicians across the empire. Although the Dominion Idea was shaken by the Great War and Great Depression, Darwin posits that during the inter-war period there was 'a shared belief among British communities around the world in the supreme attractiveness of their institutions, ethos, literary culture, and forms of civility [which] remained extraordinarily pervasive'.[52] The balance of the British world was, however, shifting.

The changing relative importance of the various metropoles can be assessed roughly by looking at when the British world's population and economy beyond Britain came to be of any significance relative to Britain's own. The combined population of the 'old' Dominions was a quarter of Britain's in 1901, just under half in 1931 and just under four-fifths in 1961; while their combined GDP was less than half Britain's in 1901, approaching two-thirds in 1931 and nearing parity in 1961.[53] In the councils of Empire-

Commonwealth, Britain was the first amongst an increasingly powerful and restless set of equals.

A symptom of this growing strength was the undermining of a previously self-confident 'Britannic' identity. This can be demonstrated by examining the collapse of the concept of imperial citizenship. For generations, Australians, Canadians, New Zealanders and (some) South Africans saw no need to define a separate citizenship. They had always been British subjects by definition. In 1935 the Irish Free State was the first Dominion to assert and define its own citizenship when it passed the Irish Nationality and Citizenship Act which classified all non-Irish subjects, including British, as aliens. This was seen as an anomaly within the newly emerging Commonwealth and Whitehall seemingly paid little attention to this petulant piece of legislation. The legal doctrine of the 'indivisibility of subjecthood' remained intact.[54] The real revolution began in 1946 when Canada introduced its own Citizenship Act, under which Canadians remained British subjects but only by dint of being Canadian citizens first. 'Indivisibility of subjecthood', which had long helped to underpin the British world, was now irrevocably severed. Australia, New Zealand and South Africa followed suit in 1948–49.[55] London's response was the British Nationality Act of 1948 that introduced a complex formula involving six categories of citizenship. This Act was not, as some have argued, a deliberate attempt to 'racialise' future British immigration policy; rather, it was meant to maintain the essence of the pre-1946 arrangements, including the right of all British subjects to enter Britain. In other words, it kept the door open for subsequent waves of non-white migration into Britain in the 1950s.[56] Conversely, long-standing restrictions on non-white migration into Canada, Australia and New Zealand were liberalised in the 1960s. South Africa was another story.

Another indication of the undermining was the rapid turnaround in the connotations of the term 'British' in official discourse. In 1939 Australia's Prime Minister, R.G. Menzies, spoke of the 'entire British world' standing up to Nazi Germany, and his successors John Curtin and Ben Chifley habitually used the odd but telling phrase, 'the British-speaking race'.[57] However, there was no doubting that the Dominions were in this war on their own terms and for their own reasons. Vincent Harlow, the Rhodes Professor of Imperial History in the University of London who had been seconded to the Ministry of Information, warned the BBC against broadcasting that the Dominions were fighting to defend the mother country as 'they look upon the war as their concern as much as ours'. During the war the BBC ruled that for broadcasting purposes the term '"British troops" cover[ed] troops from all parts of the Empire' and that when referring solely to troops from the home islands the correct term was 'United Kingdom troops', though this clumsy usage never really took hold.[58] Twenty years later, in June 1961, British Prime Minister Harold Macmillan instructed the civil service in the United Kingdom to replace the term 'United Kingdom Government' in official papers with the term 'British Government'. He argued that 'British' was no longer an appropriate adjective to use to describe Canadians, Australians and other erstwhile overseas Britons.[59]

The term dominion fell out of official use in 1949, though it persisted in popular parlance for some years.[60] The process of de-dominionisation – not to be confused with independent behaviour – was in most cases a more drawn out affair.[61] Legal and symbolic ties were eroded over several decades. The exceptions were Ireland and South Africa, which left the Commonwealth in 1948 and 1961 respectively. Canada abolished Privy Council appeals in 1949. Australia began the process in 1968 and concluded it in 1986. New Zealand has only announced the intention to do so. In 1952, Canada styled the monarch the Queen of Canada. Twenty-one years later, Elizabeth II was styled Queen of Australia. In 1965, the senior Dominion replaced its old flag, the union jack, with a new one featuring a maple leaf. It patriated its constitution in 1982. Imperial honours were abandoned in Australia in 1975 and in New Zealand in 1996; Canada had done it in the 1920s. Australia's High Court finally pronounced that Britain was legally a 'foreign' country in 1999! Nonetheless, the Crown remains a central part of the constitutions of Australia, Canada and New Zealand.[62]

Menzies, in his final years as Australia's prime minister, and a proud 'old Commonwealth' man, regretted the birth of the new Commonwealth in the early 1960s. He saw only a 'cluster of republics' which were 'more spiritually akin to Moscow than to London'. For Menzies, the end of the 'Crown Commonwealth' (those countries which acknowledged the British monarch as their head of state) finished the 'intimate association' which had prevailed before 1948 and still clung on until the matter was finalised by South Africa's leaving in 1961. Thereafter the new Commonwealth became, in Menzies' words, 'much looser' than the old, an 'association' which 'for most of its members' was now only 'functional and occasional'. This old 'intimate association' was not merely sentimental. Wayne Reynolds has shown recently that the old firm of Australia, Canada, South Africa and New Zealand co-operated closely to help Britain develop a Commonwealth atomic bomb in the early 1950s. The Suez crisis of 1956 and its aftermath, however, meant that this 'Fourth British Empire' fell to pieces almost as soon as it was started. Thereafter, to use Robert Holland's term, Britain sought its 'nuclear apotheosis' by other, non-Commonwealth, means. And the Commonwealth, under its new secretariat from 1965, in David McIntyre's term, 'de-Britannicized'.[63]

The British world was a term its inhabitants used to describe their real and imagined common origins, culture and identity. Its maximum strength was reached in the generation prior to the Great War and was probably sustained until the 1950s. Its civic and governmental institutions were moulded in the long nineteenth century and successfully defended in two world wars. It was held together not just by ties of trade, finance, and defence, but also by intricate and overlapping networks and associations of all kinds – family, occupational, professional, educational, religious, and sporting to name a few. Moreover, many of these are still with us today. Scholarly constructions of empire have had little if nothing to say about this British world over the last 50 years and we are only now beginning to turn our attention to its character and dynamics. Blinded by national historiographies and mesmerised by the exotic colonial 'other' we have lost contact with what was always the heart of the imperial enterprise, the expansion of Britain and the peopling and building of the trans-oceanic British world. It is time we reacquainted ourselves with what was once considered both vitally important and self-evident.

NOTES

1. *Rudyard Kipling's Verse: Inclusive Edition, 1885–1932*, 4th edn (London, 1937), 743–44. This poem was first published by Kipling in his *Debits and Credits* (London, 1926).
2. For a critique see Phillip Buckner, 'Was there a "British" Empire? *The Oxford History of the British Empire* from a Canadian Perspective', *Acadiensis*, 32 (2002), 110–28. A similar line of argument is explored by Andrew Thompson, 'Is Humpty Dumpty Together Again?', *Twentieth Century British History*, 12 (2001), 9–23. Also see Dane Kennedy's explication, 'The Boundaries of Oxford's Empire', *International History Review*, 23 (2001), 604–22. Other reviews include D.A. Low, 'Rule Britannia. Subjects and Empire. The Oxford History of the British Empire', *Modern Asian Studies*, 36 (2002), 491–503.
3. One partial exception is Frederick Madden (ed.), *Select Documents on the Constitutional History of the British Empire and Commonwealth*, vols.4 and 6 (Westport, CT, 1990 and 1993).
4. Volume one of *The Cambridge History of the British Empire* was published in 1929 with most of the subsequent volumes appearing in the 1930s. The exceptions were volumes two and three, which were published in 1940 and 1959 respectively. The first two volumes of the five-volume *Survey of British Commonwealth Affairs*, published in 1937 and 1942 respectively, were written by W.K. Hancock and dealt with the inter-war period, especially problems of nationality (vol.1) and the economy (vol.2). Volumes three and four were written by Nicholas Mansergh and appeared in 1952 and 1958 respectively. They focused on problems of external policy in the 1930s and on wartime co-operation and post-war change (1939–52). The final volume (vol.5) was written by J.D.B. Miller and appeared in 1974. Its remit was decolonisation and the emerging Commonwealth between 1953 and 1969.
5. Sir Charles W. Dilke, *Greater Britain: A Record of Travel in English-Speaking Countries during 1866 and 1867*, 2 vols. (London, 1868); Sir John R. Seeley, *The Expansion of England* (London, 1883).
6. Ronald Robinson and John Gallagher with Alice Denny, *Africa and the Victorians* (London, 1961); and Ronald Robinson, 'Non-European Foundations of European Imperialism: Sketch for a Theory of Collaboration', in Roger Owen and Bob Sutcliffe (eds.), *Studies in the Theory of Imperialism* (London, 1972), 117–42.
7. David Fieldhouse, *Economics and Empire 1830–1914* (London, 1974).

12 THE BRITISH WORLD

8. P.J. Cain and A.G. Hopkins, *British Imperialism*, vol.1 *Innovation and Expansion, 1688–1914* (London, 1993); vol.2 *Crisis and Deconstruction, 1914–1990* (London, 1993). See also Raymond E. Dummett (ed.), *Gentlemanly Capitalism and British Imperialism* (London, 1999).
9. J. Gallagher, *The Decline, Revival and Fall of the British Empire: The Ford Lectures and other Essays* (Cambridge, 1982). Since then, several imperial historians have accepted the challenge. Two of the best examples are John Darwin, 'Imperialism and the Victorians: The Dynamics of Territorial Expansion', *English Historical Review*, 112 (1997), 614–42; and Andrew S. Thompson, *Imperial Britain: The Empire in British Politics c.1880–1932* (London, 2000).
10. David Fieldhouse, 'Can Humpty-Dumpty be put together again? Imperial History in the 1980s', *Journal of Imperial and Commonwealth History*, 12 (1984), 9–23.
11. A.G. Hopkins, 'Back to the Future: From National History to Imperial History', *Past & Present*, no.164 (1999), 198–243.
12. Edward W. Said, *Orientalism* (New York, 1978); and, for example, Martin Daunton and Rick Halpern (eds.), *Empire and Others: British Encounters with Indigenous Peoples, 1600–1850* (London, 1999); Catherine Hall, *Civilising Subjects* (Cambridge, 2002); and Lynette Russell (ed.), *Colonial Frontiers: Indigenous–European Encounters in Settler Societies* (Manchester, 2001). David Cannadine, *Ornamentalism: How the British saw their Empire* (London, 2000) promises much and adds little to the debate. An exception in the growing literature on the colonial 'other' is the stimulating work assembled by Frederick Cooper and Ann Laura Stoler (eds.), *Colonial Cultures in a Bourgeois World. Between Nation and Colony: Rethinking a Research Agenda* (Berkeley, 1997).
13. James Belich, 'Neo-Britains', paper delivered to the conference on 'The British World: Diaspora, Culture and Identity', Institute of Commonwealth Studies, London, June 1998. He has recently developed this theme in his two-volume history of New Zealand, *Making Peoples. A History of the New Zealanders. From Polynesian Settlement to the End of the Nineteenth Century* (Auckland, 1996), and *Paradise Reforged: A History of the New Zealanders. From the 1880s to the year 2000* (Auckland, 2001), by which time 'neo-Britains' had become 'better Britains'. Toronto *Globe*, 25 Sept. 1901, cited in Phillip Buckner's chapter below. J.G.A. Pocock coined the phrase 'neo-Britains' in his 'British History: A Plea for a New Subject', *New Zealand Journal of History*, 8 (1974), 3–21.
14. Stuart Ward, 'The British World', *Australian Historical Association Bulletin*, no.94 (June 2002), 30–33; P.A. Buckner and Carl Bridge, 'Reinventing the British World', *Round Table*, 92 (2003), 77–88.
15. Pocock, 'British History'. Also see the revised version and debate in the *Journal of Modern History*, 47 (1975), 601–28.
16. Linda Colley, 'Britishness and Otherness: An Argument', *Journal of British Studies*, 31 (1992), 309–29; idem, *Britons: Forging the Nation, 1707–1837* (New Haven and London, 1992). For a critique of Colley's thesis see J.C.D. Clark, 'Protestantism, Nationalism, and National Identity, 1660–1832', *Historical Journal*, 43 (2000), 249–76. Post-colonialists and political scientists have been busy defining 'Britishness' as well. See Bill Schwarz (ed.), *The Expansion of England: Race, Ethnicity and Cultural History* (London, 1996); Keith Robbins, *Great Britain: Identities, Institutions and the Idea of Britishness* (London, 1998); David McCrone, 'Unmasking Britannia: The Rise and Fall of British National Identity', *Nations and Nationalism*, 3 (1997), 579–96; Rebecca Langlands, 'Britishness or Englishness? The Historical Problem of National Identity in Britain', *Nations and Nationalism*, 5 (1999), 53–69; Ben Wellings, 'Empire-Nation: National and Imperial Discourses in England', *Nations and Nationalism*, 8 (2002), 95–109.
17. Nicholas Canny, 'The Origins of Empire: An Introduction', *Oxford History of the British Empire*, vol.1 *The Origins of Empire* (London, 1998), 24–25.
18. J.G.A. Pocock, 'The New British History in Atlantic Perspective: An Antipodean Commentary', *American Historical Review*, 104 (1999), 490–500. Pocock's article was one of five in the AHR forum and was written largely in response to David Armitage's, 'Greater Britain: A Useful Category of Historical Analysis?', ibid., 427–45.
19. See below the essay by Stephen Constantine, 'British Emigration to the Empire-

Commonwealth since 1880: From Overseas Settlement to Diaspora?'. See also Robin Cohen, *Global Diasporas: An Introduction* (London, 1997).

20. Andy Bielenberg, 'Irish Emigration to the British Empire, 1700–1914', in Andy Bielenberg (ed.), *The Irish Diaspora* (London, 2000), 215–16.

21. Hiram Morgan, 'An Unwelcome Heritage: Ireland's Role in British Empire-Building', *History of European Ideas*, 19 (1994), 619–25; Keith Jeffery (ed.), *An Irish Empire? Aspects of Ireland and the British Empire* (Manchester, 1996); C.A. Bayly, 'Ireland, India, and the Empire, 1780–1914', *Transactions of the Royal Historical Society*, 6th series, 10 (2000), 377–97; and Donald H. Akenson, *If the Irish Ran the World: Montserrat, 1630–1730* (Liverpool, 1997).

22. Marjory Harper, 'British Migration and the Peopling of the Empire', in Andrew Porter (ed.), *The Oxford History of the British Empire*, vol.3 *The Nineteenth Century* (Oxford, 1999), 75. The latter figure is cited in Phillip Buckner, 'Whatever Happened to the British Empire?', *Journal of the Canadian Historical Association*, 4 (1993), 14.

23. Buckner, 'Whatever Happened', 17; Bielenberg, *Irish Diaspora*, 224.

24. Bielenberg, *Irish Diaspora*, 218–20.

25. Paul Hudson, 'English Emigration to New Zealand, 1839–1850: Information Diffusion and Marketing a New World', *Economic History Review*, 54 (2001), 680–98. Our thanks to Andrew Thompson for this reference. For other examples of how important the diffusion of information was to the migration process after 1914, see Marjory Harper, *Emigration from Scotland between the Wars: Opportunity or Exile?* (Manchester, 1998); Michael Roe, *Australia, Britain and Migration, 1915–1940* (Cambridge, 1995).

26. Stephen Constantine, 'Introduction: Empire Migration and Imperial Harmony', in S. Constantine (ed.), *Emigrants and Empire: British Settlement in the Empire between the Wars* (Manchester, 1990), 2; and *idem*, 'Migrants and Settlers', in Judith M. Brown and Wm. Roger Louis (eds.), *The Oxford History of the British Empire*, vol.4 *The Twentieth Century* (Oxford, 1999), 165–66.

27. Constantine, 'Migrants and Settlers', 166–67.

28. B.R. Mitchell, *British Historical Statistics* (Cambridge, 1988), 83.

29. P.J. Marshall, 'Empire and Authority in the later Eighteenth Century', *Journal of Imperial and Commonwealth History*, 15 (1987), 105–22. See also C.A. Bayly, 'Returning the British to South Asian History: The Limits of Colonial Hegemony', *South Asia*, 17 (1994), 1–25.

30. For South African constructions of multiple identities, see Saul Dubow, 'Colonial Nationalism, the Milner Kindergarten and the Rise of "South Africanism", 1902–10', *History Workshop Journal*, no.43 (1997), 53–85; *idem*, 'Imagining the New South Africa in the Era of Reconstruction', in David Omissi and Andrew Thompson (eds.), *The Impact of the South African War* (Basingstoke, 2002), 76–98. Also see Miles Fairburn, *The Ideal Society and its Enemies: The Foundation of Modern New Zealand Society, 1850–1900* (Auckland, 1989).

31. See Donal Lowry's chapter below. For examples of non-white loyalty to British values, see Bill Nasson, *Abraham Esau's War: A Black South African at War in the Cape, 1899–1902* (Cambridge, 1991); and, for a West Indian example, Anne Spry Rush, 'Imperial Identity in Colonial Minds: Harold Moody and the League of Coloured Peoples, 1931–50', *Twentieth Century British History*, 13 (2002), 356–83.

32. See Ian van der Waag's chapter below.

33. Mark C. McGowan, *The Waning of the Green: Catholics, the Irish, and Identity in Toronto, 1887–1922* (Montreal and Kingston, 1999).

34. Robert A. Huttenback, *Racism and Empire: White Settlers and Colored Immigrants in the British Self-Governing Colonies, 1830–1910* (Ithaca, NY, 1976).

35. Stephen Constantine makes some tantalising observations about labour markets and the export of skilled labour in 'Migrants and Setters', 170–72, which is expanded, in part, in his chapter below. So, too, does Jonathan Hyslop about white trade unionism in the British Empire. See Jonathan Hyslop, 'The Imperial Working Class Makes Itself "White": White Labourism in Britain, Australia and South Africa before the First World War', *Journal of Historical Sociology*, 12 (1999), 398–421. Also see Logie Barrow, 'White Solidarity in 1914', in Raphael Samuel (ed.), *Patriotism: The Making and Unmaking of the British*

National Identity, vol.1 *History and Politics* (London, 1989), 275–87.

36. Alan Lester, *Imperial Networks: Creating Identities in Nineteenth-Century South Africa and Britain* (London, 2001), and *idem*, 'British Settler Discourse and the Circuits of Empire', *History Workshop Journal*, no.54 (2002), 27–48. See also Zoë Laidlaw, 'Networks, Patronage and Information in Colonial Governance: Britain, New South Wales and the Cape, 1826–1843', D.Phil. thesis, Oxford, 2001.

37. Saul Dubow, 'The Commonwealth of Science: The British Association in South Africa, 1905–1929', in S. Dubow (ed.), *Science and Society in Southern Africa* (Manchester, 2000).

38. Andrew S. Thompson, *The Empire Strikes Back: Imperialism's Impact on Britain from the Mid-Nineteenth Century to the Present Day* (Longman, forthcoming), ch.1 entitled, 'The Empire and British Elites'. We would like to thank the author for showing us his work in progress on this intriguing subject.

39. For example, see Melanie Oppenheimer, '"The Best P.M. for the Empire in War"?: Lady Helen Munro Ferguson and the Australian Red Cross Society', *Australian Historical Studies*, 33 (2002), 108–24.

40. Eliza Reidi, 'Women, Gender, and the Promotion of Empire: The Victoria League, 1901–1914', *Historical Journal*, 45 (2002), 569–99; Elizabeth van Heyningen and Pat Merrett, '"The healing touch": The Guild of Loyal Women of South Africa 1900–1912', unpublished paper (2002); Katie Pickles, *Female Imperialism and National Identity: Imperial Order Daughters of the Empire* (Manchester, 2002). Also see Julia Bush, *Edwardian Ladies and Imperial Power* (London, 2000); Angela Woollacott, *To Try Her Fortune in London: Australian Women, Colonialism, and Modernity* (Oxford, 2001); and Lisa Chilton's chapter below.

41. There is a plethora of company histories but a relative dearth of studies of whole imperial networks. See, however, Gordon Pirie, *Aviation and Empire* (Manchester, forthcoming), Meredith Hooper, *Kangaroo Route* (Sydney, 1985); and David MacKenzie, *Canada and International Civil Aviation, 1932–48* (Toronto, 1989).

42. On cables see Robert W.D. Boyce, 'Imperial Dreams and National Realities: Britain, Canada and the Struggle for a Pacific Telegraph Cable, 1879–1902', *English Historical Review*, 115 (2000), 39–70; *idem*, 'Canada and the Pacific Cable Controversy, 1923–28: Forgotten Source of Imperial Alienation', *Journal of Imperial and Commonwealth History*, 26 (1998), 72–92.

43. K.S. Inglis, 'London Calling: The Empire of the Air Waves', *Working Papers in Australian Studies*, no.118, was a keynote address at the 1st British World Conference at the Institute of Commonwealth Studies, London, 1998.

44. Cited in Simon Potter's chapter below.

45. Quotation cited in R.G. Casey, *Double or Quit* (Melbourne, 1949), 104.

46. Ian McGibbon, *The Path to Gallipoli: Defending New Zealand, 1840–1915* (Wellington, 1991), 106–24; Carman Miller, *Painting the Map Red: Canada and the South African War, 1899–1902* (Montreal and Kingston, 1993); and Craig Wilcox, *Australia's Boer War: The War in South Africa 1899–1902* (Melbourne, 2002).

47. Jeffrey Grey, *A Military History of Australia* (Melbourne, 1999), 116; Central Statistics Office, *Fighting with Figures: A Statistical Digest of the Second World War* (London, 1995); F.W. Perry, *The Commonwealth Armies: Manpower and Organisation in Two World Wars* (Manchester, 1988); David Dilks, *Great Britain, the Commonwealth and the Wider World, 1939–45* (Hull, 1998); Avner Offer, *The First World War: An Agrarian Interpretation* (Oxford, 1989).

48. Cited in R.G. Casey, *Friends and Neighbors* (East Lansing, MI, 1955), 16.

49. Bradford Perkins, *The Great Rapprochement* (London, 1969); David Dimbleby and David Reynolds, *An Ocean Apart* (London, 1988); David Lowe, 'Percy Spender and the American Century', *The Trevor Reese Memorial Lecture 2002* (London, 2002), 31–33.

50. Robert Bickers, 'Shanghailanders: The Formation and Identity of the British Settler Community in Shanghai 1843–1937', *Past & Present*, no.159 (1998), 161–211.

51. For a recent examination of the Australian case, see Carl Bridge and Bernard Attard (eds.), *Between Empire and Nation: Australia's External Relations from Federation to the Second World War* (Melbourne, 2000). For the Irish case, see Donal Lowry, 'New Ireland, Old Empire and the Outside World, 1922–49: The Strange Evolution of a "Dictionary"

Republic', in John M. Regan and Mike Cronin (eds.), *Ireland: The Politics of Independence, 1922–49* (London, 2000), 164–216.

52. John Darwin, 'A Third British Empire? The Dominion Idea in Imperial Politics', in Brown and Louis (eds.), *The Oxford History of the British Empire*, vol.4, 64–87, esp. 85–86.

53. Calculated from relevant tables in Mitchell, *British Historical Statistics*, and in B.R. Mitchell, *International Historical Statistics: Africa and Asia* (London, 1982); and idem, *The Americas and Australasia* (London, 1983).

54. Randall Hansen, *Citizenship and Immigration in Post-war Britain: The Institutional Origins of a Multicultural Nation* (Oxford, 2000), 40.

55. Ibid., 41; Nicholas Mansergh, *Survey of British Commonwealth Affairs: Problems of Wartime Co-operation and Post-War Change 1939–1952* (Oxford, 1958), 382–87.

56. Hansen, *Citizenship*, 53. Hansen refutes Paul's and Spencer's notion that the 1948 Act was the beginning of the racialisation of British immigration policy. He shows that it was not until 1962 with the introduction of the Commonwealth Immigrants Act, which introduced limited entry, that racialisation truly began. Hansen, *Citizenship*, chs.2–4; Kathleen Paul, *Whitewashing Britain: Race and Citizenship in the Post-War Era* (Ithaca NY, 1997); Ian R.G. Spencer, *British Immigration Policy since 1939: The Making of Multicultural Britain* (London, 1997).

57. Menzies's radio broadcast as reported in the *Sydney Morning Herald*, 4 Sept. 1939, and Neville Meaney's chapter below. Menzies was still using the term 'British world' in 1959, see Stuart Ward, 'Sentiment and Self-interest: The Imperial Ideal in Anglo-Australian Commercial Culture', *Australian Historical Studies*, 32 (2001), 98.

58. Siân Nicholas's chapter below.

59. '"Britain" or "UK"', memo by Secretary of State for Commonwealth Relations, Duncan Sandys, 24 March 1961, C(61)46, Cabinet Office papers, CAB 129/104, Public Record Office (PRO), London; cabinet conclusions, CC(61)19, minute 6, 28 March 1961, CAB 128/35; '"Britain" and "British"', memos to Sandys and Macmillan by the Cabinet Secretary, Sir Norman Brook, 16 June 1961, and Macmillan's personal reply M 199/61, 20 June 1961, Prime Minister's Office papers, PREM 11/3652, PRO. The authors wish to thank Stuart Ward for directing us to the last source.

60. For an account, see W. David McIntyre, *British Decolonization, 1946–1997* (New York, 1998), 103–18.

61. Kosmas Tsokhas misuses the term de-dominionisation in his, 'Dedominionization: The Anglo-Australian Experience, 1939–1945', *Historical Journal*, 37 (1994), 861–83. For a better understanding see Jim Davidson, 'The De-dominionisation of Australia', *Meanjin*, 38 (1979), 139–53.

62. Stuart Ward, *Australia and the British Embrace: The Demise of the Imperial Ideal* (Melbourne, 2001); David Goldsworthy, *Losing the Blanket: Australia and the End of Britain's Empire* (Melbourne, 2002); *Daily Telegraph*, 8 Feb. 2003.

63. Menzies to Macmillan, 15 Jan. 1962, cited in Goldsworthy, *Losing the Blanket*, 111; Menzies's speech, *Commonwealth* [of Australia] *Parliamentary Debates*, 16 Oct. 1962; Wayne Reynolds, *Australia's Bid for the Atomic Bomb* (Melbourne, 2000); Robert Holland, *The Pursuit of Greatness: Britain and the World Role, 1900–1970* (London, 1991), 180; McIntyre, *British Decolonization*, 122.

British Emigration to the
Empire-Commonwealth since 1880:
From Overseas Settlement to Diaspora?

STEPHEN CONSTANTINE

In January 1927, to encourage British consumers to 'Buy Empire goods from home and overseas', the Empire Marketing Board (EMB) displayed on public billboards a map of the world. The British Isles were placed at the centre, in a distinctive design shaped like a half-moon. Vividly depicted in the same strong red on the surrounding satellite continents were the territories of the British Empire and unmistakably the encircling colonies of white settlement, Canada at the top and to the left, southern and eastern Africa to the bottom, Australia and New Zealand to the right. The design was much reproduced in various sizes, ranging from the huge (20 feet by 10 feet) to the modest (30 inches by 20 inches), the latter for educational use in schools.[1] Maps represent perceptions of space. Political maps like this one announce belonging. This was indeed a vision of Greater Britain, in which the ties between mother country and daughter Dominions were demographic and cultural, as well as economic and constitutional. One contemporary commentator reckoned that EMB propaganda would be an inducement to emigrate.[2] Noticeably, though with rather more sophistication, historians of the 'British world' are now again emphasising the Britishness of this Greater Britain, even in the self-governing Dominions, and the lingering appeal of empire culturally as well as politically until late in the twentieth century.[3] Their work contrasts with the writings of earlier historians of Canada, Australia and New Zealand who had opted to emphasise the historical roots of distinctive nation states.[4] The implication of this reinterpretation for our understanding of empire migration has prompted this essay.

I

The settlement overseas of large numbers of migrants from Britain, particularly over the last two centuries, indisputably created other English-speaking societies within the empire, with profound political, economic and cultural consequences. The movement, it seems, founded and then reinforced British-derived communities, sharing recognisably similar values. Moreover, the very similarity of cultures apparently eased the process of arrival and assimilation by later settlers. Movement was within the familiar. If the English and Scots were 'invisible immigrants' in nineteenth-century America,[5] how much more must that have been the case in nineteenth- and even twentieth-century colonies of white settlement within the British Empire-Commonwealth?

One implication of this perception is that the experiences of British settlers were different from those of other migrants entering what they would have found culturally alien British societies in the nineteenth and twentieth and indeed twenty-first centuries. These included, for example, European Jews, Italians, Germans and Scandinavians. Even more obviously confronting problems of assimilation or merely of integration would be non-Europeans such as those originally from China, Japan or British India seeking settlement in Canada, southern Africa, Australia and New Zealand, or, more recently, those from Asia and the Caribbean relocating in British cities.

The migration of these latter groups is often called a diaspora.[6] Etymologically, derived from the Greek, the term only means a scattering. Cohen has recently attempted to restore this purist reading so as to allow him to identify via adjectival additions a plurality of diasporic types, and hence he offers labour diasporas, imperial diasporas, trade diasporas and cultural diasporas as well as victim diasporas.[7] But words acquire connotations, and it is this last term which is closest to the conventional meaning. Diaspora is associated with the historical experience of the Jews of the Old Testament. This original concept of diaspora conjures up a sense of expulsion and exile from home, of loneliness and isolation in culturally alien places, and of a desire to return.[8] It places an emphasis on the difference between such overseas migrants and their hosts. It suggests that diasporic migrants experienced numerically and culturally a sense of oppression, prompting in reaction a resistance. Resistance might take the form of a refusal to assimilate, and a desire instead to preserve a separate identity against the dominant host culture. Moreover, diaspora in this sense implies the maintenance by such migrant groups of a cultural identity with the people in and of their country or culture of birth. A milder version would see the migrant struggling to combine a loyalty to the place of settlement with a still strong identity with their place of origin or with their ethnicity.

Yet the term diaspora is now often being used to describe the process of British emigration, but without such connotations, with no attempt at definition, indeed merely as a synonym for overseas migration and settlement. It seems almost as if historians have become too embarrassed to use terms employed by advocates of British emigration and early British historians of the process. The Empire Settlement Acts from 1922, the monthly bulletin *The Oversea Settler*, and historical texts like Plant's *Oversea Settlement* perhaps prompted the choice of an intended euphemism.[9] In 1981 the University of Kent hosted a conference on 'The Diaspora of the British', but the keynote address, entitled 'The British Diaspora', offered no definition of the term in a paper which described a process of overseas emigration and cultural transfers.[10] The conference apparently reached no consensus whether 'its subject matter was a loosely related set of "dispersals" or a "diaspora" properly integrated in cultural, economic or political ways'. That conclusion, like the papers themselves, does not suggest much regard for the historic connotations of the term.[11] The exception was the paper by Peter Lyon which conveniently drew attention to the Jewish roots of conventional usage and identified some previous uses of the word by historians and social scientists.[12] He concluded that the term could be 'a suggestive metaphor', but the implied alignment of interpretation with the Jewish diaspora seems not subsequently to have been taken up. For example, Gill Burke in 'The Cornish diaspora of the nineteenth century' employs the word only twice in her essay and without definition in an otherwise informative description of Cornish miners working overseas.[13] Similarly, Ross Johnston in his essay on 'The Welsh diaspora' does not use the word except in the title, and that is true also of Jane Sansom in the section 'The British diaspora' included in her recently published reader on *The British Empire*.[14] The Research Institute of Irish and Scottish Studies at the University of Aberdeen is currently running seven research projects within its 'Diaspora programme': clarity on the meaning and use of the term might emerge from this activity.[15] Certainly little became evident at the 'British World Conference' held at the Institute of Commonwealth Studies in 1998, although its subtitle served as an inspiration for this essay: 'Diaspora, Culture and Identity'.[16]

Perhaps the term diaspora is inappropriate because it is misleading when considering the migration and settlement of British people overseas after 1880. After all they settled overwhelmingly within an already established English-speaking world. They enjoyed an apparent ease of entry into and perhaps assimilation into British, or at least British-derived, societies and cultures, whether inside the British Empire or outside in the United States. Nevertheless, there may be merit in employing the concept of diaspora with its original connotations to explore the migration experience of the British from *c*.1880 to the present. Diaspora may have value as an analytical tool if it allows us to question the casual assumption that British emigration over the long period had a single character and that the migrant experiences of the British people settling in the British Empire-Commonwealth were, and are, necessarily and always different from those of other migrating peoples.

The interpretation offered is that, at a high level of generalisation, this long century may be divided into two phases. In the first period, from roughly the 1880s to the 1940s, British migration was primarily, though not entirely, an overseas settlement and not a diaspora. Migrants from the British Isles to the British Empire were in general reinforcing an existing wider British world and were on the whole easily assimilated into it: they experienced little sense of exile or of alienation from their new host cultures. Much more speculatively, the essay will suggest that increasingly from the 1940s, emigration from Britain to the Commonwealth probably produced experiences less like overseas settlement and more akin to a diaspora. Those who more recently went to live overseas even in English-speaking societies became aware of their intrusion into alien cultures, of difference from their hosts and from other and numerous immigrant groups. One consequence may have been a greater sense of cultural challenge, making British immigrants more conscious of themselves as distinctively British, perhaps more ready to preserve what they regarded as distinctively British cultural identities and practices, and more aware of their links with and empathy towards the institutions and values of their country of birth. Such responses may even have promoted a desire to return 'home'.

II

The conditions which in the first phase from the 1880s to the 1940s were conducive to the assimilation of British migrants into settler societies overseas include the large volume of such migrants. Each migrant or migrant family had the comfort of companionship. They were part of a British mass movement, not merely fragments of cosmopolitan flows. The figures are imprecise since no official attempt was made until 1912 to distinguish between passengers sailing from United Kingdom ports for non-European destinations, including those leaving only temporarily, and emigrants intending to settle overseas for at least one year. However, assuming the same ratio of passengers to emigrants as for the decade of the 1920s when both sets of figures were counted, calculations suggest about 1,640,000 emigrants left the United Kingdom in the 1880s, over 1,670,000 in the 1900s, and 1,816,618 in the 1920s. The flow was by no means regular. There was a spectacularly high exodus of 389,394 emigrants in the single year 1913, a virtual cessation during the war years, and a slump down to a mere 334,467 emigrants in the entire decade of the 1930s.[17] Nevertheless, the quantity overall was impressive. Underlying the outflow for most of this period remained the continuing rapid growth of the British population, from nearly 30 million in 1881 to nearly 45 million by 1931.[18] Rates of natural increase by decade were running in the 1880s at 14 per cent in England, Wales and Scotland, and not much less in the 1900s.[19]

Demography does not account for emigration. It would be an exaggeration to read diasporic consequences into population growth alone. When the National Emigration League in 1869–70 and the National Association for Promoting State-directed Colonisation in the 1880s promoted overseas settlement, they were responding to perceived overcrowded labour markets, rural poverty and urban deprivation, and not just to population growth.[20] Similarly in the 1920s, the evidence of high levels of population density only produced the Empire Settlement Act in 1922 when economic depression generated high and sustained levels of unemployment.[21] There were in these circumstances pressures to leave, and no doubt many migrants felt pushed out by diminished or unattractive prospects. However, conventional wisdom now suggests that, with some exceptions, British emigrants from the 1880s were not merely expelled from 'Israel' but perceived better opportunities overseas and could draw upon the resources to get them there. While push factors – cyclical depression and especially structural economic and social changes – might appear to threaten employment, earnings and status at home, information about better prospects relayed home by family and friends already established overseas, or conjured up by emigration propaganda, persuaded the ambitious or unsettled to leave.[22]

A further muting of diasporic features probably followed from the concentrated settlement of British migrants in specific countries from the late nineteenth century. Largely reflecting altering assessments of relative opportunities was the noticeable shift in this period from the United States to the British Empire as the chosen destination of British emigrants. Whereas in the 1880s only about one-third of British emigrants headed to empire destinations, that figure had risen to more than two-thirds by the 1920s. Especially, of course, they headed for the white settler societies of Canada, Australia, New Zealand and, to a much lesser extent, South Africa. Between 1925 and 1929, 77.7 per cent of British emigrants, 576,146 of them, headed for empire destinations, of whom 261,477 went to Canada (35.3 per cent) and 213,412 to Australia and New Zealand (28.8 per cent).[23] These were huge volumes, and since most British immigrants swarmed into towns and were not scattered across countrysides, the sense of group resettlement in British communities must have been enhanced.[24] This would have been particularly the case since at some periods the volume of immigrants contributed substantially to the population growth of the receiving societies, adding considerably to the consequences of natural increase. In New Zealand, even after the extraordinary peaks during the 1860s and 1870s, this was true of the mid-1880s and of the two decades either side of the First World War.[25] In 1921 the total population of New Zealand was 1,271,664, and of the 309,645 born overseas, 203,577 had been born in England, Scotland and Wales (plus 34,419 in Ireland).[26] Even by the 1920s, new British immigrants were therefore entering a society substantially composed of recent British immigrants. While this would be less the case in Canada and certainly in South Africa, a similar narrative with similar implications for ease of settlement applied to Australia. Australian residents born in the United Kingdom (and therefore including also the Irish) constituted 25 per cent of the population in 1891.[27]

Not only was the flow of migrants to empire substantial in this period, but the politics of emigration easily persuaded British migrants of their privileged status. One of the supposed virtues of the British Empire was freedom of movement within it. The British Nationality Act of 1914, in an apparent gesture of equality, defined British citizens to include 'any person born within His Majesty's dominions and allegiances'. This seemed to imply for all such people, whatever their geographical or ethnic origins, a perfect free market for their labour and skills anywhere in the British Empire. In truth, global migration was taking place within a highly politicised structure, in which some British citizens were more equal than others. In practice, the politics of empire were highly conducive to ease of assimilation for white British settlers until after 1945, and politics were unlikely to provoke a sense of diaspora.

Among the first powers taken by the empire's self-governing settler societies was the authority to manage the flows of immigration into their territories. Section 95 of the British North America Act in 1867, the founding document of the Dominion of Canada, made immigration a federal government responsibility. The ending of the provincial system of government in New Zealand in 1875 coincided with the centralisation of control over immigration. One of the first measures of the parliament of the federated Commonwealth of Australia in 1901 was an Immigration Act. Creating the bureaucracy of immigration management was part of the building of new states.

One role of the immigration services was negative, to screen out and indeed to deport undesirables – the unhealthy, the criminal and the politically dangerous.[28] True, some British migrants found themselves unwelcome even amongst their supposed kith and kin. British immigrants falling on hard times and needing public relief were deported, especially from Canada in the 1930s.[29] The substantial numbers of deprived British children transported between the 1860s and 1920s from orphanages in Britain and deposited as labourers on Canadian farms might legitimately interpret their fate in biblical terms. They were the often-despised 'home children', supposedly with eugenic deficiencies, who were forced to bury their origins. Like the children of Israel, they may well have felt that they dwelt among aliens.[30]

But at least they were white. For the most part British migrants were privileged because of prevailing concepts of race and the legislative consequences. Severe restrictions limited the rights of 'Asiatics' to enter the empire's settler societies, and that discrimination affected even fellow 'citizens' of the empire, such as those seeking entry from British India. Entry for non-Europeans was being made more difficult from the 1880s. The legislative model devised in Natal in 1897 was adopted by Australian colonies in 1897 and 1898, and by the Commonwealth of Australia in 1901. Similarly, legislation passed in New Zealand in 1899, by Canada in a still tighter form in 1910, and in the Union of South Africa in 1913 had the effect of depicting their portions of the British Empire as reservations for 'white' settlers only.[31]

The implicit welcome for those of good British (and that meant 'white' British) stock was made explicit by other and positive immigration policies. In various ways, governments of white settler societies set out to attract British immigrants, not least by paying some or all of their costs of travel, especially of those going to those distant territories of Australia and New Zealand. Australian colonial governments had a long history of operating assisted passage schemes before and after 1880,[32] and various schemes targeted especially at the British were operated by the New Zealand government from 1870 to 1890 and again from 1903 until the 1930s.[33] At various times, agents for the Canadian government were also active in Britain soliciting recruits.[34] Notoriously if not very successfully, the reconstruction programme in South Africa after the Boer War included attempts to induce British people to relocate in that other part of Greater Britain.[35]

Moreover, British migrants to empire may have had less sense of exile when the British government began to co-operate more actively with those in the Dominions to assist such overseas settlement. The Emigrants' Information Office set up in 1886 may have been at best neutral towards empire migration, but that changed after the First World War. British taxpayers' money then became readily available to provide free passages for ex-servicemen and their families and assisted passages and other facilities under the Empire Settlement Act of 1922. The empire partnership funded the transfer of over 86,000 British settlers under the first scheme and, by 1936, over 400,000 under the second.[36]

The propaganda, which between the 1880s and the 1930s encouraged assisted and independent emigration from Britain and settlement in the empire, was a denial of diaspora. The emphasis was on the natural harmony between the interests of Britain, dispatching migrants, and the rest of

Greater Britain, receiving them. The aims and practices of emigration and immigration authorities on the whole fitted neatly together. Demographically, Britain was judged to be over-populated, with too many people crowded into unhealthy towns, while the rural spaces of British settler societies were under-populated. In addition, gender ratios in Britain and in the new Dominions seemed mirror images of each other, with disproportionately more males than females in Britain, whilst in Australia and New Zealand, for example, the reverse was true.[37] 'Surplus women' in Britain, that is the unmarried, needed to be matched, naturally, with 'surplus men' overseas. Migration, marriage and the population growth of white settler societies formed one barely concealed element of imperial social engineering.

There was also an occupational coherence about assisted migration in this period: those leaving industrialised Britain were disproportionately workers destined for labour with rural producers or, increasingly, in ancillary urban crafts and services.[38] Labour then, like capital, was moving from the British industrial core to the, still British, rural periphery. Therefore, as a result of demographic and occupational transfers, British manufactured goods and services would be sold to empire destinations, in return for such food and raw materials as New Zealand lamb, Australian wool, Canadian wheat and South African gold.[39]

But cultural complementarity between places of origin and of destination was also emphasised. Emigration from Britain to the white settler societies of the British Empire was generally felt to be, certainly was marketed as being, merely a redistribution from one part to another of Greater Britain. Leo Amery, the architect of the Empire Settlement Act, refused to describe this process as emigration: it was merely the overseas settlement of British stock – in New Zealand, the Britain of the South; in British Australia; in British (not French) Canada; and in British colonies in southern Africa.[40] It was expected to be no more traumatic than migration from Yorkshire to Lancashire, and perhaps even less than from Scotland to England.

British migrants undoubtedly had to adjust to different physical and climatic conditions – to heat, dust, snow, flies and snakes. But it seems probable that British migrants had few difficulties from the late nineteenth century adapting to their new locations. By then, the hard work of pioneers in creating social as well as economic and political infrastructures modelled on Britain had been done. There were few alien cultural features to remind later settlers of their different and distinctive British roots. These were self-proclaimed British communities, bent upon reproducing most of the cultural products of what immigrants still thought of as home – similar business practices, equivalent political methods, familiar forms of religious observance, and recognisably similar newspapers, reading matter, sports and other recreational activities. There was little need for British immigrants to profess their distinctive Britishness when they were merely dispersed into and assimilated by this Greater Britain.

Admittedly finding negative evidence, of immigrants not behaving distinctively, is a problem. On the other hand, positive evidence of the opposite, of being self-consciously and even defensively British, might be found where the cultural dominance of the British was less assured. This appears to be the case, for example, of the British confronted by Afrikaner (and African society) within the Union of South Africa, and of British settlers in colonial Rhodesia, Kenya and India. That the British, like other immigrant communities, could be prompted to assert and preserve their cultural identities in more challenging circumstances is suggested by the response of British settlers outside the formal British Empire. For example, in a Latin culture like that of Argentina, the British community established their own distinctive schools, clubs, churches and newspapers, and British residents commonly sent their children 'home' to Britain to complete their education.[41]

Of course, an important caveat might here be entered against the argument so far advanced. It may be necessary to distinguish between the English on the one hand and the Welsh and Scots on the other. The analysis so far has grouped all under the heading 'British', excluding deliberately the Irish. However, it might be argued that Irish migration, at least from Catholic Ireland, truly constituted a diaspora, and that the Welsh and the Scots had more in common with the Irish than with the more numerous English settlers overseas.[42] Like the Irish, the Welsh (and especially the Welsh-speaking) and the Scots (and especially those from the Highlands) could claim that their nineteenth-century migration was prompted by cultural as well as, perhaps, economic oppression and the determination to preserve identities threatened by the English language or the Established Church. Certainly, the Scots especially, like the Irish, were capable of presenting themselves as mournful exiles from a homeland, however enthusiastic they might be in practice to exploit the opportunities opened up by empire.[43] If diaspora encapsulates a sense of cultural defensiveness, then Welsh and Scottish settlers demonstrated some such characteristics in, for instance, the content as well as the form of Welsh-language newspapers and in the proliferation of Caledonian societies.[44] Such identities, however, surely owed more to the sense of being persecuted minorities in English-dominated Britain than of being so treated in the less English-dominated Greater Britain overseas. Nevertheless, these distinctions need to be acknowledged here, because one might suspect that in the second period, from the late 1940s to the present, new British settlers overseas, even within the British Commonwealth, may have been made to feel more like those migrants in Argentina outside the empire or those earlier Welsh and Scottish settlers within. If so, there was a shift from British overseas settlement to British diaspora.

III

Delving more into the realm of speculation, what follows is essentially a research agenda. The need now is to unearth further evidence of a growing consciousness among later British immigrants that they had not merely transferred from Britain to another part of Greater Britain but into a different, even alien, culture. This is plausible, for three reasons.

First, emigrants from Britain to the British Commonwealth, especially in the last 40 years, have found themselves increasingly exceptional and less part of a reassuring mass movement. In this later period, after the doldrums of the 1930s and the hiatus caused by the Second World War, migration from Britain did resume, and even more British migrants went to Commonwealth as opposed to 'foreign' destinations, rising by the 1950s to 80 per cent of the total. However, the number of migrants to all destinations outside Europe never again reached earlier levels. There was a substantial surge after the war, 590,022 in 1946–49 alone, but the total of 1,327,300 in the 1950s was less than in the decades at the beginning of the century.[45]

Migration lessened partly because demographically there was no longer the same rate of population growth in Britain. Crude birth rates had fallen substantially in Britain. In 1901–05 there had been 28.2 births per 1,000 of the population in England and Wales and 29.2 in Scotland, but by 1936–40 the rate was down to 14.7 and 17.6 respectively. The figures were only a little higher after the war, and then fell further, to 12.3 and 12.7, by 1976–80. True, crude death rates had also declined since the beginning of the century. Nevertheless, the annual rate of natural increase, still in 1901–5 a remarkable 12.2 per 1,000 for England and Wales and the same for Scotland, was by 1936–40 a mere 2.5 for the former and 4.0 for the latter. By 1976–80 it was barely registering, 0.4 for England and Wales and 0.3 for Scotland.[46]

Moreover, the former harmony between British emigration and Commonwealth immigration went out of tune. Contraception was not only eliminating a demographic pressure to emigrate: it was generating in Britain a public and political concern about the apparently alarming implications of absolute population decline.[47] Indeed, after the Second World War there was an unprecedented labour shortage. The annual Ministry of Labour reports regularly recorded the pressure points. Relief for the British economy was sought by immigration, by the recruiting of 'displaced persons' from war-torn continental Europe, by huge volumes of Irish immigration, and by the arrival of immigrants from the West Indies, the first cohorts arriving aboard the *Empire Windrush* in 1948.[48] There was therefore greater official reluctance in Britain after 1945 to encourage post-war migration even to the Commonwealth.

This was especially true because British emigrants from the 1940s were drawn disproportionately from among the professional, white-collar and skilled occupational groups. The recruits sought by Australia, Canada and New Zealand were those with skills and capital, needed by industry, commerce and the professions – personnel, in other words, which British society could least afford to lose.[49] No longer was the British Empire-Commonwealth so much a harmonious economic system, featuring a core British economy and a dependent periphery. Instead, there was competition between some of the parts.

A second contextual change, which may have prompted a diasporic response, was that the composition of immigration into Commonwealth countries altered, and the privileges of the British began to decline. Initially at least, British migrants could still be persuaded that their relocation within the Commonwealth was politically endorsed and that they would be favourably received overseas as privileged incomers. A highly politicised migration strategy was revived after the war. Thanks to intensive lobbying by the Australian government and in spite of demographic and economic anxieties, the British government was persuaded to renew, repeatedly, the Empire (later Commonwealth) Settlement Act and the assisted passage scheme, but British financial support was diminished and the act was allowed to lapse in 1972.[50] The governments of Australia and New Zealand resumed their assisted passage schemes in 1947 and Canada in 1951, but the widespread propaganda in favour of those schemes depended overwhelmingly on the resources and energies of Commonwealth governments. Naturally, in couching their appeals, they emphasised the British character of British Commonwealth destinations. For example, advertising by the Australian High Commission in 1959 still insisted that 'Australia is a British land short of people' and that there was 'an open invitation to British people ... to take up life in Australia'.[51]

Nevertheless, it became increasingly apparent that British migrants were not to be uniquely privileged. The urbanised, industrialised and professionalised parts of the Commonwealth were not content to draw their essential supplies of such skilled labour from British sources alone. Demand exceeded supply. After the Second World War, more so than before, Canada, Australia and New Zealand deliberately recruited from other western and then eastern and southern European sources. Between 1945 and 1964, 271,600 immigrants arrived in Australia from Italy, 134,600 from the

Netherlands, 111,800 from Greece, and 98,000 from Germany.[52] And, subsequently, immigrants were recruited from outside Europe. The privileges for those of 'white' and therefore particularly British stock were eroded. Racial discrimination in immigration was ended, by Canada from 1962, by Australia in 1973, by New Zealand from 1974, by South Africa after 1994. Between 1966 and 1986 the percentage of immigrants entering Canada from Asia rose from 12 per cent to 42 per cent, and similarly between 1972 and 1984 for Australia from 9 per cent to 43 per cent.[53] In the five years to 2001 the biggest numerical increase in people born overseas and resident in New Zealand came from north-east Asia, up by 46 per cent.[54] As a consequence of these two developments, between 1946 and 1965 only 33 per cent of immigrants into Canada were British; between 1946 and 1976 only 44 per cent arriving in New Zealand were from the British Isles; between 1945 and 1964 only 51 per cent entering Australia were British.[55] Over the long term, to take just one example, the proportion of immigrants to Australia who came from Britain and Ireland fell from 80 per cent in 1901 to a mere 11 per cent by 1996–97.[56] Consequently the proportion of the overseas-born Australian population who had come from Britain and Ireland fell from 41 per cent in 1976 to 29 per cent by 1996.[57] Assisted passages for British immigrants to Australia were abandoned in 1982. Current ethnicity-blind (but capital and skills all-seeing) immigration policies are continuing to reduce British arrivals to one stream among several.[58]

Moreover, a third shift which may have widened the gap between immigrant and host was a reduction generally in the importance of immigrants to the demographic and labour resources of British Commonwealth countries. It was a change inevitable upon the demographic maturation of settler societies. First-generation immigrants were a declining proportion of the population. The percentage of the overseas-born in New Zealand had fallen from around 55 per cent of the non-Maori population in 1881 to around 15 per cent by 1961.[59] In 1891, 31 per cent of the Australian population was overseas-born, but only 10 per cent by 1947. Post-war recruiting lifted this figure, but only to 20 per cent by 1971 and 23 per cent by 1996, and it needs to be remembered that disproportionately more of these overseas-born were of non-British (and non-Irish) origin.[60] Britain was the birthplace of 39 per cent of the Australian population in 1861, 13 per cent in 1901, but only 6 per cent by 1996.[61] The proportion of the population of New Zealand born in Britain fell in 40-year steps from 33 per cent in 1881, to 16 per cent by 1921, to 9 per cent in 1961, to only 5 per cent by 2001.[62] By 1996, only 15 per cent of the Canadian population identified even their ancestry as British.[63]

The assumption here is that the native-born were more likely to be the makers of the cultural environment. While, of course, British-derived characteristics remained evident, and all Western societies post-war received a soaking from United States popular culture, it is probable that communities in the Commonwealth developed particular characteristics, reflecting their geographical and geo-political locations, their economic experiences, the social opportunities they offered, and not least their climates. Moreover, as a result of other migrant streams, those host populations were becoming ethnically more varied and their cultures were consequently less uniform, less British, more plural. Historians of Commonwealth nationhood may have exaggerated the speed and the spread with which new national identities were being created, and their uniformity, but they were not wrong to look for change. Over the past half-century those communities did evolve into self-conscious nation states, with new national identities and some distinctive cultural practices. Even local accents began to change, distinguishing host and immigrant by sound and vocabulary.[64] Appleyard reckoned that even in the late 1940s the character of Australia was 'only superficially British', and Sherington judged that by the end of the 1960s 'it was no longer possible to move 12,000 miles and still feel somehow at home'.[65]

If these speculations have any validity and the experiences on arrival of later British immigrants were more akin to a diaspora, then traces might emerge in several locations. Do we now find British immigrants, English as well as Welsh and Scots (and Irish), more self-aware as immigrant groups and more pressed to preserve against assimilation their ethnic identities in distinctive cultural forms, like other immigrant groups – Greeks, Italians, Vietnamese?

One place to look might be by examining the reactions of British immigrants to political change. Greater Britain was robustly denied when in South Africa the Nationalist Party took power in 1948 and the status of the British was thereafter challenged, most obviously in 1961 when the Union left the Commonwealth. A study based on 1967–68 data suggested defensive attitudes towards their nationality among a sample of British immigrants, three-quarters rejecting the idea of becoming South African citizens.[66] Similarly, the Britishness of the British community in Canada might have been challenged, if less severely, when in 1965 the union jack was dropped as the Canadian national flag and the maple leaf adopted.[67] The appeal of monarchy is powerful and the motives are plural, and in Canada it may have tugged at anti-American strings and even the monarchism of French Catholicism.[68] However, one suspects that the British immigrant community might be providing some support for the Monarchist League of Canada, formed in 1970,[69] and probably contributed to the loyalist and royalist responses to the Queen's jubilee in 2002.[70] The British immigrant contribution to the frustration of the Australian republican movement in the referendum of 1999 and to the hostility to multiculturalism expressed by Pauline Hanson's One Nation party, formed in 1997, is not easy to discern. However, it is reasonable to speculate that British immigrants were a presence, and sympathetic to the 'Keep the Queen of Australia' movement, formed in 2000.[71] Similarly it would be surprising if the redefinition of New Zealand as (at least) a bi-cultural Aotearoa on the Pacific rim – with a new National Museum also entitled Te Papa Tongarewa to prove it – has not provoked critical responses from some sections of the British (including the British immigrant) community.[72]

One similarity between recent British immigrants and other diasporic communities might be the practice of congregating in particular parts of Commonwealth cities. There is some evidence of this in Winnipeg, albeit for an earlier period, before the First World War.[73] Something similar seems now to characterise settlement in Auckland, where British immigrants have clustered in the North Shore suburbs, and probably in discrete districts of other New Zealand cities.[74] The British-born have settled disproportionately in parts of such large metropolitan areas as Adelaide, Perth and Brisbane, admittedly prompted partly by government housing programmes, and in many outer suburbs elsewhere, such as around Sydney and Melbourne, and they have generated communities distinct from those where other immigrant groups and Australian-born families principally live.[75] Since British immigrants, like others, were often chain migrants, persuaded to chance their luck on the advice of family and friends, there were practical advantages in settlement in clusters, since such networks provided a 'safe landing' and perhaps information on securing housing and employment. Moreover, since later British migrants were more likely than earlier migrants to be arriving as family units, such settlement may have further encouraged the formation of communities of newcomers. The spatial separation of incomers from the host is another dimension of recent immigrant experience worthy of further inquiry.

There may also have been cultural reassurance in such clustering amongst their own kind, rather like Asian immigrant families settling in discrete parts of Birmingham, Manchester and Leicester, or Melbourne, Auckland and Vancouver. Such communities characteristically seek to reproduce familiar structures and practices. The propensity for the Welsh and Scots to express their identities overseas in cultural practices associated with 'home' is well attested for earlier periods. However, the need for cultural resistance might have become latterly more necessary, not in the face of English oppression but rather as protection against new national identities, whether Canadian or Australian or New Zealand. Alternatively, expressions of distinctive identity might be interpreted as parallels to and indeed in emulation of other minority groups in those multi-ethnic plural societies. What percentage of the founders and members of the 27 Welsh societies in Australia and the 45 in Canada today are first-generation migrants?[76] How much are immigrants contributing to the recent proliferation of pipe bands and Caledonian societies in the overseas regions of former Greater Britain? Hewitson reckons that it is 'the Scots-born or first-generation Antipodeans who cling most tenaciously to the Scottish heritage'.[77] And how self-conscious have become the English immigrants, or subsets from among them? In Sydney in 1976 there were 14 English provincial associations as well as 12 Scottish and six Welsh. In Elizabeth, a suburb of Adelaide, could be found the Merseysiders Association, the Cornish Association of South Australia, the Elizabeth Society of Yorkshiremen and the East Anglian Association, as well as the rather splendidly named Elizabeth John Bull Association.[78] Are the English reproducing English gardens in their spots of 'home from home' and are they active members of crown green bowling clubs?[79] It is not frivolous to note that English morris-dancing teams in Canada, Australia and New Zealand appear to have emerged between the late 1970s and mid 1990s. The Vancouver Morris Men 'were formed in 1982 to maintain the traditions of the Morris ... and to recreate the ritual and social activities of England's pastoral past'.[80] Are English immigrants reluctant to support the All Blacks or Australian cricketers? It would be rash to apply the Tebbit test and hang an argument concerning diaspora merely on local recruiting to the 'barmy army' of supporters of English touring cricket teams.[81] Nevertheless it is striking that a survey of recent British immigrants in 1961 concluded that 61 per cent of the men would support a British team against the Australians.[82] Individuals and communities are quite capable of expressing plural identities and holding dual allegiances. Nevertheless, comparing the way South Asian communities express their identities with the manners of British immigrants in multicultural Commonwealth countries might reveal unexpected similarities as well as obvious contrasts.

Then there is return migration. The proportions of British emigrants returning to Britain from overseas appear to have grown this century. Return rates from Australia, for example, in 1961 were as high as 20 per cent, compared with less than 10 per cent for other nationalities.[83] Explanations for return migration are complex, but they surely include difficulties of adjustment and assimilation when British immigrants discovered that these British-derived nations were not culturally merely parts of Greater Britain. A 1962 study of an admittedly small sample of migrants who had returned from Australia to Britain detected several who ascribed homesickness and an inability to adjust to Australia's social environment as the cause.[84] The distinction between immigrant and host was growing, sometimes apparent in a frosty welcome, like the spasms of hostility to new immigrants in

Canada and bouts of Pommy-bashing in Australia, which seem to have increased as the twentieth century progressed.[85] In 1946 a Gallup poll in Canada concluded that 46 per cent of respondents were opposed to immigration even from Britain.[86] One returned migrant in the 1980s reported that 'I didn't like the way Australians made fun of the British'. Another noted that 'the English migrants would stick together and so would the Greeks and the Italians'.[87] The British had become just another migrant flow into an alien community: signs of diaspora to a foreign country, one might suggest, not of overseas settlement in a Greater Britain.

IV

This essay is highly speculative.[88] It may be that the core hypothesis – from overseas settlement to diaspora – is overstated, or that the chronological divide around the 1940s is premature. Certainly, it seems that the evolution of a distinctive culture occurred first in Canada, then in South Africa, next in Australia, and more recently in New Zealand, which would add more chronological nuance to the process. It is probable that some of the recent expressions of Englishness or Britishness in former white Commonwealth societies are made not (or not only) by immigrants but by the local-born. Across the world today, in multicultural societies, ethnic groups are actively asserting distinguishing cultural identities and celebrating diversity.[89] Moreover, in comparing diasporic experiences, it would be grotesque, of course, to equate British migrant circumstances at any stage precisely with those which African and Asian immigrants endured in Greater Britain. However, these thoughts about diaspora, culture and identity have been formed in an attempt to engage with the concepts and to speculate on the changing experiences of migrants and settlers when British Empire evolved into British Commonwealth and then onwards to become merely loosely linked multi-ethnic nation states. Eventually, British immigrants perhaps found and find themselves prompted to defend their cultural identities against that of a dissimilar host and amongst a plurality of competitors.

NOTES

1. Public Record Office, London, Colonial Office papers, CO 956/734 and 537A. For the origins of the design and a reproduction of it, see S. Constantine, *Buy and Build: The Advertising Posters of the Empire Marketing Board* (London, 1986), 8 and plate 1.
2. Reginald Wilson, General Secretary of the British Empire Union, to EMB, 2 Nov. 1926, CO 758/104/1.
3. See for example P. Buckner, 'Whatever Happened to the British Empire?', *Journal of the Canadian Historical Association*, 4 (1993) 3–32.
4. For example, D. Creighton, *Dominion of the North: A History of Canada* (Toronto, 1944);

R. Ward, *The Australian Legend* (Melbourne, 1958); K. Sinclair, *A Destiny Part: New Zealand's Search for National Identity* (Wellington, 1986). See also J. Eddy and D. Schreuder (eds.), *The Rise of Colonial Nationalism* (Sydney, 1988).

5. C. Erickson, *Invisible Immigrants: The Adaptation of English and Scottish Immigrants in 19th Century America* (Leicester, 1972).

6. For example, see P. J. Marshall, 'The Diaspora of the Africans and Asians', in P.J. Marshall (ed.), *The Cambridge Illustrated History of the British Empire* (Cambridge, 1996), 280–95, although the term is not there defined.

7. R. Cohen, *Global Diasporas: An Introduction* (London, 1997): his chapter on victim diasporas is concerned with Africans and Armenians. See also his essay, 'Diasporas, the Nation-State, and Globalisation', in W. Gungwu (ed.), *Global History and Migrations* (Oxford, 1997), 117–43.

8. I have benefited in my thinking from Paul Basu, 'Roots-Tourism as Return Movement: Semantics and the Scottish Diaspora', paper given to the 'Emigrants Homecoming Conference', University of Aberdeen, 2001.

9. G.F. Plant, *Oversea Settlement: Migration from the United Kingdom to the Dominions* (London, 1951).

10. H. Tinker, 'The British Diaspora', in *The Diaspora of the British* (London, 1982), 1–9.

11. 'Introduction', in *Diaspora*.

12. P. Lyon, 'On Diasporas – The Jewish, the British and Some Others: A Note', in *Diaspora*, 72–80.

13. G. Burke, 'The Cornish Diaspora of the Nineteenth Century', in S. Marks and P. Richardson (eds.), *International Labour Migration: Historical Perspectives* (London, 1984), 57–75.

14. W. Ross Johnston, 'The Welsh Diaspora: Emigrating around the World in the Late Nineteenth Century', *Llafur*, 6 (1993), 50–74; J. Sansom, *The British Empire* (Oxford, 2001), 139–61.

15. http://www.abdn.ac.uk/riiss/projects.hti. (All websites cited in this essay were 'live' on 19 Jan. 2003.)

16. Held at the Institute of Commonwealth Studies, University of London, June 1998. I am grateful to the organisers and participants for their responses to my original paper.

17. Calculations derive from N.H. Carrier and J.R. Jeffery, *External Migration: A Study of the Available Statistics, 1815–1950* (London, 1953); and Plant, *Oversea Settlement*, 174–75. See also S. Constantine (ed.), *Emigrants and Empire: British Settlement in the Dominions between the Wars* (Manchester, 1990), 1; and idem, 'Migrants and Settlers', in J.M Brown and W.R. Louis (eds.), *The Oxford History of the British Empire*, vol.4 *The Twentieth Century* (Oxford, 1999), 164–65. These figures are gross numbers: net emigration was of course lower.

18. N.L. Tranter, *British Population in the Twentieth Century* (London, 1996), 3.

19. *Idem, Population and Society 1750–1940* (London, 1985), 44.

20. H.L. Malchow, *Population Pressures: Emigration and Government in Late Nineteenth-Century Britain* (Palo Alto, 1979).

21. K. Williams, '"A way out of our troubles": The Politics of Empire Settlement, 1900–1922', in Constantine (ed.), *Emigrants and Empire*, 22–44.

22. For a review of the extensive literature, see D. Baines, *Emigration from Europe 1815–1930* (London, 1991); and also M. Harper, *Emigration from North-East Scotland*, 2 vols. (Aberdeen, 1988), and *idem, Emigration from Scotland between the Wars* (Manchester, 1998).

23. Figures derive from Plant, *Oversea Settlement*, 174–80.

24. For a study of failed attempts to establish British immigrants on rural settlements, see K. Fedorowich, *Unfit for Heroes: Reconstruction and Soldier Settlement in the Empire between the Wars* (Manchester, 1995).

25. See diagram 1, A.H. McClintock (ed.), *An Encyclopaedia of New Zealand* (Wellington, 1966), 131.

26. Calculated from G.T. Bloomfield, *New Zealand: A Handbook of Historical Statistics* (Boston, MA, 1984), 78–79.

27. Calculated from G. Sherington, *Australia's Immigrants*, 2nd edn (Sydney, 1990), 59.

28. For example, Canada's Immigration Acts, 1869 and 1872, and New Zealand's Undesirable Immigrants Exclusion Act, 1919.
29. H.F. Drystek, '"The simplest and cheapest mode of dealing with them": Deportation from Canada before World War II', *Histoire sociale – Social History*, 15 (1982), 407–41; see also B. Roberts, 'Shovelling out the "mutinous": Political Deportation from Canada before 1936', *Labour – Le Travail*, 18 (1986), 77–110.
30. J. Parr, *Labouring Children: British Immigrant Apprentices to Canada, 1869–1924* (London, 1980); K. Bagnell, *The Little Immigrants: The Orphans Who Came to Canada* (Toronto, 1980); G. Wagner, *Children of the Empire* (London, 1982).
31. R.A. Huttenback, *Racism and Empire: White Settlers and Colored Immigrants in the British Self-Governing Colonies, 1830–1910* (Ithaca, NY, 1976); P.S. O'Connor, 'Keeping New Zealand White', *New Zealand Journal of History*, 2 (1968), 41–65.
32. J. Jupp, *Immigration*, 2nd edn (Melbourne, 1998), 11–15, 23–26; Sherington, *Australia's Immigrants*, 39–40, 43, 106–10; M. Langfield, '"The ideal immigrant": Immigration to Victoria between Federation and the First World War', *Australian Studies*, 8 (1994), 1–14.
33. McClintock, *New Zealand*, 132–33.
34. D.F. Harris, 'The work of Canadian emigration agents in Shropshire, 1896–1914', Dacscub papers, Birmingham University, 1991.
35. M. Streak, *Lord Milner's Immigration Policy for the Transvaal, 1897–1905* (Johannesburg, 1970).
36. Constantine (ed.), *Emigrants and Empire*, 15–16 and primary sources cited there.
37. For gender ratios, see N. Tranter, *Population since the Industrial Revolution* (London, 1973), 105; and B.R. Mitchell, *International Historical Statistics: The Americas and Australasia* (London, 1983), 47, 53, 57, 77–79.
38. See, for example, data in S. Constantine, 'Immigration and the Making of New Zealand, 1918–1939', in *Emigrants and Empire*, 140–41.
39. S. Constantine, 'Empire Migration and Imperial Harmony', in *Emigrants and Empire*, esp. 7–10.
40. L.S. Amery, *My Political Life*, vol.2 *War and Peace 1914–1929* (London, 1953), 183.
41. O. Marshall, 'British Communities in Latin America', paper to 'Diaspora, culture and identity' conference, 1998; A. Graham-Yooll, *The Forgotten Colony: A History of the English-Speaking Communities in Argentina* (London, 1981).
42. That Irish migration was experienced as a diaspora, as defined in this essay, is suggested by the evidence in K.A. Miller, *Emigrants and Exiles: Ireland and the Irish Exodus to North America* (New York, 1985); and D. Fitzpatrick, *Oceans of Consolation: Personal Accounts of Irish Migration to Australia* (Ithaca, NY, 1994).
43. On the opportunities offered by Empire to the Scots and the Irish, see J.M. MacKenzie, 'On Scotland and the Empire', *International History Review*, 15 (1993), 714–39; and K. Jeffery (ed.), *An Irish Empire? Aspects of Ireland and the British Empire* (Manchester, 1996), esp. 16–17 and references there cited.
44. On the Welsh, see L. Lloyd, *Australians from Wales* (Caernarfon, 1988); B. Jones, 'Welsh identities in Ballarat, Australia, during the late nineteenth century', *Welsh History Review*, 20 (2000), 283–307; and the essay below by Aled Jones and Bill Jones.
45. Calculated from Plant, *Oversea Settlement*, 174–75; and B.R. Mitchell, *International Historical Statistics: Europe, 1780–1988* (London, 1992), 132 and 135. Comparisons with later figures are problematical since the basis for making calculations changed after 1964, but the recorded annual average for emigrating British citizens to all countries, including Europe, fell from 150,800 in 1978–82 to 119,000 in 1983–87, rising only to 134,200 in 1988–92: *Social Trends*, 24 (1994), 29.
46. A.H. Halsey and J. Webb (eds.), *Twentieth-Century British Social Trends* (London, 2000), 34.
47. Tranter, *Population since the Industrial Revolution*, 181–83.
48. C. Holmes, *John Bull's Island: Immigration and British Society* (London, 1988).
49. See data in A.H. Richmond, *Post-war Immigrants in Canada* (Toronto, 1967), 41; R.T. Appleyard, *Emigration to Australia* (London, 1964), 40; New Zealand Department of Labour, 'Assisted Immigration 1946–1964', *Labour and Employment Gazette*, 14 (1964),

8–11; and comparison of occupational data on British emigrants 1946–49 with census for 1951 in Constantine, 'Migrants and Settlers', 186.

50. S. Constantine, 'Waving Goodbye? Australia, Assisted Passages, and the Empire and Commonwealth Settlement Acts, 1945–72', *Journal of Imperial and Commonwealth History*, 26 (1998), 176–95.

51. *Facts About Assisted Passages to Australia*, edition no.9, Jan. 1959. For an effective and well-illustrated comparative study of official Australian immigration literature, see A. Ribchester, 'Marketing Australia: Information for Migrants from Britain, 1901–1924 and 1945–60', MA thesis, University of Lancaster, 2000.

52. W.D. Borrie, *The Growth and Control of World Population* (London, 1970), 109–10. *Net* Australian immigration 1947–69 was only 42 per cent British (and Irish), 12 per cent Northern European, 15 per cent Eastern European, 25 per cent Southern European, 6 per cent elsewhere: Sherington, *Australia's Immigrants*, 149.

53. B. Proudfoot, 'The Setting of Immigration Levels in Canada since the Immigration Act, 1976', *British Journal of Canadian Studies*, 4 (1989), 253; Sherington, *Australia's Immigrants*, 168.

54. Statistics New Zealand, 2001 Census, 'Snapshot 14, People Born Overseas', www.stats.govt.nz.

55. Richmond, *Post-War Immigration to Canada*, 5; R. Farmer, 'International Migration', in R.J.W. Neville and C.J. O'Neill, *The Population of New Zealand: Interdisciplinary Perspectives* (Auckland, 1979), 45; Borrie, *World Population*, 109. See also Sherington, *Australia's Immigrants*, 134.

56. *Guardian*, 13 June 1998, 19.

57. Australian Social Trends 1997, http://www.abs.gov.au/Ausstats.

58. See websites of the immigration authorities of Canada (http://www.immigration.ca), Australia (http://www.immi.gov.au), New Zealand (http://www.immigration.govt.nz), and South Africa (http://www.southafrica-newyork.net/consulate/immigration.htm).

59. McClintock, *New Zealand*, 138–39.

60. Jupp, *Immigration*, 191.

61. Ibid., 192.

62. Calculated from Bloomfield, *New Zealand*, 78–79, and Statistics New Zealand, 2001 Census, 'Snapshot 1, Cultural Diversity', www.stats.govt.nz.

63. Calculated from 'The Daily, Statistics Canada', http://stacan.ca/Daily/English.

64. The ABC in 1962 decided to use speakers with 'Australian' and not 'English' accents: K. Inglis, 'The Empire of the Airwaves', paper to the 'Diaspora, culture and identity' conference, 1998. See also T. Deverson, '"Criticising New Zealand speech unkindly": attitudes to New Zealand English', *British Review of New Zealand Studies*, 3 (1990), 65–75.

65. R. Appleyard, *The Ten Pound Immigrants* (London, 1988), 82; Sherington, *Australia's Immigrants*, 152.

66. J. Stone, *Colonial or Uitlander? A Study of the British Immigrant in South Africa* (Oxford, 1973), 215–19: political apathy was also a characteristic response.

67. A.B. Fraser, 'A Canadian Flag for Canada', *Journal of Canadian Studies*, 25 (1990–91), 64–80.

68. See also the essay by Donal Lowry below.

69. For information on the League but not unfortunately on its membership, see http://www.monarchist.ca.

70. See 'Messages to Her Majesty the Queen', http://www.canadianheritage.gc.ca/special/jubilee/messages (26 Dec. 2002).

71. http://www.geocities.com/keepqueenofoz.

72. The problems of re-presenting in a national museum the national identity of a society now perceived by its curators as diverse and plural are discussed in J. Phillips, 'Our History, Ourselves: The Historian and National Identity', *New Zealand Journal of History*, 30 (1996), 107–23.

73. A.R. McCormack, 'Networks among British Immigrants and Accommodation to Canadian Society: Winnipeg, 1900–1914', in *Diaspora*, 55–71. This essay was later reworked and published in *Histoire sociale – Social History*, 17 (1984), 357–74.

74. J. Belich, *Paradise Reforged: A History of the New Zealanders. From the 1880s to the Year 2000* (Auckland, 2001), 539.
75. I.H. Burnley, *The Impact of Immigration on Australia* (Melbourne, 2001), 298–335; Jupp, *Immigration*, 96–97.
76. National Assembly for Wales, 'Known Welsh Societies around the World', http://users.globalnet.co.uk/~aberarthcrafts/welshsocieties.html.
77. J. Hewitson, *Far Off in Sunlit Places: Stories of the Scots in Australia and New Zealand* (Edinburgh, 1998), 9. He estimates that there are over 100 Scottish clubs, clan societies and organisations in Sydney, 274.
78. Burnley, *Impact of Immigration*, 311, and similar for Perth, 316, and Brisbane, 323.
79. For links to 48 bowling clubs in Australia see http://www.abcbowling.co.uk.
80. http://www.morrisdancing.org/ and links to morris dancing websites.
81. The former British Conservative minister, Norman Tebbit, argued that the Asian communities in Britain were not 'British' because they supported visiting cricket teams from South Asia against the 'home' team: *The Times*, 21 April 1990, 1 and 16.
82. A. Richardson, *British Immigrants and Australia* (Canberra, 1974), which also concluded that among British immigrants 'full assimilation … is relatively infrequent': cited in Jupp, *Immigration*, 94.
83. Appleyard, *Ten Pound Immigrants*, 39. D. Baines, *Migration in a Mature Economy* (Cambridge, 1985), 126–40, estimated that return migration to Britain between 1861 and 1914 was not much less than 40 per cent, but it needs to be remembered that the calculation of necessity was based on passenger figures only and was largely from across the Atlantic, especially from the United States.
84. R.T. Appleyard, 'Determinants of return migration – A Socio-Economic Study of United Kingdom Migrants who Returned from Australia', *Economic Record*, 38 (1962), 352–68.
85. S. Jackel (ed.), *A Flannel Shirt and Liberty: British Emigrant Gentlewomen in the Canadian West, 1880–1914* (Vancouver, 1982), xx–xxi; Jupp, *Immigration*, 87 and 92–3; Appleyard, *Ten Pound Immigrants*, 151, and 128–33 for some oral testimony.
86. B. Broadfoot, *The Immigrant Years: From Europe to Canada 1945–1967* (Vancouver, 1986), 2.
87. B. Zamoyska, *The Ten Pound Fare: Experiences of British People Who Emigrated to Australia in the 1950s* (London, 1988), 128 and 133.
88. More robust conclusions are likely to flow from the British–Australian Postwar Migration Research Project being managed jointly by Dr Alistair Thomson and Dr Jim Hammerton from, respectively, the universities of Sussex and La Trobe. The working title 'Very Familiar and Awfully Strange', derived from the testimony of one migrant, is suggestive. Also see Andrew Hassam, 'The Whingeing Poms and New Australians', unpublished paper presented at the 'End of the Affair?: Britain and Australia since 1945' conference, Sir Robert Menzies Centre for Australian Studies, London, July 2002.
89. See, for example, M.C. Waters, *Ethnic Options: Choosing Identities in America* (Berkeley, 1990).

A New Class of Women for the Colonies:
The Imperial Colonist and the
Construction of Empire

LISA CHILTON

Over the past decade and a half, a great deal of literature has been produced to counter a weighty tradition of imperial history writing that has largely excluded women. Historians of women and of gender have shown how women – as actors and as ideological constructs – played roles of key importance in the evolution of the British world. Recent work on the gendered identities of Britain's white settler societies explores how feminine depictions of the colonies were used to promote British emigration and establish desired relations with the 'mother' country.[1] Historians of women have illustrated the myriad ways in which British and non-British women in various colonial contexts promoted, resisted and reshaped imperialism,[2] while Anna Davin's path-breaking article, 'Imperialism and Motherhood', like the more recent work of Anne McClintock and others, has shown that the lives of women (and of men) in Britain were profoundly affected by Britain's imperialist practices and ideologies.[3]

Historians of nineteenth- and early twentieth-century British female emigration have also made an effort to redress the male-centred nature of imperial history. Studies which focus upon female emigrants have underscored that imperial migration was not the monopoly of male Britons. Similarly, they have emphasised that women experienced migration and settlement in ways that were significantly different from men.[4] The late nineteenth- and early twentieth-century work of female imperialists who promoted and facilitated the emigration of large numbers of single women has been reviewed by historians who have used their findings to reinterpret British women's socio-political roles and identities.[5]

Until recently, female imperialists' emigration work has been understood by historians as fundamentally conservative in regard to emigrant women's socio-economic roles and gender relations. James Hammerton's study, *Emigrant Gentlewomen: Genteel Poverty and Female Emigration, 1830–1914*, set the tone for discussions of the politics of female migration in 1979. Hammerton found in the work of the Female Middle-

Class Emigration Society in the 1860s and 1870s a clear example of feminist effort, after which imperial female migration work reverted to a disappointingly un-feminist project, informed first and foremost by a commitment to a separate spheres ideology.[6] Since then, most studies of organised British female emigration have either assumed or enlarged upon Hammerton's argument that the second wave of female emigration societies purposefully channelled female emigrants into domestic work.[7] A slightly different, though equally damning, interpretation of female emigration work has been provided by Rita Kranidis. In her introduction to *Imperial Objects: Essays on Victorian Women's Emigration and the Unauthorized Imperial Experience*, Kranidis argues that middle-class female emigrants from Britain were 'commodified' in debates between Britons and colonials. According to her, these 'undesirable, "superfluous" English women' had no '*practical* assignment of imperial duty in the colonies – they were being exported as surplus commodities.'[8]

Readings of the female emigrators' work as un- or even anti-feminist have been somewhat undermined by Julia Bush's recent work on Edwardian female imperialists – a group of elite British women that included members of the female emigration societies.[9] Although Bush emphasises that most female imperialists were not feminists, and that their associations were not fuelled by feminist agendas,[10] she does argue that the female imperialist associations were 'powerfully linked to a broader British women's movement, fed by the mingled currents of feminist equal rights activism and gender-conscious social reform'.[11] She shows how women with divergent views on such critical questions as women's suffrage could amicably work together to promote female imperialist agendas.

I

Bush's exploration of the relationships among female imperialists, Edwardian society and the women's movement provides a useful context for a review of the discourses that were constructed in and around *The Imperial Colonist*, founded in 1902 as the official organ of the British Women's Emigration Association and the South African Colonisation Society (and from 1911 the Colonial Intelligence League for Educated Women), and incorporated into *The Oversea Settler* in 1927. A widely disseminated journal produced by women, concerning women, *The Imperial Colonist* was designed to promote female emigration to the colonies, to applaud the female imperialists' work, and to educate Britons and colonists alike about the empire and its needs.[12] The following discussion builds upon Bush's argument that middle- and upper-class British women's female emigration work was a politically complicated project that should not be dismissed as simply conservative. Female emigration societies were motivated by the ideologies and political agendas of a privileged set of British women, women of middle- and upper-class backgrounds with close ties to men in positions of power within the Anglican Church and within the British and Dominion governments. These women espoused political views that had much in common with their male counterparts. The members of these emigration societies shared their confidence that British imperialism was a force of enlightenment and civilisation, designed both to uplift colonised peoples and to reform people of British heritage long settled overseas. They also shared a sense of their own class and racial superiority. Yet a close reading of the literature that the female imperialists wrote about the educated home help in order to promote the emigration of middle-class women to Canada, Australia, New Zealand, South Africa and Rhodesia reveals an imperialist discourse that is strikingly different from most other imperialist discourses of their day, in that it aimed to recreate and empower British women in the colonial context.

The emigrators' alternative view of empire evolved both within and against a broad-based masculine imperial context. Historians of women and imperialism point to a general assumption that empire-building was men's work: women were barred from holding formally recognised posts within the state-building institutions of the empire; female imperialists and adventurers had to fight against insinuations of impropriety, amateurism and manliness in their efforts to get involved in the imperial venture; and women's informal relationships with colonised imperial subjects were regularly portrayed in the press and by the British and colonial governments as detrimental to the imperial project.[13] In fact, by the end of the nineteenth century, colonial frontiers held a mythical manly status. In fiction and in documentary-style travel literature, they were represented as masculine spaces in which danger and adventure, mateship and rugged independence thrived.[14] The frontier was presented enthusiastically as an environment in which men could shed the negative effects of an over-populated, over-civilised homeland. For instance, Anne McClintock describes the imperialist venture as a masculine enterprise, one in which male dominance was asserted over symbolically feminised peoples and territories. She describes the imperial order, a 'Family of Man – a family that admits no mother.'[15] As Anne Windholz has noted, by the end of the nineteenth century, 'the literature of empire ... permeated fin-de-siècle popular culture, not least as an antidote to the degeneracy perceived as threatening British manhood and, by extension, nationhood'.[16] This 'literature of empire' taught boys and men that time spent on the margins of the empire would transform them into real men – men who, unhampered by feminine influences, were free to rediscover their masculine identities.

Yet the assumption that imperialism should be a male monopoly was not shared by everyone. As Adele Perry's study of colonial British Columbia shows, a variety of 'missionaries, politicians, journalists, and freelance do-gooders' worked to reform the rough homosocial culture of the empire's frontier.[17] For many of these reformers, the presence of more white women was essential to the formation of a civilised society. They saw white settler societies' frontier spaces as problematic for the very reasons that these spaces excited the imaginations of the authors of adventure narratives and their readers. In the masculine discourse of empire, the absence of British women from the frontier was presented as a bonus. For those men and women who wished to turn frontier spaces into civilised outposts of the British Empire, the absence of appropriately respected female settlers was a central part of the frontier problem. Reformers regarded with scepticism the idea that the average British man was capable of acting as an effective civilising agent. They argued that the young British men who went out to civilise these raw spaces and their peoples were more likely in the process to lose their own typically British masculine virtues of self-discipline and control than to enhance them. They noted that the absence of respectable British women in the relatively sparsely populated parts of the white settler societies ensured the emergence of lawless, immoral bush cultures, in which alcohol, gambling, violence and mixed-race and illicit sex were prevalent. Reformers emphasised that frontier environments nurtured the least savoury of male attributes; without the right sort of women, white male settlers could not maintain civilised identities. The argument that the colonies[18] needed more white women before they could achieve the status of civilised societies was made by a variety of reformers. The women who joined the female emigration societies became key figures in this project to reform Britain's masculine empire. Their emigration programmes, and the politics that lay behind them, had much in common with those of male-dominated reform organisations.

Yet certain aspects of their vision of the empire differed significantly from those presented by most male promoters of increased female migration.[19] Unlike other emigration promoters, the members of the female emigration societies were determined to oversee the settlement of large numbers of women above the working class in the colonies. The female emigration promoters conceived of the empire as a space in which cultured femininity was a dominant force, and they saw themselves as the empire's grand matriarchs, working from the centre to ensure that the right class of women would be in place to domesticate the periphery appropriately. Whereas the male version of the literature of empire showed how, on the frontier, men would rediscover and reassert masculine power, the literature produced by the female imperialists claimed that those parts of the white settler societies that were in the process of being claimed and civilised were ideal locations for women to demonstrate what it meant to be a true woman. On the frontier, the right sort of women would be free to impose their civilising brand of imperialism, while carving out fulfilling lives for themselves.

From the 1860s, female emigration promoters were consistent in their arguments that the emigration of the wrong sort of woman served only to impede the proper domestication of the empire. The members of the British Women's Emigration Association (BWEA) and affiliated societies took it as a point of pride that they facilitated only the movement of respectable, capable young women. In their annual reports and in their published essays and lectures, they claimed that they discouraged as many, if not more, women than they encouraged to emigrate; more important than sheer numbers was the 'quality' of the female emigrants who would settle in the colonies.[20] The emigrators' arguments about 'quality' reflected their concerns about the emigrants' class and ethnicity. Within the published and unpublished documents created by the female emigration promoters may be seen a well-established system of rank by which the missionising and civilising potential of prospective female emigrants were assessed: firm Christian (but preferably not Catholic) religious convictions were considered a definite asset; emigrants from England and Scotland were ranked above those from Ireland.[21] Working-class women, properly schooled in humility, patience and respectability, were viewed as excellent prospective emigrants. The women who ran the emigration societies wrote positively about how, if carefully selected, such women would do a great service to the empire both as domestic servants and, later, as the wives and mothers of loyal colonial citizens. But they also made it clear that few women of this class could hope to compete with the civilising and missionising power of women of a higher class.

The female emigration societies' promotional literature focused disproportionately on women of a class above that of the average domestic servant. Yet the reality of colonial employment was such that emigration was largely synonymous with domestic service for single women. Most single immigrant women went into domestic service work when they first arrived in the colonies in spite of the increasing tendency of young women in Britain and the colonies to shun domestic service, and in spite of the efforts of British female emigration societies to find alternative careers for single women heading overseas. Throughout this period the colonies had insatiable appetites for British women who were willing to undertake domestic service, but offered few alternative occupations to prospective female immigrants. Again and again the women involved in promoting and facilitating the emigration of women to the colonies tried to scout out unconventional occupations for the women who came to them with the intention of emigrating, but who did not relish the idea of domestic work. Their efforts met with limited success.[22] The occupations available to women were few and gendered female. Women who wished to work outside of the domestic sphere might be employed as factory workers, shop assistants, teachers or nurses; but openings in these fields were inconsistent, comparatively few and usually required specific training and experience. Working on the land was also a limited occupation for women who were discouraged by popular opinion and by legislation from undertaking what was commonly considered men's work.[23]

The reality of women's work options did not fit well with the female imperialists' agenda to populate the colonies with educated women. This incongruity made for some difficulties in promoting emigration. The colonies did not want educated women for domestic servants, and educated women did not find the idea of colonial domestic service appealing. The female emigration societies' promotional literature thus had three aims: it had to convince the colonies that the immigration of educated 'home helps' would be to their benefit; it had to sell colonial emigration to women with appropriately 'gentle' class backgrounds; and it had to help transform women who technically did not match their definitions of a refined, well-educated lady into female emigrants who approximated genteel home helps in outlook and behaviour.

II

From at least the beginning of the nineteenth century, leading residents of the British colonies had publicised their understanding of the best sorts of immigrants for their communities. Of the various groups of emigrants they actively enticed (through advertising, free land and subsidised fares), the only category of unmarried female that was consistently sought was the domestic servant. Even at that, established colonials made it clear that single female immigrants ought to be respectable members of the working class, who had already been trained or were likely to be easily trained to play the part of a subservient female labourer. Colonial administrators were emphatic in their assertion that educated gentlewomen were not one of the preferred categories of immigrants. Gentlewomen were seen as superfluous and thus raised fears that without ready friends and family they would become burdens on the colonial public. Colonials noted that there were many jobs for capable domestic servants, but few jobs for well-educated but poorly trained lady's helpers. Critics of the projects to send educated women to the colonies argued that individuals who had been raised to be gentlewomen could not adapt to long and hard physical labour. Well-educated 'helps' expected to do lighter work and have more privileges than their employers found desirable or even possible. Moreover, educated British women's expectations that they would reform and civilise the communities into which they settled were not well received overseas.

The women who ran the female emigration societies were well aware that the opinions of prospective employers in the colonies were hugely influential in directing the flow of female migration. Not only did they determine what jobs were available and under what circumstances they would be offered, but they were also an effective lobby group *vis-à-vis* government immigration policies. The emigration promoters attempted to win over colonial employers to their cause by showing them the logic behind educated home helps. S.R. Perkins offered a typical analysis of the problematic shortage of colonial domestics in an article published in *The Imperial Colonist*. She pointed out that from 'nowhere in the world, and certainly not from Great Britain, can an adequate supply of domestic servants be obtained' for the colonies. 'Only under the new conditions of treating those who help in the household on a footing of equality can a sufficient supply of helpers now be secured', she claimed. Under these circumstance, it was obvious that 'the more refined the woman helper is the better for the family she enters'. Colonial employers of domestic help could decide the matter for themselves, Perkins argued. 'If ... they remember the inevitable loneliness of the woman ... if they make her feel at home, see that she has society and reasonable recreation, her descriptions of her new life will lead others at home to follow her example. It is only thus that the tide of women's emigration will rise to what we and the Colonies alike would wish to see it.'[24]

The promoters of the educated home help argued that employing gentlewomen immigrants made good sense beyond the fact that the severely restricted domestic labour market meant that colonials could not afford to pick and choose. They explained in detail how educated women made better domestic helps for cultured employers than did *bona fide* working-class servants in the colonies' less populated regions. Educated women could provide lonely housewives of the servant-hiring class with valuable companionship to an extent that could never be true for employees of a lower class. In an article on 'Home Helps', Kathleen Saunders outlined the sort of relationship that she expected would develop between the colonial mistress and her educated home help. She painted a picture of a young woman who 'will make her employer's interests her own, and who will work for her as the good elder daughter would do who is always looking out and anxious to save her mother in every way she can think of'. In cases where the lady of the house was closer in age to her employee, Saunders saw the relationship as rather like that of two sisters. Delighted by her

NEW CLASS OF WOMEN FOR THE COLONIES

vision, Saunders gushed, '[What] a happy life can be led by two young women working together with the baby as a common bond of interest!'[25]

Educated women were supposed to make good domestics because they were of similar class backgrounds to the women for whom they worked, and could thus provide valuable social interaction. But there were many other reasons why hiring an educated domestic helper made good sense. Because of her similar class background, the home help could be employed in homes where there was no possible provision of a private room for the employee. Her social education made it more likely that she would succeed in 'the sometimes difficult place of "one of the family"'.[26] The home help was also a better bet than a working-class servant because she was a bargain. An examination of the wages offered to different classes of domestic workers, as listed in *The Imperial Colonist*, reveals that educated home helps could expect to receive significantly less remuneration for their services than would domestic servants of the working class.[27] The emigrators also argued that educated women made better domestic workers than women lacking formal education, as they could tackle their labour with 'brains as well as hands'.[28] According to the female emigration promoters, in return for low wages and some social generosity, a colonial employer could gain herself a competent and willing worker and a fine companion, all in one.

The women who ran the emigration societies were aware that the promotion of the educated domestic help would not be enough to undermine the colonials' reservations; they also had to diminish the negative stereotype of the 'gentle' female immigrant. Conscious of colonials' sensitivity to attitudes of English superiority in particular, the emigration promoters encouraged their female emigrants to practise inconspicuous colonisation. The editors of *The Imperial Colonist* emphasised this point by publishing the opinions of interested colonials. 'Do bear in mind and send out quiet, sensible, level-headed English girls to uphold the character of their race', pleaded an unnamed correspondent from Toronto. 'The Scotch and North Irish get on much better and are both loved and respected.' Some English girls are so 'ignorant', she continued, 'that they imagine they only have to teach the inhabitants, and you can imagine that this is not a popular attitude, or a true one either'.[29] In her reflections upon the issue of colonial household labour, Katherine Pease took this theme one step further by asserting that South Africans desired household workers 'of sufficient education to know that South Africa is not England'.[30] Female emigrants were warned that colonials would know best how work ought to be done in colonial conditions, and that any attempt to enforce home-country practices would not go over well.[31] The emigration promoters encouraged female emigrants to understand their colonising mission in terms of inculcating colonials with the spirit, tone and ideals of respectable Britishness rather than informing colonials' technical knowledge about the performance of daily tasks.

If colonial employers were dubious about well-educated women transforming into contented domestic servants in the less-populated regions of the empire, so too were the young women who were targeted as the ideal type of emigrant. In their promotion of imperial migration to educated women, the women who ran the female emigration societies focused upon three interconnected themes: they explored how single gentlewomen's precarious economic and social status could be salvaged by emigration; they published narratives of female emigrants' lives filled with adventure and romance; and they encouraged young women to believe that by emigrating, they would be doing something worthwhile, even heroic, with their otherwise 'wasted' lives. They would not be domestic servants, they were told. Rather, they would work as 'companion helps', which would entail no loss of social status. Prospective emigrants were told that by choosing to go to a colony they would find financial security, an improved social identity and a chance at self-fulfilment and lasting happiness. Moreover, they would be doing a great service for the empire.

The turn of the century was an appropriate moment for the enthusiastic construction and promotion of the female imperialists' discourse about the educated home help.[32] This was a period in which class and gender definitions and identities were in flux.[33] Images of the New Woman were busily circulating in British society, stimulating discussions about women's roles, potentials and limitations. Similarly, in Britain and the colonies movements were afoot to alter fundamentally the nature and status of domestic work. Through scientific management and new technologies, reformers toiled to transform household work into a less labour-intensive, 'cleaner' occupation.[34] These efforts to transform the physical labour involved in the maintenance of the domestic sphere were allied with attempts to 'elevate Housecraft to the dignity of a Fine Art'.[35] The timeliness of the message to start life anew as a useful home help in one of the colonies was not lost on the emigrators who made extensive use of the rhetoric of feminist reformers and domestic science advocates to promote their emigration agendas.[36]

The emigration promoters recognised that domestic service did not appeal to educated women. The stated missions of the female emigration societies clearly indicate that finding employment other than domestic service for single women was a central aim of their work, and the minutes of their meetings reveal their frustration about their inability to find sufficient alternative occupations for educated women. Caroline Grosvenor, the chairman of the Colonial Intelligence League and the author of its first annual report, conceded that in their efforts to direct educated women towards the colonies, the members of the CIL faced 'very special difficulties'.[37] Prospective emigrants were informed that other employment options were severely limited, so that only the most qualified women could hope successfully to find such work. By contrast, opportunities for paid employment within the domestic sphere were abundant. Because of the lack of alternative work options for single women in the colonies, the society had 'first to bring home to the lady who desires to try her fortune in the Colonies the absolute necessity of complete and efficient training in the [household] arts'.[38] '[U]nder certain circumstances', Grosvenor wrote, 'this work is absolutely suitable to the educated woman.'[39] The 'certain circumstances' to which Grosvenor referred were those which would decrease or eliminate the educated woman's sense of loss of caste upon taking up domestic labour.

In her biography of Maria Rye, Marion Diamond explores the difficulties of the emigration promoter's work of navigating through the class status implications of domestic service for educated women. As Diamond notes, although a woman's occupation could be of critical importance to her social status, class identity was also determined by 'many subtle indications relating to education, accent and manner'.[40] In Britain, crossing the divide between respectable and working-class employment was impossible for those women who desired to maintain their relationships with people of their own class. But by emigrating to the colonies the possibilities for combining paid domestic work with a gentlewoman's status were presumably greatly enhanced. In this gendered 'class ambiguity', Maria Rye and those who would follow her in this work saw a vast field of opportunities for adaptable, well-educated women.

In order for the educated home help to feel that she had not irredeemably lost her genteel social status, her employment had to take place in a particular social environment. According to the emigrators, only in rural areas could such environments be found. As Grosvenor noted, 'in the large towns (in Eastern Canada, for instance), where class distinctions have already taken root and flourish vigorously, we do not recommend this particular kind of work for educated women'.[41] Nor would any rural space do. Some colonial destinations were explicitly promoted in preference to others.[42] British Columbia was consistently favoured as a destination for educated home helps because of the large number of English emigrants of 'gentle' birth who had settled there, and because British Columbians were particularly enthusiastic about employing educated women in their homes.[43] For a short period, immediately after the second Anglo-Boer War, South Africa supplanted British Columbia as the emigrators' favourite destination for educated women. The special attention given to the emigration of educated women to South African farm communities in the first decade of the twentieth century was largely due to the emigrators' imperialist politics. But the presence of a large population of Africans was also critical to South

Africa's promotion, as the emigrators believed that African workers would eliminate the most onerous manual labour from white women's daily chores.[44] Domestic work with the more unpleasant tasks performed by someone else could more easily be made appealing to prospective emigrants.[45]

In the literature produced by female emigration promoters, prospective home helps were told that they would be found situations where they would be treated as one of the family. Young women would be attracted to working in such contexts, wrote the editor of *The Imperial Colonist*, as they would not have to worry about 'losing caste by having to associate with those who are less educated than themselves'.[46] 'The real lady feels no degradation' in performing household work, Grosvenor claimed. Rather, 'what she does dislike and rightly, is to find that by reason of her work she is considered to have sunk in the social scale and is no longer treated as an equal by those of her own class'.[47] In order to assure educated home helps that they would be employed in the right sort of household – one in which the employers were of the appropriate class themselves, and where the help would be treated like a lady – the intervention of the emigration societies and their colonial representatives was essential. Local colonial committees of 'ladies' who were willing to welcome educated home helps and facilitate their appropriate employment were critical to the emigrators' promotion of various destinations to women above the 'domestic' class.[48]

The promoters of educated women's emigration made extensive use of testimonies from emigrant women and from colonial employers to prove their point that gentility and working as a home help were not incompatible. A letter from E.S., a home help working in Caribou, British Columbia, is typical of those that were published in *The Imperial Colonist* and in the societies' annual reports. 'I have now been here almost two months', E.S. wrote, 'and feel I can safely say that I am settled. I am doing the work for, and looking after an elderly lady and gentleman, and am treated just as a daughter ... I have felt quite at home from the first day.'[49] Ostensibly private letters from prospective employers to the emigration promoters were published in *The Imperial Colonist* to make the same point. 'I may tell you I want a young lady more for companionship than help, for I am devoted to the work, but I am right away in the country – a widow – living alone, and I should much appreciate a companion', reads one such letter. The author, a recent English emigrant herself, declared that she was looking for a surrogate daughter as hers had all married and moved away.[50] In a long article entitled 'Are Educated Women wanted in Canada?', Georgina Binnie-Clarke, who had had first-hand Canadian experience and was considered an authority on the position of women in Canada, cited an example of one English lady-help with whom she had become acquainted, to press home the point that in Canada, 'No woman of refinement need hesitate to take up domestic service.' Despite a hard day of work, the young lady in question

> always contrived to appear at table as neatly and becomingly attired as a woman of leisure. She was always included in any invitations that came to my host and hostess, and was a very welcome guest among the neghbours [sic]. She took part in all the amusements and recreations that came to cheer one on one's way, and she also enjoyed the privilege of keeping her own pony, and rode whenever a successful navigation through the daily round permitted.[51]

In their publications, the emigration promoters emphasised that educated women with the right sort of personalities would not lose status by performing the work of a domestic helper, because they would be doing the same sort of work that was done on a daily basis by their employers. In the colonies' rural districts, all women performed such work, as they had no option, readers were told. 'Many delicately nurtured gentlewomen, not being able to procure the help upon which they have always depended, have trained themselves to do every kind of work', declared Mrs Skinner, the BWEA's corresponding secretary for British Columbia. These women 'have found, too, that the refinements of education, which they at first thought so useless in the colony, were really a help in the end. The broader intelligence linked with willing hands soon brought-forth splendid results.'[52] Moreover, in the country districts of the colonies, expert housewives had transformed housekeeping into a highly respectable career. In an article on 'Farm Homes in Canada', Mrs Alfred Watt explained why educated women were better suited to the work of running a farm home than were women of a lower class:

> She is away from big libraries and must be herself a 'reference' for the children ... Her emergency chest must have the home remedies which she must know how to make. Her knowledge of agricultural operations must be sufficient to make her an intelligent help-meet in what is an arduous and complicated method of earning a living. Her knowledge of home nursing and home sanitation and sanitary appliances must be practical. And she must know food values and the common symptoms of diseases ... this is only part, and only the house and practical part, for the farm woman is nearly always in charge of the vegetable and fruit garden and poultry ... [Greater] still, she has the responsibility of the mental and moral wellbeing of the family.[53]

Watt depicted educated women as having skills and knowledge that could transform pioneers' household work into a career eminently suitable (even best suited) to women of their class.

III

Although home help employment was enthusiastically promoted by the women who ran the emigration societies, such a career was seldom presented as an end in itself. The emigration societies never lost their interest in finding alternative occupations for educated women. 'Not that we could on any account belittle the profession of Home-help', the editor of *The Imperial Colonist* hastened to assure her readers; 'some women find the position so agreeable that they do not wish to exchange it for any other'.[54] But the reality was that most women could not envision themselves working as home helps for life. This work was thus often promoted as a stepping stone to bigger and better things. Home help employment was recommended for women with a wide range of aspirations. 'Real talent is certain to find its outlet in the end', but in the meantime, the home help will be 'saved by the shelter of home-life from many sharp experiences in a new country', wrote M. Montgomery-Campbell.[55] By working as home helps, young single women could become acclimatised to their new physical and social environments while living in contexts that provided financial security and (at least in theory) a degree of emotional support.

Although the topic of heterosexual love and marriage was avoided by many of the women who wrote promotional literature for the female emigration societies, it was clearly in the back of most emigration promoters' minds as a powerful incentive for single women to emigrate. On this topic, there was often a discrepancy between what the emigration promoters said in their private correspondence and what they put in print.[56] Negative public reactions to the mid-century work of Caroline Chisholm and Maria Rye, due to press representations of female emigration work as husband-finding missions,[57] had taught the female emigration promoters of the late nineteenth century that references to marriage ought to be dealt with carefully in their writing. Too much enthusiasm about marriage in their promotional literature could once again create problems. Yet the assumptions that most young women desired to become wives and mothers, and that marriage was more likely to be attainable in the colonies' less populated regions, is a theme that runs through the literature produced by female emigration societies from the 1840s to the end of the 1920s, regardless of the extent to which the image of pining, marriageable bachelors on farms was based in reality. As one article reproduced in *The Imperial Colonist* put it, 'Many girls in this country know that in the West there are prospects of marriage to farmers. This is indeed an attraction. Why should it not be? Few girls are worth their salt ... if they hope not one day to be queen of a home.'[58] As the announcement of an emigrant home help's impending marriage made clear, emigrants who married well after spending time as domestic helps were admirably fitted for their future work as the mistresses of their own homes. 'Possessing both education and a complete knowledge of the management of a home', the ex-home help had 'every chance of a happy life before her.'[59]

Marriage predominated in published lists of the emigration societies' 'successes'.[60] But women-owned business and farming ventures were the focus of greater interest in the journal's articles, and letters from women running their own businesses were highlighted as correspondence particularly worthy of the readers' notice. Businesses more easily gendered female were especially promoted in *The Imperial Colonist* as likely avenues of success for capable and energetic educated women. Farms specialising in poultry, fruit production and bee keeping received regular attention in this journal, as did boarding houses, bakeries and businesses related to needlework. But women's involvement in farming activities that were more usually considered the preserve of men also received enthusiastic support in *The Imperial Colonist*. Success stories of women who struck out on their own as colonial farmers in the face of social and physical impediments may be found throughout the quarter century of the journal's publication. Successful female farmers were depicted as smart, plucky and overflowing with vitality. In spite of the obviously feminist implications of many of these stories, care was taken to emphasise that femininity was not sacrificed. Two English sisters, who made a 'brilliant success' of farming in Manitoba, operated '1,120 acres of mixed-farm' completely by themselves. 'Even to-day when they are rich and prosperous and there is no longer any reason why they should not hire male help extensively, they prefer to perform themselves all the tasks of the large establishment', wrote the author of 'Some Canadian Women Pioneers'. 'Here "man" is never seen', she joked, 'save as an admiring visitor.'[61] The cautions about the difficulties that had to be overcome before a lady farmer could be a success that usually accompanied these stories would have served, if anything, to increase the hero status of these vigorous women.

Educated women were encouraged to see emigration to the colonies and employment in someone else's home as a logical path to financial stability, self-fulfilment and sanctified heterosexual love. But the promotional literature was not all so serious. Life as a colonial home help was also presented as jolly good fun. Emigration was held out as an adventure, or, as the letters of young female emigrants described it, 'a picnic'. Gentlewomen in the colonies had the freedom to be unconventional (within strict parameters), unbound by archaic social conventions and the dictates of respectable society. The life of the home help was especially indicated for the 'girl who declared that most hardships would be compensated for by freedom from veils and gloves'.[62] The female emigrants' letters revealed that rural life did not mean isolation. Horse riding (a much commented-upon activity) allowed for a never-ending round of outings to dances and other social events. The beauty of the new settler's physical environment was the focus of a great amount of attention, as was the belief that the climate and physical activities tended to improve the health and physical attractiveness of the young women who moved out to the colonies' rural spaces. Whether a woman's destination was Australia, South Africa, New Zealand or Canada, she was informed that the environment would suit her better than that of her homeland. A rural home help existence would turn young women into more vibrant, healthy, 'interesting' versions of their former selves.

The emigration promoters worked hard to make a success of their programme to settle a new class of women in the colonies. Through their published writing, public lectures and private interactions with prospective emigrants, the emigrators encouraged single women of the appropriate social backgrounds to emigrate. They wheedled and bullied colonials into giving their carefully selected home helps a trial, and they established extensive systems of support for these women overseas. They actively discouraged educated women from choosing destinations that they considered to be unsuitable, and they were untiring in their promotion of colonial communities that were particularly hospitable to educated home helps. They carefully instructed their chosen emigrants about how educated home helps ought to behave and what sorts of attitudes they should hold. In their lectures and writing, the emigrators emphasised that all reasonable steps had been taken to ensure the emigrants' success. The rest, the departing women were told, was up to them.

The failure of individual women to settle comfortably into the colonial home help identity was usually explained in terms of personal character flaws. 'The qualifications for success in Canada', Ellen Joyce wrote to her female emigrants, 'are adaptability, capability, courtesy ... "grit and grace".'[63] If a woman was not a success, she obviously lacked one or more of these traits. Central to the literature promoting the career of colonial home help was the assumption that British women of gentle birth would be equal or superior in culture and refinement to the colonial women they were going out to serve. As one group of women departing for South Africa were reminded, it was their duty to 'raise the tone' of their future homes.[64] Yet to show any evidence of such an assumption was presented in the emigration promoters' literature as evidence of a lack of good breeding – a clear sign that the woman was wanting in courtesy.

Educated women who chose the occupation of home help in the colonies were expected to take their decision very seriously. The women who encouraged and facilitated their settlement in the colonies told them in no uncertain terms that failure in their new careers would not only affect themselves, but would also have a negative affect upon the organisations' future efforts to help out financially troubled gentlewomen. As one correspondent put it, 'So much depends on the girls themselves. If they are capable, sweet-tempered and adaptable, they not only succeed themselves, but make the way so much easier for others who shall follow.'[65] The identities that educated female emigrants formed as household workers and as citizens would determine both the extent of colonial employers' demands for their labour and the likelihood that educated home helps would receive government subsidised transportation to the colonies. Upon these emigrants lay the ultimate failure or success of the home help project as a whole, and, by extension, the female imperialist agenda to 'civilise' the empire.

The assertion that, 'There is no greater or better civilising power in the world than that which a truly good woman possesses',[66] might well have been *The Imperial Colonist*'s motto. In the female emigration promoters' imperialist writing, women were empowered to act as agents of empire. The emigrators showed women engaged in colonial adventures as heroes, civilising uncivilised native peoples and white men, and conquering harsh physical environments. The image of a British woman, empowered by her intellect and by her femininity, subduing and improving man and nature, could work for female imperialists of various political leanings. As a part of a campaign to promote female emigration, it was also an image that could be made attractive to younger women from a wide range of social backgrounds.

The literature produced by the emigration promoters aimed to do more than entice educated women to move to the colonies. It was also prescriptive. The emigration promoters were clear about what constituted the ideal prospective emigrant. However, few 'ideal' women were forthcoming, and even the young women who came from the ideal social background for making a success of a home help career required some special coaching about how to approach their new social roles. The images that were evoked in this literature were thus designed both to entice prospective emigrants and to inspire those who had already made the decision to settle in the colonies to become, by example, key components in a programme of benevolent colonisation. Through their writing and through their personal interactions with emigrant women, the emigrators taught British women how to be both genteel and successful in the colonies, while undertaking the noble mission of improving colonial society.

IV

In this essay, it has been argued that domestic service was not necessarily the preferred focus of the female emigration societies' promotional efforts. Rather, their endorsement of household work was the result of unavoidable constraints imposed by the gendered nature of the labour economy. An examination of *The Imperial Colonist* reveals that domestic service was primarily a means to an end – the end being the proper feminisation of the wider British world. The female emigration societies had to overcome a number of obstacles in order to implement their imperialist programme. The high costs of transportation and settlement were a constant source of difficulty for the emigration promoters who usually dealt with women who had limited financial resources. Similarly, the women that they were most interested in seeing settled in the colonies were not easily convinced to leave their British homes. The appeal of the colonies was particularly undermined by the fact that domestic service consistently dominated the colonial employment scene for women. The emigration promoters worked hard to secure funding from colonial governments, colonial employers and philanthropically minded colonial and British citizens to support female emigration. They also endeavoured to open up alternative career options for women emigrating to the colonies, and to improve the image of colonial domestic service. The emigrators had to pacify their project's critics, win converts to their vision of the empire, and convince single women that emigration would prove rewarding and fulfilling. As a result, the authors of promotional literature did not merely offer their own perspectives on these themes. They also responded, at least rhetorically, to the demands of a number of other interested parties.

The women who ran the British female emigration societies in the early twentieth century were motivated by political opinions that were every bit as racist, classist and imperialistic as their male counterparts. Historians who have worked in this field have also shown that the societies' programmes for single female emigrants of lower-class backgrounds tended to restrict these emigrants' movements and waged work options.[67] Yet an examination of the promotional literature which was aimed at the emigrators' 'ideal', middle-class female emigrants reveals a discourse that, if traditionally gendered in many ways, was designed to be essentially empowering. Indeed, these female emigrants were assigned an 'imperial duty' of critical importance, at the same time as they were provided with a vision of comparative freedom and self-fulfilment in the colonies. In a cultural context in which imperialism, colonisation and frontier adventure were considered the *métiers* of men, the emigrators' determination to highlight and celebrate 'heroic' women enthusiastically embracing life in the rougher parts of the empire was seriously alternative. The female imperialists had unbounded faith in the abilities of suitably educated women to be successful in whatever venture they might undertake. They assumed that, if educated women were forced by financial difficulties and a limited range of employment options into domestic work, they would be able to turn the situation to their advantage. They depicted the colonies as environments in which educated British women could thrive, to the benefit of themselves and, more importantly, to the communities into which they settled. Given space to prove their worth, they argued, educated women would use their inherent personal advantages to carve out strong roles and identities for themselves in the mutable environment of the colonial frontier, to civilise and extend the boundaries of the British world.

NOTES

The author would like to thank Bettina Bradbury, James Hammerton, Kathryn McPherson, James Moran, Camille Soucie and Nick Rogers for comments upon earlier versions of this article.

1. See D.D. Alessio, 'Domesticating "the Heart of the Wild": Female Personifications of the Colonies, 1886–1940', *Women's History Review*, 6 (1997), 239–69. Kate Darian-Smith presented a paper on this subject entitled, 'Exhibiting Identities: Australian Women, Nationalism and the Empire', The British World Conference, University of Cape Town, South Africa, 9–11 Jan. 2002.
2. See, for example, H. Callaway, *Gender, Culture and Empire: European Women in Colonial Nigeria* (New York, 1987); N. Chaudhuri and Margaret Strobel (eds.), *Western Women and Imperialism: Complicity and Resistance* (Bloomington, 1992); P. Grimshaw, Marilyn Lake, Ann McGrath and Marian Quartly, *Creating a Nation, 1788–1990* (Toronto, 1996); C. Midgley (ed.), *Gender and Imperialism* (New York, 1998); A. Perry, *On the Edge of Empire: Gender, Race, and the Making of British Columbia, 1849–1871* (Toronto, 2001); M.L. Pratt, *Imperial Eyes: Travel Writing and Transculturation* (New York, 1992); Margaret Strobel, *European Women and the Second British Empire* (Bloomington, 1991); and V. Ware, *Beyond the Pale: White Women, Racism and History* (London, 1992).
3. A. Davin, 'Imperialism and Motherhood', *History Workshop Journal*, no.5 (1978), 9–65; A. McClintock, *Imperial Leather: Race, Gender and Sexuality in the Colonial Contest* (New York, 1995); A. Burton, *Burdens of History: British Feminists, Indian Women, and Imperial Culture, 1865–1915* (Chapel Hill, NC, 1994); B. Bush, '"Britain's Conscience on Africa": White Women, Race and Imperial Politics in Inter-War Britain', in Midgley (ed.), *Gender and Imperialism*, 200–23; and C. Midgley, 'Anti-Slavery and the Roots of "Imperial Feminism"', ibid., 161–79.
4. For different national examples, see J. Gothard, *Blue China: Single Female Migration to Colonial Australia* (Melbourne, 2001); M. Harper, *Willing Exiles: Emigration from North-East Scotland*, vol.1 (Aberdeen, 1988); P. Jackson, 'Women in 19th Century Irish Emigration', *International Migration Review*, 18 (1984), 1004–21; M. Langfield, 'Gender Blind? Australian Immigration Policy and Practice, 1901–1930', *Journal of Australian Studies* (2003), forthcoming; C. MacDonald, *A Woman of Good Character: Single Women as Immigrant Settlers in Nineteenth-Century New Zealand* (Wellington, 1990); and J.J. Van Helten and Keith Williams, '"The Crying Need of South Africa": The Emigration of Single British Women to the Transvaal, 1901–10', *Journal of Southern African Studies*, 10 (1983), 17–38.
5. See, for example, Julia Bush, *Edwardian Ladies and Imperial Power* (New York, 2000); A.J. Hammerton, *Emigrant Gentlewomen: Genteel Poverty and Female Emigration, 1830–1914* (London, 1979); and R. Kranidis, *The Victorian Spinster and Colonial Emigration:*

Contested Subjects (New York, 1999).

6. Hammerton, *Emigrant Gentlewomen*, esp. chs.5 and 6.
7. See, for example, M. Barber, *Immigrant Domestic Servants in Canada* (Ottawa, 1991); M. Langfield, '"A Chance to Bloom": Female Migration and Salvationists in Australia and Canada', *Australian Feminist Studies*, 17 (2002), 287–303; and B. Roberts, 'Ladies, Women and the State: Managing Female Migration', in Roxana Ng, Gillian Walker and Jacob Muller (eds.), *Community Organization and the Canadian State* (Toronto, 1990), 108–30.
8. R. Kranidis, *Imperial Objects: Essays on Victorian Women's Emigration and the Unauthorized Imperial Experience* (New York, 1998), 14 (original emphasis). See also Kranidis, *Victorian Spinster*.
9. In a recent article that reassesses female emigration work, Hammerton indicates that Bush's publications have made it imperative that we struggle to understand the emigrators' gender politics as more complicated than his earlier work had allowed. See A.J. Hammerton, '"Out of Their Natural Station": Empire and Empowerment in the Emigration of Lower-Middle-Class Women', in Kranidis (ed.), *Imperial Objects*, 144–45.
10. Bush, *Edwardian Ladies*, 179.
11. Ibid., 175.
12. Throughout the Victorian period and the early twentieth century, the female emigration promoters published their views in a range of journals, newspapers, and pamphlets. But after its creation in 1902, *The Imperial Colonist* quickly became the central site of their female imperialist discourse's construction, evolution and dissemination. Prospective emigrant women were expected to read the journal. Copies were standardly left in the women's hostels' lounge areas for use by migrating women.
13. Mary Procida provides an excellent discussion of the antipathy towards women's imperial involvement in her dissertation, 'Married to the Empire: British Wives and British Imperialism in India, 1883–1947', Ph.D. thesis, University of Pennsylvania, 1997.
14. For discussions of the empire and masculinity, see Anna Davin's review article, 'Historical Masculinities: Regulation, Fantasy and Empire', *Gender and History*, 9 (1997), 135–38; S.L. Blake, 'A Woman's Trek: What Difference Does Gender Make?', in Chaudhuri and Strobel (eds.), *Western Women and Imperialism*, 19–34; J. Bristow, *Empire Boys: Adventures in a Man's World* (London, 1991); G. Dawson, *Soldier Heroes: British Adventure, Empire, and the Imagining of Masculinities* (London, 1994); and J.M. MacKenzie (ed.), *Imperialism and Popular Culture* (Manchester, 1986).
15. McClintock, *Imperial Leather*, 4.
16. A.M. Windholz, 'An Emigrant and a Gentleman: Imperial Masculinity, British Magazines, and the Colony That Got Away', *Victorian Studies*, 42 (Summer 1999–2000), 631.
17. Perry, *On the Edge of Empire*, 79.
18. The term 'colonies' was used by the female emigration promoters indiscriminately to denote those places that had ties to the British Empire, regardless of whether or not they had become independent Dominions. For convenience I shall also refer to Canada, Australia, New Zealand and South Africa as colonies, and their white populations as colonials, even though these terms are technically incorrect.
19. One context in which this difference between male promoters of female emigration and the women who ran the female emigration societies is particularly clear is that of South Africa in the post-Anglo-Boer War period. For discussions of this, see B. Blakeley, 'Women and Imperialism: The Colonial Office and Female Emigration to South Africa, 1901–10', *Albion*, 13 (1981), 131–49; and Van Helten and Williams, '"The Crying Need of South Africa"'.
20. Various government bodies also tried to limit female emigration by imposing 'quality' controls. But, the ways in which 'quality' was defined by government agencies differed significantly from those of the female emigrators, discussed here. For an example of early government efforts to select 'quality' female emigrants, see R.F. Haines, *Emigration and the Labouring Poor: Australian Recruitment in Britain and Ireland, 1831–69* (London, 1997).
21. As Julia Bush has shown, these societies and their leaders were unshakeably English-centric. See Bush, *Edwardian Ladies*.
22. Flurries of correspondence on this subject were initiated by the Female Middle-Class Emigration Society in the 1860s; the Colonial Intelligence League in the 1910s; and the

Society for the Oversea Settlement of British Women in the period immediately after the First World War.

23. See Susan Jackel, 'Introduction', in Georgina Binnie-Clarke, *Wheat and Women* (Toronto, 1979).

24. S.R. Perkins, 'Emigration', *The Imperial Colonist*, 3, 35 (Nov. 1904), 127.

25. K. Saunders, 'Home Helps', *The Imperial Colonist*, 6, 61 (Jan. 1907), 5.

26. Miss Johnson, 'Domestic Helps in Natal', *The Imperial Colonist*, 2, 4 (April 1903), 43.

27. See, for example, the June (p.69) and Nov. (p.126) issues of *The Imperial Colonist* of 1904, in which the monthly salaries that domestic workers might expect were listed in Canadian dollars as follows: mother's help, $12–$15; nurse-housemaids, $15; lady helps, $15; servants, $20; cooks, $20–$25.

28. Taken from *The Times*, quoted in *The Imperial Colonist*, 6, 74 (Feb. 1908), 9–10.

29. 'The New Hostel at Toronto', *The Imperial Colonist*, 9, 115 (July 1911), 338.

30. K. Pease, 'Experiences of an English Worker in South Africa', *The Imperial Colonist*, 2, 2 (Feb. 1903), 21.

31. See, for examples, *The Imperial Colonist*, 7, 87 (March 1909), 41; 9, 109 (Jan. 1911), 226–27; and 18, 214 (Jan. 1920), 6.

32. Earlier efforts to settle educated women in the colonies met with much less success. For an example, see Perry, *On the Edge of Empire*.

33. See S. Ledger, *The New Woman: Fiction and Feminism at the Fin de Siècle* (New York, 1997); and E. Showalter, *Sexual Anarchy: Gender and Culture at the Fin de Siècle* (New York, 1990).

34. For a discussion of 'The Rationalization of Housework' during the nineteenth century, see L. Davidoff, *Worlds Between: Historical Perspectives on Gender and Class* (Cambridge, 1995), ch.5.

35. This quotation comes from an article on the National Guild of Housecraft that was published in *The Imperial Colonist*, 13, 156 (Jan. 1915), 13.

36. Even Ellen Joyce, who was one of the more conservative emigration promoters in terms of her ideas about the women's sphere, made use of the current rhetoric about 'new' understandings of women's place in society to promote her cause. As she noted in a paper on 'Openings for Educated Women in Canada', not only were young women coming around to the understanding that economic independence and self-fulfilment through work were preferable to a parasitic existence, but so too was the 'new father', who had come to know that 'his girls will lead happier lives if they are filled with work than empty with idleness.' E. Joyce, *Openings for Educated Women in Canada* (n.p., n.d.), 2.

37. *First Annual Report of the Colonial Intelligence League (For Educated Women)* (n.p., 1911), 8.

38. Ibid.

39. Ibid., 10–11.

40. M. Diamond, *Emigration and Empire: The Life of Maria S. Rye* (New York, 1999), 81.

41. *First Annual Report of the Colonial Intelligence League*, 11.

42. New Zealand and most of the Australian states seldom gained sustained attention as possible destinations for educated female emigrants. For a short discussion of efforts to settle educated women in these locations, see K. Pickles, 'Empire Settlement and Single British Women as New Zealand Domestic Servants during the 1920s', *New Zealand Journal of History*, 35 (2001), 29–30.

43. For a fuller discussion of this, see M. Barber, 'The Gentlewomen of Queen Mary's Coronation Hostel', in B.K. Latham and R.J. Pazdro (eds.), *Not Just Pin Money: Selected Essays on the History of Women's Work in British Columbia* (Victoria, BC, 1984), 141–58.

44. On female emigration to South Africa, see Blakeley, 'Women and Imperialism'; C. Swaisland, *Servants and Gentlewomen to the Golden Land: The Emigration of Single Women from Britain to Southern Africa, 1820–1939* (Providence, RI, 1993); and Van Helten and Williams, '"The Crying Need of South Africa"'.

45. South African employers tried to put a stop to emigration promotion literature that indicated that African labour would make life easy for white domestic servants. They argued that on many grounds, this sort of promotion was problematic. See for example 'Notes of the

Month', *The Imperial Colonist*, 4, 41 (May 1905), 49–50.

46. 'Some Situations Offered for Useful Helps', *The Imperial Colonist*, 3, 34 (Oct. 1904), 117.
47. *Third Annual Report of the Colonial Intelligence League (For Educated Women)* (n.p., 1913), 11.
48. The relationships between colonial committees of women and the British female emigration societies are discussed at length in L. Chilton, 'Emigrators, Emigrants and Empire: Women and British Migration to Canada and Australia in the Nineteenth and Early Twentieth Centuries', Ph.D. thesis, York University, 2002, ch.4.
49. E.S., quoted in *The Imperial Colonist*, 7, 86 (Feb. 1909), 26.
50. Letter published in *The Imperial Colonist*, 7, 87 (March 1909), 42.
51. G. Binnie-Clarke, 'Are Educated Women wanted in Canada?', *The Imperial Colonist*, 8, 98 (Feb. 1910), 23.
52. Mrs Skinner, 'In British Columbia', *The Imperial Colonist*, 3, 30 (June 1904), 67.
53. Mrs Alfred Watt, 'Farm Homes in Canada', *The Imperial Colonist*, 13, 159 (April 1915), 61.
54. *The Imperial Colonist*, 8, 100 (April 1910), 51.
55. M. Montgomery-Campbell, 'Ca-na-da. A Contradiction in Terms', *The Imperial Colonist*, 2, 2 (Feb. 1903), 18.
56. See Julia Bush's comment on this in *Edwardian Ladies*, 156–59.
57. See Diamond, *Emigration and Empire*, 86; and Perry, *On the Edge of Empire*, ch.6.
58. 'English Girls for Canada', taken from the *Imperial Review*, reproduced in *The Imperial Colonist*, 7, 86 (Feb. 1909), 23–24.
59. *The Imperial Colonist*, 7, 88 (April 1909), 52.
60. See for example, 'Educated Girls in Winnipeg', *The Imperial Colonist*, 23, 3 (March 1925), 46–48.
61. E.L. Chicanot, 'Some Canadian Women Pioneers', *The Imperial Colonist*, 23, 10 (Oct. 1925), 197–98. See also, for example, the April 1910 edition of *The Imperial Colonist*, which contains several articles on farming for women in the colonies.
62. L.E. Foster, 'A Bird's-Eye View of Canada', *The Imperial Colonist*, 5, 52 (April 1906), 47.
63. E. Joyce, *Ventures within the Empire: To Women of the 20th Century* (n.p., 1913), 10.
64. 'Parting Words', reported by Adelaide Ross, *The Imperial Colonist*, 2, 1 (Jan. 1903), 6.
65. Mrs Skinner, 'Report of Work in BC', *The Imperial Colonist*, 7, 88 (April 1909), 52. See also *The Imperial Colonist*, 2, 4 (April 1903), 45; 6, 62 (Feb. 1907), 7; and the *1923 Annual Report of the Society for Oversea Settlement of British Women*.
66. The quotation comes from Mrs Skinner, the British Columbian associate of the BWEA. *The Imperial Colonist*, 2, 4 (April 1903), 41.
67. See especially: Gothard, *Blue China*; Langfield, 'A Chance to Bloom'; and P. Hamilton, 'The "Servant Class": Poor Female Migration to Australia in the Nineteenth Century', in E. Richards (ed.), *Poor Australian Immigrants in the Nineteenth Century. Visible Immigrants: Two* (Canberra, 1991), 117–31.

The Welsh World and the British Empire, c.1851–1939: An Exploration

ALED JONES and BILL JONES

Wales has sometimes been described as England's first colony,[1] whilst at the same time, from the sixteenth century onwards, the people, institutions and economy of Wales have played a formative role in the British imperial project. In this respect Wales, like Ireland and Scotland, presents something of a paradox in having being regarded as both imperial and colonial, though the relationships between the two were perhaps more complex and diverse than a straightforward colonised/coloniser dichotomy might suggest.[2] Historians of Wales have to some degree focused on the increasingly close ties between Wales and the British Empire, especially from the mid-nineteenth century onwards, and have seen it as part of the metropolitan core of empire rather than a colonial dependency.[3] During that period Wales's growing economic importance created by its dominant coal export sector, its greater political assertiveness, the founding of its own 'national' institutions such as the University of Wales, National Library and National Museum, the growth in the number of Welsh speakers, and the 'cultural renaissance' of Welsh-language literature, education, publishing and music took place within an accepted British Imperial framework. There have been references to 'Imperial South Wales' and the existence of an 'imperial Welshness' in the years before the First World War.[4] While some historians have stressed the extent of sympathy and support in Wales for imperialism, and the important role the empire played in the construction of a British identity, others have explored Welsh voices which dissented from imperialist sentiment.[5]

As yet, however, very little attention has been paid to the diversity of Welsh people and institutions in British colonies overseas. The general tendency among Welsh historians, at least until recently, has been to marginalise the experience of the Welsh overseas in general, and to concentrate more on the impact on Wales of in-migration rather than on those who crossed its borders in the other direction. In a post-war historiography of the nineteenth and twentieth centuries dominated by the study of overwhelmingly male political, labour and social institutions, the colonial, largely middle-class and female nature of the Welsh missionary field, for example, attracted the attention of few professional historians.[6] Nor, one might add, did the need to engage with the evangelical and theological, rather than the political, dimension of Nonconformity appeal to a more secular generation of post-war historians eager to emerge from the shadow of nineteenth-century Methodism.[7] Another explanation for this marginalisation may stem from the rejection of British colonialism that defined the dominant socialist and nationalist currents within post-war Welsh politics. An unease with a history of participation in, or, to borrow from an Irish parallel, of 'collaboration' with, British imperial expansion may have served as a powerful motive for avoiding the integration of colonial activity fully into the history of modern Wales.[8] Given the paucity of historical work on Welsh involvement in the empire during this period, the main aim of this essay is to survey the evidence, identify and explore some avenues of enquiry, and consider some appropriate methodological approaches.

I

The Welsh involvement in the British Empire during the nineteenth and early twentieth centuries was a multi-faceted phenomenon. As Marjory Harper has commented, this was true of British migration generally during the nineteenth century.[9] One obvious manifestation was the emergence of a relatively small Welsh – and at least in the early years a largely Welsh-speaking – migrant presence, and the formation of Welsh settler communities that, initially at least, supported a distinctive Welsh-language religious and cultural life. Welsh emigrants to empire destinations generally confined themselves to the white settler societies of British North America, Australia and New Zealand and South Africa. The lack of a separate and comprehensive official statistical record, largely due to what Ged Martin and Benjamin E. Kline have called the 'statistical indignity of being lumped in with the English', prevents precision regarding the size and direction of the outflow.[10] However, it is clear that Canada attracted the most Welsh, followed by Australia, South Africa and New Zealand. Figures for native-born Welsh in 1901 and 1921 are: Australia: 12,800 and 13,490; Canada: 13,421 and 41,952; and New Zealand: 1,765 and 2,575 respectively; whilst in 1926 the South African census recorded 4,328 persons in the Union born in Wales.[11] Those Welsh who went to the colonies were easily outnumbered by their countrymen and women who emigrated to the United States, and even more so by those who moved across the border into England.[12] On the other hand, more emigrated to Canada, Australia or South Africa than the 3,000 or so who went to *Y Wladfa*, the Welsh colony in Patagonia, established in 1865 to preserve the Welsh language.[13] It should be remembered that these Welsh migrant streams to the British colonies were themselves diverse in terms of their composition, motivations and destinations, although we might note the pull of the mining areas as one common denominator. Further, although well-known centres of Welsh concentration – such as the Victorian goldfields or the Hunter Valley coalfield in the case of Australia – inevitably dominate the picture to some extent, Welsh migrant experiences in the empire seem also to be characterised by high rates of spatial mobility and isolated, scattered settlement.

As in the cases of England, Ireland and Scotland, as well as sending out sizeable numbers of permanent settlers to the colonies and Dominions, Wales also supplied many of the empire's 'career migrants': its soldiers, administrators, educators, industrialists, businessmen, engineers, surveyors and religious missionaries.[14] In 1891 Rev. John P. Jones, head of the Madura Mission in Southern India, remarked that:

> Our nation is almost as ubiquitous as the Irish. I know of no country where the Welshman is not found. I have met him on the banks of the rivers Mississippi, Hudson, Thames, Tiber, Nile, Ganges, as upon the streams of Gwyllt Gwalia. During my twelve years' stay in India I have seen there not a few of my countrymen in the different walks of life. Some of them are high in governmental positions, and are bearing manfully the heavy burdens of authority and responsibility in that land of teeming millions of people.[15]

Our current level of understanding of the Welsh dimension to the running of the empire derives mainly from accounts of individual personalities and careers,[16] but mythology, too, as the continuing debate over Rorke's Drift testifies, has played its part.[17] We need note just a few examples of prominent and influential imperial servants. In the first two decades of the twentieth century the Chief Justices of both Bengal and Hong Kong were native-born Welshmen, whilst the career of Sir John Lewis Jenkins, who entered the Indian Civil Service in 1877, culminated in his reading of the All-India address of welcome to George V during the latter's visit to the Coronation celebrations at the Durbar in 1911.[18] Welsh soldiers included General Sir William Jones, who rose to prominence during the siege of Delhi in 1857, whilst the first motor car in Calcutta (and the second in India) was owned by the Aberystwyth-born David Edward Evans, the Superintendent Engineer for all Bengal operations of Ralli Brothers' jute manufacture and export empire.[19]

As Keith Jeffery has commented of Irish members of this category, a catalogue of Welsh people who achieved distinction within the empire does not significantly advance our understanding and 'may simply be a contribution to the "just fancy that" school of history'. What is needed, as he rightly points out, is an investigation of whether the *Welshness* (in our case) 'of imperial servants and settlers, both individually and as a group, made any specific difference to their experience and service'.[20] Indeed, to some extent, this essay takes up this challenge. Research into the Welsh contribution to providing what has been called the empire's 'steel frame'[21] is extremely undeveloped and we need more detailed work before we can assess, for example, whether, proportionately, Welsh people were more likely to act in these capacities than those from the other Celtic nations. In the cases of both the administrative and military spheres this did not apply, though these points need to be emphasised.[22]

First, the impression from these biographies and other contemporary sources is that the introduction of open competition in the Civil Service from the mid-nineteenth century onwards, and the growth in literacy and developments in secondary and higher education in Wales, led to an increase in the number of Welsh imperial officials overseas.[23] The likelihood, therefore, is that there was much greater Welsh involvement in administering the empire towards the end of the century than had been true of earlier periods, and that this trend continued in the early twentieth century. Second, although unlike the Scots the Welsh do not seem to have acquired a substantial wider reputation for empire-building,[24] there was a growing Welsh self-perception in the late nineteenth century that imperial service overseas was not only increasing but becoming essential to the empire. In the early twentieth century, articles in the influential *Wales* and *Welsh Review* magazines, edited among others by Welsh MPs, gloried in debating 'The Place of Wales in the Empire' and 'The Welsh: A Neglected Imperial Asset'.[25] As well as insisting, as Rev. John Thomas did in 1912, that no-one 'should imagine that national patriotism in respect of Wales is incompatible with true British patriotism on the part of Welshmen', these and similar articles also suggested that Wales should aspire to be 'a breeding place of leaders' for the empire.[26] Further, they maintained that the Celtic characteristics of the Welsh, and especially their religious devotion, 'may yet save England from materialism' and the empire had benefited enormously from 'the working of the leaven of Celtic genius, Celtic aestheticism, and Celtic love of first principles, and last, but not least, Celtic altruism upon the more practical, more industrious, more selfish, and more material mass of the Anglo-Saxons'.[27] In similar vein it was also suggested that one justification for Welsh imperial involvement was that Wales's own experience made it more sympathetic to the subjects of empire: 'Being free of the normal prejudices of the English ruling caste their Celtic blood was often the secret of an abundant sympathy and understanding of the East.'[28] Finally, we should not over-emphasise the distinction between career migrants and ordinary settlers as far as the presence of the Welsh language and Welsh cultural activity in both the formal and informal empires was concerned. Small communities of military personnel, administrators, businessmen, divines and educators and their families sustained Welsh societies such as those in Bengal, Ceylon and Shanghai.[29] Further, world wartime conditions considerably expanded the range of locations in which, for example, St David's Day (1 March) celebrations were held and the scale of the gatherings. Welsh soldiers celebrated Wales's patron saint in Bombay in 1918 and a year later in the American Mission Hall in Alexandria.[30] Between 1943 and 1945, the Welsh Society of Cairo's Welsh-language magazine *Seren y Dwyrain* (The Star of the East) served Welsh members of the armed forces stationed in Egypt, Israel, Syria and other parts of the Middle East.[31]

While the diversity of Welsh experience in the empire warns against generalisations that imply the existence of a single Welsh imperial mindset, it remains evident that similar motivational, linguistic, cultural and religious impulses were shared by a significant proportion of the actors involved. This complexity may best be investigated by conducting comparative research into the dissimilarities and parallels of Welsh imperial presence in different parts of the British Empire. The remainder of the essay will consider the experiences of two groups, economic migrants in Australia and religious missionaries in India, both of which in different ways sought to create and define 'Welsh colonies' within the structures of the empire. The dynamic relationship between the two, particularly in relation to the roles performed by Nonconformity in community building, will also be explored. Particular attention will be paid to the Welsh expatriate press, which was intended to help to construct and maintain a sense of Welsh identity abroad, and to explain to the Welsh elsewhere, including those in Wales, the different forms and purposes of Welsh communities in Australia and India. By reading the content of such titles as *Yr Australydd* (The Australian) and *Y Cenhadwr* (The Missionary), and uncovering the networks of writers who sustained them, historians acquire insights not only into the activities, attitudes, and aspirations of the Welsh in Australia and India, but also into the linguistic, religious and gendered social structures of these new 'imperial' communities. The comparative study of these two particular Welsh imperial experiences, and their divergent forms of self-expression and cultural production, poses new questions about the 'Welsh world' in the British imperial context during the nineteenth and early twentieth centuries.

II

The gold rush in Victoria in 1851 was crucial in stimulating emigration from Wales into the colony, and into Australia generally.[32] The number of people in Australia who had been born in Wales rose from about 1,800 in 1851 to 9,500 in 1861, whilst the Welsh-born population of Victoria increased from 377 in 1851 to 2,326 in 1854, 6,055 in 1861, and peaked at 6,614 in 1871.[33] In the goldfields, sizeable Welsh populations developed in new cities such as Ballarat, Bendigo, Castlemaine and Maldon, while Melbourne itself also attracted significant numbers of Welsh. In geographic, occupational and social terms, the Welsh influx was diverse and represented a wide cross-section of Welsh society, although working-class migrants were clearly in the majority. Most were male, either single men or those who left wives and families at home. Indeed it seems that the Welsh contingent had a higher proportion of men than other nationalities. In 1871, of the Welsh-born inhabitants of Victoria, 4,189 were males and 2,425 females, which represented a higher proportion of males to females in Victoria than was the case for other national groups from Britain.[34] Personal testimonies suggest that most came with the intention of 'getting rich quick' and returning to Wales. However, more ended up staying than had intended, some settling in the goldfield towns, others taking up farming or moving to other mining and industrial centres in Australia when the gold industry began to decline in the 1870s.[35] Although there was much mobility between gold diggings in Victoria, and sporadic settlement in isolated areas, the Welsh presence was not altogether a transitory one. Gold seeking and the new opportunities created by rapid urban and commercial expansion in places such as Ballarat, Bendigo and Melbourne itself attracted medical men, professionals and merchants among others, and a Welsh business community developed. The existence of this group is crucial because it was from its ranks that a largely self-appointed Welsh community leadership was drawn.

The Welsh contingent in Victoria became the centrepiece of Welsh-language religious and cultural life in Australia into the 1870s and beyond.[36] One manifestation of this presence was the building of Welsh churches in Ballarat, Melbourne and elsewhere, most of them established by the Presbyterian Church of Wales, otherwise known as the Welsh Calvinistic Methodists.[37] They constituted Wales's largest, most powerful Nonconformist denomination, with their adherents in Wales rising in number from 163,158 in 1855 to a peak of 347,758 in 1906, in the immediate aftermath of the 1904–05 Revival. (By 1963 the figure had returned to the 1855 level.)[38] Victoria's Welsh linguistic, religious and cultural presence was also reinforced by the formation of Welsh societies like the Cambrian Society, and frequent holding of the *Eisteddfod*, the

Welsh literary and cultural gathering.[39] Although there are no statistical records to support it, it is likely that the majority of Welsh migrants into Victoria in the middle years of the nineteenth century were Welsh-speaking, while biographical evidence reveals that some, at least, were monolingual. The existence of a Welsh-language public profile – with items in Welsh occasionally appearing in the Melbourne and Ballarat newspapers as well as in religious services and cultural events like the *eisteddfodau* – needs emphasis for its wider significance.[40] As Michael Clyne has reminded us, Melbourne, and even more so the goldfields, were linguistically diverse in the late nineteenth century.[41] Yet such public display of the Welsh language could cause tensions. An editorial on the Ballarat *Eisteddfod* in the *Ballarat Courier* in February 1886 may reveal much about influential colonial opinion makers' attitudes towards Welsh. The leader greatly commended the *Eisteddfod* and its cosmopolitan character, although it insisted that, 'when the Welsh portion of the entertainment comes on, there is an unpleasant twinge or twist on the countenance of those present who don't know Welsh, and find a difficulty in distinguishing it from Chinese'.[42]

A decade before the first Welsh gold seekers arrived in Australia, Thomas Jones, from Aberriw, Montgomeryshire, arrived in the Khasi Hills in Assam. His appearance there in June 1841 marked the beginning of the Welsh mission in north-east India.[43] The mission was organised by the Welsh Calvinistic Methodists, who, as we have seen, were Wales's largest, most powerful Nonconformist denomination, and who a year earlier had launched their own separate overseas missionary society. Although other missionaries from Wales were at work in other parts of the world, in France, the islands of the Pacific, the Caribbean, parts of western and southern Africa, and China, those in north-east India formed the largest, most continuous project funded and organised by any Welsh-based denomination.

If Welsh Victoria was the creation of an economic mass migration, then the Welsh experience in India was that of a small group of ideologically motivated, dedicated and educated middle-class men and women, operating often as individuals or couples. This relatively small-scale enterprise rarely employed more than 50 missionary workers in the field at any one time, who formed only a tiny proportion of the 10,000 or so British missionaries who were on active service abroad in 1900. They included evangelical preachers, doctors, nurses and teachers, and substantial numbers of them, constituting at times a clear majority, were lay women, mostly young and unmarried. In the mission field, the effects of their presence were strikingly uneven, leaving a powerful religious mark on the Khasi Hills. The Khasi Christian community grew from 1,796 in 1881 to 6,766 a decade later. By 1901 the figure had reached 15,937 and by 1905, the year of the Welsh

Revival, the missionaries had established a following of some 23,000.[44] However, they made little impression on other areas of the field such as Sylhet. In 1909 the mission field as a whole could count 9,569 communicants, with a total Sunday School attendance of twice that figure, out of a total population of about 3 million.[45]

The two major responsibilities of the missionaries were, first, to take Welsh Calvinistic Methodism to the Assamese and Bengalis, and second, to keep the Welsh informed of their activities, and moreover, of crucial importance, to do so in such a way that stimulated the church to make greater missionary efforts at home and to attract sufficient voluntary donations to finance their work in the field. As in the case of the Welsh in Australia, the part the Welsh language played in the mission's work in India needs emphasising. Virtually all its evangelical activity was conducted in indigenous languages, and missionaries were expected to become fluent in the language of their chosen field within three years of their appointment.[46] But most written and oral communication with the home church and its members was conducted in Welsh, which effectively excluded it from outside scrutiny.

Clearly there were important class, gender, motivational and contextual differences between these two Welsh experiences. But for the purposes of this analysis it is also necessary to stress common characteristics and influences. Crucial here are, first, the Welsh language as a medium of communication and expression of nationality, and second, the bond of Welsh religious Nonconformity and especially Welsh Calvinistic Methodism. The same spiritual impulse that prevailed among Welsh missionaries in India also manifested itself in the opening of Welsh chapels in Victoria, Australia. In the goldfields in particular Welsh religiosity was seen, not only as an integral element of a Welsh civilising mission that would benefit colonial society, but also as an affirmation of the strength of their highly specific brand of Nonconformity, a further manifestation of the successful transplantation of Welsh culture and identity in a virgin land, and even as further proof of the existence of a Welsh 'world' within and beyond the parameters of the British Empire.[47] In 1854, in response to reports that Welsh-language religious services were being held in Australia, *Y Drysorfa* (The Treasury), the Wales-based periodical of the Welsh Calvinistic Methodists, declared:

> It is a remarkable and very comforting feature of the Welsh that wherever they go if there are a number of them together, they will set up communal worship in the Welsh language. In the large cities of England, in the coal mines and iron works of Scotland, in the various states of America, and now in the gold fields of Australia, emigrants

from Wales must hear about the greatness and good works of the Lord in their own language.[48]

Nevertheless, shared impulses should not be taken to imply complete harmony within this international Calvinistic Methodist nexus. Wider clashes of interests between white colonial governments and the British government were also mirrored in the relations between individual national groups in those respective locations. Throughout the late nineteenth and early twentieth centuries, Welsh churches in Melbourne and the Victorian goldfields collected money to fund Welsh missionaries in India and elsewhere. Nevertheless, the importance religious leaders in the homeland attached to the Indian endeavours, and the resources devoted to them, further exacerbated existing tensions between Welsh colony and Welsh metropole created by the latter's apparent neglect of the need for Welsh-language preachers in Australia. This competitiveness suggests that the relationships binding these three points of a religious, cultural and linguistic triangle were at best unequal and even hierarchical. In 1865, while on a visit to his homeland, Rev. William Meirion Evans of the Welsh Calvinistic Methodist Church in Sebastopol, Ballarat, and soon to be one of the editors of *Yr Australydd*, was exasperated to discover the level of ignorance regarding Welsh religious and cultural life of the Welsh in Australia. He also found he had to defend '*i'r eithaf*' (to the hilt) the religious character of the Welsh there in the face of accusations regarding the scale of the continent's ungodliness. He complained that the Calvinistic Methodist denomination was prepared to spend any amount of money to equip its overseas missions, but none on sending Welsh preachers to Australia to relive the shortage of ministers there.[49] Ten years earlier, although clearly ignoring the existence of similar tensions within the international Gaelic religious community for maximum effect, a Ballarat religious elder suggested that:

A question which is often asked is why do the Highlanders of Scotland, that is the '*Gaelic*', get ministers to preach for them in their own language? and the Irish get priests and churches everywhere they settle? whilst we the Welsh are without any minister which has been sent out by any denomination. Thousands of young men and women who were bred with such religious care are here … sinking into becoming slaves to their lusts and passions, while there is a big fuss over collecting and sending out missionaries to … wear themselves out in order to return to the fold some superstitious Pagan.[50]

III

It follows, therefore, that the persistence of highly differentiated forms of Welsh presence in British imperial expansion and settlement during the nineteenth and early twentieth centuries raises some key questions about the ways in which empire was comprehended culturally, both by the peoples of Britain and by those they colonised. Some Welsh migrants sought to escape from the empire, others to profit from it, still others to transform it into a moral agency. As the work of a number of recent historians suggests, the non-English trajectories of Britishness in relation to imperial expansion not only complicate the story of the empire itself, but may also oblige us to reconsider the ways in which the different parts of the United Kingdom were interconnected and how their individual histories were shaped.[51] There are some important general issues for imperial history to be found here, issues that are not by any means confined to the territorial or cultural histories of Wales or Ireland or Scotland. Scottish historians have done some pioneering work in this respect, as have some in Ireland. Far less has been heard from Wales. In terms of the number of its people engaged in settling the colonies, Wales was the least significant of the three. Yet its extensive, one might say insistent, use of a different language from English means that the Welsh experience of empire makes us address a distinctive set of issues. If language structures experience, as some have argued, then the use of the Welsh language alongside and within English-speaking imperial societies is a subject that deserves further investigation. At the very least, it renders the 'contact zone', where colonisers and colonised became 'entangled', an even more complicated place.[52]

In some parts of the empire, it is evident that British languages other than English were not only seen and heard, but could at times be perceived as embodying and representing imperial power. Traces of these other imperial languages are to be found, for example, in the surviving records of Welsh voluntary organisations, particularly cultural and religious institutions such as the *eisteddfod* or Nonconformist religious denominations, or letters and personal recollections that exist in a variety of forms. But in terms of chronological range, consistency and sheer size, the most abundant single source from which we can build a picture of the Welsh presence in the empire are Welsh-language newspapers and periodicals. In their pages, language, religiosity and a sense of place combine to produce a complex, reflexive and, until very recently, an astonishingly neglected subject to be interrogated by imperial historians. For one thing, historians will be eager to quarry this source for its vast amount of empirical information. The Welsh-language press contains biographical references to individuals, accounts of the activities of institutions, details of the rise and fall of political movements, and the forms and content of cultural events, much of which is unavailable in other types of historical source. Often the information it contains may be cross-referenced only by consulting other periodicals. As a result of their self-referentiality in that very specific sense, to read newspapers historically is to enter a virtual world, a textual web whose purpose was the production of meaning by communicating with an indefinable audience, a 'public' of potential readers.

Regarded in these ways, newspapers and journals may be seen less as useful empirical sources and more as structuring institutions, as deliberate attempts to offer particular and subjective readings of experience of which we too, as historians reading these old papers in the present, are consumers. There should be nothing new in any of this. For a decade or more the 'linguistic turn' has focused attention precisely on the extent to which history is the study of language. But what is surprising is how little thought has been given to the ways in which different languages structure readings of shared experiences in diverging ways, and the ways in which language is perceived by contemporaries themselves to be more than a value-free communication medium. An investigation of the contrasting phenomena of Welsh-language journalism in India and Australia may enable some of these issues to be opened up to closer scrutiny.

In Australia, Welsh migrants produced two Welsh-language monthly titles: *Yr Australydd*, published between 1866 and 1872 and edited by Rev. William Meirion Evans and Theophilus Williams; and *Yr Ymwelydd* (The Visitor), which was edited by Evans alone in Melbourne and lasted from 1874 to 1876. (One issue of a pilot journal *Yr Ymgeisydd* (The Candidate) also appeared in 1865.) A number of other individuals in Victorian cities and settlements, especially Ballarat and Melbourne, were involved in the production of both at various times, but both ventures appear to be essentially the initiative and efforts of Evans himself.[53] It is unclear why *Yr Australydd* ceased publication in 1872, but *Yr Ymwelydd* was closed in 1876 because its printer moved from Victoria and a replacement with sufficient knowledge of Welsh to continue its printing could not be found in the colony.[54] It is curious to note that the title of the first emphasised its affinity to the country where it was produced, while the second suggested a more fleeting visit. Whether this was intentional is unknown. Other newspapers and journals bearing this title appeared in Wales and the United States during the nineteenth century, and an alternative intended meaning may have been a paper that was a regular visitor to households. Nevertheless, if not deliberate, the title of the Welsh-Australian *Yr Ymwelydd* is certainly symbolic of the transience – in both geographic and cultural terms – of significant sections of the Welsh population in Victoria during the colonial era.[55]

Research into the individual histories of these two papers and the dynamics of their relationships with the wider Welsh ethnic group in Australia is continuing, but some central features of their nature, content, and role have already been established.[56] It is no accident that they were published during the period when the Welsh presence in Victoria was at its peak and most active, and their appearance testifies to a certain but by no means complete degree of maturity and stability among the Welsh community at that time, and not least the demand for some form of inter-community medium of communication.[57] Indeed, one reason for embarking on a Welsh-language paper in 1866 was that a leaflet in Welsh printed for the Welsh Calvinist Methodist connexion by an Australian company in 1863 had contained an embarrassingly high number of grammatical and spelling errors, and the connexion had been forced to consider establishing its own printing venture.[58] Robert Tyler has correctly pointed out that these papers were the mouthpieces of a social and cultural leadership that sought to formulate and diffuse ideas of Welshness, but equally that they were by no means solely restricted to such an elite. Both papers were modestly priced (6d per issue) whilst their content and other evidence reveals that ordinary gold miners and other manual workers were represented among their contributors. It further appears that the papers had a respectable circulation, and Tyler suggests that they were remarkably successful in reaching a large proportion of their potential audience. In 1866 and 1867, for example, lists of sums of money received from distributors that were printed in *Yr Australydd* suggest that the number of copies sold by this means alone ranged from 200 to 496.[59]

The umbilical link between Welsh Calvinistic Methodism and both *Yr Australydd* and *Yr Ymwelydd* needs to be emphasised. They were the creation of the Calvinistic Methodist connexion in Victoria, and throughout their existence they were sponsored and partly funded by it. According to a content analysis undertaken by Robert Tyler, religious matter featured prominently in both the Australian periodicals. Theological writing accounted for some 22 per cent of the content of *Yr Australydd* in 1866–67, and 13 per cent in 1871–72, while some 46 per cent of *Yr Ymwelydd* in 1876 may be categorised as religious material.[60] Both periodicals were an antipodean extension of a denominational press that developed close ties across the Atlantic in mid-nineteenth-century Wales.[61] And in many respects the format and content of the Australian dimension to this international network of reportage and comment resembled *Y Drysorfa* in Wales and *Y Cyfaill o'r Hen Wlad* (The Friend from the Old County) in the United States. Like their counterparts in Wales and the United States, neither *Yr Australydd* nor *Ymwelydd* was *exclusively* religious. In its first issue in July 1866 the former's editors declared their ambition to 'gwasanaethu ein *cenedl mewn llenyddiaeth, moesoldeb a chrefydd'* (serve our nation in literature, morality and religion), and took pains to call not just for religious contributions but poetry, reports of literary and religious meetings and of notable occurrences in various parts of the colony.[62] And to a significant extent they received them. The poems, short stories and sketches that were published await in-depth analysis. This is regrettable, as it is evident that some of them attempt to combine metaphors, imagery, expressions and language forms of Australian usage of English as it was developing on the Victorian goldfields into their Welsh-language literary products. Prime examples here are the serialised novel '*Cymro yn Awstralia*' (A Welshman in Australia), which appeared in *Yr Australydd* during the whole of 1870, and the work of the critic 'Hen Lag'. The latter enlivened his commentaries with frequent use of words adapted from the vocabulary of gold mining such as '*sliwsio*' (sluicing), '*puddlo*' (puddling) and '*prospect*'. In terms of content if not in vocabulary, these writers were expanding the range of Welsh-language literature itself.[63]

In contrast to this evidence of what one might be tempted to call the Australianisation of Welsh-language content in *Yr Australydd* and *Yr Ymwelydd*, at no time did news from Wales account for more than 3 per cent of the content of either periodical.[64] Indeed, as a result of a reciprocal arrangement with the North American Welsh-language newspaper *Y Drych* (The Mirror), *Yr Ymwelydd* on occasion carried more material relating to the Welsh in the United States than in Wales.[65] One reason for this relative absence, Tyler suggests, is that the leaders of the Welsh community in Victoria were, in part through their journalism, developing a distinctly Australian form of Welsh identity founded on religious orthodoxy and the use of Welsh.[66] It was these loyalties, then, rather than a commitment to a particular territory, that formed the core components of their self-image as a community, and as a result they saw no contradiction in giving allegiance to a new country while at the same time retaining a distinctive sense of cultural identity. An editorial on '*Gwerth Teimlad Cenedlaethol*' (The Value of National Sentiment), which appeared in *Yr Australydd* in April 1871, epitomises this mindset:

> The position of the Welsh in the Australian Colonies is a subject which should receive the special attention of every Welshman as a good patriot and citizen. Some try to persuade themselves that all national feeling – Welsh, Scottish, and Irish, etc. – is less than useless in a mixed [cosmopolitan] country such as this ... Some [believe] that all walls built on the basis of nationality should be thrown down in order to lay the foundations of a superior nation of Australians ... [But] is this necessary or advantageous for the foundation and

progress of Australia ... Nationality ... is one of the most important
elements in the success of all nations. If we are to assist in placing a
South Asian nation on permanent foundations – if the Welsh of the
colonies want to leave their mark on the world and the ages to come,
then they should nurture and breed strong and enlightened national
feelings, acquaint themselves with the famed ancient literature of
Wales ... and adopt the spirit of the old fathers.[67]

In line with this set of self-perceptions, in both papers most column
space is devoted to the activities of Welsh communities in Australia
(especially in Victoria) and the cultural events which they hosted and the
literature which they produced. It is devoted, too, to reflection on the nature
of being Welsh in Australia. The pages of *Yr Australydd* and *Yr Ymwelydd*
were sites of contest between diverging interpretations of the present and
future condition of Welshness in the colony, and they are thus invaluable
testimony to the processes of cultural negotiation and identity formation.
Articles and letters in both periodicals drew attention to a seemingly rapid
process of cultural and linguistic change.[68] Some bemoaned this, and
accused the Welsh of gross apathy in neglecting to teach their children
Welsh.[69] Others believed that maintaining religious services was more
important than maintaining language; consequently Welsh children should
be taught in English in Sunday schools.[70] A complex picture thus emerges:
debates over the degree to which the Welsh language was central to a Welsh
identity were nevertheless articulated in *Welsh*. Equally the mutually
beneficial cross-fertilisation that obtained from faith in both Welsh
religiosity and the Welsh language could at times undermine as well as
nurture a distinctive Welsh identity and the priorities it had to establish in a
new economic, social and cultural environment away from the homeland.
   Welsh missionaries in north-east India produced a very different form of
journalism, which addressed an entirely different audience. Most of it was
in Welsh, which effectively excluded it from scrutiny by converts, or those
who drew on missionary services in the field, or indeed the agencies of the
imperial power itself. With the exception of the field journals, which were
printed in English, or bilingually in English and Bengali, communication
with the home church and its members was in Welsh and was intended to
flow only in the one direction. The transmission of these communications
took a number of forms. Institutional reports were submitted annually for
publication in the *Report of the Foreign Mission*, but news also seeped into
the public domain in Wales by means of letters, the contents of which at
times filtered through to the newspaper press. News coverage of events in
India during the rebellion of 1857, for example, provides a telling
illustration of the way in which editors in Wales used missionaries

effectively as foreign correspondents. Material intended for public consumption was printed in the monthly denominational journal *Y Drysorfa*, which included from 1847 a separate missionary report section, *Y Cronicl Cenhadol* (Missionary Chronicle), a periodical within a periodical, where accounts from the mission fields were regularly included alongside other religious news and comment. Lectures and sermons given by missionaries on furlough, with occasional visits by converts, were widely publicised, as were special fund-raising chapel events. Touring exhibitions of Indian villages and bazaars were intended further to excite the sympathies of their audiences. These were augmented in the 1920s by missionary films, shown in schools and chapels, such as the one shot by Mostyn Lewis, son of the Liberal MP Sir Herbert Lewis, in 1928.[71] Furthermore, missionaries produced their own communications media within the mission field. John Pengwern Jones launched the *Friend of Sylhet* and *The Friend of the Women of Bengal* in 1899, and Helen Rowlands started *The Link* in 1933. But the most important missionary periodical was without doubt *Y Cenhadwr*, published wholly in Welsh between 1922 and 1974, and aimed at a popular Welsh audience at home.[72] Initially edited by the Rev. J. Hughes Morris, and published at monthly intervals from the denomination's printing centre at Caernarfon, north Wales, it offered a miscellany of articles, reports, essays and photographs from the mission fields. Missionaries themselves contributed the vast majority of items. No reliable circulation figures are available, but we do know that the journal was distributed principally through the chapels and by subscription.

Most of the contributors were women. This partly reflects the high numbers of women missionaries in the field, particularly from the turn of the twentieth century. In 1924, for example, of 56 Welsh missionaries in the field, 37 (66 per cent) of them were women; 21 of them, or 38 per cent of the total number of missionaries of both sexes, were unmarried women.[73] The troubled history of some of the early male missionaries may have contributed to the gender imbalance. Dr Richards, an early medical assistant to the first of the Welsh missionaries, Thomas Jones, was expelled in 1845. Then, in October 1847, Jones himself found his connection with the church abruptly terminated. By all accounts, he had re-married without church permission, had taken up farming, and had introduced to the Khasis the distilled form of alcohol and improved techniques for brewing beer.[74] Twenty years later, William Pryse, who had first extended the mission south to Sylhet, was excommunicated, though church records are coy about the reasons for this.[75] Significantly, however, both he and Jones remained in their adopted homes until their deaths.

A more compelling reason for the size of the female contingent was their capacity to proselytise among other women. As one communication from the field had observed, 'women are the real Hindus', and, as the 'main defenders'[76] of the religion, women were regarded not necessarily as the main targets for conversion, but certainly as the essential agency by means of whose influence Christianity might be normalised or made acceptable in Hindu households. Demand for women missionaries increased as greater priority was given to work in the *zenanas*, a policy favoured by missionary societies, especially in Bengal, since at least the 1840s,[77] in schools, and in women's hospitals. Many of these young women were drawn from the reservoir of enthusiasts generated by the 1904–05 religious revival in Wales, and from the new University Colleges, especially Aberystwyth and Bangor, which from around the turn of the century were starting to produce a new generation of university-educated women who clearly regarded missionary work not only as a spiritual activity but also as a valid career choice. These women were responsible not only for carrying out missionary work in the theatre of the public sermon, the *zenanas*, the schools and the hospitals, but also for writing most of the articles printed in *Y Cronicl Cenhadol* and its successor, *Y Cenhadwr*. Although their role in governing the mission field through the District Committees was limited, it can be said that, from the 1890s, they became the mission's most consistent and effective correspondents. It was their constructions of India, and the sense which they made of the missionary presence there, that formed the most significant proportion of the missionary journalism consumed by readers at home. At their best, these examples of women's writing appear less zealous and doctrinaire, and more open and exploratory, than other contemporary forms of Welsh literature.

These articles also served what were clearly propagandist purposes, communicating the otherness of India while defending the legitimacy of missionary activity there. Much of this was communicated in topographical and anthropological descriptions. Mary Louise Pratt has described 'the portrait of manners and customs' found in travel writing as 'a normalizing discourse, whose work is to codify difference, to fix the other in a timeless present where all "his" actions and reactions are repetitions of "his" normal habits'.[78] Accounts in *Y Cenhadwr* of Indian religious practices, for example, caricature Hindu beliefs by essentialising them in the way Pratt suggests. Other ethnographic accounts work in a similar fashion, particularly those that describe dress, social codes of behaviour, diet and occupation. In 'The Indian Barber', which forms part of an ambitious series on work and street life, Dilys Edmunds describes the social and religious significance of the *napit*, but it too 'fixes' the 'intellectual' barber in an essentialist way, and attributes his social power to the Hindu 'superstitions' which, she seeks to persuade her readers, her school for Hindu girls in Karimganj was committed to eradicating. Since religion and caste, as

Bernard Cohn has argued, 'were the sociological keys to understanding the Indian people', these articles appear to fit a pattern of colonising writing.[79]

News of political processes and cultural events form a substantial proportion of the contents of *Y Cenhadwr*. Thus readers in Wales received regular accounts during the 1930s and 1940s on the progress of the Congress Party, the activities of Gandhi, the proliferation of symbols of Indian nationhood and, in 1947, a series of extraordinary descriptions of the human cost of Partition, the most notable being Helen Rowlands's reports from Karimganj, positioned on the new border between India and East Pakistan. In other accounts of journeys through the mission field, which included descriptions of landscapes, vegetation, animals, forms of transport, fields, street scenes, markets, and of the men, women and children they encountered, missionaries employed rhetorical strategies which both emphasised the otherness of India and which encouraged a sympathetic identification with it on the part of their readers. 'How different Sylhet is from Wales!' exclaimed Miss E.A. Roberts in 1902,[80] yet the very contrast was intended to produce a closer affinity. The missionaries clearly wanted readers at home to care about their work, and about the people they were in contact with. Welsh and Bengali place names are intertwined in these narratives, and comparisons are made between features of the landscape in the two regions. Other kinds of encounters demanded a different, more subtly nuanced use of language. An essay by Helen Rowlands entitled 'The Rain', which describes a journey taken downriver with a group of her school pupils during the flood season in Sylhet in 1925, resonated with the vibrancy of colour, the scent of flowers, the softness of skin, and the sensual textures of hair and cloth.

> In the morning, as dawn breaks, the waters wait shyly but with quiet expectation for the first kiss of the sun. And who at sunset could describe the shadows that turn the water ruddy and purple? A moonlit night on the rivers and the land covered by water – it is full of enchantment and magic.[81]

The tenderness of the writing contrasts strongly with the language of Calvinistic Methodism, even in early twentieth-century Wales, and by describing their encounter with India, the bonds that for more than a century had tied literary style to religious orthodoxies were being loosened while new, fresher forms of writing were beginning to appear.

Missionaries innovated with established cultural forms in other ways too. In 1901 John Pengwern Jones organised the first *Eisteddfod* in Sylhet, while Helen Rowlands later began in Karimganj an annual *eisteddfod* in Bengali.[82] Hymns were written in, or translated into, indigenous languages, and these were used in much the same devotional way within the order of

the service in the field as they were in the home church. J. Arthur Jones, sent
to Shillong in 1910 by the *Manchester Guardian*, was struck by the
combination of Indian landscape and Welsh religiosity:

> While I sat at my dinner in the dark bungalow, a familiar strain came
> to my ears. Mingling with the fire-flies ... floated the minor cadences
> of an old Welsh tune. They were singing in the chapel which stood on
> the hill opposite. The timbre of the voices were a little strange, but
> apart from this I could have imagined myself in some Welsh village
> where the 'Seiat' was being held in Bethel or Saron. Yet the singers
> now were Khasis, a Mongolian hill folk of Assam, once worshippers
> of demons ... The Khasis have adopted Welsh Methodism with
> scarcely a variant.[83]

In the first issue of *Y Cenhadwr* in 1922, Thomas Charles Edwards had
confidently announced that the Welsh Calvinistic Methodists had 'to date
created in India a Methodist Church in our own image'.[84] The re-creation of
a little Wales in India, however, went some way beyond the devotional. In
an account of Christmas at her home for orphaned girls in Silchar in 1922,
E.M. Lloyd described how they had 'spent an evening in Wales!'. Pictures
and maps of the country had been pinned to the walls, the children were
dressed in old Welsh costume, and the choir sang *Hen Wlad Fy Nhadau*
(Land of My Fathers, the Welsh national anthem) and a number of Welsh
folk songs, 'in Welsh'.[85] Equally significantly, Helen Rowlands, writing in
The Link in 1935, explicitly described the Bengali mission field as 'a colony
of Welsh people'.[86]

IV

A comparative study of these two forms of expatriate, colonial Welsh
journalism raises a number of issues. The first is their similarities. Both
were concerned with the task of transplanting the moral and ethical
elements of their culture into colonial locations, both were infused with the
Calvinism of their producers, and both insisted that the Welsh language was
an intrinsic and inseparable component of their faith and identity. Again,
religion and language formed the most fundamental characteristics of a
highly portable sense of Welsh cultural identity quite distinct from any
reference to nationality or territoriality. Finally, both acknowledged their
reliance on the colonial administrative, commercial and military structures
of the British Empire. But there were also some marked differences between
them. The Australian papers were produced in Australia for a Welsh-
Australian readership. The missionary journals were written in India but
were printed in Wales predominantly for a domestic Welsh audience. The

main purpose of the first was to build a new cultural community, the aim of the second was to educate a distant audience about the realities as they saw them of social, political and cultural life in British India, to justify missionary work, and to generate funds for its continuation. The first deliberately distanced itself from the concerns of the metropole, the other sought to involve its readers emotionally and intellectually, as well as financially, in the British imperial project, or at least in its informal Christianising dimension. These differences are important, and point to the diversity of the Welsh experience of empire and the Welsh contribution to the British world.

At the same time, both were also capable of expressing something of the cultural ambiguities of the British presence in the colonies. They occupied quasi-autonomous positions within the imperial power-structure and mindset, and deliberately distinguished themselves as much from the other British as from the colonised 'other'. On occasion, this emphasis on difference enabled elements within at least one of these migrant communities to question the legitimacy of the entire imperial project and to elide one set of nationalist assumptions with another. But that response was rare. What may be more significant was the way in which these communities, largely by means of their public modes of communication, cut across empire – and in the Australian case effectively cut out British Wales – to develop an international if virtual Welsh network focused above all on the American Welsh and their powerful and comparatively well-funded print media, particularly the weekly newspaper *Y Drych*.[87]

The divergent experiences of these two Welsh communities within the British Empire, particularly with regard to the ways in which those experiences were shaped and articulated by their respective journalisms, provide us with a means of disinterring what have been, for far too long, conveniently buried aspects of both Welsh and Imperial history. The Welsh clearly did participate in the expansion and consolidation of the British Empire, and the history of that participation needs to be more fully researched and its implications and consequences addressed. But by uncovering that involvement, we also complicate our understanding, in certain areas at least, of the manner in which the Imperial mission may have been practised and perceived. The Welsh language and its cultural forms, which in mid-Victorian Britain had still been regarded as 'semibarbarous' obstacles to the political and cultural integration of the United Kingdom,[88] were increasingly being associated with imperial 'modernity' and the 'civilising' mission of British power in the colonies. In both India and Australia, Welsh missionaries, industrial workers and farmers were regarded above all as regional variants of the English, situated at, or very near, the top of the religious and racial imperial hierarchy. At the same time, the language, its cultural priorities, and the Calvinist mental world they embodied distinguished the Welsh in important ways from the remainder of Protestant Britain. The language enabled the Welsh to develop a distinctive presence within the empire, one in which barriers of incomprehensibility protected its internal affairs from external scrutiny, and which effectively turned even its most public forms of expression, its journalism, into a very private affair. What begins to emerge are the outlines of a hidden Welsh world, driven by a combination of language, religion and proximity to British state power, whose aim was to create and sustain interconnected centres of Welsh life within – and beyond – the broader British world.

NOTES

1. C.A. Bayly, *Imperial Meridian: The British Empire and the World 1780–1830* (London, 1989), 81; Keith Jeffery, 'Introduction', in *idem* (ed.), *'An Irish Empire'? Aspects of Ireland and the British Empire* (Manchester, 1996), 1.
2. In writing this essay we have benefited greatly from comparative insights suggested by reading David Fitzpatrick, 'Ireland and the Empire', in Andrew Porter (ed.), *The Oxford History of the British Empire*, vol.3 *The Nineteenth Century* (Oxford, 1999), 494–521; Jeffery, 'Introduction'; and John M. MacKenzie, 'Essay and Reflection: On Scotland and Empire', *International History Review*, 15 (1993), 714–39.
3. See discussion in Neil Evans, 'Internal Colonialism? Colonization, Economic Development and Political Mobilization in Wales, Scotland and Ireland', in Graham Day and Gareth Rees (eds.), *Regions, Nations and European Integration: Remaking the Celtic Periphery* (Cardiff, 1991), 235–64.
4. Gwyn A. Williams, 'Imperial South Wales', in his *The Welsh in their History* (London, 1982), 171–87; Prys Morgan, 'Keeping the Legends Alive', in Tony Curtis (ed.), *Wales: The Imagined Nation: Essays in Cultural and National Identity* (Bridgend, 1996), 19–41, 38.
5. Baruch Hirson and Gwyn A. Williams, *The Delegate for Africa: David Ivon Jones 1883–1924* (London, 1985).
6. Most histories are by retired missionaries, the most informative being the following three-volume series: Ednyfed Thomas, *Hanes Cenhadaeth Dramor Eglwys Bresbyteraidd Cymru. Cenhadaeth Casia. Y gyfrol gyntaf, Bryniau'r Glaw* (Caernarfon, 1988); J. Meirion Lloyd, *Hanes Cenhadaeth Dramor Eglwys Bresbyteraidd Cymru. Cenhadaeth Mizoram. Yr ail gyfrol, Y Bannau Pell* (Caernarfon, 1989); D.G. Merfyn Jones, *Hanes Cenhadaeth Dramor Eglwys Bresbyteraidd Cymru, Cenhadaeth Sylhet-Cachar. Y drydedd gyfrol, Y Popty Poeth a'i Gyffiniau* (Caernarfon, 1990). See also two novels by D.G. Merfyn Jones, *Ar Fryniau'r Glaw* (Swansea, 1980), and *Eryr Sylhet* (Denbigh, 1987). Other useful studies include J. Meirion Lloyd, *Nine Missionary Pioneers: The Story of Nine Pioneering Missionaries in North-East India* (Caernarfon, 1989); and Ioan W. Gruffudd (ed.), *Cludoedd Moroedd: Cofio Dwy Ganrif o Genhadaeth* (Swansea [?], 1995). See also Siân Rhys Morris, 'Dwy ar Daith i'r Dwyrain: Cenadesau Cymru yn yr India, 1889–1914', BA Hons dissertation, Department of History and Welsh History, University of Wales, Aberystwyth, 1994; Aled Jones, '"Meddylier am India": tair taith y genhadaeth Gymreig yn Sylhet, 1887–1947', *Transactions of the Honourable Society of Cymmrodorion 1997*, new series, 4 (1998), 84–110; and Jane Aaron, 'Slaughter and Salvation: British Imperialism in Nineteenth-Century Welsh Women's Writing', *New Welsh Review*, 38 (1997), 38–46. In an otherwise admirable account of religious movements in modern Wales, D. Densil Morgan, *The Span of the Cross: Christian Religion and Society in Wales 1914–2000* (Cardiff, 1999), 17, makes only one reference to the Indian mission.
7. A notable exception, Robert Pope, *Building Jerusalem: Nonconformity, Labour and the*

Social Question in Wales, 1906–1939 (Cardiff, 1998), reinserts the religious impulse into the history of early twentieth-century Welsh labour politics.

8. On the reluctance of historians in the Celtic countries to address their involvement in Empire, Patrick O'Sullivan observes that, 'aspects of the missionary enterprise are rarely discussed within Irish writing, nor is the concomitant effect on non-European ethnic groups. It might be thought that a nation, part of whose nation-building myth involves criticism of an invader who vilified Irish religion and culture, would at least think twice about so happily doing precisely that to other peoples ... This is clearly an area where the sensitivity of the subject matter creates "gaps in the literature".' Patrick O'Sullivan (ed.), *The Irish World Wide: History, Heritage, Identity*, vol.5 *Religion and Identity* (London, 1990), 13.

9. Marjory Harper, 'British Migration and the Peopling of Empire', in Porter (ed.), *Oxford History of the British Empire*, vol.3, 75–87, 78. See also Stephen Constantine, 'Migrants and Settlers', in Judith M. Brown and Wm. Roger Louis (eds.), *Oxford History of the British Empire*, vol.4 *The Twentieth Century* (Oxford, 1999), 163–87.

10. Ged Martin and Benjamin E. Kline, 'British Emigration and New Identities', in P.J. Marshall (ed.), *The Cambridge Illustrated History of the British Empire* (Cambridge, 1996), 254–79, 265. They have described the Welsh as being 'rarities everywhere' in the Empire. See also David Williams, 'Some Figures Relating to Emigration from Wales', *Bulletin of the Board of Celtic Studies*, 7 (May 1935), 396–415; ibid., 8 (May 1936), 160.

11. James Jupp and Barry York, *Birthplaces of the Australian People: Colonial and Commonwealth Censuses, 1828–1991* (Canberra, 1995); Wayne K.D. Davies, 'The Welsh in Canada: A Geographical Overview', in M.E. Chamberlain (ed.), *The Welsh in Canada* (Canadian Studies in Wales Group, 1986), 1–45, 3; Heather Hughes, 'How the Welsh Became White in South Africa: Immigration, Identity and Economic Transformation from the 1860s to the 1930s', *Transactions of the Honourable Society of Cymmrodorion 2000*, new series, 7 (2001), 112–27; Williams, 'Some Figures', 160.

12. The 1890 United States census recorded around 100,000 Wales-born persons, and according to the 1901 British census, 265,000 people who had been born in Wales were living in England, with major concentrations in Liverpool, London, the Midlands and the North East. For the Welsh in the United States, see William D. Jones, *Wales in America: Scranton and the Welsh, 1860–1920* (Cardiff and Scranton, 1993). For England, see Emrys Jones (ed.), *The Welsh in London 1500–2000* (Cardiff, 2001); and R. Merfyn Jones and D. Ben Rees (eds.), *The Liverpool Welsh and their Religion* (Liverpool, 1984).

13. See Glyn Williams, *The Desert and the Dream* (Cardiff, 1975).

14. Harper, 'British Migration', 78.

15. *The Cambrian*, 11 (June 1891), 163–64.

16. See, for example, W.R. Owain-Jones, 'The Contribution of Welshmen to the Administration of India', *Transactions of the Honourable Society of Cymmrodorion* (1970), 250–62.

17. See Norman Holme, *The Noble 24th* (London, 1999), 265–372; and David Berry, *Wales and Cinema – The First Hundred Years* (Cardiff, 1994), 266–67, for discussions of the film *Zulu*.

18. *Wales*, Jan. 1912, 33; and Aug. 1914, 332; D.E. Lloyd Jones, 'David Edward Evans: A Welshman in India', *Transactions of the Honourable Society of Cymmrodorion* (1967), 132–41, 133.

19. *Wales*, June 1913, 91–94.

20. Jeffery, 'Introduction', 17.

21. Judith Brown, 'War and the Colonial Relationship: Britain, India and the War of 1914–18', in M.R.D. Foot (ed.), *War and Society* (London, 1973), 85–106, 89.

22. Official government statistics relating to the army did not distinguish between English and Welsh nationality until 1905. Between 1905 and 1913 the percentage of non-commissioned officers and men in the army who were born in Wales varied between 1.4 and 1.8 per cent, a significant under-representation as Wales contained approximately 5 per cent of the population of the British Isles in 1901. H.J. Hanham, 'Religion and Nationality in the Mid-Victorian Army', in Foot (ed.), *War and Society*, 159–81, 178. The difficulties the British army encountered in recruiting in Wales in the late nineteenth and early twentieth centuries is discussed in Neil Evans, 'Gogs, Cardis and Hwntws: Region, Nation and State in Wales, 1840–1940', in *idem* (ed.), *National Identity in the British Isles* (Harlech, 1989), 67–68.

23. See *Wales*, June 1913, 105; and Feb. 1914, 242; Owain-Jones, 'Contribution', 254. Fitzpatrick, 'Ireland and Empire', 509–10; MacKenzie, 'Scotland and Empire', 722. See also Bayly, *Imperial Meridian*, 251, for the opportunities Empire presented to a 'revived aristocracy' in Wales, as elsewhere in the British Isles, in the late eighteenth and early nineteenth centuries.

24. MacKenzie, 'Scotland and Empire', 721–22.

25. Owen Rhoscomyl, 'The Place of Wales in the Empire', *Wales*, July 1912, 369–71; Canon Edwards-Rees, 'The Welsh: A Neglected Imperial Asset', *Wales*, July 1912, 396–402.

26. Rhoscomyl, 'Place of Wales', 371.

27. Harry Jones, 'Glimpses of Welsh History and Character', *Welsh Review*, 1 (June 1906), 81–83; Lord Justice Vaughan Williams, 'The Celtic Character', *Wales*, Feb. 1913, 57–61, 61. See also D. Wynne Evans, 'Cambria's Part in Empire Building', *Wales*, Aug. 1911, 173–76.

28. Owain-Jones, 'Contribution', 261.

29. Programmes and other material relating to *Cymdeithas Gwladol y Cymry yn yr India* [National Society of the Welsh in India], which existed 1898–*c*.1903, and *Cymdeithas Cymry Bengal*/Bengal Welsh Society, inaugurated 1909, Ex 887, National Library of Wales, Aberystwyth (NLW); *Australian Association of Welsh Societies News Letter*, 1, 4 (July 1936), 7; unidentified press cutting re Easter Banquet for Welsh in Calcutta, 1892, in Revd Tudur Lloyd Frimston, 'Y Cymry a Ymfudasant ac a Godasant i Enwogrwydd yn America a'r Trefedigaethau Prydeinig' [*c*.1893], MS 19216C, NLW; *Welsh Outlook*, Aug. 1925, 213–14. See also Lloyd Jones, 'A Welshman in India', 136–40.

30. *Y Drych*, 27 June 1918; *The Druid*, 1 May 1919.

31. *Seren Y Dwyrain*, 1943–45; 'Ar drywydd y llythyren "Y" yn yr Aifft', *Y Casglwr*, 33 (Christmas 1987), 3. See also programmes, minutes etc. relating to Delhi Welsh Society 1944–48, MS 14983D, and the Welsh Language Society of Rangoon 1945–46, Ex 1111, NLW.

32. The following discussion is largely based on Bill Jones, 'Welsh Identities in Ballarat, Australia, during the Late Nineteenth Century', *Welsh History Review*, 20 (2001), 283–307; *idem*, 'Welsh Identity in Colonial Ballarat', *Journal of Australian Studies*, no.68 (2001), 34–43; and Kerry Cardell, Cliff Cumming, Peter Griffiths and Bill Jones, 'Welsh Identity on the Victorian Goldfields in the Nineteenth Century', in Kerry Cardell and Cliff Cumming (eds.) *A World Turned Upside Down: Cultural Change on Victoria's Goldfields 1851–2001* (Canberra, 2001), 25–60. See also Arthur Ffestin Hughes, 'Welsh Migrants in Australia: Language Maintenance and Cultural Transmission', Ph.D thesis, University of Adelaide, 1994, 142–51; Lewis Lloyd, *Australians from Wales* (Gwynedd Archives, 1988); Bob Reece, 'The Welsh in Australian Historical Writing', *Australian Studies*, 4 (1990), 88–104, and in Gavin Edwards and Graham Sumner (eds.), *The Historical and Cultural Parallels and Connections between Wales and Australia* (Lewiston, *c*.1991); Robert L. Tyler, '"A Handful of Interesting and Exemplary People from a Country Called Wales". Identity and Culture Maintenance: The Welsh in Ballarat and Sebastopol in the Second Half of the Nineteenth Century', Ph.D thesis, University of Melbourne, 2000.

33. Jupp and York, *Birthplaces*, 27; *Census of Victoria*, 1871, *passim*.

34. *Census of Victoria*, 1871, 226; *Y Gwladgarwr*, 16 April 1859; *Yr Australydd*, June 1871, 7; April 1872, 2; Letters from Mary Jones, Ballarat, to her sister in Llanfihangel-y-Pennant, Wales, 185[5?]–61, MS 22846D, NLW. See also Hughes, 'Welsh Migrants', 146–50; and W. Vamplew (ed.), *Australians, Historical Statistics* (Broadway, NSW, 1987), 11–16; and especially the discussion in Tyler, 'Interesting and Exemplary', 254–67.

35. *Yr Australydd*, March 1867, 129–37; *Yr Ymwelydd*, 16 March 1875, 142; 16 May 1875, 189–90; Ebeneser Morris to William Meirion Evans, 20 April 1876, MS 21817, NLW; Mary Jones to her sister, 13 Nov. 185[5?], 24 Oct. 1856, 14 Aug. 1859, 22 Sept. 1860, MS 22846D, NLW.

36. For contemporary accounts of the development of Welsh religious institutions in Victoria, see 'Achosion crefyddol Cymreig yn Australia', *Y Beirniad*, 14 (1873), 146–58, 263–76, 338–47; W.M. Evans, 'Trem ar agwedd crefydd ym mysg Cymry Victoria Awstralia', *Y Cyfaill o'r Hen Wlad*, Sept. 1864, 276–78.

37. Welsh Calvinistic Methodism combined a belief in election through God's grace, the morally

purifying power of the Welsh language, a socially conservative ethos, a revivalist style, and a highly structured internal organisation. It has only existed within Wales itself, among the Welsh outside Wales, and in its overseas missions. Efforts to create an English-language variant met with only limited success.

38. John Williams (ed.), *Digest of Welsh Historical Statistics*, vol.1 (Cardiff, 1985), 294–95. For the political and social power of Calvinistic Methodism in nineteenth- and early twentieth-century Wales, see Kenneth O. Morgan, *Wales in British Politics* (Cardiff, 1963); and *idem*, *Rebirth of a Nation: Wales 1880–1980* (Cardiff, 1981).

39. Records of the Cambrian Society of Victoria, Welsh Church, Melbourne, Archive; notebook of William Griffith Parry, Ballarat, containing records of early meetings of the Gymdeithas Lenyddol, Facs 449, NLW; *Y Diwygiwr*, July 1856, 212–13; *Argus* (Melbourne), 4 March 1856; *Ballarat Miner and Weekly Star*, 20 and 27 March 1857; Theophilus Williams and J.B. Humffray (eds.), *Ballarat Eisteddfod: Report of the Meetings Held in Ballarat in 1885–86 with Introductory and Historical Notes* (Ballarat, 1886). See also reports of meetings in *Yr Australydd*, 1866–72 and *Yr Ymwelydd*, 1874–76, *passim*.

40. See, for example, Welsh-language column in *The Banner* (Melbourne), 4, 11 and 18 Aug. 1854; *Argus* (Melbourne), 10 July 1855.

41. Michael G. Clyne, 'Multi-Lingual Melbourne Nineteenth Century Style', *Journal of Australian Studies*, 17 (1985), 69–81. See also Kerry Cardell and Cliff Cumming, 'Scotland's Three Tongues in Australia: Colonial Hamilton in the 1860s and 1870s', *Scottish Studies*, 31 (1993), 40–62; Cliff Cumming, '"In the Language of Ossian": Gaelic Survival in Australia and New Zealand – A Comparison', *Australian Studies*, 12 (1997), 104–22.

42. *Ballarat Courier*, 25 Feb. 1886.

43. The following account is largely based on Aled Jones, *Welsh Missionary Journalism in India, 1880–1947*, Currents in World Christianity Position Paper no.123 (Cambridge, 2000). The Welsh missionaries' efforts were concentrated into a divided region which sat astride the frontier between Assam and Eastern Bengal, and which in 1947 was to become the international border separating India from East Pakistan.

44. B.C. Allen, C.S., *Assam District Gazeteer*, vol.2, Sylhet (Calcutta, 1905), 90.

45. *Report of the Foreign Mission of the Welsh Calvinistic Methodists*, 1910, xv. For other statistics, see *Blwyddiadur, neu Lyfr Swyddogol y Methodistiaid Calfinaidd*, published annually from 1898.

46. The Welsh Calvinistic Methodists' Foreign Mission Society, *Regulations for the Guidance of the Directors and Missionaries of the Society* (Salford, 1870), 36–38. See also Nicholas Thomas, *Colonialism's Culture, Anthropology, Travel and Government* (Cambridge, 1994), 39.

47. Jones, 'Welsh Identities', 299–304.

48. *Y Drysorfa*, Aug. 1854, 276–77. 'Mae yn beth hynod a thra chysurus yn nodweddiad y Cymry, eu bod, i ba le bynag yr elont, os bydd rhyw nifer o honynt gyda'u gilydd, yn sefydlu addoliad cymdeithasol yn yr Iaith Gymraeg. Yn nhrefi mawrion Lloegr, yn y gweithfäoedd glo a haiarn yn Scotland, yn ngwahanol daleithiau America, ac yn awr yn aur-gloddfeydd Australia, rhaid i ymfudwyr o Gymru gael clywed yn eu hiaith eu hun am fawrion weithredoedd Duw yn iachawdwriaeth gras.' All quotations from Welsh-language sources have been translated by the authors.

49. Eiflyn Peris Owen, 'Tair Wythnos yn Liverpool a Chymru', *Cylchgrawn Hanes y Methodistiaid Calfinaidd*, 7 (1983) 43–52.

50. *Y Diwygiwr*, 21, 252 (July 1856), 213. 'Gofyniad ag sydd yn cael ei ofyn yn fynych yw, Pa fodd y mae trigolion Ucheldiroedd Scotland, sef y "Gaelic," yn cael gweinidogion i bregethu iddynt yn eu hiaith? a'r Gwyddelod yn cael offeiriaid ac eglwysi yn mhob man y byddont yn sefydlu ynddo? tra yr ydym ni y Cymry heb yr un gweinidog yn perthyn i un enwad crefyddol wedi cael ei ddanfon allan. Miloedd o fechgyn a merched a fagwyd â chymaint o ofal crefyddol, sydd yma ... yn syrthio yn ysglyfaeth i'w blys a'i nwydau, tra y mae ffwdan mawr, a chasglu er danfon canadon allan i ... [d]reulio eu hunain allan er ceisio dychwelyd rhyw Bagan coelgrefyddol.' See also Cumming, 'In the Language of Ossian', 109–11.

51. Linda Colley, *Britons: Forging the Nation 1707–1837* (London, 1992), esp. 117–31. Also see previously cited works by Fitzpatrick, Jeffery and MacKenzie.

52. For the concept of colonial 'entanglement', see Nicholas Thomas, *Entangled Objects: Exchange, Material Culture, and Colonialism in the Pacific* (Cambridge, MA, 1991).

53. *Yr Awstralydd*, July 1866, 1–2; English-language translation of an unattributed, and apparently lost, biography of William Meirion Evans, 94–7, Facs 680, NLW. A second copy of the biography can also be found in the Welsh Church, Melbourne, Archive.

54. *Yr Ymwelydd*, Dec. 1876, 282–83, 286; 'Gweithrediadau Cymanfaol Trefnyddion Calfinaidd, neu Henaduriaid Australia', 25–27 Nov. 1876, 131, Welsh Church, Melbourne, Archive.

55. Letters written to William Meirion Evans on various matters relating to *Yr Ymwelydd* c.1874–76 and deposited in the Welsh Church, Melbourne, Archive, contain numerous references to subscriptions being stopped because subscribers had moved away or could not be traced to collect payment.

56. See also Geraint Evans, 'Welsh Publishing in Australia', *Biblionews and Australian Notes and Queries*, 18 (1993), 105–11; Tyler, 'Interesting and Exemplary', 204–13; Myfi Williams, *Cymry Awstralia* (Llandybie, 1983), esp. 82–90.

57. It appears that there was some discussion in Welsh circles in Victoria at the time regarding the need for a weekly newspaper, but it was felt to be wiser to embark on a monthly in the first instance. *Yr Australydd*, July 1866, 1–2; Evans biography, 94–97, Facs 680, NLW.

58. 'Gweithrediadau Cymanfaol Trefnyddion Calfinaidd', 24–26 July 1863, 10.

59. Tyler, 'Interesting and Exemplary', 204–13.

60. Ibid., 207–09.

61. Aled Gruffydd Jones, *Press, Politics and Society: A History of Journalism in Wales* (Cardiff, 1993); Huw Walters, *Y Wasg Gyfnodol Gymreig/The Welsh Periodical Press, 1735–1900* (Aberystwyth, 1987).

62. *Yr Australydd*, July 1866, 2.

63. See, for example, *Yr Australydd*, Nov. 1867, 112–15. See also Williams, *Cymry Awstralia*, 85–86.

64. Tyler, 'Interesting and Exemplary', 209.

65. For details of the reciprocal subscription payment arrangements, see *Yr Ymwelydd*, June 1875, 216. See *Y Drych*, 27 April, 13 July 1876, for commentaries on the contents of *Yr Ymwelydd*.

66. Tyler, 'Interesting and Exemplary', 209–10.

67. *Yr Australydd*, April 1871, 5. 'Y mae sefyllfa y Cymry yn y trefedigaethau Australaidd yn destun a ddylai gael sylw arbenigol pob Cymro fel cenedlgarwr a dinesydd da. Ceisia rhai eu perswadio eu hunain fod pob teimlad cenedlaethol – yn Gymreig, Ysgotaidd, a Gwyddelig, &c. – yn waeth na difudd mewn gwlad cymysg fel hon ... [Creda] rhai yn fyr a didrafferth, y dylai pob mur a adeiladwyd ar sail cenedligrwydd (nationality) gael ei daflu i lawr mewn trefn i osod i lawr seiliau cenedl orwech o Australiaid ... [Ond] a ydyw hyn yn angenrheidiol a buddiol er mwyn sylfaenaid a chynydd Australia? [Mae] cenedligrwydd yn un o elfenau pwysicaf yn llwyddiant pob cenedl. Os ydym am roddi cymorth i osod seiliau cenedl Deasia ar graig safadwy – os ydyw Cymry y trefedigaethau am adael eu hol ar y byd a'r oesoedd a ddeuant, bydded iddynt feithrin a magu teimladau cenedlaethol grymus a goleuedig, ymgydnabyddu â hen lenyddiaeth enwog y Cymry ... a [m]eddianu ysbryd yr hen dadau.'

68. For a fuller treatment, see Bill Jones, 'Welsh Identities'; and 'Cymry "Gwlad yr Aur": Ymfudwyr Cymreig yn Ballarat, Awstralia, yn ail hanner y bedwaredd ganrif ar bymtheg', *Llafur*, 8 (2001), 41–62.

69. See, for example, *Yr Australydd*, Oct. 1870, 227–31.

70. *Yr Australydd*, Sept. 1868, 344–48.

71. *Y Cenhadwr*, Dec. 1928, 236.

72. Numbers of Welsh speakers in Wales over the age of three totalled 766,103 in 1921, peaking at 811,329 in 1931. For further details, consult Williams, *Digest*, vol.2, 86–8. The Church Missionary Society, founded in 1799, published its Annual Proceedings from 1800 to 1922. See also *The Missionary Register*, 1813–55, and *The Church Missionary Paper* and *Record* from 1830. Both *The Church Missionary Gleaner*, est. 1841, and *Mercury and Truth*, est. 1897, ended in the early 1920s. Josef L. Altholz, *The Religious Press in Britain, 1760–1900* (New York and London, 1989), 20.

73. *Adroddiad Cenhadaeth Dramor y Methodistiaid Calfinaidd Cymreig, 1926*, CMA/GZ/2–14, NLW.
74. Nigel Jenkins, *Gwalia in Khasia: A visit to the site, in India, of the biggest overseas venture ever sustained by the Welsh* (Llandysul, 1995), 230–41.
75. For further information on the expulsion of William Pryce, see John Hughes Morris, *Hanes Cenhadaeth Dramor y Methodistiaid Calfinaidd Cymreig, hyd ddiwedd y flwyddyn 1904* (Liverpool, 1907), 300. Pryce died in India on 2 Aug. 1869.
76. Ibid., 312.
77. Aparnu Basu, 'Mary Ann Coote to Mother Teresa: Christian Women and the Indian Response', in Fiona Bowie, Deborah Kirkwood and Shirley Ardener, *Women and Missions Past and Present: Anthropological and Historical Perceptions* (Oxford, 1993), 199.
78. Mary Louise Pratt, 'Scratches on the Face of the Country; or, what Mr. Barrow saw in the land of the Bushmen', in Henry Louis Gates Jr. (ed.), *"Race", Writing, and Difference* (Chicago, 1986), 139.
79. Thomas, *Colonialism's Culture*, 38.
80. Miss E.A. Roberts, 'Y Cronicl Cenhadol', *Y Drysorfa*, Dec. 1902, 570.
81. *Y Cenhadwr*, Jan. 1925, 8–9. 'Yn y bore, fel y mae'r wawr yn torri … (m)ae'r dyfroedd i gyd fel pe'n disgwyl yn swil ond yn ffyddiog dawel am gusan gyntaf yr haul. A phwy ar fachlud haul all ddisgrifio'r cysgodau yn y dwr yn ei droi'n rhuddgoch a phorffor? … (no)son leuad ar yr afonydd a'r wlad yn orchuddiedig gan ddwr – mae yn llawn cyfaredd a hud.'
82. John Pengwern Jones introduced the Eisteddfod to Sylhet in 1904, and Helen Rowlands later held *eisteddfodau* in Bengali in Karimganj. J. Meirion Lloyd, *Hanes Cenhadaeth Dramor Eglwys Bresbyteraidd Cymru*, 7.
83. *Report of the Foreign Mission*, 1910, xiii.
84. Parch. T. Charles Edwards, 'Gair i Gychwyn, *Y Cenhadwr*, Jan. 1922, 2.
85. *Y Cenhadwr*, Dec. 1923, 189–90. See also Susan Fleming McAllister, 'Cross-Cultural Dress in Victorian British Missionary Narratives: Dressing for Eternity', in John C. Hawley (ed.), *Historicizing Christian Encounters with the Other* (Basingstoke, 1998), esp. 123–24.
86. *The Link*, March–April 1935, 18.
87. For a fuller history, see Aled Jones and Bill Jones, *Welsh Reflections: Y Drych and America, 1851–2001* (Llandysul, 2001).
88. 'The Welsh language is the curse of Wales … their antiquated and semibarbarous language … shrouds them in darkness'. *The Times*, editorial, 8 Sept. 1866.

Revisiting Anglicisation in the Nineteenth-Century Cape Colony

VIVIAN BICKFORD-SMITH

Writing about the British world should do more than merely tell us about events which happened in that world. It should necessarily involve exploring how such a world was constructed and maintained in its various geographical parts through time. To paraphrase comments made about urban historiography: writing about the British world should involve 'history-of-the-British world', not just 'history-in-the-British world'.[1] Studying the 'history-of-the-British world' is, then, in part about studying the history of British 'hegemony'. Hegemony, following Raymond Williams's definition, refers to: 'not only the articulate upper level of "ideology" nor ... only those [policies/processes] ordinarily seen as "manipulation" or "indoctrination". It is a whole body of practices and expectations, over the whole of living ... our shaping perceptions of ourselves and our world. It is a lived system of meanings and values.'[2] The establishment of British hegemony was driven by English nationalism; its ideological content, 'practices and expectations' derived from English values and customs, from Englishness itself, which was the dominant influence within Britishness.[3] Such values and customs, and resulting practices and expectations, were not of course static; and one task facing historians of the British world is to be sensitive to the chronology of change in this respect. Equally British hegemony, whatever its precise ideological content, was not established over *tabula rasa*. As Bredekamp and Ross have written while examining the history of Christianity in South Africa, 'their [i.e. indigenous South Africans] consciousness was not colonized, at least [not] in the same way as their land and their labour was colonized'.[4] Richard Elphick has expanded on this view: 'two systems of thought do not "collide"; rather, real people negotiate their way through life, grasping, combining, and opposing different elements which the scholar (but not necessarily the actor) assign to different origins'.[5] In this postmodern world it has become easier to accept that there was no simple divide between acceptance and rejection of imperial values: 'To this process people brought traditions, acquired or inherited social identities, practices and skills, and whatever they could marshal from their native cultures and the colonial cultures to which they were now continuously exposed.'[6] And the process was not necessarily one way: converts to Anglicanism, for instance, in South Africa could later switch to another, non-British, denomination, move to an African 'independent' church, or revert to 'paganism'. But it is salutary to remember that in the nineteenth-century Cape it was the British who held power. Establishing British hegemony was about preserving and increasing that power. Even if minds could not easily be colonised, 'consciousness was not power',[7] and British hegemony helped to determine – albeit in varying ways and degrees – the nature of that consciousness.

I

Twenty years ago James Sturgis wrote an article for the *Journal of Imperial and Commonwealth History* entitled, 'Anglicisation at the Cape of Good Hope in the Early Nineteenth Century'.[8] He defined anglicisation as 'the assimilation of Afrikaners into a predominantly English culture', while noting that the term was used in the nineteenth century in relation to policies aimed at incorporating either the Cape Dutch or French Canadians in this manner. Without expanding directly on his understanding of 'culture', Sturgis explained that he meant assimilation to refer not only to 'Afrikaner' adoption of the English language, but also to 'the attitudinal changes which were expected to accompany such a conversion and which would have the effect of turning the Afrikaner into something resembling the enterprising and liberal bourgeois Englishmen of the time'.[9] Both were brought about by a combination of what he calls 'direct' and 'indirect' anglicisation. The former referred to policies intended to have a near immediate effect, such as changes 'in the colonial civil service, local government and the law'; the latter to longer-term policies and processes leading to the same result, such as assisted immigration and changes in educational or religious practices. Thus the focus was on government initiatives, particularly in the 1820s and 1830s, rather than the 'informal transfer' of British culture in the form, for instance, of British sports.[10]

Sturgis was drawing from, and building on, existing liberal historiography that acknowledged and described early nineteenth-century anglicisation while, he argued, analysing neither 'its origins nor its modus operandi, nor its degree of success'.[11] Accordingly, Sturgis importantly drew attention to the personalities within both the imperial and colonial states who advocated anglicisation and provided a useful summary of the means they adopted towards this end, along the lines suggested in the previous paragraph. Yet unfortunately Sturgis is decidedly disappointing in his attempts to assess anglicisation's 'success', telling us little about the extent to which Dutch colonists did or did not in fact succumb to British hegemony.

As he himself acknowledged, the difficulty in doing so arose partly from the 'chronological limits' of his article. Thus, in a one-paragraph conclusion, he rather lamely stated that 'the market economy had taken root', accepting the view of Arthur Keppel-Jones that British predominance in the politics and culture of the Cape in the nineteenth century derived to a considerable degree from the anglicising policies begun in the 1820s, but warning that 'the obverse side of the Great Trek meant that those forces opposed to Anglicisation were never subdued'.[12] The fact is that Sturgis's ability to contribute to our understanding of the history of British hegemony in the Cape is also constrained by his failure to examine 'attitudinal changes' among 'Afrikaners', whether within his period or beyond. Such examination would, of course, have required engagement with the somewhat slippery conceptual realm of cultural change and exchange, as well as with a much wider range of primary sources beyond the official correspondence that forms the bedrock of his article. Yet he himself stated that this was the second level on which anglicisation operated, implicitly promising to reveal something of this process.

There is also the problem that Sturgis defined 'anglicisation' only in reference to policies aimed at converting the Cape Dutch to Englishness, a definition apparently in keeping with contemporary usage. He therefore ruled out the possibility of telling us anything much about how other residents of the Cape might have experienced the imposition of British rule, how they might have been affected by anglicising policies even if the latter were aimed in the first instance at the Dutch. And one might add that it is somewhat ingenuous to exclude an examination of 'informal' cultural transfers when presumably the point of an official policy of introducing immigrants from Britain was precisely to encourage these.

For all its limitations, Sturgis's article was a rare attempt within the high era of revisionist South African historiography (the 1970s and 1980s) to focus directly on the acculturation of South Africans of any region, race or ethnicity within a British world. Most revisionist historiography, given its neo-Marxist influences, was more concerned with modernising, rather than specifically anglicising, processes – such as proletarianisation or capital accumulation – even if the latter were part and parcel of establishing British hegemony. In this respect it mattered that British conquest tied the Cape, and subsequently large portions of southern Africa, to the dominant capitalist and industrialising power of the nineteenth century, with all that this might mean for strategies of protest and resistance, class formation and the growth of counter-nationalisms.[13] But with the notable exceptions of Brian Willan's work on Sol Plaatje and Bill Nasson's on black participation in the South African war, there appears to have been remarkably little concern among revisionists to understand the consequences of a specifically

British, rather than merely capitalist, hegemonic project, be it at the Cape or elsewhere in southern Africa.[14] Equally, whether in the case of revisionist or liberal historians, when dominant social identity in colonial southern Africa was considered in terms other than class, or as part of class identity, it was almost exclusively portrayed as a largely de-ethnicised or de-nationalised, but racialised, 'white' hegemony over blacks, as 'white supremacy'. In the case of Greenberg and Fredrickson, it would seem that this was at least in part to facilitate comparative studies in white racial domination across the Atlantic.[15] Comparative work between different parts of the British Empire has in contrast produced an understanding of colonial power in India, South and West Africa as inextricably bound up with British imperial discourse.[16]

These lacunae in most South African historiography occurred despite the fact that English nationalism 'was the prime nationalism of South Africa, against which all subsequent ones ... reacted' and that 'Englishness was the major symbol used to determine what was right and acceptable in the political life of the Cape Colony'. In making these observations, in a wonderfully nuanced recent work, Robert Ross convincingly, if provocatively, suggests that British hegemony has been so little studied because 'the English have been so successful in imposing it on South African society. They themselves, those who have assimilated to the English and those who have reacted against it, have all taken it for granted, have assumed that it is part of the natural order of things that English ways are the best.'[17]

Between them, Willan and Nasson establish many of the elements of British hegemonic ideology within 'Cape liberal' rhetoric that lingered into the early twentieth century among black Cape colonists: the potential or actual benefits of being 'freeborn' British citizens; the dichotomy between those deemed to be 'civilised' and 'barbaric'; the possibility of 'civilising' all citizens, irrespective of race, within the empire; the belief that a commanding knowledge of the English language and good English education were crucial to being categorised among the 'civilised'; the promise that hard work, 'progress', 'improvement' and 'respectability'[18] – in dress, manners and hygiene – could lead to acceptance as 'civilised' and the achievement of equal rights; the existence of a non-racial franchise that seemed to be proof of such a promise; the idea of a Great White Queen across the water who made no distinction of race among her subjects, who might be appealed to in case of need.[19] What Willan and Nasson also provide is a reminder that the most important agents of British hegemony came from the ranks of the 'rising class' among the colonised themselves, as was the case in West Africa and India.[20] Equally their work cautions us that adherence to British ideology (or elements thereof) among the colonised, such as expressions of patriotism during the South African war, 'should not be interpreted as the product of a simple, unmediated absorption of an imperial creed'.[21]

This raises the challenge (one not accepted by Sturgis) of attempting to discover how, as Megan Vaughan has put it while discussing the impact of colonial medical discourse in Nyasaland, 'ideas were "read" by those at whom they were directed'.[22] For the non-literate, imaginative methodology is needed to do this: whether it be perceptive readings of 'dominant class' sources such as magistrates' or missionaries' records, or by examining elements of popular culture that have survived to the present in rites, festivities, songs or oral tradition.[23] For the literate members of the Cape's indigenous rising class the task is perhaps easier, though few attempts have been as elegant or nuanced as Willan's biographical pieces on Plaatje. However, mention should be made of Janet Hodgson's path-breaking articles on Xhosa chiefs and their scions in mid-nineteenth-century Cape Town, which make particularly good use of the correspondence of youths at Zonnebloem College.[24] For instance, one pupil believed that the Xhosa leader, Maqoma, who fought the British 'was as brave as ... Duke Wellington' [sic],[25] suggesting that a number of lessons could be learnt from the study of British history. In addition, in Odendaal's and Lewis's accounts of the rise of African and Coloured political organisations respectively,[26] Cape historiography has at least detailed accounts of a process well described for India's rising subaltern class:

> By integrating society, introducing symmetric trends of social hierarchy, enumerating society, familiarizing Indians with the theory of public power and democracy, placing before them the universality of reason and the great narratives of European nation-formation and introducing the skills of forming associations, this [British] imperial discourse had also taught Indians how rationalism could be turned against the European colonizers themselves. The lessons of rationalism were learnt, unfortunately too well.[27]

And Lewis's insights into Abdullah Abdurahman, the dominant figure in Coloured politics for the first four decades of the twentieth century, combine to deliver another empathetic portrait of a leading member of the Cape's subaltern rising class to put alongside Willan on Plaatje.[28]

Despite the perceptiveness of the literature, including the imaginative contributions listed in endnote 23, there remains surprisingly little work since the 1980s that attempts to deal directly with the question of British hegemony. But there are a number of at least partial exceptions. There have been important insights provided by the creative work on conversion to Christianity by the Comaroffs and Elizabeth Elbourne.[29] Deborah Gaitskell has directly tackled the question of Victorian domestic ideology, and revealed an area of British and African male consent, in her investigation of African girls' education in the Cape.[30] Elizabeth Van Heyningen has also brought to light a great deal about British hegemonic discourse in her work on aspects of medicine, poverty and social policy in Cape Town.[31] Indeed, Cape Town has been relatively well served in terms of the amount of attention given to the infusion, not only of British hegemonic rhetoric and social practice, but also of British material culture, popular culture more generally, British literature and scientific institutions – interestingly explored by Saul Dubow – and the rise of an aggressive and exclusive Englishness in the late nineteenth century, the latter seemingly somewhat overlooked by Ross.[32] Finally, in this probably gap-ridden bibliographical sketch, Andrew Thompson has recently provided an excellent overview of the regional nature of British colonial identity, while Elizabeth Van Heyningen has provided insight into the gendered nature of such loyalism.[33] All the above insights, whether direct or indirect analyses of the nature of British hegemony, provide the possibility of rethinking Sturgis's limited definition of 'anglicisation'. They suggest a revised agenda for research in this field. It is to this consideration that the second section of this article must now turn.

II

In rethinking 'anglicisation' in the nineteenth century, an initial necessary step is surely to reconsider Sturgis's definition of the term. At the risk of being anachronistic – and one might point out that Sturgis has no problem in using the anachronistic term 'Afrikaner' for 'Dutch' or 'Boer' in his paper – it hardly seems appropriate to confine the process of British acculturation at the Cape to settlers of Dutch (or German, or French) descent. Rather, a more useful and appropriate definition of 'anglicisation' must refer to a process that included nationalist and rationalist, ideological and material, official and (Sturgis's term) informal components that affected all Cape colonists. In other words, anglicisation was about political, economic, social and cultural transformations that necessitate, as Thompson suggests, looking beyond (but incorporating) the 'high politics of the governing classes'.[34]

Such transformations obviously included the changes brought about by colonial government policies in the early nineteenth century (in the colonial service, local government, the law, religion, education and immigration) that Sturgis examined. But apart from effecting changes in such areas beyond his period – as well as religious (and accompanying ideological) change brought about by missionary activity that Sturgis addresses in a single paragraph – such transformations also included informal cultural transfers that Sturgis did not attempt to address, but whose study should be an essential part of any attempt at understanding the anglicisation process in its entirety.

The existing literature, albeit not always centrally focused on anglicisation, already provides or suggests considerable information on, and insights into, how such future research could proceed. Some of the studies, as we have implied, have already initiated the grand project, while leaving considerable room for further work, whether this be on other parts of the Cape, other periods, or even within the same place and period. Thus Dubow has mapped out the establishment of Cape literary and scientific institutions established between the 1820s and 1870s, including the *South African Commercial Advertiser*, the South African Museum, and the South African library, which were key components of anglicisation within the creation of a Cape colonial identity. Kirsten McKenzie had already demonstrated how the establishment of the *Advertiser* helped to create a 'rational public sphere … out of which a distinctive middle class identity might be formed'.[35] The point is that recognisably British values and aspirations were naturally part of such distinctiveness. Notable among them was the desire for (gender differentiated) respectability. Ross has made it abundantly clear that such a desire was not confined to the white, urban middle class.[36]

A number of scholars have noted, some even emphasised, the anglicisation of material culture. In terms of architecture and urban landscape, British influence *inter alia* wrought changes in both the outward appearance of urban public and private buildings as well as the inward arrangement of domestic space; it also led to the covering over of Dutch canals and the dismantling of stoeps in Cape Town. In rural areas it produced the installation of Christian converts in 'appropriate' houses, as well as the construction of distinctively English settler farmhouses. Such material change – and Ross has drawn attention to clothing as another important element of anglicisation in material change – was meant to convey a variety of anglicising rhetorical messages, whether about respectability, status or (would be) national dominance.[37]

In similar fashion, this author has attempted to show how the anglicisation of leisure activities included not just the importation of particular and new British games and entertainments – from archery to vaudeville – and the suppression or erosion of indigenous ones, but the ideological values that went with this process. Such values helped to inculcate British ideas about appropriately gendered behaviour, of physical and moral 'improvement', of industrial time discipline, indeed of discipline and the need to maintain social order in general. Leisure activities also bolstered a range of colonial British identities.[38] As Willan put it, 'In Kimberley, the two African clubs … were the Duke of Wellington Cricket

Club ... and Eccentrics Cricket Club ... both symbolizing qualities upon which the British empire was built', and at least the first of these names demonstrated respectful loyalty to that empire.[39] The same was broadly true of the two teams that took part in an annual competition that began in 1862 in Cape Town, 'Mother Country' and 'Colonial Born'.[40]

Indeed names and naming – of people, places, occasions or things – remain a fascinating and significant aspect of anglicisation that has been largely (and strangely) neglected in academic literature, left in the un-analytical clutches of antiquarians.[41] Of course, naming might not just be a matter of individual (or groups of individuals') choice. It could also be the result of decisions by central or local government functionaries. This is only one potential area of official, rather than 'informal' anglicisation overlooked by Sturgis, despite his rubric.

Another, also still under-researched area, is the matter of official festivities, ceremonies, holidays and other occasions that in one way or another celebrated British power, policies or achievements. Indeed comparisons between official and unofficial celebrations of the same event could be particularly rewarding for exploring the extent (and limitations/contestations) of British hegemony. As it is, what we know, in a rather haphazard and patchy way, about both kinds of celebrations – whether emancipation day commemorations by ex-slaves and their descendants;[42] or festivities from 1844 that celebrated the landing of the 1820 settlers;[43] or royal celebrations (Queen's birthday, royal wedding, royal visits or jubilee celebrations)[44] – can provide rich information on how British rule was either presented or understood, or both.

In addition we have glimpses, and we should attempt broader surveys, of particular ways in which British rulers at the Cape consciously attempted to impress their indigenous subjects with British power in more informal ways than official celebrations. Governor Sir George Grey was particularly alert to such possibilities. Thus he wanted a school for the sons and daughters of African chiefs to be located in Cape Town, at least in part because it offered 'the most striking proof of England's power' and demonstrated 'the advantages of civilization'.[45] Much the same motive lay behind Grey's insistence on bringing Chief Sandile to Cape Town in 1860, with the added advantages that Sandile was conveyed to the western Cape on the impressive warship HMS *Euryalus*, and that the visit was to coincide with the major festivities surrounding Prince Alfred's ceremonial beginning of the city's harbour construction.[46]

Beyond gaps in our information about who or what was affected by anglicisation is the matter of understanding the process more fully in terms of agency, periodisation, and extent and limitations. In other words, we still need to assess anglicisation's success, the problem side-stepped by Sturgis.

In terms of agency, it is worth reconsidering Monica Wilson's memorable comment on British missionaries, a comment that could equally apply to a number of secular advocates of British imperialism: 'the missionaries were ... mostly from Britain, and they were Victorians imbued with a conviction of the value of their whole manner of life – a conviction matched since 1918 only by communists'.[47] The passion and energy of such agents of British ideological hegemony, and their capacity to achieve seemingly nigh complete conversion of minds and bodies, should not be underestimated. But in adding to the obvious candidates responsible for spreading British hegemonic ideology, we need to include other British functionaries, notably at local state level, and also the civilian settlers themselves, whether they were professionals spreading such ideology in the fields of colonial law or medicine, employers of labour, or members of voluntary organisations. In addition, we must remember and learn from comparative literature on other parts of the British world that often the most important agents of British hegemony came from the ranks of the 'rising class' of indigenous people.

In terms of periodising anglicisation, we need to be alert to its different, or changing, or overlapping components, and how these may have had regional variations. One might, for instance, agree with Sturgis that there were both aristocratic and bourgeois components of official anglicisation in the early nineteenth century. One might also tentatively suggest that this early, largely non-consultative, process of official anglicisation gave way by mid-century to an attempt at anglicisation – and by extension government – more obviously by consent. Even so, such consensual anglicisation was increasingly threatened in the late nineteenth century by a narrower English chauvinism, so evident in Cape Town from the 1870s, and the subsequent rise of counter-nationalisms that nonetheless stressed loyalty to the crown.[48]

Finally, any study must not only be aware of the limits and extent of anglicisation, but sensitive to a range of possible explanations of such parameters. It would seem uncontroversial to argue that different experience of, or reaction to, anglicisation was in part because of (and this will be another incomplete list) cultural, gendered, class, pigmentary, ethnic, generational, and occupational differences in those it touched, or only lightly touched – allowing for the fact that such differences were partly shaped or reshaped by the process itself. Thus revealing overlapping gender, class, and ethnic prejudices, Sandile was more impressed that Prince Alfred actually worked as a midshipman on board the *Euryalus* than by the fighting potential or engineering wonders of the ship itself. As he wrote to the ship's captain:

> Up to this time we have not ceased to be amazed at the wonderful things we have witnessed, and which are beyond our comprehension.

But one thing we understand, the reason of England's greatness, when the Son of her great Queen becomes subject to a subject that he may learn wisdom ... what we have learnt shall be transmitted to our wondering countrymen and handed down to our children.[49]

But those children, in the persons of the pupils of Zonnebloem College, were in the event far more excited by the visit of Sandile, and what he represented in terms of courageous leadership against British domination, than by that of the Great White Queen's oldest son.[50]

Yet if range of experience, across groups and individuals and over time, must surely be emphasised, colonists could also be affected in similar ways by anglicisation, across seemingly wide divides – thus the ubiquitous, if hardly all-embracing, appeal of 'respectability'. Equally 'time discipline' was not just a system imposed on indigenous or (proto-) working-class South Africans, or one that was accepted eagerly by a 'rising' indigenous class, but one that white elite colonists were taught at institutions such as the South African College. In other words 'anglicisation' was not something that had happened to anyone in the womb.[51]

In conclusion, much of revisionist history has of course been centrally concerned to record 'resistance' of various kinds. And resisters in a multitude of forms have been looked for and found in the nineteenth-century British Cape Colony, whether they be Xhosa or Khoi soldiers, Xhosa millenarian cattle-killers, slaves, Cape Town dock workers or domestic servants.[52] In addition, Ross has examined 'rejection' as well as 'acceptance', and devoted a chapter in *Status and Respectability* to 'outsiders', those arguably least touched by anglicisation such as 'the Cape Town underclass', farm labourers and Muslims.[53] Others have also been interested in the relationship, the tensions and ambivalences, between respectability and 'unrespectability'.[54] But more recently there has been a tendency, in keeping with postmodern teachings, to make greater allowance for 'ambiguity and multiple meanings'. In other words, we must recognise that historical reality allowed for much greater complexity than simple or teleological 'acceptance' or 'rejection' of imperial ideologies.[55] Studying British hegemony is about understanding that indigenous peoples, as well as colonisers themselves, took part in the making of their own worlds. But also to understand the nature of the power and processes that confined their efforts within the British world itself.

NOTES

1. In terms of the distinction made in this respect in urban history between 'history-of-the-city' and 'history-in-the-city', see, for instance, Paul Maylam, 'Explaining the Apartheid City: 20

Years of South African Urban Historiography', *Journal of Southern African Studies*, 21 (1995), 20.

2. Raymond Williams, *Marxism and Literature* (Oxford, 1977), 110.
3. See R. Colls and P. Dodd (eds.), *Englishness: Politics and Culture 1880–1920* (Beckenham, 1986).
4. Henry Bredekamp and Robert Ross (eds.), *Missions and Christianity in South African History* (Johannesburg, 1995), 4.
5. Richard Elphick, 'Writing Religion into History: The Case of South African Christianity', in Bredekamp and Ross (eds.), *Missions and Christianity*, 21.
6. Bill Nasson, *Abraham Esau's War: A Black South African at War in the Cape, 1899–1902* (Cambridge, 1991), 8–9.
7. C. Clark, 'Politics, Language and Class', *Radical History Review*, 34 (1986), 85, cited in Nasson, *Abraham Esau's War*, 191.
8. James Sturgis, 'Anglicisation at the Cape of Good Hope in the Early Nineteenth Century', *Journal of Imperial and Commonwealth History*, 11 (1982), 5–32. Sturgis acknowledged that his use of the label Afrikaner was anachronistic, but preferred it to 'Dutch' or 'Boer'. The Cape Colonists became part of the British Empire in 1815.
9. Ibid., 5.
10. Ibid., 25.
11. Ibid., 6. On liberal historiography that describes anglicisation policies, see, for instance, T.R.H. Davenport, 'The Consolidation of a New Society: The Cape Colony', in M. Wilson and L.M. Thompson (eds.), *The Oxford History of South Africa* (Oxford, 1969), 272–333; K.S. Hunt, *Sir Lowry Cole* (Durban, 1974); M. Streak, *The Afrikaner as viewed by the English 1795–1854* (Cape Town, 1974); and E.A. Walker (ed.), *The Cambridge History of the British Empire*, vol.8, 2nd edn (Cambridge, 1963), 200–03, 258–60, 370–72 and 865–67.
12. Sturgis, 'Anglicisation', 27–28.
13. For a summary of some of the main players among the revisionists, and their ideological and thematic preoccupations, see Christopher Saunders, *The Making of the South African Past* (Cape Town and Johannesburg, 1988), 165–91.
14. Brian Willan, 'An African in Kimberley: Sol T. Plaatje, 1894–1898', in Shula Marks and Richard Rathbone (eds.), *Industrialisation and Social Change in South Africa: African Class Formation, Culture and Consciousness 1870–1930* (London and New York, 1982), 238–58; Brian Willan, *Sol Plaatje: A Biography, 1876–1932* (Johannesburg, 1984); Bill Nasson, 'The War of Abraham Esau 1899–1901: Martyrdom, Myth and Folk Memory in Calvinia, South Africa', *African Affairs*, 87 (1988), 239–65; and idem, *Abraham Esau's War*.
15. See, for instance, Stanley Greenberg, *Race and State in Capitalist Development* (Johannesburg, 1980); George Fredrickson, *White Supremacy: A Comparative Study in American and South African History* (New York and Oxford, 1981); and Clifton C. Crais, *The Making of the Colonial Order: White Supremacy and Black Resistance in the Eastern Cape, 1770–1865* (Cambridge, 1992).
16. Dagmar Engels and Shula Marks (eds.), *Contesting Colonial Hegemony: State and Society in Africa and India* (London, 1994).
17. Robert Ross, *Status and Respectability in the Cape Colony 1750–1870: A Tragedy of Manners* (Cambridge, 1999).
18. For a 1980s acknowledgement of the importance of 'respectability' as a concept and badge of status that could cut across class, if less easily race, divides in Cape society, see Robert Ross, 'Structure and Culture in Pre-Industrial Cape Town', in Wilmot G. James and Mary Simons (eds.), *The Angry Divide* (Cape Town, 1989), 44–45.
19. Willan, 'Plaatje', 239 and 242–43; Nasson, *Abraham Esau's War*, 6 and 8.
20. See, for instance, William Gervase Clarence-Smith, 'The Organisation of "Consent" in British West Africa, 1820s to 1960s'; and David Arnold, 'Public Health and Public Power: Medicine and Hegemony in Colonial India', both in Engels and Marks (eds.), *Contesting Colonial Hegemony*, 55–78 and 131–51 respectively.
21. Nasson, *Abraham Esau's War*, 62.
22. Megan Vaughan, 'Health and Hegemony: Representation of Disease and the Creation of the Colonial Subject in Nyasaland', in Engels and Marks (eds.), *Contesting Colonial Hegemony*, 173.

23. Bill Nasson's work on Abraham Esau is particularly instructive in this respect, while Ross's *Status and Respectability* also offers many imaginative insights drawn, for instance, from examining material culture. Perhaps the most exciting examples of an attempt to give a voice to the illiterate in the nineteenth-century Cape comes from work on slavery and emancipation. Notable amongst them is John Mason's outstanding contributions, such as: 'Hendrik Albertus and His Ex-Slave Mey: A Drama in Three Acts', *Journal of African History*, 31 (1990), 423–45; and 'Paternalism under Siege: Slavery in Theory and Practice during the Era of Reform, c.1825 through Emancipation', in Nigel Worden and Clifton Crais (eds.), *Breaking the Chains: Slavery and its Legacy in the Nineteenth Century Cape Colony* (Johannesburg, 1994), 46–77. Mention should also be made of the work of Pam Scully and Patricia Van der Spuy, which emphasises the gendered nature of the experience of slavery and emancipation, such as Scully's 'Private and Public Worlds of Emancipation in the Rural Western Cape, c1830–42', in Worden and Crais (eds.), *Breaking the Chains*, 201–24; or P. Van Der Spuy, 'Slave Women and the Family in Nineteenth-Century Cape Town', *South African Historical Journal*, 27 (1992), 50–74. There is also Chris Winberg's path-breaking, if under-developed paper, 'The "Ghoemaliedjies" of the Cape Muslims: Remnants of a Slave Culture', unpublished paper, University of Cape Town, 1992; and Robert Shell, 'Rites and Rebellion: Islamic Conversion at the Cape, 1808 to 1915', *Studies in the History of Cape Town*, 5 (1983), 1–45. For clumsier attempts, see Vivian Bickford-Smith, 'Meanings of Freedom: Social Position and Identity Among Ex-Slaves and Their Descendants in Cape Town, 1875–1910', in Worden and Crais (eds.), *Breaking the Chains*, 289–312; and 'Leisure and Identity in Cape Town, British Cape Colony, 1838–1910', *Kronos*, 25 (1998–99), 103–28. Without pretending to be comprehensive in this endnote, attention should also be drawn to Jeff Peires's use of oral tradition in his masterful reconstruction of Xhosa Cattle-Killing movement of 1856–57 in *The Dead Will Arise* (Johannesburg, 1989); and William Beinart's and Colin Bundy's achievements in giving some sense of popular consciousness in the Eastern Cape in the later nineteenth century in *Hidden Struggles in Rural South Africa* (Johannesburg, 1987).

24. Janet Hodgson, 'Zonnebloem College and Cape Town: 1858–1870', *Studies in the History of Cape Town*, 1 (1979), 125–52; and *idem*, 'Xhosa Chiefs in Cape Town in the Mid-19th century', ibid., 2 (1980), 41–74.

25. Hodgson, 'Xhosa Chiefs', 64.

26. Andre Odendaal, *Black Protest in South Africa to 1912* (Cape Town and Totowa, NJ, 1984); Gavin Lewis, *Between The Wire and the Wall: A History of 'Coloured' Politics* (Cape Town and Johannesburg, 1987).

27. Sudipta Kaviraj, 'On the Construction of Colonial Power: Structure, Discourse, Hegemony', in Engels and Marks (eds.), *Contesting Colonial Hegemony*, 44; see also Sudipta Kaviraj, 'The Imaginery Institutions of India', in P. Chatterjee and G. Pandey (eds.), *Subaltern Studies*, 7 (Delhi, 1992), 1–39.

28. See especially Lewis's review of the life and career of Abdurahman in *Between the Wire and the Wall*, 198–204. See also Mohamed Adhikari's creative exploration of the preoccupations of the writer of a satirical column in the *APO* newspaper, 'Straatpratjes', which he identifies as Abdurahman: 'Coloured Identity and the Politics of Language: The Sociopolitical Context of Piet Uithalder's "Straatpraatje's Column', in Mohamed Adhikari (ed.), *Straatpraatjes: Language, Politics and Popular Culture in Cape Town, 1909–1922* (Cape Town, 1996), 1–17; also, Mohamed Adhikari's paper to the British World Conference, University of Cape Town, January 2002, 'Ambiguity, Assimilationism and Anglophilism in South Africa's Coloured Community: The Case of Pet Uithalder's Satirical Writing, 1909–1922'.

29. For instance, see Jean and John Comaroff, *Of Revelation and Revolution: Christianity, Colonialism and Consciousness in South Africa*, vol.1 (London, 1991); Elizabeth Elbourne, 'Early Khoisan Uses of Mission Christianity', in Bredekamp and Ross (eds.), *Missions and Christianity*, 65–96.

30. Deborah Gaitskell, 'At Home with Hegemony? Coercion and Consent in African Girls' Education for Domesticity in South Africa before 1910', in Engels and Marks (eds.), *Contesting Colonial Hegemony*, 110–30.

31. For example Elizabeth Van Heyningen, 'Public Health and Society in Cape Town

1880–1910', Ph.D thesis, University of Cape Town, 1989; 'Refugees and Relief in Cape Town, 1899–1902', *Studies in the History of Cape Town*, 3 (1980), 64–113; 'Cape Town and the Plague of 1901', ibid., 4 (1981), 66–107; 'Prostitution and the Contagious Diseases Act: The Social Evil in the Cape Colony, 1868–1902', ibid., 5 (1983), 79–123; and 'Poverty, Self-Help and Community: The Survival of the Poor in Cape Town, 1880–1910', *South African Historical Journal*, 24 (1991), 128–43.

32. Nigel Worden, Elizabeth Van Heyningen and Vivian Bickford-Smith, *Cape Town, The Making of a City* (Cape Town, 1998), esp. ch.4; Kirsten McKenzie, 'The South African Commercial Advertiser and the Making of Middle-Class Identity in Early Nineteenth Century Cape Town', MA thesis, University of Cape Town, 1993; and 'Gender and Honour in Middle-Class Cape Town: The Making of Colonial Identity, 1828–1850', D.Phil. thesis, Oxford University, 1997; Bickford-Smith, 'Meanings of Freedom'; and 'Leisure and Identity'; Saul Dubow, 'An Empire of Reason: Anglophone Literary and Scientific Institutions in the 19th Century Cape Colony', paper presented to the Historical Studies Department, University of Cape Town, 1999; Vivian Bickford-Smith, *Ethnic Pride and Racial Prejudice in Victorian Cape Town* (Cambridge, 1995), esp. ch.4, which charts the rise of English ethnic mobilisation in Cape Town from the late 1870s.

33. Andy Thompson, 'The Languages of Loyalism: Constructing and Contesting a "British" Colonial Identity in Southern Africa, c.1870–1961', unpublished paper presented to the Historical Studies Department, UCT, 2001, and at the British World Conference, UCT, January 2002; Elizabeth Van Heyningen, 'The Voices of Women in the South African War', *South African Historical Journal*, 41 (1999), 22–43; and 'Imperial Women's Organisation in South Africa: The Guild of Loyal Women and the Victoria League in the Anglo-Boer War, 1899–1902', unpublished paper presented at the British World Conference, University of Cape Town, January 2002.

34. Thompson, 'Languages of Loyalism', 3.

35. Dubow, 'Anglophone Institutions'; Kirsten McKenzie, 'South African Commercial Advertiser', and 'Gender and Honour' – both works are also drawn on in Dubow, and cited in his 'Anglophone Institutions', 9 and 31.

36. As is clear from the title of his book, Ross sees 'respectability' as a key value for an ethnically and racially diverse number of Cape colonists in the nineteenth century: Ross, *Status and Respectability*.

37. Monica Wilson, 'Co-operation and Conflict: The Eastern Cape Frontier', in Wilson and Thompson (eds.), *Oxford History of South Africa*, 239. Wilson was a pioneer in her comments on the transforming nature of the missionary project in terms of material culture. See also Ross, *Status and Respectability*, 78–88, 124 and 153; McKenzie, 'Honour and Gender', 54–65; Crais, *White Supremacy*, 82, 88, 90, 104 and 136–37; also Jeff Peires, 'The British and the Cape: 1814–1834', in Richard Elphick and Hermann Giliomee (eds.), *The Shaping of South African Society, 1652–1840* (Cape Town, 1989), 487.

38. Bickford-Smith, 'Leisure and Identity'.

39. Willan, 'Plaatje', 251.

40. Bickford-Smith, 'Leisure and Identity', 111.

41. Though there are exceptions. Thus Dubow draws attention to the significance of 'South African' forming part of the name of Cape Colonial institutions in the mid-nineteenth century; and Ponelis notes that names in the 'Straatpratjes' column of *APO* reflected an 'early stage' of both the direct translation of Afrikaans surnames into English – e.g. Furtuin to Fortune, Feberwarie to February – and the adoption of English Christian names: see F. Ponelis, 'Codes in Contradiction: The Sociolinguistics of "Straatpraatjes"', in Adhikari (ed.), *Straatpratjes*, 137–38.

42. Bickford-Smith, 'Meanings of Freedom', 297–312; Worden, Van Heyningen and Bickford-Smith, *Cape Town*, 106, 108 and 195; Ross, *Status and Respectability*, 146–150.

43. Ross, *Status and Respectability*, 63–66.

44. Bickford-Smith, 'Leisure and Identity', 105–08 and 127–28; Worden, Van Heyningen and Bickford-Smith, *Cape Town*, 151–53, 155, 186, 189–91, 193, 239, 244 and 262; Willan, 'Plaatje', 242–43.

45. Hodgson, 'Zonnebloem College', 127.

46. Hodgson, 'Xhosa Chiefs', 56–61.
47. Wilson, 'Co-operation and Conflict', 266.
48. An argument suggested by Bickford-Smith, *Ethnic Pride and Racial Prejudice*.
49. Cited in Hodgson, 'Xhosa Chiefs', 58.
50. Ibid., 59.
51. Wayne K. Durrill, 'Creating a Colonial Elite: Students, Violence, and Social Relations at South African College, 1829–1914', unpublished paper presented to the Historical Studies Department, University of Cape Town, Aug. 1998.
52. For example, see Timothy Keegan, *Colonial South Africa and the Origins of the Racial Order* (Cape Town, 1996); Noel Mostert, *Frontiers* (London, 1992); Susan Newton-King, *Masters and Servants of the Cape Eastern Frontier, 1760–1803* (Cambridge, 2000); Crais, *White Supremacy*; Peires, *The Dead Will Arise*; Bickford-Smith, *Ethnic Pride and Racial Prejudice*, esp. 108–09 and 164–85.
53. Ross, *Status and Respectability*, 125–46.
54. Bickford-Smith, 'Leisure and Identity', esp. 117–27.
55. Elphick, 'Writing Religion into History', 21–22.

The Crown, Empire Loyalism and the Assimilation of Non-British White Subjects in the British World: An Argument against 'Ethnic Determinism'

DONAL LOWRY

On 4 July 1966, Queen Elizabeth II arrived in Belfast to open the new Lagan bridge. Violent nationalist protest against the Northern Ireland state had not yet begun in earnest, but there was heavy security, the biggest single policing operation since the Second World War, and known republicans were rounded up under the Special Powers Act for the duration. On her arrival she was greeted by her urbane Old Etonian prime minister of Northern Ireland, Captain Terence O'Neill. Regarded as a reformist who sought to broaden the base of unionism among Catholics, O'Neill wanted to use the sovereign's popularity among Protestants to his advantage, but he found the Queen from the outset very conscious of her position as a Protestant monarch. She omitted a reference to improved community relations in her arrival speech, but O'Neill hoped that she would be willing to refer approvingly to his efforts on her departure. He was not assisted by the fact that a Catholic labourer had dropped, on impulse, it would seem, a concrete block on the royal limousine from the fourth floor of a block of flats. 'The Catholics in Northern Ireland do not like me', she mused, 'what happens if the Protestants also turn against me?' The Duke of Edinburgh, who accompanied her, appeared to sympathise with O'Neill's desperate need to remain popular among Protestant voters and to face down his critics in the Northern Ireland House of Commons, but Her Majesty refused to endorse publicly O'Neill's reforms. O'Neill later reflected:

> The Queen, who in Ulster is more a symbol of Protestantism than an ordinary monarch, had failed to use her position in a responsible manner ... How can one drag Northern Ireland, kicking and screaming, into the second half of the twentieth century if single handed, unaided even by one's monarch.[1]

This assertion of the Protestant character of the Crown was neither unusual nor confined to Northern Ireland. Even in the somewhat more ecumenical if not indifferent religious climate of early 1980s Britain, Prince Charles was publicly prohibited by his mother to attend Mass in Rome. A decade later, the low-key celebration of Mass in the Tower of London, attended by a handful of English Catholics of impeccable loyalty, was, when it was drawn to the notice of the sovereign's private secretary, expressly forbidden. There have been other such occasions throughout the twentieth century. In 1937 the Home Office, adopting a similar attitude to that taken during George V's Jubilee two years earlier, refused to forward a loyal address to George VI presented by the English and Welsh Catholic hierarchy on the grounds that their Catholic designation and 'pretended' ecclesiastical titles were unacceptable.[2] Nor were such views uncommon in political circles. When the vice-president of the Irish Free State, Kevin O'Higgins, was assassinated in 1927, the Dominions Secretary, Leo Amery, noted in his diary:

> Poor fellow, he had many attractive personal qualities as well as great courage and patriotism. What a curse hangs over Ireland. To unravel it would be like a tale of Atreidae, but I fear the starting point is a fault in the blood, some element of ape-like savagery which has survived every successive flood of settlers ... [I attended the] Memorial service to O'Higgins. These RC services strike me as curiously barbaric and in the direct line of descent from ancient Egypt.[3]

And in 1959, having angrily read the devastating Devlin Report into the state of emergency in Nyasaland, Prime Minister Harold Macmillan noted in his diary that Lord Devlin was a clever lawyer but Macmillan had since discovered that 'he [was] (a) Irish – no doubt with Fenian blood that makes Irishmen anti-government on principle. (b) A lapsed Catholic. His brother is a Jesuit priest.'[4] The general impression of a continuing, if largely unspoken, anti-Catholicism, even in multicultural, 'politically correct', non-church-going Britain, seems to be reinforced by the apparent slowness in reforming the anti-Catholic clauses of the Act of Settlement.[5]

Not surprisingly, therefore, those who have debated both the contemporary and historical monarchy have often concentrated on its exclusive, and excluding, religious and ethnic character, particularly in those countries of the Commonwealth that remain monarchies. The recent republican debate in Australia in particular has highlighted the apparent incompatibility between the monarchy and an ethnically diverse society. Malcolm Turnbull, chairman of Prime Minister Paul Keating's republican advisory committee in the early 1990s, highlighted the anomalous relationship of a remotely situated monarchy, whose succession was exclusively Protestant, to a democratic, multicultural and secular Australian democracy.[6] Echoing Donald Horne, republican author of *The Lucky*

Country (1964), the critic Robert Hughes persuasively attributed the erosion
of monarchical allegiance to the growing ethnic diversification of Australia:

> By the beginning of the 1970s thousands of Australian kids, presently
> to be Australian voters, were reading in school the [anti-] monarchical
> arguments of Horne – along with those of Dutton and Manning Clark,
> our Michelet. Many of these kids were the sons and daughters of post-
> war migrants: folk from places like Skópelos, Dubrovnik, Beirut,
> Montealegre, Ankara, Crakow or Budapest, people who, while
> indubitably Australian now, felt only a little more innate attachment to
> Queen Elizabeth II than we Anglo-Irish Australians have been
> expected to feel to King Farouk or King Zog.[7]

Critics of monarchy could, moreover, draw on plenty of examples of the
importance of anti-Catholicism in forging identities in the colonies of
settlement, from Canada, where the Orange Order was crucial in fashioning
Canadian Britishness, to frequent conflicts over Empire Day in Australia
and the replaying of British–Irish sectarianism in New Zealand.[8] Indeed, the
colonies of settlement not infrequently amplified the prejudices of the
motherland. Catholics, Jews (stereotyped as pawnshop parasites) and the
'lower Latin type' were frequent targets of settler Anglo-Saxon 'race
patriots' in Australia. The *Bulletin* declared in 1903 that the Australian had
become 'as much a full-blown, white British subject as the Britisher
himself', perhaps more so, since the Londoner was often either a Pole or a
Jew.[9]

    In Britain itself, a country arguably more ethnically diverse than
Australia, over the past decade and more these concerns have been reflected
in debates among historians about the nature of Britishness. Linda Colley in
particular has emphasised the importance of the Catholic 'other' as an
'omnipresent menace' in forging a sense of Britishness, effectively
excluding the Irish, apart from Protestants of largely settler origin, from
Britishness because of their inveterate Catholicism.[10] It should be stressed
that anti-Catholicism was at its most virulent both in Britain and the colonial
empire when Catholicism was combined with Irishness. Indigenous English
and Scottish Catholicism, particularly in their aristocratic recusant forms,
could be regarded as harmless and quaint survivals, and therefore politically
trustworthy. But compare, for example, the uncomplicated career of English
Catholic colonial governor, Sir Hugh Clifford, with those of Sir James
Pope-Hennessy and Sir William Butler, both of whose sympathy for
underdogs was attributed, rightly or wrongly, to their combination of
Catholicism and Irish home rule sympathies.[11]

    There is always a danger, because of this evidence, of reading history
backwards. It has been pointed out that the historiographies of the

Dominions, the former 'neo-Britains', have since the 1960s been often fed by determinist nationalisms which have distorted the connections between these countries and a wider 'British' world. Certainly, at the level of popular reportage during the Australian referendum, it was commonly suggested that new societies remained loyal to the empire and its symbols only while they were dominated by descendants of British Protestant settlers. Citizens of these societies who were not of British origin, out-groups such as Irish Catholics, Jews and other European immigrants, could not feel such loyalties. Indeed, once these became more numerous, the days of British symbolism were numbered. Such arguments were frequently put forward by Paul Keating and writer Thomas Keneally, both Irish-descended Catholics, during the recent referendum.[12] Here, however, it will be argued first, that ethnic outsiders could and frequently did feel as profound a sense of loyalty to the Crown and Empire as did their Anglo-Protestant compatriots; second, that the personal nature of the monarchy was particularly suited to such political assimilation; third, that, contrary to the stereotype, the most prominent republicans in the white colonies, later Dominions, were not uncommonly of British Protestant rather than Irish Catholic or of another ethnic origin; fourth, that organised religion played an important role in securing the allegiance of 'non-British' citizens; and finally, that the erosion of British symbols in the post-war Commonwealth has more to do with wider cultural and generational changes, as well as strategic realignments, than ethnic factors.

The fact the monarchy was a personal symbol, unlike a republic, also ought not to be overlooked. A loyalty expressed in a vertical chain of allegiance to the sovereign, unlike abstract republicanism, was arguably easier for many 'non-British' subjects to accept. Indeed, it can be argued that the personal character of the monarchy, vertically acknowledged, avoided the controversies of what it meant to be a Canadian, Australian or New Zealander, in a way that a republican form of government would not have been able to do. Significantly, perhaps, the British Empire was at its most exclusively 'British', in a cultural sense, when it was under Cromwell's republic.[13]

I

This essay will focus on Catholic and also Jewish subjects of the empire, for Jews shared a long, even longer, history of persecution and marginalisation in Britain itself. Even as late as the 1950s, more benignly, British and Dominion church parades included the order: 'Jews and R[oman] C[atholic]s fall out'.[14] Both groups, as 'white' British subjects admitted to metropolitan political rights in the nineteenth century, make for interesting comparisons, in the metropole and in the settler empire. As the Protestant monopoly of political power began to falter, both groups sought to emphasise their loyalty to the throne and their political trustworthiness. On Jubilee Day 1809, for example, Catholic chapels and synagogues joined established and dissenting churches in thanksgiving for the King's health.[15] Significantly, Daniel O'Connell, architect of Catholic emancipation, within a year of his admittance to parliament, supported a bill to remove Jewish disabilities, when he acknowledged that Jews and Catholics suffered the same accusation that their sympathies and loyalties lay outside the state. While admitting that he, like the Jews, owed a spiritual allegiance abroad, 'his own Sovereign received his undivided political homage. So it was with the Jews.'[16] In a different way, in the early 1900s, Sidney Webb continued to link the two groups when he held up the spectre of a declining British birth rate, due to widespread use of contraception. 'This', he warned, 'can hardly result in anything but national deterioration, or, as an alternative, in this country gradually falling to the Irish or the Jews.'[17] And yet, we should be careful to avoid any such simplistic attempt to link ethnicity and loyalty, for the process of redefining Englishness and Britishness at home and in the empire in the late eighteenth and early nineteenth century was, it should be remembered, not inconsiderably the product of two 'non-British' politicians, Edmund Burke and Benjamin Disraeli. It was Disraeli, first-generation Christian of Jewish origin, who declared that: '[M]an is a being born to believe. And if no Church comes forward with its title-deeds of truth, sustained by the tradition of sacred ages and by the conviction of countless generations, to guide him, he will find altars and idols in his own heart and own imagination.'[18] Although Disraeli was an arch-political opportunist, it is difficult, with his Young England opinions, to attribute such views to cynicism alone. Indeed Disraeli was thus following Burke, a first-generation Protestant, who, prompted by the experience of his disenfranchised extended Irish Catholic family, abhorred rebellion and sought to undermine any support for revolution by reintegrating Catholics into the political system.

The fact that a later generation of Irish nationalists was not ultimately politically reconciled to the Crown and Empire should not blind us to the widespread willingness of Irish Catholics and their spiritual leaders to support such institutions.[19] In 1798, in the midst of a rebellion against the British that would cost over 20,000 insurgents their lives, Archbishop Troy of Dublin, fearful of atheist French Jacobinism, reminded his flock of the reason for their marginally improved political rights: 'Your loyalty, your submission to the constituted authorities, your peaceable demeanour, your patience under long sufferings.'[20]

Such beliefs often went beyond immediate self-interest. A century later,

John Healy, Archbishop of Tuam, Co. Galway, spelled out the absolute necessity of loyalty to the Crown and the 'reverence for the majesty of kings and constituted governments'. It was, he argued, a 'sacrilege' comparable to 'an indignity offered to God Himself', to violate the person of the sovereign, adding:

> It is this view of kingly rule that alone can keep alive in a scoffing and licentious age the spirit of ancient loyalty, that spirit combining in itself obedience, reverence and love for the majesty of kings, which was at once a bond of social union, an incentive to noble daring ... Such was loyalty in the Ages of Faith, when men swore and kept their oath to reverence the king, as if he were their conscience and their conscience as their king.[21]

Although a staunch cultural nationalist, and in spite of past British persecution of Catholicism, he affirmed his allegiance to the Crown, which he distinguished from the more vociferous devotion of northern loyalists.

> I hope no Irish teacher or true Irishman will ever fail to pay due honour to the toast of Edward VII, who not only royally but personally deserves that honour at the hands of every Irishman ... We, in the West of Ireland here, have always been genuine loyalists, in spite of much foolish talk; but the Orangemen of Belfast are not genuine loyalists at all ... We are loyal to King Edward ... because he is king. We owe him an absolute and unconditional loyalty as king *de jure* and *de facto*. But what of them? They have no absolute loyalty, no genuine, unconditioned loyalty. We are loyal to the King because he is the King; they are loyal to the King because he is a Protestant king.[22]

Indeed, significantly for Catholic royalists, monarchical anti-Catholicism was not unrelenting. In 1901, Edward VII forced his reluctant prime minister, Lord Salisbury, to revise for the benefit of his successors those aspects of his coronation oath that were 'gratuitously offensive' to his Catholic subjects.[23] Healy, moreover, like many missionary-minded Catholic clergy, came to regard the British Empire as providing a unique, almost providential opportunity for the evangelisation of a great portion of the world, including – in the longer term, of course – that great prize: the reconversion to the Ancient Faith of England herself. Catholic clergy were often willing to forget past persecutions, preaching a loyalty based on obedience to earthly sovereigns, even if constitutional indignities necessitated a high degree of forbearance. As Arthur Hinsley, Cardinal Archbishop of Westminster, told a Missions Week gathering to great applause in 1939: 'I want to express my joy at the freedom which Catholic missions enjoy in the lands under the British flag. In the Dominions and the Colonies we have scope for missionary work which no other people in the world can enjoy.'[24]

II

The process of assimilating 'non-British' subjects of the Crown began, however, not in Ireland but in Canada, which would become the prototype Dominion of the 'second' British Empire. Here the formula for advanced responsible government initiated by Lord Durham in 1839 became the template for settler self-government in Australasia and southern Africa over the next century. Britain came into possession of New France in 1763, when, in a settlement that would have far-reaching consequences for both loyalism and republicanism in its colonial empire, the language and religious privileges of French-speaking Catholics were guaranteed. Equally significant for the subsequent fortunes of republicanism was the exodus in 1783 of 40,000 colonial loyalists to Nova Scotia and Quebec. Canadian loyalism, founded as the ultimate negation of American republicanism, was reinforced by the deep antipathy of the Catholic Church in Quebec towards the French Revolution and reaffirmed by Canadian resistance to American and Irish Fenian invasions in 1812 and 1866. French-Canadian bishops were already grateful to enjoy the fullest range of religious freedom, as well as the preservation of tithes and old French civil law, at a time when British and Irish Catholics were still covered by penal legislation. But the anti-clerical character of the French Revolution fostered a profoundly deferential episcopal attitude towards the Crown. The Quebec Act of 1774, passed as American colonists contemplated open rebellion at Lexington and Concord, came to be regarded as 'virtually the Magna Carta of French Canadians'.[25] Although metropolitan France supported the American Revolution, French Canadians declined an invitation to the Continental Congress at Philadelphia. In the end, however, they refused to join in the rebellion, partly because of American Protestant objections to the 'intolerable' Quebec Act, but also due to ethnic differences and the geographical barrier of the Appalachians. The Act had caused a split between a largely pro-British elite and pro-American masses. If some French Canadians adopted a detached attitude towards the American revolutionaries, Bishop Briand exhorted his flock to respond generously to General Carleton's request for volunteers, since the Crown had recently guaranteed 'the practice of our laws, the free exercise of our religion, and the privileges and advantages of British subjects', although few *habitants* accompanied Carleton's southward invasion force.[26]

In 1791, the Colonial Secretary, Lord Grenville, drafted a Constitutional Act which left the privileged position of the Catholic Church unchanged, but divided Quebec into Upper Canada and Lower Canada, each with representative institutions, so that British and French would not be 'blended' and Canadian separation from Britain, which he believed to be inevitable, would be delayed. In 1793, Bishop Hubert reminded his clergy that 'the bonds which attached them to the King of France had been entirely broken, and ... all the loyalty and obedience which they formerly owed to the King of France, they now owed to His Britannic Majesty', and that it was therefore their 'duty to drive the French [republicans] from this province'.[27] Crucially, for any possible resurgence of republicanism, the British conceded that the French Canadians might be British subjects without becoming English in religion and law, and imperial historians have understandably sought in the Quebec Act the remoter origins of the multi-racial Empire and Commonwealth.[28] Indeed, many members of the French-Canadian hierarchy began to regard the British conquest as a providential deliverance from Jacobinism, as Joseph-Octave Plessis declared in 1794:

> You [British] are not our enemies, or those of our Holy Religion, which you respect ... [I]f, after having learned of the overturn of the state and of the destruction of the True Faith in France, and after having tasted during thirty-five years the mildness of your rule, some amongst us are still found so blind or so evil-intentioned as to ... inspire in the people criminal desires to return to their ancient masters, blame not on the whole what is only the vice of a small number.[29]

These loyalties also extended to the secular sphere. In 1837–38, rebellions in Upper and Lower Canada, both of which drew on republican ideas, served only to strengthen the monarchist tradition within the French hierarchy and powerful sections of the Quebec seigneurial class. Sir George-Étienne Cartier, one of the Francophone 'fathers' of Confederation, had rebelled against the Crown in 1837, but subsequently became fearful of the threat to property of the ideas of Proudhon and other socialists. He later declared that the British conquest had 'saved us from the misery and shame of the French Revolution'.[30] Sir Étienne-Pascal Taché, another former revolutionary, was appointed an aide-de-camp to Victoria, with the rank of honorary colonel of the British Army. Taché is widely credited with coining the provincial motto of Quebec, later adopted by the French-speaking Royal 22nd Regiment (the celebrated bearskinned and redcoated 'Van Doos'): *Je me souviens* ('I remember'). Significantly, the full line from which this is taken, though in more recent times misinterpreted by Quebecois separatists as an anti-British sentiment, translates: 'I remember that although I was born under the Lily [of the Bourbons], I flourished under the Rose [of England]', and it was Taché who told a cheering House of Assembly in Montreal in 1846, as he pointed to a portrait of Victoria: 'we claim to be

children of the same mother as [British Canadians] ... Be satisfied we will
never forget our allegiance till the last cannon which is shot on this
continent in defence of Great Britain is fired by the hand of a French
Canadian.'[31] This was colourful language, but Taché was not alone. Louis-
Hippolyte LaFontaine, sometime Premier of Quebec, also became
convinced that French-Canadian heritage would be best consolidated under
the Crown, but none, perhaps, described this relationship as deferentially as
Sir Adolphe Chapleau, another Quebec premier, who told an American
audience that the French Canadians were 'a people abandoned by their
natural parents, who found in the British Crown, though alien in race, in
language and religion, a friend and protector when their need was sorest,
and under whose sway they enjoyed ... liberty of the soul'.[32] In the 1860s,
the American Civil War was used by Louis LaFontaine and Sir George-
Étienne Cartier to confront the republicanism of the rationalist *Parti Rouge*
which was also increasingly banned by the Catholic Church.[33]

Examples of French-Canadian loyalism are numerous. The original
words of the Canadian national anthem, 'O Canada', were written by Sir
Adolphe-Basil Routhier and played for the first time by the military band of
the avowedly monarchist light cavalrymen of Les Voltigeurs in 1880. In the
late nineteenth century, even Wilfrid Laurier, who was opposed to the
excessive influence of the clergy, argued that free institutions had enabled
French Canadians to remain both French and Catholic under the British flag
'which floats over our heads without a single British soldier [sic] in the
country to defend it, its sole defence resting in the gratitude which we owe
it for our freedom and for the security we have found under its folds'.[34]
Louis-Honoré Fréchette, a radical in his youth, later became a founding
member of the Royal Society of Canada, of which he became president in
1900. He was widely regarded as the most notable French-Canadian poet of
his generation. In 1897 he was appointed CMG, having written a fulsome
poetic tribute to Victoria, with the grand title of *A Sa Majesté Victoria Ière,
Reine d'Angleterre et Impératrice des Indes*.[35] There was also the case of Sir
Percy Girouard, a Montreal Catholic of Franco-Irish parentage, who
attended the Royal Military College of Canada at Kingston and the Royal
Military Academy at Woolwich, before going on to a distinguished career
as governor of Northern Nigeria and East Africa.[36] Talbot Papineau provides
yet another example of this phenomenon. He was the great-grandson of
Louis-Joseph Papineau and a first cousin of Henri Bourassa. Brought up as
a freethinker, he had an illustrious career at McGill University in Montreal,
before going to Oxford as a Rhodes Scholar, where he caught the political
eye of Lionel Curtis. Returning to Canada, he developed a keen interest in
Quebec folk songs and culture. Nevertheless, on the outbreak of war in 1914
he joined the Princess Patricia's Canadian Light Infantry, in which he served

with distinction, winning the Military Cross at St Eloi in 1915. He was killed in 1917 at Passchendaele.[37] A sense of Britishness also extended, in translated form, to the parliamentary institutions of Quebec, where, in 1907, the writer André Siegfried was impressed by the House of Assembly's almost excessive pride in their affiliation to the *Mater Parliamentorum*, and was struck by how the rubrics of its debates bore no resemblance to any post-revolutionary metropolitan French assembly: "*"Monsieur l'orateur, l'honorable membre pour Québec a dit ..."* Approbation is signified by sonorous guttural cries of "Hear, Hear!" The whole impression is thoroughly British.'[38]

Irish-Canadian Catholics had also been in the forefront of Canadian loyalism and anti-republicanism. None used the American Civil War more to warn against the dangers of republicanism and the value of monarchy more vehemently than the former Irish republican gun-runner of 1848, Thomas D'Arcy McGee. By 1856 he had come to despise the French Revolution as 'that monstrous apparition', or 'that evil spirit'.[39] In the 1860s, on a visit to his native Wexford, he denounced the Fenians as 'Punch-and-Judy Jacobins whose sole school of action seems to be to get their heads broken', and he contrasted the Fenians unfavourably with the 'honest, youthful folly' of the Young Irelanders, including himself.[40] Taking an organic Burkean approach, he thought that North America was a failed laboratory for republican experimentation and the outbreak of the American Civil War appeared to sound the death-knell of republicanism, not only in North America, but in Europe as well:

> On the fate of so many republics we may surely be allowed to reason. They have been of all sizes and shapes ... [but] [i]s there one, a single one, which can be cited as an example of a 'model Republic', supposing nations to be made on models? ... If stability be essential to good government, they have not had stability, and therefore their description of government cannot be good either for themselves or for others.[41]

Until his assassination by a Fenian in 1868, D'Arcy McGee more than anyone was credited with popularising the idea of Canadian Confederation based on the monarchical principle, and he moved the parliamentary resolution calling for Confederation thus:

> We come to Your Majesty, who has given us liberty, to give us unity, that we may preserve and perpetuate our freedom; and whatever charter, in the wisdom of Your Majesty and Your Parliament, you give us, we shall loyally obey and observe as long as it is the pleasure of Your Majesty and Your Successors to maintain the connection between Great Britain and these Colonies.[42]

Canada's Irish Catholics, as Mark McGowan has recently argued, were by the end of the nineteenth century substantially integrated into a monarchical Canadian identity. They identified themselves as a loyal people, in contrast to their cousins south of the border. Despite Toronto's reputation of being the 'Belfast of North America', the bulk of Canadian Irish Catholics was not anti-British, and the exile motif, so prominent in the United States, was largely absent. During Victoria's Jubilee of 1897, the Canadian Irish Catholic *Record* thanked God 'for all the blessings we have received during the Queen's reign, and especially for the blessings of civil and religious liberty which we enjoy under the British flag'. The rector of Toronto's St Michael's Cathedral eulogised in a sermon that Victoria had been 'a good mother, a model mother', and Canadian Irish Catholic loyalism was subsequently strengthened by Edward VII's and George V's known toleration towards Catholics. When Edward died, the *Register* declared him to be a 'good friend of the Catholic Church who visited the Pope and showed him every reverence, confidence and respect', thus winning the loyalty and love of 'his Catholic subjects'.[43] Significantly, not only did the Catholic Church in Canada seek to emphasise its Canadian character, along with its staunch loyalty to the Crown, rather than its Irish roots, but it sought to ensure that newer waves of European immigrants were assimilated in the same political identity.[44] These efforts were not without success, in spite of Canadian nativist prejudice.[45] During the 1937 Coronation, for example, the Polish Falcon Society and Ukrainian dancers joined the Sons of England and the Orange Lodge in celebrations in Winnipeg, of which the highlight was the Ukrainian National Choir singing Kipling's 'Land of Our Birth'. Similarly, during the Second World War the hand missal for Canadian Ukrainian Catholic soldiers contained a prayer for 'our Gracious King George, his court and military forces'.[46]

In contrast, French-Canadian loyalism was shaken by the Manitoba Schools issue of the 1890s, when the provincial government of Manitoba, under pressure from the Orange Order, abrogated an earlier agreement to guarantee French-language rights and Catholic schools, and this decision was upheld by the courts. By the late nineteenth century, members of the Catholic hierarchy in Quebec appeared to be switching their support for the imperial connection. French-Canadian opinion was further alienated by the outbreak of the South African War, when the fiery Henri Bourassa, rising spokesman of French-speaking opinion, warned that his people could not support aggressive imperialism. But he was no Anglophobe, as he felt compelled to explain:

> I am a Liberal of the British school. I am a disciple of Burke, Fox, Bright, Gladstone, and of the other Little Englanders who made Great

Britain and her possessions what they are, and I will not desert the ranks of their true followers because Mr Chamberlain or other renegade Radicals might choose in their megalomaniac ambition to call these great men blunderers.[47]

Bourassa's anti-imperialism was to a considerable extent constrained by his much wider fear of American annexation which was shared by many Canadians across the linguistic and religious divide. Many French Canadians may have hated what they regarded as English-Canadian arrogance, but it was difficult to convert them to a principled ideological republicanism. Goldwin Smith lamented the monarchism of Quebec: 'French Canada is a relic of the historical past preserved in isolation, as Siberian mammoths are preserved in ice ... The French Canadians are an unprogressive, religious, submissive, courteous, and, though poor, not unhappy people.'[48] English Canada did little, however, to capitalise on French-Canadian loyalty. Crucially, French Canadians felt themselves culturally and religiously excluded from the militia, which might have been used to cement a stronger Franco-English bond of citizenship.[49]

In Canada, as in the other Dominions, the Great War provided an occasion for those of non-British origin to demonstrate their loyalty to King and Empire. French Canadians were still antagonised, however, by the government's language and educational policies. This was compounded by the ineptness on the eve of war of the minister of national defence and Orangeman, Sir Sam Hughes, who claimed, ironically given his Huguenot ancestry, a special sensitivity towards Catholic French Canada, and who yet forbade the 65th Carabiniers Mont-Royal to march in the traditional Corpus Christi procession. After a storm of protest he relented and allowed them to march without arms, widely regarded as a calculated insult. Nevertheless, well over 12,000 French Canadians served in the war, many of these in the newly raised Royal 22nd Regiment. Significantly, as Desmond Morton notes, many of its officers were drawn from the same background as those young idealists who had joined Bourassa's *La Ligue Nationaliste*.[50]

In spite of the inroads of Quebec separatism, the French-Canadian hierarchy generally still taught their flock to render unto the Protestant Caesar, provided there were no attempts to interfere with its educational controls. A monarchist, providential approach to Quebec history survived: the old, Catholic France of Clovis, Charlemagne, Joan of Arc and St Louis had apparently been supplanted by a series of masonic and anti-clerical republics of 'Marianne' and Rousseau. Metropolitan France had thus been irrevocably dislocated or exiled from its history, so that some French upper clergy came to see Wolfe's capture of Quebec as strangely providential. French Canadians were often more opposed to Anglo-Canadians than anti-

British or anti-monarchist. Indeed, John Buchan, now Lord Tweedsmuir and
Governor-General of Canada, had some reason to declare in 1938 that: 'The
French in Canada ... have never been anything other than monarchists.
They came to Canada long before the French Republic was thought of. We
may say, therefore, that Canada is not only a loyal nation, but a royalist
nation.'[51] During the Royal Tour of 1939 huge crowds turned out to greet the
royal couple. Montreal spent more on the visit than ultra-loyalist Toronto.[52]
'By the smile of a Queen and the French words of a King the English have
conquered once more the cradle of New France', complained the separatist
Omer Heroux, in *Le Devoir*.[53] Cardinal Villeneuve, archbishop of Quebec,
widely regarded as a nationalist in his youth, now ordered the belfries of all
the Catholic churches along the banks of the St Lawrence to ring out
joyously as the royal party arrived, and Catholic clergy and their
congregations gathered outside the churches to greet the royal visitors.
Twenty-five thousand children assembled on the Heights of Abraham
dressed as Papal Zouaves and Swiss Guards to welcome the royal couple.
The historic Church of Notre Dame in the Place d'Armes was festooned and
draped with an enormous Union Jack.[54] Cardinal Villeneuve had prepared
for the royal visit by ordering *Dieu sauve le Roi* (*God Save the King*), as
well as the usual prayer for the King and Royal Family, 'our sovereigns', to
be sung in church after all masses. The visit was freely referred to in
sermons, and Mgr Antoniutti, Apostolic Delegate to Canada, expressed the
loyalty of Catholic Canada in an address to the St Jean Baptiste Society in
Ottawa.[55] As the royal couple departed, in an emotive speech, Maxime
Raymond, a leading Quebec Liberal, pleaded that French Canadians should
realise the threat posed to their religion and political institutions by both
Nazism and communism, concluding with the words: 'God bless Canada.
God bless our King. God bless our Queen.'[56] This visit, which included the
United States, was of major political importance for Anglo-American
relations on the eve of the war, but it also possessed a singular significance
for many Catholic subjects of the Crown, moving the *Catholic Herald* of
London to remark:

> The journey of their Majesties to Canada and the United States
> reminds us of one of the greatest assets in the possession of this
> country: its spiritual power ... The Crown has been accorded high
> symbolic value and its position, above Party and the vicissitudes of
> temporal changes, is undoubtedly of inestimable value both to the
> country and to the Empire. But in these times the lives and examples
> of their Majesties have a significance that perhaps goes deeper. It will
> be recalled that at the coronation of the King the Apostolic Delegate
> [to Britain], according to his own confession, was more impressed by

the example given to their subjects by the King and Queen than by anything else. The ideals of Christian devotion, of family life, of absolute dedication to self-sacrificing service without any hope of personal gain or the serving of personal ambition – these, it seemed to him, measured the value to the country of this Royal Crown ... It is not unfair to say that the King and Queen stand today before the world as the living exemplars of the spiritual qualities which have been in the past traditionally associated with the best in British history. And when we come to ask ourselves about the real contribution to peace which this country has it in her to offer we can go some way towards finding an answer by comparing present-day Britain with the example set by her ancestors.[57]

In French Canada, during the wartime years, the tradition of loyalty was symbolically well represented by Quebec Lieutenant-Governor Sir Eugène Marie Joseph Fiset. As a medical officer, he had won the DSO while serving with the Royal Canadian Regiment in the South African War. He became a long-serving deputy minister of militia and defence (1905–21), retiring with the rank of major general. When the British high commissioner, Malcolm MacDonald, visited him in 1943, he found his loyalism undiminished, despite having lost a son during the ill-fated defence of Hong Kong in December 1941, where two Canadian battalions had surrendered to the Japanese.[58] Such monarchist sentiments were greatly weakened, it should be stressed, by the political upheavals of the 'Quiet Revolution' in Quebec during the 1960s, which, significantly, coincided with egalitarian-minded liturgical revisions throughout the Catholic Church, mirroring the wider collapse of civic-religious interpretations of loyalism in Protestant Canada.[59] No longer were Catholics throughout the sovereign's realms, from Britain to Canada to Australia and New Zealand, obliged to pray with their priest each Sunday after High Mass, as they had in less ecumenical times:

> O Lord, save Elizabeth, our Queen ... Almighty God, we pray for thy servant Elizabeth our Queen, now by thy mercy reigning over us. Adorn her yet more with every virtue, remove all evil from her path (and vanquish her enemies); that with her consort and all the royal family she may at last in grace to thee, who art the way, the truth and the life ...[60]

Still, this tradition had not entirely disappeared, not least because General Georges Vanier, the first French-Canadian governor-general of Canada (1959–67) – who won a Military Cross and a DSO, as well as losing a leg serving in the 'Van Doos' during an assault on the Hindenberg Line in 1918 – was of the old school of Canadian monarchism. He was Irish on his

mother's side and he was reared in the clericalist atmosphere of Montreal.
As governor-general, he always solemnly insisted on the royal toast to 'La
Reine' at even the smallest private gatherings at Rideau Hall or The Citadel.
His career illustrates how a Protestant monarchy could command the almost
religious reverence of an avowedly French-Canadian Catholic.[61] Another
example is provided by General Jean Victor Allard (1913–96), former Chief
of the Canadian Defence Staff. Allard, like Vanier, came from a staunchly
Francophone, Catholic and monarchist background, served with the 'Van
Doos' in Italy and the Low Countries (where he won the DSO and two
bars), and after the war became the first Canadian to command a British
division in peacetime. In 1980 he joined 224 prominent Quebeckers in
opposing René Lévesque's referendum on secession.[62] Nor were such
expressions of French monarchical feeling isolated. During Elizabeth II's
controversial visit of 1964, Ottawa's Le Droit declared:

> Elizabeth II remains juridically and legally The Queen of Canada until
> such time as Confederation disintegrates, if that ever happens, and she
> deserves, whether in her personal or official capacity, the most
> profound respect. French Canadians can, for a number of reasons,
> justifiably reproach their fellow citizens of British origin and of the
> English language, but they have no cause of complaint against The
> Queen, and certainly none against the noble and distinguished mother
> who carries that Crown today.

L'Action of Quebec also argued that, 'long before Ottawa was seized, as it
is now, of the bilingual and bicultural ferment, the Crown was established
in fact, in all its interventions in Canada, of equality between the two
languages beyond the letter of the constitution. The Queen as an ally of
Quebec nationalism? And why not? In a sense she always has been.'[63]

Even in 2001 French-Canadian monarchism had not entirely disappeared.
Liberal Senator Serge Joyal, a leading Canadian nationalist and former
Quebecois student activist – who as a young MP for Maisonneuve-Rosemont
once refused to stand for the royal anthem – defended the monarchy in
Canada against the republican-minded (and then) minister for external affairs,
John Manley, as an incontestable attribute to which parliamentarians had
pledged their allegiance. The Crown, he declared, was 'the fundamental
structuring principle of our entire system of government'. French and British
monarchs had provided Canada with 'a unique sovereign lineage'. The
Canadian Crown was 'a symbol, an institution and an organic principle ... the
transcendent essence ... the expression of the continuity of our nation'.[64]
Meanwhile, Canadian monarchists have emphasised the appointment of an
avowedly royalist governor-general of Chinese origin, Adrienne Clarkson, as
an example of the ever-widening multicultural but essentially Canadian
character of their Crown.[65]

III

The Canadian confederation formed the loose model for the establishment of the Commonwealth of Australia in 1901 as a Dominion within the Empire. Nonetheless, this was symbolically a much more democratic Dominion than its Canadian cousin. Whereas Canada possessed a 'House of Commons', Australia opted for an American-style 'House of Representatives'. Australian culture was pervaded by an egalitarian ethos. With its large Irish Catholic minority, and not insignificant immigration from elsewhere in Europe, an erosion of loyalty to the Crown might have been expected. There was, moreover, a strong tradition of republicanism and anti-monarchism which had French and British radical roots and, in contrast to Britain and Canada, a widespread admiration for American republicanism. Australian republicanism was punctuated by prominent debates and dramatic moments, from an assassination attempt on visiting royalty, through the controversies of the negotiations leading to federation, to the debate about hereditary aristocracy in New South Wales and the Eureka Stockade, to the convict ships of the late eighteenth century.[66]

Yet, as with D'Arcy McGee in Canada, it was possible for former Irish republicans to become supporters of the constitutional status quo. Charles Gavan Duffy, for example, one of the Young Irelanders who was imprisoned in 1848, emigrated to Victoria, where he became Premier in 1871 and was knighted two years later, the first of three consecutive generations of Gavan Duffys to be so honoured for service to Victoria and to Australia.[67] New Zealand's homegrown republicanism was a somewhat slight affair, even among the Irish, and Sir Joseph Ward, its Irish-descended premier liked nothing better than a title.[68] Indeed, the cause of monarchy and empire in Australia has never been simply a case of Anglo-Protestants versus the non-British, and the Irish were far less crucial to Australian republicanism than the stereotype would suggest.[69] When anti-monarchy protests occurred in Sydney during Victoria's Jubilee of 1887, Catholic and Jewish community leaders were outraged, condemning the 'riotous conduct of a disloyal minority' and pledging themselves 'to the laws, institutions, and Throne of the British Empire'.[70] Two years earlier the Irish Catholic William B. Dalley seized his opportunity as acting premier of New South Wales to demonstrate his loyalty by sending a contingent to the Sudan to avenge the death of General 'Chinese' Gordon.[71] In the context of ethnic loyalism, the example of General Sir John Monash is particularly significant, for he was commander of the Australian forces in the Great War, during which he was knighted by George V on the battlefield, and when he died in 1931, he was regarded as the greatest living Australian. In a country of 'anti-heroism' in which Ned Kelly and Sir Robert Menzies at different times enjoyed strong ethnic allegiance, no Australian, it was generally agreed, had ever attracted such devotion. Monash, who chose to be buried under the Union Jack rather than the Australian flag, was born in Melbourne of German-Jewish parents and grew up in a German cultural enclave with both Jewish and non-Jewish German-speaking friends, but he never attempted to hide his Jewish and German origins. Indeed he later became honorary president of the Zionist Federation in Australia. But when the Great War broke out he wrote to a pro-German American cousin: 'It may cause you and your people surprise that I should myself take up arms in this quarrel, but then, you must not fail to remember that I am Australian born, as is my wife and daughter, that my whole interest and sympathies are British ... and that every man who can, and is able to do so, must do his best for his country.'[72]

It might be easy to dismiss Monash's loyalty to the Crown as simply opportunistic and lacking in real sincerity, yet it is difficult to read Monash's wartime correspondence with his wife and daughter without feeling that his loyalty was not profoundly felt. When in 1915, on his way through Suez, he witnessed a display of British naval power, he called it a 'revelation of Empire'. When he observed Anzac Day at Serapeum in Egypt in April 1916, he described being moved by 'a fine stirring address by [the chaplain] ... Then the massed bands of the brigade played "The Dead March in Saul" while the parade stood to attention, then the massed buglers played the "Last Post".' In September 1916, when George V came to inspect his troops, which had been redeployed to England over the summer, he was moved by a visit from 'the King of so mighty an Empire'. He later recalled,

> I then presented to him my brigadiers, and battery and battalion commanders, and then we rode down together ... I riding on the right of the King, the Royal Standard behind us, and the rest of the retinue following. And then came the climax of it all ... as the King rode by, each unit broke into deafening cheer, raising hats aloft on bayonets.[73]

At the end of the conflict, when he attended a dinner at Buckingham Palace in honour of President Woodrow Wilson, and in the company of such dignitaries as Rudyard Kipling, Winston Churchill and South Africa's prime minister, Louis Botha, Monash, taking in the detail of the traditions and protocol, was moved by this 'most impressive and historic moment'.[74] Indeed, his own funeral reflected this attachment to the rubrics of empire in an amalgam of traditional Jewish burial ritual and neo-Anglican state ceremonial, complete with gun carriage, and riderless cavalry horse with boots reversed in the stirrups.[75]

When Monash died in 1931, it fell to another Jewish 'ethnic outsider', Sir Isaac Isaacs, first Australian-born governor-general, to pay tribute on behalf of Australia: 'With all Australia I mourn the loss of one of her ablest, bravest, and noblest sons, a loyal servant of King and country ... He served Australia and the Empire well.'[76] Again, it is difficult to attribute Isaacs's loyalty to opportunism alone. The son of a Polish tailor who had migrated from Britain during the gold rush, Isaacs had long been an anglophile. A successful lawyer, he was regarded as one of the founders of the Australian federation. Throughout his life, even when British fortunes appeared to be failing, and when British and Zionist interests appeared to clash, he remained an ardent supporter of imperial causes.[77] And it is significant to note that well into the post-Second World War period, especially during the winding up of the Palestine Mandate, the heated debates that took place within Australia's Jewish community centred not only on Zionism or its relationship to Australia, but on Australian Jews' connection to the Crown. Such was the strength of monarchical institutions in Australian Jewish immigrant culture, as well as in the wider Australian society.[78] Further evidence of the power of monarchy in the assimilation of Jews, Irish Catholics and other 'non-British' migrants is provided by the highly successful 1954 royal tour. Even allowing for the propaganda of the organisers, it is hard to dismiss such identification as wholly shallow or coldly calculating.[79]

IV

It may be useful to concentrate on recent events in Australia. In 1994, Ewan Morris, writing about the royal visit of 50 years previously, assumed that 'to Aborigines and non-British migrants the Queen probably remained a representative of an alien culture'.[80] Looked at historically, however, it can be argued that the British Empire and the imperial monarchy proved well capable of assimilating ethnic outsiders, and although it has been frequently asserted that 'non-British' immigrants have been significant in the breakdown of traditional monarchical loyalty, the ethnic evidence, in the case of Australia at least, is inconclusive.[81] True, Irish-descended Australian Catholics such as Paul Keating, Thomas Keneally and Robert Hughes have been vociferous in the ranks of republicans, but, significantly, perhaps, the republican leadership was neither especially Irish nor other European migrant stock, but they, like Geoffrey Dutton and Donard Horne before them, were substantially of white Anglo-Saxon Protestant heritage. Malcolm Bligh Turnbull, the investment banker and lawyer who led the republican campaign in the 1999 referendum, for example, was conventionally Anglo-Protestant Australian: Sydney Grammar School, University of Sydney and Rhodes Scholar at Brasenose College, Oxford. A major backer of the movement, the publishing magnate, Rupert Murdoch, was equally thoroughly Anglo-Australian establishment. Otherwise, although 'non-British' migrants formed a significant part of the argument of the republicans, they were not markedly prominent in republican ranks.

An analysis of the monarchist leadership in the campaign reveals, in contrast, that the founding director of Australians for a Constitutional Monarchy, Tony Abbott, was an Irish-descended Catholic, educated at St Ignatius's College and St Patrick's Seminary, Sydney. His successor, Kerry Jones, was also an Irish-descended Catholic, educated at the Loretto College of New South Wales. Other leading monarchists included James Miltiadis Samios MLC, deputy leader of the Liberal Party, whose shadow ministry had included the ministry of multicultural and ethnic affairs, and Helen Sham-Ho, the first Australian-Asian MP and federal parliamentary adviser on aboriginal legislation. One of the most prominent monarchists was Neville Bonner, a Jagera aboriginal elder and former senator, who doggedly opposed the creation of a republic as a betrayal of aboriginal constitutional trust. Another leading advocate of the monarchy was Sir David Smith, distinguished lawyer and official secretary to successive governors-general from 1975 to 1990. Smith might not seem to qualify immediately for the category of 'non-British', but despite his anglicised name, he is of Polish-Jewish ancestry, a heritage which he readily claims. Yet the Crown in Australia has no stronger advocate.[82] A generation earlier, one of the most ardent champions of the monarchy in Australia in the 1970s was Sir Johannes Bjelke Petersen, later discredited premier of Queensland, who was a New Zealander of Danish descent, and who defiantly entrenched the Crown in the Queensland constitution.[83] Similarly, in Canada, while many republican advocates are of British Protestant origin, it may be significant to note that the leading academic apologist for monarchy is a French-Canadian Jesuit.[84]

Plenty of similar examples can of course be cited elsewhere in the colonies of settlement, including southern Africa. In South Africa, as Mordechai Tamarkin has highlighted, there were the Cape Afrikaners who, for all their ethnic and linguistic links to their republican cousins in the north, saw advantage in remaining within the empire and were deeply reluctant to believe that Rhodes had betrayed them in the Jameson Raid. The old Cape Dutch dynasties of Cloetes and van der Byls became – literally – 'Anglicaners', producing generations of Anglican clergy and imperial soldiers.[85] Further north there was Sir Charles Coghlan, leader of the Rhodesian Responsible Government Association, who was a Catholic of Irish and German descent and former advocate of Irish home rule, but who grew to despise Sinn Féin on imperial grounds.[86] Sir Roy Welensky, prime minister of the Federation of Rhodesia and Nyasaland (1956–63), once described himself as half-Jewish, half-Afrikaner, but 'a hundred per cent British'. The first action of his premiership was the pledge of Rhodesian support for the Anglo-French invasion of Egypt; while in the years of Rhodesia's Unilateral Declaration of Independence, when non-British Rhodesians became more central to political life, there was none more prominent than the Greek-descended Divaris brothers, whose careers as Rhodesian Front parliamentarians were aided by distinguished wartime service in the Rhodesian Armoured Car Regiment.[87] In terms of allegiance, there must surely have been many more Welenskys, Monashes and Cloetes and the like scattered throughout the settler empire. It also might be questioned whether Ronald Robinson's term 'collaboration', with its unfortunate Second World War connotations, can adequately describe these connections. As with medieval feudalism itself, self-interest and self-protection may indeed lie at the heart of such allegiances, but as has been argued here, there does seem to be a point when these loyalties became internalised and were often accorded religious approval, and that these attachments seem to have gained a considerable momentum of their own. This was particularly apparent in time of war, when such institutions and allegiances are put to their most severe test.[88]

How do we explain the phenomenon of 'non-British loyalism'? The case of Australia suggests that mainly those Australians of unchallengeable British establishment origin have felt sufficiently secure and confident to advocate breaking with the Crown, while non-British immigrants have had so much more to prove. Moreover, as the historian J.D.B. Miller observed, even in the late 1980s, Greek, Italian and Hungarian immigrants and their children were willing to accept what honours, including knighthoods, Australia had to offer. Education, sport and common law, he contended, assimilated the children of immigrants into Australian culture as well as into a wider English-speaking culture. As he reminds us, 'Stratford-on-Avon and the Edinburgh Festival attract hordes of Americans whose names suggest no Anglo-Saxon link'.[89] Such factors, it is argued here, also apply to British colonies of settlement. The military career of distinctly un-Anglo-Saxon-sounding Bert Hoffmeister of Vancouver provides a case in point. A British Columbian of German origin, he joined the Seaforth Highlanders of Canada during the Second World War, in which he won the DSO (with two bars) fighting the Germans in Italy. He retired with the rank of major general and became Agent-General in London for British Columbia in 1958–61.[90] Also, let us not forget another veteran of the Italian campaign, the New Zealand Major General Sir Howard Karl Kippenberger. Born of German parents, he fought with distinction in both world wars.[91]

Adoptive nationalism has often proved powerful enough to transcend national origins. We can see how in the United States the children of recent immigrants can be made to feel as patriotic on the Fourth of July as they would be had their ancestors fought at Lexington or Yorktown. In the same way, in the settler Dominions the monarch's portrait in the immigration building, the oaths of allegiance, the militia regiment, the sports club and the masonic hall could play equally effective roles in the political assimilation of the Ukrainian immigrant to Canada and the Baltic immigrant to South Africa into conventional settler institutions of loyalty and notions of honour and duty. The monarchy could be imagined selectively by various groups of imperial subjects. Thus, for example, the Orangemen of Ontario could emphasise the Crown's Protestant character, while, simultaneously, French Canadians and Irish Catholics could stress the monarch's protective concern for their language rights and religion. Notwithstanding the constitutional requirement to uphold the Crown's Protestant character in the metropole, the secret of the monarchy's imperial success was its ability to juggle conflicting and contradictory allegiances across the empire. Where possible, as John Buchan recognised in the Canadian case, the monarchy had to avoid too explicit an identification with its natural constituency of British-descended Protestants, if French and Irish loyalties were not to be alienated. The traumatic years 1916–21 in Ireland provided a warning of what might happen when the Crown was discredited by its association with robust military action, or appropriated by the Protestant cause. As the symbols of Britishness fade in the former dominions, it can be argued that the weakening of these ties in Australia and, to a lesser extent, Canada and New Zealand, has had more to do with such factors as Britain's entry into the European Common Market, the secularisation of society, the decline both of deference and the erosion of monarchical mystique, and with the apparent loss of faith in such connections among dominant British Protestant-descended elites, than with any inherent inability of monarchy to recruit supporters from among the ranks of the 'non-British' in the British world.

NOTES

The author thanks the AHRB for the award of a conference grant to enable him to present a draft of this paper at the British World Conference in Cape Town. He also wishes to thank Professor Jacques Monet SJ, Dr Anne Summers, Professor Roy Foster and John Stewart for their assistance in discussing several themes.

1. Terence O'Neill, 'The Queen's visit', July 1966, Terence O'Neill papers, Public Record Office of Northern Ireland, Belfast; *Daily Mirror*, 4 July 1966; *Belfast Telegraph*, 4 July 1966; *Irish Times*, 5 July 1966. I am very grateful to Marc Mulholland of St Catherine's College, Oxford, for these references. For further explorations of the relationship of monarchy to Protestantism in Northern Ireland, see James Loughlin, *Ulster Unionism and British National Identity Since 1885* (London, 1995), 17–19, 40–45, 163–67, 222–24; Donal Lowry, 'Ulster Resistance and Loyalist Rebellion in the Empire', in K. Jeffery (ed.), *'An Irish Empire'?: Aspects of Ireland and the British Empire* (Manchester, 1996), 191–215.

2. *The Times*, 21 May 1937.
3. J. Barnes and D. Nicolson (eds.), *The Leo Amery Diaries*, vol.1 *1896–1925* (London, 1980), 515–16, entries for 10 and 13 July 1927.
4. Quoted in R. Lamb, *The Macmillan Years 1957–1963: The Emerging Truth* (London, 1995), 237.
5. But see Mary Ann Sieghart, 'The quiet rebirth of Catholic England', *The Times*, 21 Dec. 2001.
6. Malcolm Turnbull (ed.), *The Reluctant Republic* (Melbourne, 1993), 5.
7. Robert Hughes, 'Introduction', in Turnbull, *Reluctant Republic*, xv. See also Mary Kalantzis and Bill Cope, 'Republicanism and Cultural Diversity', in W. Hudson and D. Carter (eds.), *The Republican Debate* (Kensington, 1993), 130–37; R. Rivett, 'The Monarchy and the Migrant', in G. Dutton (ed.), *Australia and the Monarchy* (Sydney, 1966), 62–85.
8. See, for example, J.R. Miller, 'Anti-Catholic Thought in Victorian Canada', *Canadian Historical Review*, 66 (1985), 474–94; M. French, 'The Ambiguity of Empire Day in New South Wales', *Australian Journal of Politics and History*, 24 (1978), 61–74; P.S. O'Connor, 'Sectarian Conflict in New Zealand, 1911–1920', *Political Science*, 19 (1967), 3–16.
9. D. Cole, 'The Crimson Thread of Kinship: Ethnic Ideas in Australia, 1870–1914', *Historical Studies*, 14 (1971), 515–17.
10. L. Colley, 'Britishness and Otherness: An Argument', *Journal of British Studies*, 31 (1992), 309–29. The literature on Britishness is now extensive, but in particular see L. Colley, *Britons: Forging the Nation, 1707–1837* (London, 1992); B. Bailyn and P.D. Morgan (eds.), *Strangers within the Realm: Cultural Margins of the First British Empire* (Chapel Hill, NC, 1991); A. Grant and K.J. Stringer (eds.), *Uniting the Kingdom? The Making of British History* (London, 1995); D. Hempton, *Religion and Political Culture in Britain and Ireland: From the Glorious Revolution to the Decline of Empire* (Cambridge, 1996).
11. K. Lowe and E. McLaughlin, 'Sir John Pope-Hennessy and the "native race craze"', *Journal of Imperial and Commonwealth History*, 20 (1992), 223–41; B. Nasson, *The South African War 1899–1902* (London, 1999), 72–73. For Sir Hugh Clifford, see K. Tidrick, *Empire and English Character* (London, 1992), ch.3. More generally see D.G. Boyce, '"The marginal Britons": The Irish', in R. Colls and P. Dodd (eds.), *Englishness, Politics and Culture 1880–1920* (London, 1986), 230–53. While Irish Protestants were well represented among colonial governors, under ten per cent were Catholics or Jews. See Anthony Kirk-Greene, *Britain's Imperial Administrators, 1856–1966* (London, 2000), 17.
12. For teleological assumptions in Australian and Canadian historiography, see N. Meaney, 'Britishness and Australian Identity: The Problem of Nationalism in Australian History and Historiography, *Australian Historical Studies*, 32 (2001), 76–90; P. Buckner, 'Whatever Happened to the British Empire?', *Journal of the Canadian Historical Association*, 4 (1993), 3–32.
13. For a very useful discussion of the personal aspects of monarchical loyalty, see Thomas Hennessey, *Dividing Ireland: World War I and Partition* (London, 1998), xi–xxi.
14. See Colin Holmes, *Anti-Semitism in British Society, 1876–1939* (London, 1979), 1–9; M.C.M. Salbstein, *The Emancipation of the Jews in Britain: The Question of the Admission of Jews to Parliament* (New Brunswick, 1982).
15. Colley, *Britons*, 231.
16. Daniel O'Connell, 'On a Bill for the Removal of Jewish Disabilities (1830)', in A. Burton (ed.), *Politics and Empire in Victorian Britain* (New York, 2001), 6–7.
17. S. Webb, 'The decline of the birth-rate', *Fabian Tract*, 131 (1907), quoted in D. Read, *England 1868–1914: The Age of Urban Democracy* (London, 1979), 384.
18. Benjamin Disraeli, 'Address delivered in the Sheldonian Theatre, Oxford, 25 November 1864', quoted in R.J. White (ed.), *The Conservative Tradition* (London, 1964 edn.), 108.
19. For Irish nationalist anti-imperialism, see H.V. Brasted, 'Irish Nationalism and the British Empire', in O. MacDonagh (ed.), *Irish Culture and Nationalism, 1750–1950* (Canberra, 1983), 83–103. For Irish involvement in Empire, see D. Fitzpatrick, 'Ireland and the Empire', in A. Porter (ed.), *The Oxford History of the British Empire*, vol.3 *The Nineteenth Century* (Oxford, 1999), 495–521.
20. Quoted in A.C. Hepburn (ed.), *Ireland 1905–25*, vol.2 *Documents and Analysis*

(Newtownards, 1998), 22.
21. P.J. Joyce, *John Healy: Archbishop of Tuam* (Dublin, 1931), 67–69.
22. Ibid., 274–75. Healy himself shared a school bench at Summerhill, Athlone, with Sir Antony MacDonnell (later Baron MacDonnell of Swinford), who became lieutenant-governor of the North-Western Provinces and Oudh and a distinguished adviser to the Government of India. In spite of his Catholicism and Liberal sympathies, the prejudices that had impeded Pope-Hennessy and Butler do not appear to have had any significant impact on his career. He served as permanent under-secretary for Ireland under George Wyndham. MacDonnell's career, Healy's biographer speculates, 'no doubt impressed [Healy] in after life with some of the temporal advantages of Ireland's imperial connexions'. MacDonnell, like Healy, and many other 'ethnic outsiders' throughout the Empire, were generally very comfortable with the decentralised imperial structures advocated by the Liberal Party in the late Victorian and Edwardian years. Joyce, *Healy*, 6; H.V. Lovett, 'Antony Patrick MacDonnell', in J.R.H. Weaver (ed.), *The Dictionary of National Biography, 1922–1930* (Oxford, 1937), 530–35.
23. S. Heffer, *Power and Place: The Political Consequences of King Edward VII* (London, 1999 edn.), 108–09. See also 158–62, 271–73.
24. *Catholic Herald*, 30 June 1939. For other examples of this general outlook, see T. Johnstone and James Hagarty, *The Cross on the Sword: Catholic Chaplains in the Forces* (London, 1966), esp. chs.1–5.
25. M. Wade, *The French Canadians, 1760–1945* (Toronto, 1956), 63.
26. Ibid., 68.
27. Ibid., 99.
28. Ibid., 66–67, 74, 81, 87.
29. Ibid., 100.
30. B. Young, *George-Étienne Cartier: Montreal Bourgeois* (Kingston, 1981), 73.
31. J. Monet, *The Last Cannon Shot: A Study of French Canadian Nationalism, 1837–1850* (Toronto, 1969), 3, 228–29. See also *idem*, 'The Personal and Living Bond, 1839–1849', in W.L. Morton (ed.), *The Shield of Achilles: Aspects of Canada in the Victorian Age* (Toronto, 1968), 62.
32. Monet, 'Living Bond', 45–50; K. Munro, *The Political Career of Sir Adolphe Chapleau, Premier of Quebec* (Quebec, 1992), 153.
33. Monet, 'Living Bond', 84.
34. Wade, *French Canadians*, 367; Kenneth Munro, 'The Crown in French Canada: The Role of the Governors-General in Making the Crown Relevant', in Colin M. Coates (ed.), *Imperial Canada, 1867–1917* (Edinburgh, 1997), 109–21.
35. Ibid., 385.
36. A.H.M. Kirk-Greene, 'Canada in Africa: Sir Percy Girouard, Neglected Colonial Governor', *African Affairs*, 83 (1984), 207–40.
37. C. Murrow, *Henri Bourassa and French-Canadian Nationalism: Opposition to Empire* (Montreal, 1968), 34. The author is indebted to John Darwin for this reference. Sandra Gwyn, *Tapestry of War* (Toronto, 1992), 85–106, *passim*. For a history of the PPCLI, see Jeffery Williams, *First in the Field: Gault of the Patricias* (London, 1995).
38. André Siegfried, *The Race Question in Canada* (London, 1907), 178–79, quoted in N. Mansergh, *The Commonwealth Experience*, vol.2 *From British to Multi-Racial Commonwealth* (Toronto, 1982), 244.
39. C. Murphy (ed.), *D'Arcy McGee, 1825–1925: A Collection of Speeches and Essays* (Toronto, 1937), 67, 81.
40. L. O'Broin, *Charles Gavan Duffy: Patriot and Statesman* (Dublin, 1967), 116–17.
41. Quoted in Wise and Brown, *Canada Views the United States*, 85–86.
42. Quoted in Murphy (ed.), *D'Arcy McGee*, 265–66.
43. See Mark McGowan, *The Waning of the Green: Catholics, the Irish and Identity in Toronto, 1887–1922* (Montreal, 1999), 202–04.
44. M.G. McGowan, 'The De-greening of the Irish: Toronto's Irish-Catholic press, imperialism and the forging of a new identity, 1887–1914', *Historical Papers* (1989), 118–45.
45. Howard Palmer, *Patterns of Prejudice: A History of Nativism in Alberta* (Toronto, 1985), 58–59; Donald Avery, *'Dangerous Foreigners': European Immigrant Workers and Labour*

Radicalism in Canada, 1896–1932 (Toronto, 1983).
46. John Herd Thompson and Allen Seager, *Canada 1922–1939: Decades of Discord* (Toronto, 1988), 315, 327–28; Professor Richard Toporowski to the author, 26 Nov. 2001.
47. See also Wade, *French Canadians*, 512–13.
48. E. Wallace, *Goldwin Smith: Victorian Liberal* (Toronto, 1957), 153, 241. Such views were not uncommon. See R.G. Moyles and Doug Owram, *Imperial Dreams and Colonial Realities: British Views of Canada, 1880–1914* (Toronto, 1988), ch.4.
49. D. Morton, 'French Canada and the Canadian Militia, 1868–1914', *Histoire sociale – Social History*, 3 (1969), 32–50.
50. See D. Morton, 'The Limits of Loyalty: French Canadian Officers and the First World War', in Edgar Denton (ed.), *The Limits of Loyalty* (Kingston, 1980), 81–97.
51. Lord Tweedsmuir, 'The Monarchy and the Commonwealth', in *Canadian Occasions* (London, 1940), 94–95.
52. Wade, *French Canadians*, 856.
53. Thompson and Seager, *Canada 1922–1939*, 327.
54. *Montreal Daily Star*, 17 May 1939.
55. *Catholic Herald*, 19 May 1939.
56. Wade, *French Canadians*, 521.
57. Michael de la Bedoyere, 'The Royal Journey – Spiritual Example of Their Majesties', *Catholic Herald*, 19 May 1939.
58. MacDonald to Halifax, 26 Feb. 1943, Malcolm MacDonald papers 14/8/28–9, University of Durham. The author is indebted to Kent Fedorowich for this reference.
59. David J. Cheal, 'Ontario Loyalism: A Socio-Religious Ideology in Decline', *Canadian Ethnic Studies*, 13 (1981), 41–51.
60. *The Manual of Prayers* (London, [1886] 1953 edn.), 65.
61. Robert Speaight, *Vanier: Soldier, Diplomat and Governor-General* (London, 1970).
62. 'General Jean Allard', *Daily Telegraph*, 4 May 1996.
63. Speaight, *Vanier*, 428–29.
64. Monarchist League of Canada website: http://www.monarchist.ca/cmn/summer0114.htm.
65. 'Canada's Lady in Pink raises a Royal Flag', *Sunday Times*, 31 Oct. 1999; 'Little Snowdrop keeps Canada safe for the Queen', *Independent on Sunday*, 31 Oct. 1999.
66. See M. McKenna, *The Captive Republic: A History of Republicanism in Australia, 1788–1996* (Cambridge, 1996), esp. chs.5, 7–8; G. Martin, *Bunyip Aristocracy: The New South Wales Debate of 1853 and Hereditary Institutions in the British Colonies* (London, 1986); A. Taylor, *'Down with the Crown': British Anti-Monarchism and Debates about Royalty Since 1790* (London, 1999), 153.
67. O'Broin, *Duffy*, 126.
68. R.P. Davis, *Irish Issues in New Zealand Politics, 1868–1922* (Dunedin, 1974); M. Bassett, *Sir Joseph Ward: A Political Biography* (Auckland, 1993), 122.
69. Taylor, *'Down with the Crown'*, ch.5; McKenna, *The Captive Republic*; D. Lowry, 'Republicanism in the British Colonies of Settlement in the Long Nineteenth Century', in D. Nash and A. Taylor (eds.), *Republicanism in Victorian Society* (Stroud, 2000), 125–39.
70. Quoted in R. Birrell, *A Nation of Our Own* (Melbourne, 1997), 70–71.
71. K.S. Inglis, *The Rehearsal* (Sydney, 1985).
72. G. Serle, *John Monash: A Biography* (Melbourne, 1983), 202.
73. F.M. Cutlack (ed.), *War Letters of General Monash* (Sydney, 1934), 12, 112, 131, 135.
74. Ibid., 285–6.
75. Serle, *John Monash*, 202.
76. 'Sir John Monash', in F. Johns (ed.), *Australian Biographical Dictionary* (Melbourne, 1934), 250.
77. Some of these tensions within Zionism were reflected among Jews living in the Palestine Mandate in these years, including British administrators of Jewish origin. See Tom Segev, *One Palestine, Complete: Jews and Arabs Under the British Mandate* (London, 2000), 192.
78. See W.D. Rubenstein, *The Jews in Australia. A Thematic History*, vol.1 *1788–1945* (Melbourne, 1991), 361–9, 552–75; vol.2 *1945 to the Present* (Melbourne, 1991), 383–91, 511.

79. Jane Connors, 'The 1954 Royal Tour of Australia', *Australian Historical Studies*, 25 (1993), 371–82. For earlier parallels, see K. Fewster, 'Politics, Pageantry and Purpose: The 1920 Tour of Australia by the Prince of Wales', *Labour History*, 38 (1980), 59–66.
80. E. Morris, 'Forty Years On: Australia and the Queen, 1954', *Journal of Australian Studies*, 40 (1994), 13.
81. M. Goot, 'The Queen in the Polls', in J. Arnold, P. Spearritt and D. Walker (eds.), *Out of Empire: The British Dominion of Australia* (Melbourne, 1993), 295–311; D. Charnock, 'National Identity, Partisanship and Popular Protest as Factors in the 1999 Australian Republican Referendum', *Australian Journal of Political Science*, 26 (2001), 271–91.
82. See, for example, Sir David Smith, 'Some thoughts on the monarchy republic debate', http://www.monarchist.org.au/smith1.htm. The author is indebted to Dr John Fleming for alerting him to Smith's ethnic origin.
83. G. Bolton, *The Oxford History of Australia*, vol.5 *The Middle Way 1942–1995* (Oxford, 1996), 224–25.
84. See J. Monet, *The Canadian Crown* (Toronto, 1979); idem, 'The Canadian Monarchy: "Everything that is best and most admired"', in C. Berger and R. Cook (eds.), *The West and the Nation* (Toronto, 1976), 321–35.
85. See Mordechai Tamarkin, *Cecil Rhodes and the Cape Afrikaners* (London, 1996).
86. J.P.R. Wallis, *Sir Charles Coghlan and the Liberation of Southern Rhodesia* (London, 1950).
87. See Sir Roy Welensky, *4000 Days* (London, 1964).
88. R. Robinson, 'Non-European Foundations of European Imperialism: Sketch for a Theory of Collaboration', in Wm. Roger Louis (ed.), *Imperialism and the Robinson and Gallagher Controversy* (London, 1976). For a useful summary of the hierarchy of loyalties in the middle ages, see Otto Friederich von Gierke, *Political Theories of the Middle Ages* (Cambridge, 1958 edn.), 30–37. The author is grateful to Professor Rodney Davenport for this reference.
89. J.D.B. Miller, 'People to People', in J.D.B. Miller (ed.), *Australians and British: Social and Political Connections* (North Ryde, NSW, 1987), 187–88.
90. 'Major-General Bert Hoffmeister', *Daily Telegraph*, 7 Dec. 1999.
91. Glyn Harper, *Kippenberger: An Inspired New Zealand Commander* (Auckland, 1997).

Britishness and Australia: Some Reflections

NEVILLE MEANEY

Do you realize that, if you go in England from one county to another, men speak with a different accent ...? Yet you can go from Perth to Sydney, and from Hobart to Cape York, and find men speaking the same tongue with the same accent ... We are all of the same race, and speak the same tongue in the same way. That cannot be said of any other Dominion in the Empire, except New Zealand, where, after all, it can be said only with reservations, because that country has a large population of Maoris. We are more British than the people of Great Britain, we hold firmly to the great principle of the White Australia, because we know what we know.[1]

William Morris Hughes
Prime Minister of Australia, 1919

Recent scholarship has suggested that Australian nationalist historiography based on the Bush and Anzac Legends and radical Labor mythology has distorted our understanding of Australian identity and that British race patriotism was dominant until the 1970s. Australian nationalism was not 'thwarted'; rather, it was based on a local patriotism which saw itself as part of a pan-Britishness. This Britishness was probably stronger in Australia than in Britain itself: Australians had, in the words of the original 'Advance Australia Fair', a 'British soul'. Anglo-Australian differences – and these were often profound ones over foreign, defence, immigration and trade policies – were merely conflicts over interest. They neither derived from cultural difference nor led Australians to create a separate myth of themselves as a unique people.[2] In order to underpin this argument it is important to discuss three issues. The first is conceptual, namely the problem of nationalism in history. The second is contextual, namely Britishness in British historiography. And the third, and more specific, is the 1941–49 period in Australian history, which is seen by the great majority of nationalist historians, especially the 'radical nationalists', as either marking Australia's break with Britishness or setting the pattern for the subsequent achievement of independence.

I

To begin, then, with the problem of nationalism. The idea of Britishness is first and foremost about nationalism. Yet while those scholars who have addressed the British question implicitly accept this, very few have given thought to the conceptual phenomenon which defines their subject and informs their conclusions. As a result historians, or at least those historians concerned with ideas of political community and culture, still tend to interpret their subject within the parameters set by nationalism's own teleological view of the past, namely that all history has been directed towards fulfilling the destinies of unique peoples, of achieving their self-realisation, most commonly in sovereign states.

This approach, however, ignores the relatively recent findings of Western political theorists who have in different ways rejected nationalism's own essentialist claims and therefore its view of history. They have argued, by contrast, that nationalism was socially constructed and historically contingent, that it was a product of a particular set of social conditions and a particular time in history. These scholars have maintained that the stories which served nationalism's purpose and gave meaning to each people's belief in its separate and exclusive identity were myths about 'imagined communities', to use Benedict Anderson's rather well-worn phrase.[3]

It may well be that this critique of nationalism is itself a response to new times and a new social psychology. Benedetto Croce's maxim that 'All history is contemporary history' contains more than a grain of truth. It is only when new times and new circumstances undermine established orthodoxies they become historical problems. It would seem that this is what is happening to nationalism in the Western world. Nationalism, which arose first in the West, has now almost run its course there. The great nations that from the late nineteenth century fought at great cost 'total wars' of peoples against peoples have for the last 40 years been engaged in building a European Union. It is a new political structure which, unlike all its nineteenth- and early twentieth-century forebears, is held together not by a national myth but by a shared commitment to liberal civic values and what might be called a modern way of life. The great historians of the nineteenth century who created national myths for their respective countries, such as George Bancroft in America, Jules Michelet in France, J.A. Froude in Britain, and Helmut von Treitschke in Germany, are now read, if at all, as documents revealing the ideological character of their time.[4]

Nationalism has become a major problem for the social sciences.[5] Western historians have not only removed nationalism from its proud position at the centre of the discipline but also are beginning, even if tentatively, to respond to the new insights into the nature of nationalism.

Some from the older generation bemoan the fact that national identity is under challenge, while younger members of the profession seek a way of coming to terms with the end of nationalism.[6] In the aptly-titled work *Imagined Histories: American Historians Interpret the Past*, which shows the influence of Anderson, its editors, Anthony Molho and Gordon S. Wood, admit that it was 'Only at this moment [1999] – when the identity of the United States and the discipline of history are shifting in profound ways – are we able to perceive clearly the peculiar ways Americans have written about the past.' Here in this book Wood, a previously committed nationalist historian, begins, even if uncertainly, the process of unpacking nationalism's assumptions and opening up new ways of understanding America's mythology.[7] Britishness has not escaped this process.

II

Although there can be no question but that this interrogating of Britishness is connected to the broader examination of nationalism in the Western world, its immediate origins can be traced to Britain joining the European Economic Community. J.G.A. Pocock's clarion call for a new subject called 'British History', which began the whole enterprise, was issued from Christchurch, New Zealand in 1973.[8] He, as a New Zealander, has subsequently confessed that the lecture

> was composed and delivered after the great divorce which occurred when you [the British] told us that you were now Europeans, which we as New Zealanders were not ... What you did, of course, was irrevocably and unilaterally to disrupt a concept of Britishness which we had supposed that we share with you ... In effect, you threw your identity, as well as ours, into a condition of contingency, in which you have to decide whether it is possible to be both British and European ..., while we have to decide in what sense if any we continue to be British or have a British history.[9]

British scholars, in reacting to Pocock's plea and the problems of identity raised by Britain's entry into the European Community have, however, confined their research and writing to the history of the United Kingdom and Ireland and to its connection to British North America. In the last 20 years there has been a plethora of works dealing with the origin and nature of English or British nationalism and the relation of the Celtic peoples to England. By contrast there has been hardly any work on Greater Britain or, for that matter, on the classical era of British race patriotism at the end of the nineteenth century which shaped the British-settled colonies' sense of identity.[10] Indeed, the indifference to this period highlights the failure of the

historians engaged in the 'New History' to reflect on the concept of
nationalism and, more to the point here, to take seriously the problem of
Britishness for the latter-day, that is nineteenth- and twentieth-century,
British diaspora. It is noteworthy that Pocock himself has not shown any
desire to fill this gap: his scholarly endeavours have been devoted almost
entirely to civic humanism and republicanism in the seventeenth- and
eighteenth-century Anglo-American world.

The burden of Pocock's complaint is that Britain by going into Europe
had cut itself free from a global sense of Britishness which had given New
Zealanders their identity. In his article he expressed New Zealanders'
resentment at British indifference to their cultural fate – 'we were to learn
that you cared as little for our past as for our future' – sentiments which had
their echoes, even if in more subdued tones, in Australia and Canada. In a
1999 *American Historical Review* forum on 'The New British History in
Atlantic Perspective', Pocock, returning to the initial impulse that had
started this hare running, could not forbear from repeating the old refrain:

> One of the origins of the 'New British History' lies in the perceived
> need they (the colonies of settlement – the former dominions or neo-
> British) are under to rewrite British history, in order both to enhance
> their own understanding of their own and to point out to the United
> Kingdom British that there is a history of common substance, which
> Europeanisation must not be allowed to write out of existence.

For Pocock this wider British history should not be limited to eighteenth-
century North America. Australia, New Zealand and South Africa, even if
the latter was an unsuccessful venture, needed to write 'their own histories
and their own British history'. And he concluded defiantly, 'There was a
British world, both European and oceanic, in the nineteenth and twentieth
centuries: it had a history, which will have successors.'[11]

Pocock's call for such a new British history has fallen mostly on deaf
ears in the antipodes as well as the United Kingdom. Australian and New
Zealand historians, no less than their British counterparts, have evinced
little or no inclination to take up this cause.[12] For Australians and New
Zealanders their British past has become something of an embarrassment.
On the one hand, a new breed of social historians responding to the decline
in nationalism's appeal has focused on its victims, that is those who had
been marginalised by nationalist history, and developed in its place a
pluralist alternative. On the other, those still captive to nationalism's claims
have recognised that, after the United Kingdom had abandoned its fellow
Britons across the sea, they could no longer define themselves through a
history the core of which had rejected them. In the case of Australia these
historians have sought to create a new exclusive nationalist history written

against Britain and its supposed betrayals. The new teleological history, frequently given a radical slant, has seen Australia's past as a story of 'thwarted' nationalism, a thwarting which was the result of British manipulation, Anglo-Australians' subversion and security dependence.

III

The decade of the 1940s is seen by most Australian nationalists as the crucial period in which Australia, under the greatest provocation, moved to cut the British ties and affirm its own identity. It was, according to this quasi-nationalist view, the decade in which Australians realised or ought to have realised – there is a confusion here which betrays the scholarly difficulties of the argument – themselves as a distinct people. Under the leadership of the Curtin and Chifley Labor governments – and for the radical historians the Labor Party and the labour movement are the heroes of the teleological story – it is claimed that Australia was or ought to have become a nation at last. The titles of David Day's two major works on Australia in the Second World War, namely *The Great Betrayal* and *Reluctant Nation*,[13] reveal this approach. Down to the fall of Singapore Britain showed no interest in Australia's fate and exploited Australia's loyalty for its own ends. Subsequently, however, despite Australia's resentment of British behaviour and its insistence that Australia's forces should be used in the south-west Pacific to defend it against Japanese aggression, Day had to recognise reluctantly that somehow these events did not produce a popular demand for a separate Australian nationalism and the severing of the links that bound Australia to Britain. The curious title, *Reluctant Nation*, expressed Day's disappointment that the salutary lessons of wartime had not been translated into a crusade for independence which he seems to have believed was the natural culmination of this history.

Why then were Australians so unwilling to claim their independence from Britain and its Empire? The answer is clear. They, even under the testing circumstances of the Second World War, could not think of themselves as other than a British people. The idea of Britishness which Australians had embraced at the end of the nineteenth century, at the outset of the modern nationalist era, was so deeply embedded in the society that no alternative was seriously contemplated. John Curtin, the Labor Prime Minister, who has been seen as the putative symbol of this national emancipation, cannot fulfil the role. Australian nationalists have often cited his New Year message at the end of 1941, in which he famously called on Australia to turn to the United States 'free of any pangs as to our traditional links or kinship with the United Kingdom', as a cry for independence. It cannot serve the purpose. In his early years while on the periphery of politics Curtin had espoused socialist and pacifist causes and shown little interest in nationalism of any kind. But, propelled into the centre of the country's political life, he could not, as wartime prime minister, avoid the issue and he responded with the language of the heroes of Federation and all their successors. He, like them, believed in a white British Australia. Following the Japanese attack on Pearl Harbor and Australia's declaration of war on Japan Curtin in a radio broadcast asserted that 'We Australians … shall hold this territory and keep it as a citadel for the British-speaking race.'[14]

'British-speaking' may sound odd but, though a malapropism, it did say something about Australia's idea of itself.[15] Australia's myth was not English but British, as William Morris Hughes proudly proclaimed in 1919. Australians, as the British myth would have it, believed in some incongruous way that those of English, Scottish, Irish and Welsh descent shared one culture and one history, and in Australia where they were all mixed together this was the 'race' to which they belonged. Thus since nationalism required that each 'race' of people had to have its own distinct culture and language Australia as a British people must have a British language. This phrase was not a slip of the tongue. Curtin repeated it many times, even in England, and his successor as Prime Minister, Ben Chifley, followed Curtin's usage. In Britain, where Britishness never had the same resonance, this curious effort to nationalise language for British nationalist purposes never appeared. Churchill's history was a history of the English-speaking peoples. In the United Kingdom, English dominance meant that England could be used for the whole. Since the need for a modern nationalism was never felt there in the same degree as in Australia, there was no great demand that the distinct country, county and local loyalties give way absolutely to a British one.

Australia's Britishness was a white Britishness and Curtin wholeheartedly endorsed this full version of national identity. In an Australia Day address in January 1942, at the time when the fear of a Japanese invasion seemed imminent, Curtin declared that 'We carry on the purpose of Captain James Cook: we maintain the tradition of Captain Arthur Phillip. This Australia is for the Australians: it is a White Australia, with God's blessing we shall keep it so.'[16] Here, by looking back to a British explorer hero and the first British governor, the teleological story of Australia gained its legitimacy. Curtin admitted that he 'felt intensely the horror of a Japanese invasion because of the incompatibility of race and blood'. But his desire to continue the work of making Australia 'a second Britannia in the Antipodes' was imperilled not only by the immediate Japanese danger but more generally by the 'teeming millions of coloured races to the north of Australia'. To meet this future it was imperative to hold fast to Australia's racially exclusive immigration policy and at the end of the war to encourage substantial numbers of white British to settle in the country.[17]

In harmony with these assumptions about Australia Curtin also looked forward to closer ties with Britain and the other Dominions. His answer to Britain's so-called 'betrayal' was not independence and separation but more effective arrangements for Dominion participation in the making of a united empire's defence and foreign policy. For this purpose he wanted at the end of the war a reformed British Empire with permanent machinery for consultation and information. And he took these proposals with him to the Prime Ministers' conference which was held in London in May 1944.[18] Arriving in London he again and again expressed in fulsome language Australia's British race ideal. To the Empire Parliamentary Association he stated that:

> Numerically – because Australians are over 90 per cent British stock – and in every other aspect, the Australian people are a replica of Britain and the way of life in Britain. In the southern hemisphere 7,000,000 Australians carry on a British community as trustees for the British way of life in a part of the world where it is of the utmost significance to the British-speaking race that such a vast continent should have as its population a people and a form of government corresponding in outlook and in purpose to Britain.[19]

In this rendering of the 'New Britannia' the newness was not in its adaptation to its peculiar history and geography but in its latter day founding. It was a 'replica' of the old country. Its destiny was to be a trustee of British civilisation in the South Pacific. Yet, despite Curtin's rather naive hopes, the Commonwealth Prime Ministers poured cold water on his plans. For Churchill his proposals were embarrassing. The British leader had no desire to give the Dominions a greater share in imperial policy-making. He also knew that the Canadian, South African and Irish Prime Ministers, who in the previous two decades had carried through a constitutional revolution which had been designed to obtain autonomy, would have none of it. As a result Curtin's proposals for a more closely integrated empire failed at the first hurdle. Returning home, even though he had not achieved the co-operation of Britain and the other Dominions, he maintained that Australia's future role in the world would be as an 'integral part of the British Commonwealth'.[20]

The Labor Prime Minister's conception of Australia and its relation to Britain was consonant with that which had held sway since the end of the nineteenth century. The imagery invoked by Curtin of a 'New Britannia' menaced by 'teeming millions to the north' drew on the orthodox language depicting Australia in the world. Similarly, Curtin's attempt to deal with British slights or failures by seeking better means of influencing the British government's decisions and so ensuring that the unity of the British race would not again be fractured was in accord with earlier leaders' practice in meeting similar problems.[21] Curtin's oratory and behaviour cannot be explained away by opportunist arguments, whether political or strategic. Suggestions that Curtin adopted the language of British race patriotism merely to win elections will not stand up to the most superficial scrutiny. Given that Curtin spoke and acted in this way it has to be asked: 'why might he think it would be useful?' And the answer must be that he believed that Australians generally identified themselves with this British race tradition, that is, that Britishness was indeed Australians' national myth. Furthermore, if this is so, then it must also be asked, 'how did they come to accept the myth?' And if the answer is that they were acculturated into accepting it, then since Curtin was himself part of the same society, he could not have easily escaped the process, and there is no evidence that he did. Curtin did not select the language of Britishness for certain audiences, whether in Australia or the United Kingdom. He had no choice. There was no alternative Australian myth he could offer the people in rallying them against the foreign foe.

In the post-war era Australia had to deal with a set of interconnected policy questions. These included European immigration, citizenship and naturalisation, the Irish Free State's withdrawal from the British Commonwealth, India's joining the renamed 'Commonwealth' as a republic, and Anglo-Australian co-operation in regional and global defence, all of which tested Australia's Britishness. To all of these the Chifley government gave answers that followed from the assumptions with which Curtin and all his predecessors had approached the world. Chifley as well as senior members of his cabinet such as Dr H.V. Evatt, Minister for External Affairs, and Arthur Calwell, Minister for Immigration, all spoke the same language of British race nationalism. Chifley, though less hyperbolic than Curtin, nevertheless expressed the same sentiments as his former leader. In the 1946 election campaign he described the Australia which he hoped to lead as 'the great bastion of the British-speaking race south of the equator'.[22]

It was this British self-definition which underpinned the Chifley government's treatment of those topics which touched on Australia's relations with Britain, the British Commonwealth and the world. In introducing the government's post-war immigration policy, which extended a welcoming hand to non-British as well as British Europeans, Calwell maintained that he hoped that 'for every foreign migrant there will be 10 people from the United Kingdom', and that these foreign migrants would quickly assimilate themselves into a British Australia.[23] When Canada passed legislation providing for a distinct Canadian citizenship and thereby nationality, Australia in the light of the changing nature of the Commonwealth was prompted to address the question. From the time of federation no Commonwealth parliament had thought it necessary to provide for an Australian citizenship. The concept had no standing in law. Indeed in 1906 the High Court had stated that, 'We are not disposed to give any countenance to the novel doctrine that there is an Australian nationality as distinguished from a British nationality.'[24] In the late 1940s the Australian people showed no interest in exchanging their status as British subjects for that of Australian citizens. At the end of 1947, 65 per cent of Australians in a Gallup opinion poll said that they would prefer to keep a British nationality rather than have a separate Australian nationality.[25] When in 1948 the Chifley government introduced its Nationality and Citizenship Act, Calwell, as the responsible minister, assured parliament that it was not designed in any way 'to make an Australian any less a British subject'.[26] The Act was pre-eminently intended to lay down the conditions for naturalising the large number of non-British Europeans who were to enter the country under the new migration programme. British migrants continued to enjoy all the privileges of citizenship without becoming naturalised.

The negotiations accompanying the admission of India to what became the Commonwealth of Nations and the withdrawal of Eire from the British Commonwealth compelled the Australian government to reflect upon the meaning it gave to Britishness. Both these new developments disturbed the foundations of Australia's faith in the British Commonwealth. Although the Irish question was the more straightforward, Australia desperately wanted to avoid the breach. It exerted its influence to prevent Britain taking a hostile position and treating Ireland as a foreign country. Eire's severance of ties with the Commonwealth was both politically and culturally dangerous. It challenged Australians' idea of Britishness. Those of Irish Catholic descent would no longer be able so easily to fit under this cultural umbrella. It was the view of both Evatt and Chifley that, even after separation, if that could not be averted, Irish citizens should continue to be treated as though they were British subjects.[27] And this was provided for in the Nationality and Citizenship Act. Likewise they were to be entitled to all the privileges enjoyed by British Europeans under the nation's migration policy. It was the Chifley government's hope that Eire at some future time would want to rejoin the Commonwealth and they wished to ensure that the measures accompanying separation would place as few obstacles as possible in the way of achieving that end.

India's case was the more taxing. The newly independent India, which was not British, either ethnically or culturally, would accept membership only if it were admitted as a 'Republic' and the word 'British' was omitted from the title of the body. These conditions, if conceded, would represent a fundamental change in the character of the Commonwealth. Nevertheless both Britain and Australia, for economic and strategic reasons, desired that India should be associated with the Commonwealth in some form, if that proved to be practicable. Australia, more than Britain, still found the Indian terms difficult to swallow. Evatt, along with the New Zealand Prime Minister, Peter Fraser, resisted almost to the end of the negotiations. Evatt urged that everything possible be done to convince India to become a member of the Commonwealth on the existing basis. He wanted 'British' retained in the title and India to acknowledge the position of the Crown as the focus of loyalty and unity.[28] Cabling Chifley from London on 18 December 1948, after representatives of the 'Old Commonwealth' governments had discussed among themselves India's proposal, Evatt put forward a compromise:

> What is developing is an idea I have long entertained and you have frequently expressed, namely, that there is a group of British Commonwealth nations with intimate associations such as the United Kingdom, Australia and New Zealand, and that equally there are other Nations with associations which are not so intimate. This may lead to two classes of membership of the Commonwealth – full membership and what might be called associate membership.[29]

This idea of a two-tier Commonwealth did not find favour with the other governments. At the April 1949 Prime Ministers' Conference Chifley, under pressure from the United Kingdom, finally accepted India's terms. Nevertheless he made it clear to the Indian Prime Minister, Pandit Nehru, that 'there would be no weakening of the links now joining Australia to the Crown'. In explaining Australia's position he stated that, 'There were sentimental, historic, economic, defence and other reasons which ensured effective assistance to the United Kingdom if required of it, perhaps even in some cases irrespective of rights and wrongs of the case.'[30] Chifley was echoing Edmund Barton's words at the time of the Boer War when the leader of the Federation movement had declared for the empire, 'right or wrong'. After the event the Labor ministers continued to speak of the 'British Commonwealth' as though to their mind no change had occurred.

The Chifley government also desired to give effect to Australia's Britishness in policy-making, most notably in defence. As nationalism itself prescribed, Chifley, like all his predecessors, wished to be united with the other British peoples in facing the world. Indeed the post-war Labor government showed a greater willingness to collaborate with Britain on defence in peacetime than any previous administration. It readily agreed to co-operate in the Guided Missile Project at Woomera and in its Joint Military Intelligence machinery. At the 1946 Commonwealth Prime Ministers' conference Chifley accepted that Australia should join with the United Kingdom and New Zealand in defence planning. He regretted that the British Commonwealth was losing its unity and therefore its position in the world. At a Council of Defence meeting in March 1947 he observed that 'the United Kingdom has not the capacity and strength she formerly possessed', that 'India appears to be on the way out', and 'Canada and South Africa are non-co-operative'. As a result it was only Britain, Australia and New Zealand that were 'prepared to take measures and co-operate in a plan'.[31] Although discouraged, especially by the attitude of the Canadians and the South Africans, he still remained convinced that Australia and New Zealand, those Dominions which were wholly British, should continue to work with the United Kingdom in seeking a joint policy for both regional and global defence.

Yet, as in the case of Curtin, the British government, while seeing some advantages in fostering such ideas, was disturbed by the Australian insistence that such co-operation should be restricted to Australia and New Zealand. In London in July 1948 when the British ministers were endeavouring to persuade Chifley that the Commonwealth countries should work together to resist Soviet expansionism, they were much troubled by Chifley's view that: 'The United Kingdom, Australia and New Zealand were the only parts of the Commonwealth which fully represent the British tradition', and by implication that they were the only members who could therefore be relied upon to work together in meeting an external threat. The British were not only looking towards a close association with the Canadians in an Atlantic security arrangement but also hoped that the new South Asian members of the Commonwealth could be induced to assist with the defence of the Middle East. Thus the British Cabinet Secretary, after learning of Chifley's attitude, wrote to Clement Attlee, the British Prime Minister, suggesting that he should try to convince Chifley that Australia, no more than Britain, could 'afford to see the Commonwealth reduced to those countries which he regards as [and he quoted Chifley's words from the previous day's meeting] "fully representing the British tradition and outlook".'[32] Britishness meant more to the Australians than to the British themselves.

At the Commonwealth Prime Ministers' meeting later that year when the British government appealed to the assembled leaders to join together, in association with the United States and Western Europe, to combat Soviet aggression, Evatt acting on Chifley's authority was of all the Commonwealth representatives the most supportive. Evatt declared that Australia was 'in general agreement' with the British proposals and confirmed that: 'If war came it would not be a regional war: and consultation on defence should take place on the Commonwealth as well as a regional basis.'[33] Unlike the Canadians, South Africans and the Indians, who responded rather coolly or negatively, the Australians for sentimental reasons wanted to be united with the United Kingdom in facing up to the world crisis.

In the era of the Cold War, as in every preceding era since Federation, however, this sentimentally driven desire for making common cause with Britain was frustrated by the fact that Australia and Britain held two different views of the empire. Whereas Britain tended to treat the British-settled countries as subordinate colonies and to see them as expendable resources available for the protection of the heart of the empire, Australia thought of the empire as being made up of separate and equal British peoples all of whose interests were entitled to the same degree of security. Curtin had when reaffirming Australia's British identity and loyalty underscored the point by insisting that Australia was 'a Dominion not a colony'. Consequently Chifley, in responding to Britain's post-conference requests to begin regional and global defence planning – it particularly wanted Australian assistance in the Middle East – followed this tradition, and informed Attlee that though Australia had an interest in regional planning the Australian government would require '[s]omething more than the statement of the United Kingdom's Chiefs of Staff ... that "we consider the threat in the Pacific can be adequately matched by American naval and air strength" before it would consent to participate in global arrangements which might involve Australian forces being used outside its immediate neighbourhood'.[34] Since Britain itself lacked the power to guarantee Australia's security in the Pacific, only an American commitment similar to that which the United States was negotiating for Western Europe would serve. Without such an assurance the Chifley Labor government, like all its predecessors in peacetime, would not ahead of time give the British any promise of assistance. It is worth noting that the succeeding Menzies government similarly rejected British overtures to have Australian forces stationed in the Middle East until after the ANZUS pact was signed in September 1951.

IV

To conclude. First, since nationalism is a product of particular times and circumstances, of a particular stage in history, it does not establish the 'essence' of a state or a society. It was preceded by and will be replaced by different dominant loyalties and identities. Indeed in the Western world, including Australia, this latter process may now be well under way. Second, following from this, it is not impossible to believe – and it would not demean Australians to accept – that Britishness was more important in Australia than in Britain. And finally, Australians cannot hope to come to terms with Britishness in their past unless they face up to its importance in what might be called the nationalist period of their history, and so free themselves from the trammels of British race and culture orthodoxies, the legacy of which still haunts the present in many different and obfuscating ways. Until then Australians will be unable to deal properly with their British inheritance, which is not the same as Britishness. It may be, as Pocock has asserted for New Zealand, that Australia needs a new British history which incorporates the Oceanic Greater Britain into its tale. Thirty years after Pocock's appeal, however, there is no sign that British historians are likely to heed this plea. Perhaps Australians and New Zealanders have to do this for themselves.

NOTES

1. *Commonwealth* [of Australia] *Parliamentary Debates* [hereafter *CPD*], 10 Sept. 1919, p.12175.
2. Neville Meaney, 'Britishness and Australian Identity: The Problem of Nationalism in Australian History and Historiography', *Australian Historical Studies*, 32 (2001), 76–90; and Stuart Ward, *Australia and the British Embrace: The Demise of the Imperial Ideal* (Melbourne, 2001). See also Stuart Ward, 'Sentiment and Self-interest: The Imperial Ideal and Anglo-Australian Commercial Culture'; Richard White, 'Cooees cross the Strand: Australian Travellers in London and the Performance of National Identity'; John Rickard, 'Imagining the Unimaginable?'; and Jane Connors, 'Identity and History', *Australian Historical Studies*, 32 (2001), 91–108, 109–27, 128–31 and 132–36 respectively.
3. Benedict Anderson, *Imagined Communities: Reflections on the Origin and Spread of Nationalism* (London, 1983); Eric Hobsbawm and Terence Ranger (eds.), *The Invention of Tradition: A Study in its Origin and Background* (Cambridge, 1983); Ernest Gellner, *Nations and Nationalism* (Oxford, 1983); and Walter Connor, *Ethnonationalism: The Quest for Understanding* (Princeton, 1994). It is rarely recognised that Hans Kohn in his work, *The Idea of Nationalism: A Study in its Origins and Background* (New York, 1945), that is almost 40 years earlier, had already anticipated this relativist view of the origin and nature of nationalism, declaring it to be 'a state of mind' which had arisen in the nineteenth century out of a peculiar set of social forces. But Kohn's astute intellectual insight had no impact on either the scholarly or political world of his day. The times were not propitious for such a challenge to nationalism.
4. Stefan Berger, Mark Donovan and Kevin Passmore (eds.), *Writing National Histories: Western Europe since 1800* (London, 1999).
5. Anthony D. Smith, *Nationalism and Modernism: A Critical Survey of Recent Theories of Nations and Nationalism* (London, 1998), gives an overview of the extraordinary extent of the debate which has emerged since the 1970s.
6. Even United States historians have been affected by this critical approach to nationalism. While veteran scholars whose *weltanschauung* was formed in the high era of nationalism could protest against the failure of their American vision (see Arthur Schlesinger Jr., *Disuniting of America*), many more, such as Joyce Appleby in her presidential address to the Society of American Historians in 1995, celebrated the collapse of the hegemonic myth.
7. Anthony Molho and Gordon S. Wood (eds.), *Imagined Histories: American Historians Interpret the Past* (Princeton, 1998), 3.

8. J.G.A. Pocock, 'British History: A Plea for a New Subject', *New Zealand Historical Journal*, 8 (1974), 3–21.

9. *Idem*, 'Conclusion: Contingency, Identity, Sovereignty', in Alexander Grant and Keith J. Stringer (eds.), *Uniting the Kingdom? The Making of British History* (London, 1995), 297. For the impact of Britain joining the EEC on Australia, see Ward, *Australia and the British Embrace*.

10. For surveys of works on Britishness which have been published since 1973, see Grant and Stringer (eds.), *Uniting the Kingdom?*; and Tony Claydon and Ian McBride (eds.), *Protestantism and National Identity: Britain and Ireland, c.1650–1850* (Cambridge, 1998). David Cannadine in his chapter on 'British History as a "new subject": Politics, Perspectives and Prospects', in Alexander and Stringer (eds.), *Uniting the Kingdom?*, 24, commenting on the dearth of studies on Britishness in the nineteenth and twentieth century, has remarked, 'How odd it is that "British history" as a subject should be at its weakest for the very period when British history itself in many ways reached its zenith.' Norman Davies, in his iconoclastic attack on the careless use of the word 'British' in *The Isles* (London, 1999), has a chapter on 'The British Imperial Isles, 1707–1922', but its treatment of the British settled colonies and Dominions is perfunctory and superficial. Pocock's ambition to have a British history which would incorporate the British settled colonies has to overcome the United Kingdom historians' predisposition to see these colonies as part also of the dependent Empire and therefore, given their size and significance, especially when compared to India, to pay them little attention. Douglas Cole's pre-Pocock article, 'The Problem of "Nationalism" and "Imperialism" in British Settlement Colonies', *Journal of British Studies*, 10 (1971), 160–82, remains the only serious attempt to deal with the conceptual questions, but his work still does not show how these ideas of British race nationalism were generated in England and the degree of their acceptance in the United Kingdom.

11. 'The New British History in Atlantic Perspective: An Antipodean Commentary', *American Historical Review*, 104 (1999), 499–500.

12. James Belich, *Making Peoples: A History of the New Zealanders. From Polynesian Settlement to the End of the Nineteenth Century* (Auckland, 1996); and *idem*, *Paradise Reforged: A History of the New Zealanders. From the 1880s to the Year 2000* (Auckland, 2001), are perhaps exceptions.

13. David Day, *The Great Betrayal: Britain, Australia and the Onset of the Pacific War 1939–42* (Melbourne, 1988); *idem*, *Reluctant Nation: Australia and the Allied Defeat of Japan 1942–45* (Melbourne, 1992).

14. *Sydney Morning Herald*, 9 Dec. 1941.

15. 'British-speaking race' is unknown to the Oxford Dictionary and those working on its revision. The Macquarie Dictionary editors also have no references to the phrase. The Macquarie editors have only one related reference, namely to 'British-speaking man', which appeared in an obscure work, *Australia Limited*, by A.J. Marshall, which was published in 1942 in Australia.

16. *Digest of Decisions and Announcements and Important Speeches by the Prime Minister* [hereafter *DDS*] (Canberra, 1942), 24 Jan. 1942, cited in James Curran, '"More than Empty Words?": Prime Ministerial Rhetoric and Australian Nationalism, 1972–1996', Ph.D thesis, University of Sydney, 2001, 46.

17. David Day, *John Curtin* (Sydney, 1999), 518; and *Reluctant Nation*, 179.

18. *Documents on Australian Foreign Policy 1937–1949* [hereafter *DAFP*] (Canberra, 1988), vol.7 *1944*, 263. At the meeting of the Prime Ministers on 3 May 1944, Curtin explained that while he made no apology for asking for American assistance when Australia was 'seriously threatened', the result of American support had been that 'a continent which was an integral part of the British empire, and was occupied and defended by British people, had been held through a period of grave peril'. He maintained that 'The acceptance of American help had in no way affected the Australians' deep sense of "oneness" with the United Kingdom.'

19. Cited in Curran, '"More than Empty Words?"', 47.

20. *Current Notes on International Affairs*, 15 (1944), 153.

21. Neville Meaney (ed.), *Under New Heavens* (Melbourne, 1988), 393–425.

22. Curran, '"More than Empty Words?"', 50.

23. The Coalition government which came to power in December 1949 fully endorsed this aim. The Minister for Immigration, Harold Holt, in addressing a Citizenship Convention declared that: 'Australia, in accepting a balanced intake of other European people as well as British, can still build a truly British nation on this side of the world.' See James Jupp (ed.), *The Australian People* (Sydney, 1988), 858.
24. *Attorney-General for Commonwealth v Ah Sheung* (1906), 4 *Commonwealth Law Reports*, 951.
25. *Australian Gallup Polls*, 470–77 (Nov.–Dec. 1947). Only 28 per cent opted for a separate Australian nationality.
26. *CPD*, Sept. 1948, p.1060.
27. Cables, Evatt to Chifley, 14 and 17 Oct. and 23 Nov. 1948, and Heydon to Burton, 17 Nov 1948, *DAFP*, vol.14 *1948–1949*, 129–35.
28. Raj and Janis Darbari, *Commonwealth and Nehru* (New Delhi, 1983), 53.
29. *DAFP*, vol.14 *1948–1949*, 115. On 7 November Chifley, in an address to the nation about the changing Commonwealth, had spoken of 'the willingness of purely British units like Britain, Australia and New Zealand; units like Canada and South Africa which have large French or Dutch sections; and units like India, Pakistan and Ceylon, proud of old civilizations long pre-dating any British links, to work closely and effectively for common ideals and concrete objectives.' See *DDS*, No.140, 12 Oct.–21 Nov. 1948, 17. See also Frank Bongiorno, 'Commonwealthmen and Republicans: Dr H.V. Evatt, the Monarchy and India', *Australian Journal of Politics and History*, 46 (2000), 33–50.
30. Cable, Australian High Commission, London, to E.J. Holloway, 22 April 1949, *DAFP*, vol.14 *1948–1949*, 119.
31. Minute, Council of Defence, 12 March 1947, *DAFP*, vol.12 *1947*, 302–06.
32. Minute, Sir Norman Brook to Attlee, 9 July 1948, Cabinet Office papers [hereafter CAB], CAB 21/1793, Public Record Office, London.
33. Minutes of the third, ninth, and eleventh meetings of the Commonwealth Prime Ministers Conference, 12, 19, and 20 Oct. 1948, including confidential Annex and British Memorandum, 'The World Situation and its Defence Aspects', PMM(48)1, attached to the minutes of the eleventh meeting, 20 Oct. 1948, CAB 133/88.
34. Cable, Chifley to Attlee, 7 Feb. 1949, *DAFP*, vol.14 *1948–1949*, 204. For a more detailed account of the episode, see Neville Meaney, *'Primary Risks and Responsibilities' in the Pacific: The Problem of Japan and the Changing Role of Australia in the British Commonwealth, 1945–1952* (London, 2000).

Hugh Wyndham, Transvaal Politics and the Attempt to Create an English Country Seat in South Africa, 1901–14

IAN VAN DER WAAG

The British Empire throughout the nineteenth century was a fast-expanding enterprise, which required numerous government and colonial officials, for whom it held the prospect of power, prestige and possible wealth. It also formed an enormous playground for the patrician class. During the last quarter of the nineteenth century, genteel globe-trotting was endemic: more patricians were travelling more often and to destinations more exotic than ever before. The Wyndhams of Petworth were typical and several of Hugh Wyndham's relatives journeyed extensively. His uncle, Lord Rosebery, visited the German spa towns regularly, purchased a Neapolitan villa in 1897, and spent much time sailing among Aegean islands. Numerous cousins were equally mobile though not always travelling for pleasure. Alfred Douglas fled to the continent to avoid social disgrace at the time of the Oscar Wilde trial. Wilfred Scawen Blunt visited Algeria in 1874 and, attracted to the Bedouin life, espoused the cause of Egyptian nationalism and eventually established an Arabian stud at Crabbet. Aubrey Herbert took up the cause of Albanian nationalism. The Union Castle Company plied patricians to South Africa. Hugh's brother, Reginald Wyndham, arrived in 1896 for adventure and big game hunting in *ante bellum* Transvaal.[1]

Yet by the century's end, several successive, largely coinciding forces set most patrician families on a steady decline. The agricultural revolution brought enormous financial losses upon large, land-owning, wheat-producing families whose privileged position was increasingly assailed by the democratic revolution and undermined by a society that was more plutocratic and a gentry more plebeian. For a land-based aristocracy this was of extreme concern.[2] From the 1870s, facing fewer opportunities in Britain, younger sons and even heirs left Britain for the colonies: some for a vocation or adventure, others for health reasons. The few with independent means attempted to recreate vanishing lifestyles where agricultural land was cheap, positions more prominent than those to which they could lay claim at home could be enjoyed, and genteel occupations could still be pursued. Here they would, largely unsuccessfully, make a go of it for themselves and in the process build new countries and have a good time.[3]

In many ways, the Hon. Hugh Wyndham (1877–1963), fourth son of the second Lord Leconfield was atypical. He migrated to South Africa, which, unlike British East Africa and Canada, was not conducive to aristocratic settlement. While climate and terrain were good, the natives, black and white, were 'unfriendly'. South Africa, with a large European population, also held the danger of incompatibility in an egalitarian environment and the maintenance of geographical and social distance would be difficult. The Boers of the former republics, in particular, would be mesmerised less easily by British grandiloquence. As a result, the transfer of power to a responsible government could only be staved off until sufficient Britons had settled and a transfer of British values had taken place. After serving the British High Commissioner for South Africa, Viscount Alfred Milner, for two years, Wyndham built a country house at Kromdraai, Standerton district, where he led the life of a landed gentleman. Here he bred and raced horses, wrote extensively and even commanded his own regiment. He built, rebuilt, remodelled and improved – all aristocratic diversions. After an unsuccessful attempt at Standerton in 1907, he won the Turffontein seat as a Unionist in 1910, a seat that he held until beaten by 'a labour man' in 1920. By the mid-1920s, there was no limelight – only 'a little hard grind in the dark for S. Africa' – and with 'no great national British question at stake' South African politics had become 'dull and degrading'.[4] Disillusioned by developments in South Africa, he returned permanently to England in 1930 and in 1952 succeeded, as the fourth Lord Leconfield, to what remained of the family's estates.

The foci of this chapter are threefold. First, it will explain why Wyndham migrated to South Africa in October 1901. Second, it will show why he established an English-style country house on the Transvaal highveld. And, finally, it will evaluate the return, political and otherwise, on this rather expensive investment.

I

As a younger son in a society that was preferentially primogenital Hugh Wyndham was barred from a stable niche within the aristocracy. His childhood passed in the princely surroundings of Petworth but he would have to find his own way in a world, where his success would depend on the exploitation of family ties and on his own exertion.[5] His only status was that of a gentleman, albeit one with connections, and he could rely on little more than an education and a financial leg-up into a career. Throughout the eighteenth, nineteenth and early twentieth centuries the Wyndhams packed most of their younger sons off into the armed forces, with one in each generation sitting in the House of Commons. The armed forces did not have the stigma of trade, were financially more rewarding than the Church, and, as Charles Wyndham's (1796–1866) father pointed out, they also held the prospect of 'tailors & uniforms & all the pomp of war'.[6] Wyndham sons tended to rise to colonel, with half passing through to general's rank.

Wyndham sons were educated at Eton. Hugh went on to New College, Oxford, where he read history and the classics, and made the acquaintance of John Buchan, Robert Brand, Philip Kerr and others, all of whom were later drawn to South Africa by Milner.[7] These men had no fortunes of their own. Many, like Wyndham, were younger sons or the sons of younger sons of gentry, who, needing to make their own way, went out to South Africa to assist in the exciting task of reconstructing the former Boer republics.[8] Eagerly they left the country houses and the palaces of Park Lane for a Johannesburg where everything was 'new, raw, and fortuitous'.[9]

And so, in 1901, at the age of 23 and with the best imperial education behind him, Hugh set out to seek his fortune in South Africa. With the process of aristocratic decline almost imperceptible at Petworth, Hugh, in 1901, had no reason to leave England, other than for health and imperial adventure.[10] For the moment he would assist Milner in establishing British ascendancy in this newest outpost of the empire and share digs with Buchan and others.[11] He suffered from tuberculosis and South Africa's drier climate – according to Buchan 'one of the healthiest places in the world'[12] – would do him good. George Wyndham, Under Secretary for War, former chairman of the South Africa Association (the main jingo pressure group in England), and leader of the Milnerites in the Commons, was Hugh's cousin and eased his appointment to Milner's staff, as indeed he had done for Westminster, his ducal stepson.[13] Hugh was given 'the position of Assistant Private Secretary (unpaid), and plenty of work'.[14] He was offered independence and a free hand to 'devil' for Milner. And, after a year or two, he planned to strike into South African politics on his own account, which, according to George Wyndham, was 'the best way now into Imperial politics at Westminster'.[15] However, judging from his correspondence with his sister, Lady Mary Maxse, return migration was the furthest thing from his mind in 1901 and the years immediately after.

Fired with the confidence of newly acquired knowledge, personal ambition and the romance of empire-building, the Kindergarten provided the Transvaal with a fine administration, eager to restructure the country politically, rebuild it economically and engineer social and cultural change.[16] Although, as Leo Amery pointed out, it was not beyond making mistakes,[17] the Kindergarten managed the repair of the ravages of a total war: whole towns were destroyed, some 30,000 farmhouses burned and more than 250,000 refugees displaced. They had to be rebuilt, repatriated and resettled. The goldmines were returned to production. Progressive agriculture was introduced and the country restocked with horses, cattle and sheep. Government departments were recreated. An agricultural research station was set up at Potchefstroom. Breeding programmes were run in Standerton, a district earmarked as a future centre for the horse industry.[18] Some farmers received grants, others compensation. Land was purchased for new settlers, who, Milner hoped, would form a useful element – in Wyndham's words, 'a new leaven'[19] – in the agricultural population. Milner was resolute that 'the old condition of things should not be reproduced in which the race division coincided almost completely with a division of interests, the whole country population being virtually Boer, while the bulk of the industrial and commercial population was British'.[20] He explained to his Military Secretary, Major John Hanbury-Williams, late in 1900:

> The majority of the agricultural population will always be Dutch. This does not matter, provided there are some strong English districts and that, in most districts, there are a sufficient number of British to hold their own ... The only way to achieve this is by large purchase of land on the part of the Government with a view to reselling ... to suitable settlers ... Men willing to risk some capital of their own should be preferred, and they should be planted on large or middle-sized farms ... Our great hope is in getting a considerable number – several thousands – of settlers of a superior class, and placing them in districts where there is already a British nucleus ... Well-selected settlers will flourish there and raise large families.[21]

Yet much of this failed. The Milner government was autocratic, had only contempt for everything that was not English, and most of all they failed to see that good governance did not necessarily win hearts and minds. The 'new settlers' – the overwhelming majority with no independent finance or prior farming experience – were placed on isolated farms among an irrepressible Boer population. Mutual support was difficult, a British presence could not easily form in small localities and the consolidation of sentiment 'in the general interests of the Empire' was not possible.[22] Sensing a threat to their interests and future political power, Boer magnates – many of whom, like Louis Botha, C.F. Beyers and Coen Brits had considerable political ambition – held onto their enormous estates, closed ranks and denied or attempted to deny British access to the *platteland*. They, like Milner, realised that the Boer system would survive if the new settlers were politically insignificant when the Transvaal obtained self-government.[23]

Wyndham did not remain on Milner's staff for long. Buchan found his work satisfying and exhilarating: Wyndham's position was an unpaid stepping-stone. Buchan could put his heart into his work because, on the whole, he liked the Boers and got on well with them.[24] Wyndham did not share this admiration but instead, like Milner, saw their shiftiness and farming manners which were not those of polite society: he saw the unruly peasant instead of the republican farmer.[25] And then there were the religious differences between the High Churchman and the Calvinist, a problem Buchan did not face. In Buchan's words: 'I think a Scotsman is always more adaptable than an Englishman – he is more of a humanist.'[26] The time had come for Wyndham to strike out into South African politics. Yet, as he confided to his sister, Lady Mary Maxse, he was 'no friend with that strange conglomeration of nations known as the Uitlander population',[27] who, according to the wife of a close friend, were 'ambitious for money, & society, pushing to a degree & knowing where & when to push'.[28] He chose to settle in the country and explained to Lady Maxse in December 1902 that the labour question, which would never be satisfactorily resolved, was 'sure to wreck the political influence of Johannesburg from any Imperial point of view [and] as far as I can see the best thing to do will be to get out of it as soon as possible'.[29]

II

On 17 August 1903, Wyndham acquired Kromdraai, a farm some eight kilometres from Standerton, a town situated on the banks of the Vaal some 156 kilometres by road south-east of Johannesburg. Buchan thought these fertile grassy plains at an elevation of over 1,500 metres 'magnificent breezy upland country'.[30] To John Dove, another of Milner's Kindergartners, they were 'ugly but bracing and cold: the place for sheep and healthy children'.[31] Here Wyndham would seat himself, establish a stud, plant crops, raise cattle and sheep and perhaps a family, and launch himself into Transvaal politics. He and the Marquess of Graham, who in 1903 was also in the market for a farm in the region of £6,000, were attractive propositions: they were of that 'superior class', had independent finance and had been exposed to progressive farming methods in Britain.[32]

At Kromdraai much work was required. There was little water, sufficient only for stock, and wells had to be sunk and tanks made to render practically the whole cultivatable.[33] A house, commensurate with Wyndham's perceived status, had to be built. He and R. Ruxton, his agent, set about the task in earnest. Wyndham was abroad, staying at the Bachelor's Club in London, when he heard of the allotment to him of Kromdraai and building commenced while he was still in England: the house was still uninhabitable when he returned to South Africa at the end of January 1904 to inspect progress.[34]

In March 1904 Wyndham spent a week on the farm, indicating that the house was now habitable, and attended a race meeting at Standerton, which was rained out. The same month he commenced his first harvest and negotiated his first sale of produce: 50 tons of oat hay. Yet he felt cut off from society with access to very little news, 'as a farmhouse on the veldt, is not a place to pick up political information'.[35] He would have to establish Kromdraai as a centre of hospitality, useful for the making of political alliances, and providing him with the right kind of people to talk to and play with. Geoffrey Robinson, another member of Milner's coterie, who spent a weekend with Wyndham at Kromdraai in May 1904, thought the then five-room house a 'small ugly stone affair'.[36] In Wyndham's circle, ownership of a country house was still an essential qualification for membership of the local elite, and to join their number he had to establish at Kromdraai an outward symbol of his dignity and authority. He needed a device for living the life of an English country gentleman, even if in another part of the world, and this he created as the 'small ugly stone affair' grew into a village-like farmstead. Lawrence Stone, in his study of gentry families in three English counties, found that country houses fulfilled several functions. They were administrative centres, showplaces for the display of authority, centres of hospitality, venues for a great deal of outdoor activity, and places where time could be whiled away in pursuit of pleasure.[37] The new Kromdraai performed most of these functions for its mobile and ambitious owner.

The house at Kromdraai was first the centre for the administration of a large farm, which produced a good deal of the food and drink for consumption in the house and, to a lesser extent, Wyndham's Johannesburg residence. And a formidable amount of supplies were needed by an establishment consisting of Wyndham (from February 1908 his wife too) and a constant flow of guests. Visiting members of the Wyndham and Lyttelton families and other visitors brought their own servants, all of who had to be fed and accommodated.[38] This meant that Kromdraai had a business room, from where Wyndham's agent managed the complex, and possibly another, where Wyndham met with his agent. There he monitored breeding programmes and poured over the pedigrees of his horses,[39] arranged race meetings and the improvement of his breeds of cattle and sheep, and the quality of his crops. He may also have had a separate record room where breeding, financial, political and legal archives were housed as well as his growing collection of books and the official archives of the Eastern Rifles.

Wyndham seemingly could not be bothered with the day-to-day running of Kromdraai: the allotment of the farm had been approved by the Central Land Board with exemption from the residential clauses of the Settlers' Ordinance, subject to his placing an approved representative on the farm.[40]

In Ruxton, a Mr Spiller and J. de Mestre he found competent and honest agents: Spiller perhaps too efficient. Their thoroughness enabled Wyndham to pursue interests that drew him away, sometimes at great distance, from Kromdraai: to Johannesburg for politicking, to Durban for the races, for extended social flits across the Transvaal or 'stamping the country a good deal' in anticipation of the 1907 election.[41] Poorer farmers lived a vastly different life. The Adelaide-born poet and farmer, Leonard Flemming, who took up his 'thousand acres of treeless, birdless veld' in the Orange River Colony in 1903, 'had no manager, no assistant, no one here to advise me or to relieve me'.[42]

The establishment at Kromdraai was also the showplace for the display of Wyndham's social power. The recreation of Kromdraai, which had undoubtedly suffered during the war, was profound. It was built in several stages and exorbitantly, at a cost of some £43,000, 'on bare veldt', and inhabited in a manner that would impress visitors.[43] The real extravagance took place here and not in his town house in Parktown. Without a *point d'appui* in Johannesburg, Kromdraai provided the only means of exercising authority: it was an essential element of his existence and a prime justification for his claim to deference. And, at a macro level, imperial security, hollow at the best of times, depended to a large extent upon men like Wyndham, whose lifestyles mesmerised indigenous collaborators with a display of British 'energy, success, and apparent omniscience' and reinforced the thin red line.[44]

Wyndham needed a home of ample size and imposing appearance, and was probably influenced by Milner, who believing that good homes and impressive edifices foster a love of country, encouraged good architecture.[45] The much-expanded house, probably designed by Sir Herbert Baker, was placed prominently and the linked public rooms offered opportunities for formal entertainment on a generous scale, a platform for ceremonial hospitality and deference and the clinching of deals.[46] The dining room catered for 40 dinner guests and the public rooms opened onto a broad veranda with sweeping views over the orchards and gardens, planted before the house was even habitable.[47] Roads were diverted to open up the prospect and when infuriated neighbours objected Wyndham simply remarked that 'the whole thing [would] blow over'.[48]

He was playing the lord of the manor. His dealings were often high-handed and he did not bother to nurture friendship with people from 'the backveldt', whom he believed should be excluded from the suffrage: *bywoners* and carpetbaggers were 'uninteresting', 'ignorant' and 'dependant'. For them – 'those looking in' – the house offered an imposing appearance, with architectural features that inspired the appropriate sense of awe. Wyndham had an interest to preserve in the country. He had future voters to impress, neighbours to treat and labour to woo, inducements to display his riches to the lower classes. Wyndham was (at this time) no absentee landlord and, in July 1905, thought he could secure the farming vote in a future election 'mainly because I live on my farm, & have spent money in the district'.[49] Kromdraai was built with a view to success in public life. Political ambition meant the exercise of patronage and Kromdraai was the centre from which to direct it. Wyndham is a wonderful lens through which to view class relations in turn-of-the-century Transvaal.

His paternalism emanated from the main residence, which dominated the collection of stables, service buildings and servants' quarters. This complex – or 'Wyndhamsdorp' as he referred to it in several letters to his mother – represented a sort of village, all dominated by the great house.[50] The service buildings included an electric plant – installed in July 1905, the workings of which 'much engrossed' him[51] – stables, laundry, dairy, barn and stores to supply the household and provide transport, repairs, food and drink. These ancillary buildings took up a significant amount of the total cost of house building and the maintenance of the establishment. In May 1904, he wrote to his mother that he was 'very busy here just now, as [he was] now taking steps to get [his] stables & buildings up, & [was] employed in marking out the ground'.[52] The pursuit of pleasure, giving of hospitality and proclamation of importance did not come cheaply.

Wyndham also had to court labour, which in 1904 was scarce, and here, due to his command over land, he had fewer difficulties: 'I have comparatively no difficulty in getting labourers on the farm, though I have to pay them what I know to be an excessive wage.'[53] Away from the house the servants had their quarters. In May 1904, he announced that he had just 'obtained 2 native families to come & squat on the farm & work' for him. Their first act was to erect dwellings: 'one out of turf sods with a rush roof, which looks very appropriate – the other family, however, very proudly brought along with them some corrugated iron, which I fear will result in a fearful eye sore being erected.'[54] Africans did not enter Wyndham's daily life except as servants or labourers. They were mostly perceived in their occupational role, a one-dimensional perception that denied their human feelings and needs and their having thoughts and opinions.[55]

Wyndham was not dependent financially upon the revenue of the farm: he received a monthly income from England and on this he largely relied. His wealth allowed him to sell his first crop of oat hay at three pennies below market price and, in 1914, when his flow of money to South Africa was threatened by war, his wife Maud dreaded the ensuing frugality: there would be fewer luxuries, no new outfits.[56] This meant that there was no close relationship between the size of the house and the farm administered from it, as he indicated in his evidence before the Transvaal Supreme Court in 1907. He built to outdo his neighbours and thereby earn the prestige that could be transplanted into power. As in any English county, the Standerton country elite had its internal struggle for pre-eminence. A little way off, General Louis Botha had his fine estate of Rusthof, from where he spent the immediate post-war years re-establishing his personal finances and assisting poverty-stricken Boers, with party politics as the longer-term object.[57] A great rivalry, culminating in February 1907 in the Transvaal election and a defamation suit, ensued between Wyndham and Botha and his propagandists. From the lofty heights of his table, Wyndham misread the Transvaal political environment entirely. Blinded by class he was to do this again and again.[58]

Kromdraai's third function was to act as a centre of hospitality: 'in part a function of sociability, in part a method of displaying generosity and authority, and in part a way to make useful political and matrimonial contacts'.[59] Hospitality was a necessary, albeit expensive, way of enhancing prestige in the neighbourhood and of providing themselves with company and playmates.[60] Since Transvaal roads were bad – muddy and rutted – and visitors, without motorised transport, could only travel at the speed of a horse-drawn carriage, guests from almost any distance often had to be put up for the night.[61] Plenty of spare bedrooms were therefore provided as well as rooms for the servants of the visitors, and special space and kitchen staff to feed them all. Some guests even brought pet animals.[62] While very expensive, this did help to break the tedium of country life and, in any case, generous hospitality was a hallmark of a gentleman. Their letters show, quite clearly, that the Wyndhams liked to entertain 'interesting' people, mostly the working of business and political connections, though often reinforced through Kindergarten and family relations.

From the government experimental farm at Potchefstroom Wyndham acquired his fruit and other trees. His contacts in the Transvaal Agriculture Department, which included its director, F.B. Smith, arranged the sale to him of 'a certain number of the best' of the government cattle on the Crocodile River, at the set price of £15 per animal.[63] However, under Lord Selborne, Milner's successor as High Commissioner, the Transvaal government became less co-operative. Selborne, 'accused in some quarters of being a Pro-Boer',[64] refused to join Wyndham's Australian sheep importing syndicate. Wyndham's stipulation that the government only sell its merinos 'to approved and progressive [i.e. British] farmers' had no appeal, although Selborne did allow a reduction of half the railway rates from the coast to the Transvaal and felt obliged to attend the shearing exhibition at Kromdraai.[65]

After 25 February 1908, when Wyndham married Maud Lyttelton, fresh connections were made, old ties reinforced and the flow of visitors to

Kromdraai increased. The Lytteltons were closely connected to some of the most prominent families in England – the Cavendishes, the Howards and the Cecils – and were themselves renowned as statesmen, soldiers, bishops and cricketers. Maud's brother, Jack Lyttelton, was not only Selborne's private secretary but also the son-in-law of Charles Leonard, chairman of the Progressive Association. Her uncles included General Sir Neville Lyttelton (General-Officer-Commanding South African Military Command, 1902–04) and Alfred Lyttelton (Colonial Secretary, 1903–05). George Wyndham (Under Secretary for War, 1900–02, and later Chief Secretary for Ireland, 1902–05), Neville Talbot (Bishop of Pretoria), Sir Arthur Lawley (lieutenant governor of the Transvaal, 1902–05), and Herbert Gladstone (South Africa's first governor general, 1910–14) were their cousins. Kindergarteners John Buchan, Lionel Hichens and Geoffrey Robinson all later married cousins. The marriage also cemented ties with the Tennants, whose brother-in-law, Herbert Asquith, became British prime minister in the year of the Wyndham marriage. Undoubtedly, the Hugh Wyndhams and their relatives formed an 'Imperial connection' in South Africa.[66]

Without a professional occupation, Wyndham had a great deal of time on his hands. There were, of course, administrative responsibilities at Kromdraai, the local party circuit (less extensive than in England), the races and evening cards: the Drummond Chaplins, Dr L.S. Jameson and other Unionists providing one or more foursomes after dinner get-togethers.[67] There was also the care of his tenants, the distribution of charity in the district – probably never a significant sum in comparison with his overall income and expenditure – and his duties as a justice of the peace and member of the St George's Society and the Standerton Liquor Licensing Court.[68]

At Kromdraai Wyndham also had his horses. His first recorded social activity in Standerton was attendance at a race meeting in March 1904. He enjoyed the pleasures of field sports and the stud at Kromdraai and the improvement of his breeds of cattle and sheep, and the quality of his crops undoubtedly took much of his time. Judging from his correspondence with his mother, he bought several mares, mostly from Natal, between 1904 and 1908. He made a scientific study of their pedigrees and monitored the breeding programmes closely, and this led to the publication in 1924 of his early history of the thoroughbred horse in South Africa.[69] Seemingly prompted by his mother, he also experimented with horticulture and set out avenues of trees and planted orchards: in June 1906 he planted 470 fruit trees and a month later 'got in' some oaks, walnuts and mulberries. During her visits, his mother, an avid gardener, set up a garden of bushy-green privets.[70]

When the tedium of Kromdraai and the Standerton circuit became too
much for him, Wyndham escaped to friends in Johannesburg or to Durban
for the races. Racecourse construction was invariably a priority in new
colonies: the first meeting at Turffontein was held in December 1889, and
after the Anglo-Boer War race meetings re-opened in 1903. Although
drawing large crowds from all classes of society, the races provided an
opportunity to rub shoulders with equals in the privacy of their boxes.
Moreover, the promotion of British sport and the creation of similar taste in
amusement, according to Milner's predecessor as High Commissioner, Sir
Hercules Robinson, would lead to 'common sympathy in more important
matters'.[71] Selborne, unlike Milner, attended the races regularly and in state,
which Wyndham thought 'a very good thing'.[72] Wyndham had his first
victory on the turf in September 1905, which although 'a fluke ... was very
satisfactory'.[73] This was the British world as outdoor relief.

Wyndham's military career also took him away from Kromdraai, for
short but frequent periods. Having served with the Rand Rifles from 1901,
he was appointed in September 1905 to the command of the Eastern Rifles,
which in 1906 had a strength of 720, 33 of whom took part that year in the
suppression of the Bambata uprising.[74] War was a source of glory and
another justification of the special status of the officer-gentleman, for whom
command was both recreation and duty: 'It is really very good fun training
the Boer in the methods of British Cavalry. They are immensely keen but
have not the smallest idea as to what the object of it all is. Their turn out is
also sometimes very remarkable. Generally spurs upside down & so forth.'[75]
There were volunteer encampments and bivouacs, church parades and
military balls.[76] Many of these events were held at Kromdraai, the house
serving as regimental headquarters and ad hoc officers' mess. In May 1906,
Wyndham hosted a mock battle, followed by a gymkhana, which registered
no fewer than 39 competitors for tent pegging. Forty invited guests – and
ten gatecrashers – sat for lunch on the second day, many of whom entered
the 'smoking concert in the evening' and all 'went to bed much
exhausted'.[77]

The Eastern Rifles was amalgamated with the Western Rifles in 1907 to
form the Southern Mounted Rifles, with Wyndham as commander. Yet,
although deemed 89.91 per cent efficient in 1909, this was no easy
command. The Eastern Rifles comprised six mounted squadrons and three
infantry companies and, although the headquarters was at Standerton, the
recruitment area stretched across the Eastern Transvaal, including the towns
and districts of Barberton, Heidelberg, Standerton, Wakkerstroom, Piet
Retief, Ermelo, Carolina and Swaziland. This made regimental
concentrations difficult and, as a result, turnout was often not the best and
Wyndham was frequently on the road.[78] Service, however, implied a

willingness to accept pain and privation, particularly by the common soldier who it was assumed would serve under the command of their social superiors. Burghers, many of them republicans blooded during the South African War, accepted the command of a relatively inexperienced 28-year-old from England with difficulty. Some, after a series of not so subtle acts of insubordination, had to be booted out.[79] This sort of thing eroded the entertainment value: 'This volunteer business is really becoming no joke. I am up to the chin in rows.'[80]

The enrolment books show that the regiment in 1911 was overwhelmingly 'British': some 531 men. A further ten were 'English', three 'Irish', one 'Scotch', and one 'Colonial New Zealand'. There were 69 'Dutch' and five 'British Dutch', categories replaced from 1908 by 'Africander' of whom there were 20. There were a further 67 'British Subjects', three 'South Africans' and five 'Colonials', one of whom had served in the Boer forces. Farmers were by far a majority: 434 as opposed to 16 clerks in next position. And of the four attorneys, Daniel Oosthuizen from Piet Retief described himself as 'British' and Arnt Leonard Reitz, the son of the former president of the Orange Free State, F.W. Reitz, gave himself as a 'British attorney'.[81] Such were the complexities of British identity.

The Southern Mounted Rifles and other regiments of the Transvaal Volunteers cemented together the small, often isolated pockets of British settlers and formed a British presence in remote localities: in the Bethal troop 'all except four [were] Boers'.[82] The Piet Retief troop was 'very strong – numbering 150 – nearly all Boers – but all very keen & really very efficient'.[83] Many Afrikaners in exposed, isolated areas, particularly on the always-insecure borders with Swaziland and Zululand, rushed to the colours for reasons of personal security rather than any feeling of Britishness. Yet military training and socialisation fostered individual Boer–British relations and most probably consolidated at least some sentiment 'in the general interests of the Empire'.[84]

III

Milner and his Kindergarten, while visionaries, failed to grasp the realities of colonial Transvaal. They moved in relatively closed circles: working, living and playing in the cocoons of Government House and private residences like Kromdraai. Expatriates, according to Hyam, 'behaved more swaggeringly, more grandly and unfeelingly than they would or could have done in Britain ... and this gave a touch of unreality and theatricality to all their lives'.[85] Social conventions imported from Britain encouraged snobbery, pretentiousness and self-conscious class distinctions, none of which endeared Wyndham and his set to the broad Transvaal electorate, which, as John Darwin has noted, had 'generally little sympathy for what they regarded as an over-rigid class system at home'.[86]

Wyndham knew the Transvaal would receive responsible government. This was promised in the peace treaty and first demanded by the returned *uitlanders* – 'unattractive as a class' – who considered themselves the real victors and entitled to the spoils of the war and government office.[87] They thought the Milner administration expensive, wasteful and aloof and over-regulating; according to one 'neglected colonial' they were brusque novices, 'young men imported from England'.[88] Their lobbying led to the draft constitution designed by Alfred Lyttelton, as Colonial Secretary, to give representation but with executive power remaining in the hands of British officials.[89]

The Boer leadership, revitalised and headed by Louis Botha, hastened the tempo. Organised at first under the cover of agricultural societies, a unified Afrikaner party, chaired by Botha, appeared under the name *Het Volk* in January 1905. Consolidation centred on the mobilisation of history and the use of the British settlers as the main punchbag.[90] *Het Volk* had an elaborate organisation, comprising a network of committees. This was the old commando system with the military component ostensibly removed: ward committees elected by the people; district committees elected by the ward committees; and all falling under an all-powerful head committee.[91] The South African War failed to disrupt the continuity of Boer politics and in many instances the men who saw to the election of Paul Kruger in 1892 undertook the same task for Botha 15 years later.[92] Yet one former *uitlander* agitator, Charles Leonard, who referred in February 1905 to *Het Volk*'s opposition as 'the fire of burning scorn', was still confident that 'we are strong and skilful and well-captained enough to carry it to the finish without their aid'.[93] This was not to be. Selborne – who 'concedes too much to the Boers' – succeeded Milner in April 1905.[94] The British Conservatives suffered a major electoral defeat early in 1906 and the Liberals promised immediate responsible government, which, according to Wyndham, 'would make no difference to the inimitable attitude of the Boers, & would enormously weaken the Imperial position'.[95] There were insufficient British settlers, scattered across the Transvaal and divided between four political parties.

The Progressive Association, virtually the political embodiment of Milner and the Chamber of Mines, was the chief of these. It was unionist, pro-British, a proponent of provisional self-rule, and supporting the principle of 'one vote, one value'. Manhood suffrage would admit *bywoners* who, according to Wyndham, were 'poor & of no sort of influence or independence [and] will be led like sheep'.[96] He, like many of his class, thought that national affairs were best left in the hands of 'great families' – like the Cavendishes, Cecils and Wyndhams – many of whom believed in parliamentary government but one representing landed (and later moneyed) interests. To Lord Salisbury, democracy was a threat to individual liberty – the 'right of the majority to impose its will on others ... for the majority represented tyranny rendered confident by superior numbers'.[97] To such patricians, political equality was meaningless, short of allowing an inevitably ignorant majority the right to elect those few, who ought to have made politics their profession.[98] Within British ranks, the Responsible Government Association, formed by self-made men of the middling sort who branded the Progressives as 'no more than a capitalist cabal', provided their greatest competition.[99]

Wyndham first proposed to stand as an independent and so attract Boer votes without alienating the Progressives – tactics that Buchan thought too Machiavellian[100] – but soon joined the Progressives and fought the Standerton seat on a platform 'calculated to bring about the ultimate federation of South Africa under the British flag'.[101] He took up the cudgels on behalf of the British settlers (whom he thought generally apathetic), lobbied the Ridgeway Commission, and eventually got a clause inserted into the constitution 'protecting the settlers against the possibility of a *Het Volk* government boycotting them'.[102] Wyndham also scurried to draw the British settlers into a farmers association, which was formed at a meeting held in Pretoria in July 1906.[103] Rushing from settler meetings in Klerksdorp and Nylstroom to volunteer manoeuvres at Bronkhorstspruit, he was very busy during the last months of 1906 and for the first time he missed the mail: an abnormal *caesura* in his dutiful correspondence with his mother.

In September he lamented that the Progressive Association was 'in rather a poor way'. This did not surprise him. It was a mistake running the party purely on the finances of the big houses and he feared that the nearer the elections came the less influence actual party politics would have: 'people will go a great deal more for individuals, especially as there is nothing either for a candidate or a party to indulge in except vague generalities'. There were still no real questions before the country and 'nobody seems in a hurry to have them'.[104] Frans Engelenburg, editor of *De Volkstem* and Botha's chief advocate, too believed there was '*een grote gelykluidendheid*' (a large consonance) between the party manifestos.[105]

Wyndham's troubles with the volunteers increased as the election approached. In Vereeniging 'resignations have been flying about like locusts';[106] while in Standerton, the headquarters of his regiment, 'very few turned up' for a bivouac.[107] The boundary commission in the meantime decided that Standerton return two members to the Legislative Assembly: one for the town and the Klipriver area, and another for the remainder of the district. And as Wyndham was sure to note, the first was the only ward where an Englishman 'will have a chance of getting in'. Wyndham hoped the British vote would not be divided as 'the Boer ... is rather a broken reed to rely on'.[108] He lay low and awaited the publication of the constitution and delineation of the constituencies. This was a 'hopeless period of delay & inaction', but he did not want to suffer burn out before the election and so refused to get 'onto his legs' until the Constitution was published and 'everything settled'. He held his shearing exhibition at Kromdraai on 21 November with some of the merinos imported from Australia. He received several hundred visitors and made his 'first attempt at a short oration in Dutch': 'a grand opportunity to do a little quiet politics'.[109]

The second week of December brought a mixed bag of news. Wyndham's settler clause was inserted into the Constitution but the imperial board would last only five years and he worried that it 'may quite easily be washed out by an unsympathetic Governor & a Boer Ministry'. No provision was made for further land settlement.[110] He spent Christmas with the Drummond Chaplins and found that he had to instil an optimistic view into his hostess, who was 'very gloomy' and feared that Britain would 'have to fight the war over again in 10 years time or else retire from the country'.[111] While Wyndham was more optimistic he did not think the progressives would be able 'to cover the retreat of the Home Government'.[112] He predicted electoral defeat as well as the ruin of Selborne and the leader of the National Party, Sir Richard Solomon, which were no small solaces.

The second week of December 1906 also saw Louis Botha confirmed as his opponent in Standerton.[113] The seat was particularly hard-fought: he was heckled and in late January 1907 was convinced he would be beaten but not without putting up 'a very good fight'.[114] Coen Brits, 'who is a mere bully, & who is also the local Het Volk magnate', took pleasure in disrupting Wyndham's meetings in the eastern end of the constituency.[115] No less than 80 per cent of the Standerton electorate turned out to vote: the highest for any constituency in the election and, with 74 per cent of votes cast, Botha won Standerton convincingly.[116] On 25 February 1907 Hugh wrote to his mother: 'As you know the election here ended disastrously for me. I suppose it was really only to be expected, as of course the Dutch vote, in spite of all promises, went very nearly solidly against me, & they polled to a man, whereas, naturally, there was a considerable apathy amongst some of the British.'[117]

Wyndham's name was also still closely associated with Milner and as a result he, like other progressives, was politically compromised. His lifestyle, furthermore, was better suited to the nineteenth century, when voters were hustled and could be impressed by the exercise of patronage. In 1907, the 'backvelder', whom Wyndham did not bother to nurture, had little appreciation for airs and graces.[118] Instead of inspiring the appropriate sense of awe he and Kromdraai became convenient punchbags. While all sides whipped up 'racial' emotion and character assassination was frequent, Botha's propagandists, Engelenburg and Gustav Preller, both seasoned electioneers, found his opponent at Standerton an easy target. They canvassed the opinion that Kromdraai was given to Wyndham while on Lord Milner's staff – 'that it was a disgraceful government job'.[119] On 6 February a special *Volkstem* billboard confronted Standertonians: 'How the Hon. WYNDHAM BECAME LANDOWNER. BY CIRCUMVENTION OF THE LAW!' Free copies of the day's paper, containing a leading article on 'The Wyndham Scandal', were dumped all over the district.[120] Although Wyndham considered this a good sign – the Botha camp were 'becoming seriously alarmed' – it was libellous and if 'repeated often enough some people are bound to end by believing there is something in it'. He took legal advice and his attorneys were for action. After all, 'the only way to affect these people in any way is to make them pay damages & costs, & I am not going to be satisfied with a mere apology and withdrawal if there is a good chance of retaliating on them'.[121] He was learning that his class could, at times, be a hindrance.[122]

A summons was served upon Engelenburg, as editor of *De Volkstem* and a director of Wallach's Printing and Publishing Company: Wyndham filed for £10,000 in damages plus costs. Although he won his case before Chief Justice Rose Innes, nothing of it is mentioned in Engelenburg's biography of Botha. The archival residue of *De Volkstem* is also silent on the matter.[123] The political situation gave him less satisfaction. As he predicted, *Het Volk* obtained an absolute majority over all other parties in the new Transvaal legislative assembly. This was followed in November 1907 by an even larger setback in the Orange River Colony, and in the Cape Colony, Jameson's Progressive government fell within three months and John X. Merriman, a sworn foe of Milnerism, replaced him. A total political metamorphosis in British South Africa occurred between 1907 and 1908.

IV

The electoral defeats and, more importantly, the apparent weakness and failure of the British government, had an enormous effect on the position of the British population in South Africa. The atmosphere had become 'very uncongenial': the resident magistrate at Wolmaransstad wished 'to leave this awful service [and] leave this county'.[124] The Kindergarten was affected directly and several were summarily dismissed: Dougal Malcolm, Selborne's private secretary, was in 1909 the only member of the Kindergarten still in government employ. Others had drifted back to

England. John Dove moved to Pretoria, where as chairman of the Transvaal Land Settlement Board he took charge of various schemes promoted by Hugh Wyndham, other Progressives and their friends in England to increase the flow of British settlers into rural South Africa and protect them from the Boer governments. Milner suggested that his disciples appraise the situation realistically and look after their own careers. They had known of his pessimism for some time. Yet by late 1907 at least some of them had accepted a far more optimistic view and a scheme was devised which they hoped might even bring their mentor's dream of a unified South Africa under a British flag to fruition.[125]

Wyndham stayed on in South Africa. He returned to his horses and achieved eminence as a progressive farmer and breeder of thoroughbred stock and took a leading part in public and sporting affairs, both in Standerton and in Johannesburg. He won the Turffontein seat as a Unionist in 1910, which brought an end to many of his wonderful, aristocratic pastimes. Advocating stronger ties with Britain, he called for the integration of imperial and dominion defence and the design of a Union Defence Force for South Africa along British lines.[126] He was for ten years (1910–20) shadow defence minister and, as a member of the parliamentary select committee on defence, an architect of the South Africa Defence Act (1912).

During the First World War he served as Chief Intelligence Officer for the Union, as official historian of the German South West Africa campaign, and from 1917 to 1921 on the Defence Council, where he voiced ideas on land, naval and air power. A prolific writer and astute thinker, Wyndham contributed to the shaping of early twentieth-century South Africa and, more particularly, of the Union Defence Force. His lifestyle, already cramped by his parliamentary duties – 'We lead a very limited life here between the hotel & the house' he complained to his mother in March 1914[127] – was severely restrained by the First World War, which brought his first real employment. He lived in khaki and toiled – again unpaid – 'in that horrid hole of a Pretoria': Maud thought it 'funny how work suit[ed] him'.[128]

Hugh Wyndham's unsuccessful bid to establish an English country seat on the South African veldt epitomised the overall failure of Milner's 'anglicisation' policy that had been a key component of his reconstruction programme. The inability of Milner's administration to introduce large numbers of British immigrants to leaven the Afrikaner lump in the *platteland* was mirrored by Wyndham's chronic incapacity to read correctly the significant changes that were occurring on the local political landscape in the south-eastern Transvaal. Although not one to admit defeat, privately Wyndham's decision to withdraw from rural politics must have rankled. Correspondingly, as part of the gradual reduction of the British garrison in South Africa, Standerton was evacuated as a military base in February 1909, which coincided with the shift of Wyndham's political interest toward the Unionist strong hold of Johannesburg, where he found electoral sanctuary in 1910. Like Milner, Wyndham's dreams of transplanting a British world into rural South Africa had foundered on the rocks of a resurgent Afrikaner political identity.

NOTES

My thanks to Lord Egremont & Leconfield for granting access to the Petworth House Archives; to Mrs Alison McCann for facilitating this access; and to Bill Nasson, Ross Anderson, Deon Visser and Iain Smith. Thanks also to the Research Development Division of the University of Stellenbosch which provided a grant in aid of research.

1. D. Cannadine, *The Decline and Fall of the British Aristocracy* (London, 1996), 370–73, 382–83; Hannah Rosebery to Constance Leconfield, 25 July 1880 and 18 Aug. 1880, Petworth House Archive [hereafter PHA], 9680, West Sussex Record Office, Chichester [hereafter WSRO]; Coloniale Secretaris Kaapstad Verzoekt dat permit verleend worde aan zekeren Heer Wyndham om zijne revolvers binnen dezen staat mede te bregen, 1896, CR 6353/96, archives of the Commandant General, Transvaal Archive Depot [hereafter TAD], South African National Archives [hereafter SANA], Pretoria. See also R. Hyam, *Britain's Imperial Century, 1815–1914* (Basingstoke, 1993), ch.5; *idem, Empire and Sexuality: The British Experience* (Manchester, 1991), ch.4.
2. In 1904, Hugh Wyndham was 'very distressed' about the Crewe finances and considered the purchase by Lord Crewe of a London house just before as 'extraordinary'. His cousin, Lady Margaret Primrose, married the Marquess of Crewe, as his second wife in 1899. Hugh Wyndham to Constance Leconfield, 7 May 1904, PHA, WSRO; Marquis de Ruvigny, *The Titled Nobility of Europe* (London, 1914, reprinted 1980), 542.
3. Cannadine, *British Aristocracy*, 429.
4. Sir Charles Crewe to Sir Lewis Michell, 11 Dec. 1925, Sir Lewis Michell collection, vol.1, South African National Archives, Cape Town [hereafter KAB].
5. L. Stone and J.C. Fawtier Stone, *An Open Elite? England, 1540–1880* (Oxford, 1986), 148. For a brief, longitudinal study of the Wyndham family, see Ian van der Waag, 'Hugh Archibald Wyndham (1877–1963): His Ancestry and Family Connections', *Historia*, 47 (2002), 315–44.
6. Earl of Egremont to Colonel Charles Wyndham, undated (*c*.1828), Wyndham MSS, Lilly Library, University of Indiana, Bloomington.
7. Eton School reports for Hugh and Edward Wyndham, 1895–1901, PHA 1700 and 1701, WSRO. On the Kindergarten, W. Nimocks, *Milner's Young Men: the 'Kindergarten' in Edwardian Imperial Affairs* (Durham, NC, 1968).
8. Cannadine, *British Aristocracy*, 426.
9. J.A. Smith, *John Buchan: A Biography* (London, 1965), 113.
10. P. Blackwell, '"An Undoubted Jewel": A Case Study of Five Sussex Country Houses, 1880–1914', *Southern History*, 3 (1981), 183–200. See also Humphrey Wyndham to Mary Maxse, 7 Aug. 1916; Lord Leconfield to Mary Maxse, 11 Sept. 1914; Edward Wyndham to Mary Maxse, 14 Nov. 1915, Maxse papers 455, WSRO.
11. Milner to Joseph Chamberlain, 22 Sept. 1902, archives of the Private Secretary to the Governor [hereafter GOV] 543, PS 167, 'Housing of Government Officials', TAD, SANA; Nimocks, *Milner's Young Men*, 27 and 46; Smith, *Buchan*, 107.
12. Smith, *Buchan*, 107.
13. George Wyndham to Milner, 9 Aug. 1898, Viscount Alfred Milner papers, MSS Eng. Hist. 205, ff.245–48, Bodleian Library, Oxford; George Wyndham to Milner, 5 Oct. 1898, ibid., ff.290–91; George Wyndham to Hugh Wyndham, 17 June 1901, PHA, WSRO.

14. Milner to Hugh Wyndham, 1 Aug. 1901, PHA, WSRO.
15. George Wyndham to Hugh Wyndham, 17 June 1901; Milner to Hugh Wyndham, 1 Aug. 1901, PHA, WSRO.
16. Welby to Curtis, 11 Sept. 1900; Hichens to Curtis, 27 Nov. 1900, Lionel Curtis papers, MSS Curtis 1, Bodleian.
17. Smith, *Buchan*, 133.
18. *British Parliamentary Papers* [hereafter *BPP*], Cd.1463, *Further Correspondence relating to Affairs in South Africa* (1903), Director of Agriculture, Transvaal, to Assistant Private Secretary to Governor, Transvaal, 30 Oct. 1902.
19. Lord Leconfield, 'The Formation of the Union, 1901–1910', in E.A. Walker (ed.), *The Cambridge History of the British Empire*, vol.8 *South Africa, Rhodesia and the High Commission Territories*, 2nd edn. (Cambridge, 1963), 644.
20. *BPP*, Cd.1163, *Further Correspondence relating to Affairs in South Africa* (1902), Milner to Chamberlain, 30 Dec. 1901.
21. C. Headlam (ed.), *Milner Papers*, vol.2 *South Africa 1899–1905* (London, 1933), 242–43 (Milner's emphasis).
22. *BPP*, Cd.1163, *Further Correspondence* (1902), Milner to Chamberlain, 25 Jan. 1902.
23. Ibid., 30 Dec.1901; S. Trapido, 'Landlord and Tenant in a Colonial Economy: The Transvaal 1880–1910', *Journal of Southern African Studies*, 5 (1978), 27.
24. Smith, *Buchan*, 122.
25. See the sentiments in Hugh Wyndham to Constance Leconfield, 29 July 1905 and 4 Aug. 1905, PHA, WSRO. Also see R.H. Brand (ed.), *The Letters of John Dove* (London, 1938), 19 and 133.
26. As quoted by Smith, *Buchan*, 125–26.
27. Hugh Wyndham to Lady Mary Maxse, 21 June 1902, Maxse papers 50, WSRO.
28. Diary of Lady Marguerite Chaplin, 27 Oct. 1896, Drummond Chaplin papers, BC 831, University of Cape Town Archive and Library [hereafter UCTAL]. Lady Chaplin was referring to the Goldmann brothers, Richard and Charles, who were mine directors and financiers. Charles van Onselen, *Studies in the Social and Economic History of the Witwatersrand 1886–1914*, vol.1 *New Babylon* (Johannesburg, 1982), 171; *Dictionary of South African Biography*, vol.4 (Pretoria, 1981), 187–88.
29. Hugh Wyndham to Lady Maxse, 15 Dec. 1902, Maxse papers 50, WSRO.
30. Plaintiff's Declaration, 13 March 1907, archives of the Supreme Court of the ZAR and the Supreme Court of the Transvaal Colony [hereafter ZTPD] 5/634, f.73/1907, TAD, SANA; Smith, *Buchan*, 119–20.
31. Brand (ed.), *Letters of John Dove*, 3.
32. W.R. Ball, Land and Estate Agent, to Michell, 8 Jan.1903, Michell papers, vol.1A, KAB, SANA. See Wyndham's evidence in his claim for damages against Wallach's Printing and Publishing Company, ZTPD 5/634, f.73/1907, TAD, SANA.
33. H.C. Lister, Recorder of Crown Lands, to Hugh Wyndham, 10 July 1903, ZTPD 5/634, f.73/1907, TAD, SANA; Wyndham to Constance Leconfield, 30 July 1906, PHA, WSRO.
34. Lister to Wyndham, 31 Aug. 1903; hand-written note by Wyndham, 30 Sept. 1903, ZTPD 5/634, f.73/1907, TAD, SANA.
35. Wyndham to Constance Leconfield, 14 March 1904, PHA, WSRO.
36. Diary of Geoffrey Dawson, 21 May 1904, MSS Dawson 10, Bodleian.
37. As quoted by Stone and Fawtier Stone, *An Open Elite?*, 199. Also see ch.9.
38. Wyndham to Constance Leconfield, 30 Sept. 1905, PHA, WSRO.
39. F.B. Smith to Wyndham, 8 May 1906, and Wyndham's reply, 11 May 1906, archives of the Transvaal Agriculture Department [hereafter TLD] 574, G 1517/06, TAD, SANA.
40. Lister to Wyndham, 31 July 1903; and extract from the Executive's Council Resolution no.690 of 17 Aug. 1903 attached to Lister to Wyndham, 31 Aug. 1903, ZTPD 5/634, f.73/1907, TAD, SANA. Most aristocrats found their business affairs irksome and fatiguing. See also Cannadine, *British Aristocracy*, 490, and *passim*. Craig Sellar battled with the household 'troubles' when they shared accommodation in Johannesburg. Wyndham to Lady Maxse, 15 Nov. 1901, Maxse papers 50, WSRO.
41. Wyndham to Constance Leconfield, 8 Sept. 1905 and 21 July 1906, PHA, WSRO.

42. L. Flemming, *The Call of the Veld* (Bloemfontein, 1927), 167.
43. See Wyndham's evidence in his case against Wallach's printing company, ZTPD 5/634, f.73/1907, TAD, SANA; Wyndham to Constance Leconfield, 31 March and 9 June 1906, PHA, WSRO.
44. B. Vandervort, *Wars of Imperial Conquest in Africa* (London, 1998), 37–40; Hyam, *Britain's Imperial Century*, 281–82.
45. Headlam (ed.), *Milner Papers*, vol.2, 368.
46. Stone and Fawtier Stone, *An Open Elite?*, 204–06.
47. Wyndham to Constance Leconfield, 31 Jan. 1904 and 25 May 1905, PHA, WSRO.
48. Ibid., 31 Jan. 1904 and 4 Aug. 1905, PHA, WSRO.
49. Ibid., 16 July 1905, PHA, WSRO.
50. Ibid., 30 Sept. 1905, PHA, WSRO. See also Trapido, 'Landlord and Tenant', 26–57, for a good introduction to rural class relations in colonial Transvaal.
51. Wyndham to Constance Leconfield, 16 July 1905 and 29 July 1905, PHA, WSRO.
52. Ibid., 7 May 1904, PHA, WSRO.
53. Ibid., 25 March 1904, PHA, WSRO. See also T. Keegan, 'The Sharecropping Economy, African Class Formation and the Natives' Land Act of 1913 in the Highveld Maize Belt', in S. Marks and R. Rathbone (eds.), *Industrialisation and Social Change in South Africa: African Class Formation, Culture, and Consciousness, 1870–1930* (London, 1982), 195–211.
54. Wyndham to Constance Leconfield, 19 May 1904, PHA, WSRO.
55. S. Dagut, 'Paternalism and Social Distance: British Settlers' Racial Attitudes, 1850s–1890s', *South African Historical Journal*, 37 (1997), 4–8; Trapido, 'Landlord and Tenant', 28.
56. Wyndham to Constance Leconfield, 14 March 1904, 7 May 1904, 4 and 11 Aug. 1914, PHA, WSRO.
57. Daniel Grove to Louis Botha, 23 Aug. 1903, Dr Gustav S. Preller collection, A787, vol.89, TAD, SANA.
58. Compare, for example, two letters by Wyndham to Constance Leconfield, 7 July 1905 and 25 Feb. 1907, PHA, WSRO.
59. Stone and Fawtier Stone, *An Open Elite?*, 211.
60. R. Porter, 'Material Pleasures in the Consumer Society', in R. Porter and M.M. Roberts (eds.), *Pleasure in the Eighteenth Century* (Basingstoke, 1996), 21.
61. Wyndham to Constance Leconfield, 11 Nov. 1905, 8 April and 31 Dec. 1906, PHA, WSRO. June 1906 marked Wyndham's first 'attempt' to journey from Johannesburg to Standerton by motor car.
62. Maud Wyndham to Constance Leconfield, 25 July 1914, PHA, WSRO.
63. Smith to Wyndham, 15 July 1904, 'Hugh Wyndham Re Cattle', TLD 417, G 1248, TAD, SANA.
64. Wyndham to Constance Leconfield, 11 Aug. 1905, PHA, WSRO.
65. Wyndham to Selborne, 24 Aug. 1906; Jack Lyttelton to Smith, 25 Aug. 1906, and Selborne's reply, 29 Aug. 1906, 'Stock Importation of Sheep by Hon Hugh Wyndham', GOV 1025, PS 73/14/06; Smith to Selborne, 27 Aug. 1906, and Selborne's reply, 27 Aug. 1906, 'D.G.V. Dalgety Importation of Sheep', GOV 931, file 8/19/06, TAD, SANA.
66. Cannadine, *British Aristocracy*, 237; and J. Abdy and C. Gere, *The Souls: An Elite in English Society, 1885–1930* (London, 1984), 35, 37–39, 185.
67. Wyndham to Constance Leconfield, 24 Oct. 1910, PHA, WSRO.
68. Justice of the Peace, H.A. Wyndham vice Kelby, archives of the Transvaal Land Department [hereafter LD] 747, AG 2610/04, TAD, SANA; Wyndham to Lady Maxse, 15 Oct. 1904, Maxse papers 50, WSRO; cancellation of the commissions as justices of the peace granted to A.J. Malherbe, C. Power and the Hon. H.A. Wyndham, archives of the Transvaal Executive Council, URU 75, file 99, TAD, SANA.
69. Smith to Wyndham, 8 May 1906, and Wyndham's reply, 11 May 1906, TLD 574, G 1517/06, TAD, SANA. See H.A. Wyndham, *The Early History of the Thoroughbred Horse in South Africa* (Oxford, 1924).
70. Wyndham to Constance Leconfield, 9 June 1906 and 21 July 1906, PHA, WSRO; and G.

Jackson-Stops, *Petworth House, West Sussex* (London, 1978), 33.
71. As quoted by Hyam, *Britain's Imperial Century*, 295. See also D.C. Allen, 'Beating them at their own game: Rugby, the Anglo-Boer War and Afrikaner nationalism, 1899–1948', *Proceedings of the War and Society in Africa conference* (CD ROM), South African Military Academy, 12–14 Sept. 2001.
72. Wyndham to Constance Leconfield, 1 Jan. 1906, PHA, WSRO.
73. Ibid., 25 Sept. 1905, PHA, WSRO.
74. Wyndham to Lady Maxse, 15 Nov. 1901, Maxse papers 50, WSRO; Volunteer Returns Strength and Distribution. Commandant of Volunteers, Transvaal, to Assistant Colonial Secretary, 7 Dec. 1906, archives of the Colonial Secretary, Transvaal, CS 2182/1905; archives of the Private Secretary to the Governor of Transvaal Colony, ministerial minute, 8 Feb. 1909, PS 68/5/1909, Volunteers Reorganisation, TAD, SANA.
75. Wyndham to Constance Leconfield, 17 Dec. 1906, PHA, WSRO.
76. Ibid., 9 Dec.1905, 1 Jan., 4 June and 16 Sept. 1906, PHA, WSRO.
77. Ibid., 25 May 1906, PHA, WSRO.
78. Ibid., 11 Nov. 1905, PHA, WSRO.
79. Ibid., 31 March, 8 April and 16 June 1906, PHA, WSRO.
80. Ibid., 22 April 1906, PHA, WSRO.
81. Enrolment Book of the Southern Mounted Rifles, Transvaal Volunteers, 50B, TAD, SANA.
82. Wyndham to Constance Leconfield, 17 Dec. 1906, PHA, WSRO.
83. Ibid., 3 Dec. 1909, PHA, WSRO.
84. *BPP*, Cd.1163, *Further Correspondence* (1902), Milner to Chamberlain, 25 Jan. 1902.
85. Hyam, *Britain's Imperial Century*, 281.
86. David Cannadine, *Ornamentalism: How the British Saw Their Empire* (London, 2002), 137.
87. Hand-written notes by Lionel Curtis, 3 March 1903 (or 1904?), MSS Curtis 1, Bodleian; Wyndham to Lady Maxse, 21 June and 15 Dec. 1902, Maxse papers 50, WSRO.
88. A Colonial Officer, *Twenty-Five Years' Soldiering in South Africa* (London, 1909), 445.
89. G.H.L. Le May, *British Supremacy in South Africa 1899–1907* (Oxford, 1965), 155.
90. Circular from Louis Botha, Nov. 1903, Preller collection, vol.92, f.561, TAD, SANA.
91. Transvaaler (*nom de plume* for Geoffrey Robinson), 'Political parties of the Transvaal', *The National Review*, 45 (May 1905), 480–81; N.G. Garson, 'Het Volk: The Botha-Smuts Party in the Transvaal, 1904–11', *Historical Journal*, 9 (1966), 129.
92. Garson, 'Het Volk', 103. Engelenburg led Kruger's campaign in the 1892 presidential election. Preller's father was his electoral agent for Wakkerstroom. Engelenburg to Ribbinck, 30 Aug. 1892, register herkiezing President Kruger, H. Orban collection, W18, TAD, SANA.
93. The *Leader*, 14 Feb. 1905, quoted by B. Spoelstra, 'Die Bewindsaanvaarding van die Botha-regering oor Transvaal as selfregerende Britse Kolonie in 1907', *Archives Year Book for South African History*, vol.2 (1953), 328.
94. Wyndham to Constance Leconfield, 26 Nov. 1905, PHA, WSRO.
95. Ibid., 1 July 1905, PHA, WSRO.
96. Ibid., 20 Aug. 1906, PHA, WSRO. See also Sir West Ridgeway to Botha, 11 May 1906, Preller collection, vol.89, ff.13–15, TAD, SANA.
97. Paraphrased by Lord David Cecil, *The Cecils of Hatfield House* (London, 1973), 242.
98. Lord David Cecil quoted by J. Carter Brown, 'Power, Privilege and Patronage', *Heritage, The British Review*, 7 (1985/6), 24.
99. Transvaaler, 'Political parties of the Transvaal', 474–76; A.A. Mawby, 'Capital, Government and Politics in the Transvaal, 1900-1907: A Revision and a Reversion', *Historical Journal*, 17 (1974), 410 *passim*.
100. John Buchan to Lady Leconfield, 6 Dec. 1905, PHA, WSRO.
101. Transvaal Progressive Association Principles, Dr F.V. Engelenburg collection, A140, vol.7, f.43, TAD, SANA.
102. Wyndham to Constance Leconfield, 4 June 1906, PHA, WSRO; Garson, 'Het Volk', 110–15.
103. Wyndham to Constance Leconfield, 15 July 1906, PHA, WSRO.
104. Ibid., 16 Sept. 1906, PHA, WSRO.

105. Engelenburg to Jan Smuts, 18 Oct. 1906, Engelenburg collection, vol.7, f.2, TAD, SANA.
106. Wyndham to Constance Leconfield, 22 Sept. 1906, PHA, WSRO.
107. Ibid., 8 Oct. 1906, PHA, WSRO.
108. Ibid.
109. Ibid., 19 and 26 Nov. 1906, PHA, WSRO.
110. Ibid., 17 Dec. 1906, PHA, WSRO.
111. Diary of Lady Chaplin, 24 March 1906, Chaplin collection, BC 831, UCTAL; Wyndham to Constance Leconfield, 24 Dec. 1906, PHA, WSRO.
112. Wyndham to Constance Leconfield, 24 Dec. 1906, PHA, WSRO.
113. Ibid., 17 Dec. 1906, PHA, WSRO.
114. Ibid., 27 Jan. 1907, PHA, WSRO. See also H. Spender, *General Botha* (London, 1919), 178, where Spender states that Botha 'was fought very keenly by a young Englishman, the Hon. Hugh Wyndham, who had a large farm at Standerton ...'.
115. Wyndham to Constance Leconfield, 11 Feb. 1907, PHA, WSRO.
116. *BPP*, Cd.3528, *Further correspondence regarding the affairs in the Transvaal and Orange River Colony* (1907), Selborne to Elgin, 25 March 1907.
117. Wyndham to Constance Leconfield, 25 Feb. 1907, PHA, WSRO.
118. During the Anglo-Boer War, the poet Jan F. Celliers addressed an elderly, uneducated 'uncle in arms': 'Worthy old ox! With a sage nod of the head and the smile of one who has never awoken I am often warned by you against reading so many "bits of paper", because it results in weightier matters – like grilling meat and cooking porridge – not receiving sufficient attention.' As quoted and translated by F. Pretorius, *Life on Commando during the Anglo-Boer War 1899–1902* (Cape Town, 1999), 122.
119. Wyndham to Constance Leconfield, 27 Jan. 1907, PHA, WSRO. Botha was himself a victim of character assassination in 1907. Minister of Justice to Bok, 3 March 1927, Engelenburg collection, vol.60, TAD, SANA.
120. Illiquid case for Damages, Hugh Archibald Wyndham versus the Wallach's Printing and Publishing Company Limited, 1907, ZTPD 5/634, f.73/1907, TAD, SANA; Nimocks, *Milner's Young Men*, 67–68.
121. Wyndham to Constance Leconfield, 11 Feb. 1907, PHA, WSRO.
122. The matter arose again in the 1915 election, when Wyndham's labour opponent 'said that Turffontein people were such snobs they would follow a doll if it had Hon. to its name'. Maud Wyndham to Constance Leconfield, 29 Sept. 1915, PHA, WSRO. See also, Cannadine, *Ornamentalism*, 137 *passim*.
123. F.V. Engelenburg, *General Louis Botha* (Pretoria, 1929), 144; Brieweboek van die Volkstem 1893–1911, Orban collection, 18/1, TAD, SANA.
124. P. Jourdan to Michell, 12 Sept. 1907, Michell collection, vol.1, KAB, SANA.
125. F. Edmund Garrett, 'Lord Milner and the Struggle for South African Union', *National Review* (Feb. 1906), 1123; G.L. Beer, 'Lord Milner and British Imperialism', *Political Science Quarterly*, 30 (1915), 302–03; Nimocks, *Milner's Young Men*, 68–75, 138.
126. H.A. Wyndham, 'Some Aspects of South African Defence', *The State*, 2 (June 1909), 644–51; and 2 (July 1909), 96–103.
127. Wyndham to Constance Leconfield, 6 March 1914, PHA, WSRO.
128. Ibid., 23 Nov. 1914, PHA, WSRO.

Casting Daylight upon Magic:
Deconstructing the Royal Tour of 1901
to Canada

PHILLIP BUCKNER

On 16 September 1901 George, Duke of Cornwall and York and heir apparent to the throne of Great Britain, arrived in Canada to begin a 35-day royal progress, which would involve crossing the country twice, from Quebec City to Victoria and back again to Halifax. For a whole generation of Canadians this was one of the most memorable public events to take place during their lifetimes. Certainly this was the view of contemporary Canadians, who turned out in unprecedented numbers to view their future King and Queen. The streets of Toronto, reported the *Telegram*, were 'aglow with happy boys and girls who will ever remember the visit of the Duke of Cornwall, as their parents remember the visit of his father to Toronto 41 years ago'.[1] The Toronto *News* described the Duke's arrival as 'one of the biggest days in Toronto's history'.[2] Similar comments were made in newspapers across the country, which carried lengthy daily reports about every aspect of the tour. Five British and 11 Canadian journalists as well as four photographers were carried on board the royal train at government expense and hundreds more tracked the tour across Canada.[3] No fewer than three books about the tour were published by British journalists, another by Sir Donald Mackenzie Wallace, who had accompanied the tour as its official chronicler, and a fifth by Sir Joseph Pope, the chief Canadian civil servant involved in organising the tour.[4] The Edison Company even produced the first (albeit rather short) moving picture of a royal tour to Canada.[5] Hector Charlesworth, one of Canada's best known journalists, described the tour in his reminiscences as 'One of the most interesting of all the assignments I covered while a reporter'.[6] John Castell Hopkins, author of a range of popular histories and a member of the organising committee when the Duke visited Toronto, included a lengthy description of the tour in his biography of Edward VII.[7] Stephen Leacock, a member of the welcoming committee in Orilla, always remembered the day he had met the future George V.[8] Thousands of Canadian homes once contained memorabilia of the tour and scrapbooks lovingly collected to be handed on to the next generation. The importance of the tour seemed self-evident to all who had been there.

Its importance has not appeared equally self-evident to later Canadian historians and one looks largely in vain for even a brief mention of the tour in recently published studies of Canada at the turn of the century.[9] In part this scholarly void simply reflects the general lack of interest among Canadian scholars in the monarchy and its significance in Canadian history, despite the fact that during the second half of the nineteenth century popular enthusiasm for monarchy grew steadily stronger in Canada. Queen Victoria's birthday (24 May) became one of the most significant public holidays, and the celebrations of Queen Victoria's Golden Jubilee in 1887 and her Diamond Jubilee in 1897 were marked by widespread ceremonies across the country. Victoria became the most popular place name in Canada and virtually every Canadian urban centre acquired a Victoria Street and usually an Albert, Edward and George as well. The Jubilees and Victoria's death led to a host of public buildings and public monuments being dedicated to her memory.[10] If one is to believe the newspapers, Canadians were overcome with grief at the death of Victoria in 1901 and equally overcome with joy at the coronation of her son as Edward VII in 1902.[11] Yet all this public enthusiasm for the monarchy is generally dismissed as essentially meaningless – indeed, almost irrational. The classic example of this attitude can be seen in Robert Stamp's *Kings, Queens and Canadians* – one of the few historical studies to recognise the significance of popular royalism in Canada. Yet Stamp's subtitle – 'A Celebration of Canada's Infatuation with the British Royal Family' – tells it all.[12] Canadian enthusiasm for what was essentially a foreign institution – the 'British' monarchy – could only have been an 'infatuation'.

A more sophisticated approach argues that the popularity of the monarchy was essentially the product of indoctrination by the Canadian social elite, who had their own reasons for collaborating with the imperial authorities, a classic example of what Marxist historians would call the creation of a 'false consciousness', in the interests of maintaining hegemonic control. Most Canadian historians (and the same could be said of their Australian and New Zealand counterparts) would prefer simply to ignore the whole issue and to focus on the gradual evolution of a distinct and separate Canadian national identity with its own separate and distinct national symbols. They are deeply embarrassed by the fact that Canadians have for so long been committed to the preservation of the monarchy and that this enthusiasm was shared by men and women of virtually every class and ethnic group in Canada. But if forced to confront the appeal of popular royalism, as Jane Connors has argued about Australian historians, Canadian historians would prefer to interpret this enthusiasm 'in terms of conscious manipulation on high and an audience of "cultural dopes" down below'.[13]

Ironically, until recently, even in Britain there were few serious studies of the nineteenth-century monarchy. This pattern began to change with the publication of Eric Hobsbawm and Terence Ranger's *The Invention of Tradition*, which included David Cannadine's stimulating study of 'The Context, Performance and Meaning of Ritual: The British Monarchy and the "Invention of Tradition", 1820–1977'.[14] Cannadine may have downplayed the historical roots of some of the traditions that were 'invented' or perhaps one should say re-invented or renovated during the late nineteenth century.[15] But his argument that much of the modern pageantry surrounding the monarchy is a late nineteenth-century 'invention' designed to strengthen the monarch's popularity and its usefulness as a symbol of national unity and national identity is irrefutable. Yet for all of its strengths the 'invention of tradition' approach has some severe weaknesses, particularly in the hands of less sophisticated scholars than Cannadine.[16] Obviously all traditions have to be invented by someone at some time for some purpose, but it is not always easy to say with precision when a particular cultural tradition or symbol was manufactured, by whom and for what purpose. Even if one can establish the precise roots of an historical tradition, this 'does not explain the imaginative appeal of a symbol nor its subsequent mutations over time'.[17] Moreover, it is easy to assume that the public plays little part in the evolution of successful traditions and can be manipulated more or less at will by elites. One arrives at this conclusion teleologically, by emphasising the traditions that are successfully 'invented' while ignoring those efforts at the conscious invention of tradition that fail. The 'invention of tradition' approach also glosses over the ways in which different groups may support the same tradition for different – indeed, diametrically opposed – purposes. In fact, the 'invention of tradition' approach cannot really answer the question of why certain traditions can be invented (or re-invented) while others cannot. This is why Terence Ranger, one of the inventors of the 'invention of tradition' concept, now prefers to talk about 'imagining' (rather than 'inventing') traditions.[18] If in 1901 the majority of Canadians had not been able for logical reasons of their own to 'imagine' the British monarchy as an institution which belonged to them, no amount of propaganda and pressure, external or internal, could have persuaded them to embrace the monarchy as embodying an historical tradition which was part of their heritage and which continued to have relevance to them.

I

This is not to deny that in 1901 there was an attempt at conscious manipulation of royal symbolism. But in the case of a complex cultural event like a royal tour, there are always a variety of agendas, frequently conflicting agendas, at work. In 1901 Canadian monarchists liked to claim that it was Queen Victoria herself who 'devised and designed' her grandson's tour.[19] In reality the Queen only unenthusiastically and under considerable duress agreed to allow the Duke of Cornwall to embark on a lengthy trip around the globe. In the 1860s there had been official tours by members of the royal family to both Canada and Australia, and for years Canada and some of the Australasian colonies had requested another formal tour by the Queen or by the heir to the throne. Queen Victoria had consistently rejected their appeals. The decisive pressure that changed her mind came from the Secretary of State for the Colonies, Joseph Chamberlain, the one-time republican mayor of Birmingham who had been transformed into a committed imperialist and monarchist. Julian Amery has argued that the 1901 tour was 'his idea from the start'.[20] This too is a partial truth. During 1900 Chamberlain was involved in negotiating the terms of union with delegates from the Australian colonies and it was the Australians who expressed the wish for a tour to open the first Australian Parliament in 1901. Chamberlain was easily persuaded since he saw the formation of the Australian Commonwealth as an important opportunity for promoting imperial solidarity and for thanking the Australian colonies for their support in the war in South Africa.[21] When New Zealand, Canada and the South African colonies asked for the tour to be extended to include them, Chamberlain supported their requests, hoping to turn the tour into a triumphal march around the British Dominions and a ringing endorsement of his policy in South Africa. The Queen was less easily convinced to part with her grandson. Reluctantly, under pressure from the Prime Minister, Lord Salisbury, the Queen agreed that the Duke of Cornwall might go to Australia and New Zealand but initially she refused to allow the tour to include Canada. In December 1900 Victoria was persuaded by Chamberlain to allow a 'short visit' to Canada to show her gratitude to the Canadians for the sacrifices 'made in her cause in South Africa, where the bravery of her Canadian soldiers had been so conspicuous'.[22]

Early in 1901 the arrangements for the tour ground to a halt with Victoria's death. Edward VII had undertaken the first official royal tour by a member of the royal family to a colony – to Canada in 1860 – and he remembered the tour affectionately since it was one of the few times in his life that he had earned even grudging respect from his royal parents. But although he had previously supported Chamberlain's request to the Queen to allow George to undertake the tour, after her death he was reluctant to see his only surviving son leave England for such an extended period of time and he only agreed to allow the tour to go ahead under pressure from the cabinet. Arthur Balfour, soon to replace his uncle as Prime Minister, was delegated to read the King a lesson in the responsibilities of being an Imperial monarch. The King, he pointed out, 'is no longer merely the King of Great Britain and Ireland and of a few dependencies whose whole value consisted in ministering to the wealth and security of Great Britain and Ireland. He is now the greatest constitutional bond uniting together in a single Empire communities of free men separated by half the circumference of the Globe.' The citizens of this empire, Balfour perceptively noted, 'know little and care little for British Ministries and British party politics. But they know, and care for, the Empire of which they are members and for the Sovereign who rules it.'[23] Faced with the determination of the cabinet, Edward agreed that the tour should take place.

The Duke of Cornwall and York – the future George V – had already agreed to go. Like his father and elder brother he had made a number of visits to the colonies (including two brief visits to Canada) but prior to 1901 he had never shown any great interest in colonial affairs. The real love of his life was the Royal Navy and he had been perfectly happy as a serving naval officer when the unexpected death of his elder brother suddenly transformed him from just another prince into the potential heir to the throne and he was compelled to retire from active service in the navy. But after retiring he had little to command his attention except his passions for hunting and for stamp collecting, although he did take seriously his responsibilities to represent the crown as a patron of worthy causes. When approached by Chamberlain, George agreed to undertake the long tour, which became even longer as more countries were added, but there was considerable truth in the comment of the London *Daily Express*: 'That the whole thing will be a bore to the Duke goes without saying; that the Duchess will cordially enjoy it, it is also unnecessary to remark.'[24] This judgement is a bit unfair to George. He did take 'keen and continuous' interest in the elaborate outfitting of the HMS *Ophir*, the ship that was selected to carry the royal party around the globe.[25] It was also his idea to carry out to the colonies the medals to be given to the colonial veterans of the South African War and to present them himself. But in many respects George was temperamentally unsuited for his new career; he did not enjoy meeting people, disliked the popular press, was a reluctant public speaker and had a limited interest in royal ceremonials, though he was a stickler in matters of protocol. When consulted what he might like to do in Canada he is reputed to have replied: 'I want a day's duck shooting, and I want to see a lacrosse match.'[26] Both the royal wishes were granted. He attended a lacrosse match during his visit to Ottawa. The Montreal committee also arranged for him to see a baseball game but the programme was too crowded and it was dropped from the itinerary. The Governor-General, Lord Minto, justified this decision on the grounds that baseball 'is looked upon as an American game and is not at all popular in Canada – moreover it has fallen entirely out of the hands of amateurs and has been taken over by the very low American professional element'.[27] The shooting party – George actually insisted on at least two day's shooting – proved somewhat more difficult to arrange. The Duke was determined to keep the number of official ceremonies to a minimum and the Canadian government was very concerned that if the Duke were to go hunting in Ontario when he had declared that he did not have time to visit a number of important communities, there would be a public outcry.[28] In the end Lord Minto arranged to hold the shooting party at a remote spot in Manitoba, where the Duke spent two happy days killing Canadian wildlife.[29] On the first day in five hours he bagged 52 ducks and expressed 'great pleasure' at the excursion.[30] The two day total for the royal hunting party was estimated at 742 ducks and 70 snipe.[31] He also added considerably to his growing stamp collection, since he was presented with complete sets of stamps of the various colonies he visited and the duties of one of his aides-des-camps was to make selective purchases for his collection. Much of the long voyage from Australia to Canada he spent pasting into albums the stamps collected in Australia.

Much of the rest of the time George was bored, especially during the repetitious welcoming ceremonies which he had to endure at each stop in the tour. Even the scenery did not normally interest him, although during the trip across the Rockies he noted in his diary that the scenery was 'so grand & so magnificent that it baffles description'.[32] George did not mind the various military ceremonies. Massive military parades were organised in Quebec city, Toronto and Halifax and smaller ones arranged at other stops. One of the most common photographs of the tour was of the Duke reviewing colonial troops or handing out to South African veterans the medals from the Imperial government which he had arranged to bring with him. On such occasions he usually wore the uniform of the Royal Fusiliers, one suspects because it included an enormous busby which helped to disguise the fact that he was only 5 feet 4 inches tall. The public image of George promoted in the press and by the books published after the tour was an extremely flattering one, emphasising his sense of duty, his dedication to meeting his subjects, and his tact and lack of pretence. In private many of the officials surrounding the Duke were less flattering. In his personal journal (but not in the book he published about the tour) Sir Joseph Pope noted that:

> The Duke of York improves on acquaintance. He is somewhat slow of thought, destitute of wit, humour or sarcasm, blunt to rudeness, says just what he thinks without much regard for anyone's feelings – in

short, he is a spoiled boy. At the same time, he has, I would judge, a
great sense of duty, and is disposed to be kindhearted if he can be so
without inconvenience to himself. I dare say he possesses a fair share
of common sense, but he knows very little. Is really meagrely
educated – would never learn, I am told. Is wholly without tact.[33]

These sentiments were echoed by Lord Wenlock, the member of the royal
household responsible for acting as the liaison between George and the
various colonial governments. At one point he wrote to his wife that, 'The
Duke and Duchess are getting terribly weary of these constant functions –
and I can well understand it, but they are, so to speak, paid for the job.'[34]
Fortunately for George, his lack of tact in dealing with subordinates could
be hidden and his lack of interest in royal ceremonial and rather gruff
personality could be portrayed by the press as endearing characteristics of a
simple and straightforward man who did not like to put on airs.

Nonetheless, the real star of the 1901 tour was the Duchess of Cornwall.
Mary – or May as she was commonly referred to – genuinely loved the
attention showered upon her. The long sea voyage was for her a real
hardship as she suffered from severe seasickness. Initially she had also to
overcome her natural shyness, but over the duration of the tour her self-
confidence grew steadily. This was the first royal tour to the self-governing
colonies on which a prince was accompanied by his consort, and Mary's
presence enabled colonial women to be far more involved in the tour than
in any previous one. At every major stop the Duchess was presented with
addresses, bouquets and frequently with expensive gifts from the women
who formed part of the local elite and from various groups, including
branches of the Imperial Order Daughters of the Empire, the National
Council of Women, and the Young Women's Christian Association. The
women's columns in the newspapers discussed at great length what the
Duchess was wearing and, while George was the focal point at military
reviews and at formal ceremonies, Mary took centre stage when visiting
hospitals, exhibitions, schools and art galleries. She was not widely read but
she was more widely read than George and had considerably more interest
in the arts. In Britain one of the ways in which the monarchy increasingly
earned its popularity was by becoming patron for a host of worthy causes.[35]
Indeed, while in Canada George raised $250,000 ($200,000 of it donated by
Lord Strathcona) for a British hospital fund.[36] In Canada a host of charitable
and philanthropic organisations eagerly sought to acquire a royal patron and
the Duke and Duchess lent their names to a variety of good causes, although
their generosity rarely extended to donating any of their private income.
Mary took a particular interest in women's and children's hospitals,
frequently visiting them without the Duke, chatting with individual patients

and donating photographs of herself and her children. Press reports made a good deal of the ease with which she moved among ordinary people. They did not focus on the fact that she was extremely class-conscious and socially very conservative. She had nothing but scorn for the women's suffrage movement. The press stressed that she was 'a womanly woman'.[37] The Kingston *Daily British Whig* noted that, 'It is said she does not admire the mannish woman. Who does?'[38] Indeed, for all her supposed sympathy for the poor, Mary was not interested in the problems of working women nor unduly sensitive to the life of toil that was the lot of most working people. In Melbourne when workers marched past with signs supporting the eight-hour day, she proclaimed how lucky they were and wished that she and George had such an easy life.

Certainly while on tour the Duke and Duchess were compelled to put in long hours. The tour included lengthy visits to Australia, New Zealand, South Africa and Canada, as well as brief stops in Aden, Malta, Ceylon and Mauritius. There was some discussion of visiting the United States, but fears that American security might be inadequate and a desire to promote imperial unity meant that the Duke went round the globe without ever leaving British soil. The royal progress – 'the like of which Caesar had never dreamed' – would last from 25 March until 2 November, making it the longest in history.[39] The Duke would travel over 50,000 miles, receive 544 addresses, deliver 86 speeches, lay 21 foundation stones, inspect 62,000 troops, and award 4,329 South African medals and 142 investitures and knighthoods. It was estimated that he shook 35,000 colonial hands.[40] The cost of the tour was enormous. The colonies being visited were expected to absorb the bulk of the costs but the British Government spent £126,000 in hiring and another £56,000 in refurbishing the *Ophir*. Even this was only the tip of the iceberg since the Duke travelled with an enormous entourage, with special carriages and horses to pull them, and with a substantial naval escort. Minto estimated that the tour was costing the British Government £70,000 per month.[41] When it was asked in the House of Commons why the Duke could not afford to contribute to the costs of the tour out of the substantial revenues he received from the Duchy of Cornwall and from the civil list, the member was told by the Chancellor of the Exchequer that all the costs were to be 'provided by the nation' because of the immense advantages of the tour in consolidating the empire and 'in instructing the future ruler as to the greatness of his responsibilities'.[42]

II

One of the results of the 1901 tour was, as Chamberlain had hoped, to increase public interest in Britain in the 'little Britains' overseas and to strengthen the monarchy's identification with the unity of the empire. Both the Duke's departure and his return to Britain were turned into elaborate public ceremonies, extensively covered in the British press. Five British journalists accompanied him around the globe, and for most of the summer and autumn of 1901 British newspapers carried stories about the tour and numerous photographs. In the aftermath of the tour the Imperial Institute held a special exhibit of the various addresses and gifts the royal couple had collected during their trip.[43] Chamberlain certainly viewed the tour as 'an unqualified success'.[44] The reception that the Duke and Duchess received, especially in Canada and Australia, strengthened Chamberlain's belief in imperial federation; indeed, it led him to overestimate the degree of support for closer imperial union in the self-governing colonies. The tour also reinforced the image that the empire was solidly behind the war in South Africa, strengthening Chamberlain's position at home. George did return with a far greater sense of his Imperial responsibilities. Upon his return a special dinner was held by the city of London to honour the Duke, and in his speech he called upon Britons at home to 'Wake up' to the importance of the empire.[45] Edward VII also thought the tour a great success and used it as the justification for making his son Prince of Wales. When he inherited the throne as George V, he emphasised his imperial responsibilities and encouraged frequent trips to the colonies by his sons, Edward and Albert (the future George VI), a practice continued by his granddaughter, Queen Elizabeth II, whose commitment to the Commonwealth is indisputable.[46] The tour also had a profound impact upon Mary, who saw her role as ensuring that the members of her family lived up to 'what she considered the proper royal attitude'.[47]

Yet it is important to remember that the real pressure for the tour to Canada came not from the British government nor from the crown but from the colonial politicians. Canada was added to the Duke's itinerary because of lobbying from the Canadian government. In December 1900 Lord Minto sent an official invitation declaring that the proposed visit to Australia 'has stirred the hearts of your loyal subjects in Canada' and asking that the tour be extended to Canada, where 'their visit will tend to strengthen, if possible, those ties of union that bond a loyal and patriotic people to their much loved sovereign'.[48] Minto was a strong imperialist who was concerned to promote imperial federation, but as Minto's letter made clear he was offering the invitation on the advice of his Canadian ministers. Indeed, the decision to invite the Duke could not have been taken without the consent of the Prime Minister of Canada, Sir Wilfrid Laurier, and the government's financial support. Laurier's motivation was undoubtedly political. In initially opposing the pressure to send a Canadian force to South Africa Laurier had misread English Canada's increasing determination to participate more

actively in the empire and he had paid a heavy price in the election of
1900.[49] Although he had won the election, his party had lost considerable
popular support in Ontario and the west, the areas of the country where the
Duke would spend most of his time in 1901. At every public function
Laurier and his ministers would be seen standing side by side with the
royals. Newspapers described Laurier as 'the pilot of the Duke and
Duchess' and the 'master of ceremonies', who 'could hobnob with Royalty
on easy terms'.[50] Liberal papers in the West took special pains to note that
this was Laurier's first official visit to the region in seven years, while
Conservative papers complained that Liberal papers 'placed Sir Wilfrid
Laurier into [their] royal pictures much more prominently than the duke'.[51]
For Laurier there was a price to pay in associating himself so clearly with
the royal visitors.[52] Several of the published accounts of the tour mention
Laurier's enthusiasm in singing 'God Save the King'. They do not recount
what Laurier must have felt on hearing for the hundredth time 'Rule
Britannia' or 'The Maple Leaf Forever', which was sung with gusto by
massed choruses of children at virtually every whistle stop in English
Canada. During the Duke's visit 'The Maple Leaf Forever', which
emphasised the permanency of the imperial connection, was 'sung by
millions of Canadians scattered from Quebec to Victoria' and became, in
effect, English Canada's national song.[53] The author of 'The Maple Leaf
Forever', Alexander Muir, was honoured at a special ceremony in Toronto
at which 'a young maple tree gaily decorated with Union Jacks' was planted
by the Duke with Muir's 'assistance'.[54] Nor is it clear how enthusiastically
Laurier cheered the veterans from South Africa who were presented with
medals at each stage of the tour, a ceremony inevitably accompanied by
speeches praising Canada's generous contribution of troops to assist Britain
in its hour of need and calling for greater imperial unity in future.

Perhaps this is being too cynical. By 1901 Sir Wilfrid had moved a long
way from his *rouge* roots and there is no reason not to accept his enthusiasm
for the monarchy at face value. But there is also no question that the tour
was designed to bring political benefits to the Liberals and to undermine
attempts to impugn Laurier's loyalty to the monarchy and the empire.
Although Laurier seems to have been a restraining influence on some of his
Liberal followers who sought to turn the Duke's visit into a partisan event,
he was not above paying off a few political debts. In a private letter Pope
wrote to Laurier suggesting that some recognition should be given to the
veteran Quebec Conservative politician Sir Hector Langevin, who as Mayor
of Montreal had received the Duke's father during the Prince of Wales's
1860 tour. 'He is old and broken now', Pope wrote, 'and not likely to have
many opportunities of a like nature.' Laurier bluntly wrote back: 'I do not
at all share your views. My opinion is to leave him severely alone.'[55] Clearly

the Liberals did attempt to manipulate the tour in order to shore up their political support in English Canada but surely this is a very strange kind of 'conscious manipulation from on high', since Laurier (though this was not true of some of his English-Canadian colleagues) was leading Canadians in a direction in which he did not really want to go. As Minto repeatedly stressed in his private letters home, Laurier did not share the English-Canadian enthusiasm to play a greater role in the empire; Laurier, Minto reported to the Queen, was 'a broad-minded and extremely able' man, but 'his dream is not an Imperial one'.[56] During the period of mourning after Queen Victoria's death, Minto declared to Chamberlain: 'The feeling of sorrow amongst the Canadian people has been very deep, but I can not help feeling that Sir Wilfrid Laurier does not feel as we feel.'[57] Ironically, in the aftermath of the tour, Laurier would spend much of his energies trying to hold back the enthusiasm for closer imperial integration to which the tour had contributed both in Canada and in Britain.

Lord Minto undoubtedly also hoped the tour would enhance the prestige and influence of the office of governor-general. Indeed, he was offended when it was indicated that the Duke would take precedence over him in Canada, even though Minto as governor-general was the direct representative of the King. Minto appealed to the Colonial Office but his complaint was referred to Edward VII, who personally approved the decision for his son to take precedence.[58] Partly to avoid embarrassing issues of precedence Minto decided not to accompany the tour across the country (although Lady Minto did). He was, however, determined to be the primary channel of communication with the Duke and the latter's staff in organising the tour. In late February Chamberlain confirmed that the tour would go ahead and the dates when the Duke and Duchess would visit. Other than a visit to Niagara Falls and a day's shooting the itinerary was left to the Canadian government to plan.[59] But disputes immediately arose over the point of arrival since the Canadian ministers wished the Duke to sail from Australia to Vancouver and begin the tour there. When it became clear that the Duke would land at Quebec city and would spend only 32 days in Canada, much less than he had spent in Australia, several members of the cabinet thought the tour should be cancelled since it was not possible to see all of Canada in such a short time and 'a hurried attempt ... would do more harm than good'.[60] But Laurier was not prepared to withdraw the invitation and he appointed a cabinet committee chaired by the Minister of Finance, W.S. Fielding, to prepare the itinerary for the royal tour and to work out the arrangements for accommodation and hospitality with the governor-general. The committee seems to have met only once.[61] Although Minto had not objected to the idea of a committee so long as he chaired it, he wrote to Laurier to insist that, while 'in a bigger sense the visit must be regulated by the wishes of my Ministers', there must be 'some central authority to whom reception Committees can refer for information and to whom they can submit their proposals', and he suggested to Laurier that he and the Prime Minister constitute the central committee.[62] In fact, it was agreed that all invitations would be submitted to the Department of Secretary of State and all the programme arrangements to Minto.[63] In practice, this division of labour was impracticable and all of the details were worked out in the governor-general's office. Minto's Military Secretary, F.S. Maude, occasionally went to see the Secretary of State, R.W. Scott, 'as I thought it would please him, if he were told something from time to time'.[64] But Minto was aware of the need to submit all of the key decisions to Laurier for his approval and several changes and additions were made at the latter's request. On only one issue did Laurier and Minto seriously disagree – on the awarding of honours. Minto had hoped to use the Duke's visit as the excuse to bestow knighthoods on Frederick Borden and William Mulock, the staunchest imperialists in the cabinet who had strongly supported the decision to send Canadian volunteers to South Africa, but he was forced to defer to Laurier and withdraw the recommendations.[65] Minto was, however, able to overrule Laurier and make Thomas Shaughnessey, the head of the Canadian Pacific Railway, a Knight Bachelor, ostensibly because of the assistance he had given to the royal tour. Laurier appealed to Chamberlain against the recommendation because of the unpopularity of the CPR in western Canada and argued that 'purely social considerations ought not to prevail against political issues', but was informed by Chamberlain that the award had already been announced and that in any event it was being given on entirely non-political grounds.[66] Ironically it was not Laurier but Minto who suffered the political consequences of this decision since Liberal papers across the country made clear that the decision had been taken over Laurier's objections.

After the arrangements had been approved by Laurier, they had then to be submitted to the Duke for his approval. In the previous royal tour to Canada by the Prince of Wales in 1860 the ultimate control over the itinerary had been determined by the Secretary of State for the Colonies, the Duke of Newcastle, who had accompanied the Prince as his political adviser. By 1901, however, real control had passed from the imperial to the colonial officials. The Duke of Cornwall was accompanied by an official from the Colonial Office, John Anderson, but he was a civil servant, not a minister representing the British government. Although Anderson's salary was paid by the British government, he was considered as one of the Duke's private staff and could not therefore correspond, publicly or privately, with Chamberlain or the Colonial Office on official matters during the tour unless directed to do so by the Duke.[67] By 1901 the monarchy's own staff had become increasingly adept at organising royal events and the Duke was also accompanied by Arthur Bigge, his private secretary, and by Lord Wenlock, the head of the household staff. Bigge, Wenlock and Anderson met with the Duke to examine the proposals submitted by Lord Minto and went over every detail,[68] but their role was largely a negative one. Their primary concern (other than ensuring a hunting expedition for the Duke) was to limit the Duke's commitments and to ensure that the rigid rules of court procedure were followed to the letter. There was little more they could do since the royal party had limited knowledge about Canada and Canadian politics. When supplied with the itinerary for Quebec city, which included a visit to Canada's pre-eminent French-Canadian university, Wenlock cabled back to ask: 'What is Laval?'[69]

The burden of organising the tour fell upon Minto, who – subject to Laurier's consent – decided where the Duke would go and how long he would spend in each place. The decision about what the Duke would do within each province was primarily the responsibility of the lieutenant-governors, who organised the provincial programme in consultation with the premiers of the provinces and the municipal governments of the cities and towns fortunate to be graced with a royal visit. All the provincial plans had to be approved by Minto, who had to make the arrangements for transporting and housing the royal party. Most of the real burden fell upon Minto's military secretary, Major F.S. Maude. Maude had been involved in organising the 1897 jubilee celebrations in London, and at Minto's request he was detached from Kitchener's staff in South Africa in the spring of 1901 and sent to Canada. Maude handled most of the negotiations with the provincial and municipal authorities and he came under considerable criticism for being too rigid in his application of the rules of precedence and for overruling local committees.[70] The *Brantford Courier* complained that Maude was 'about to issue a brochure on the proper way to part with the Canadian sneeze'.[71] But Joseph Pope, the Canadian civil servant who worked closely with Maude, denied that Maude was responsible for these decisions, declaring that in 33 years of government service in Ottawa he had never met an imperial official 'more capable, hardworking, modest and adaptable to his environment than Major Maude'. Pope pointed out that even if they sought to alter any of the rules of procedure they would be prevented from doing so by the Duke's advisers, who would 'insist on the correct ceremonial being adhered to'.[72] As the volume of criticism grew, Pope asked the editor of the Toronto *Globe*, John Willison, to set the record straight and in an editorial Willison, while complaining that there was 'too much red tape and too much "precedence" to suit a democratic country', pointed out that the rules were not invented by the governor-general and his secretary but simply reflected 'ancient usages, which they have no power to vary'.[73] How ancient many of these rules were and how inalterable are both issues open to doubt, but it is clear that Minto and Maude were only obeying guidelines laid down by the Duke and his advisers when they insisted that the rather rigid rules of court dress and court procedure be followed.

Joseph Pope was the other important behind-the-scenes official involved in organising the tour. Pope's grandfather, his father and his uncle had all been active politicians on pre-Confederation Prince Edward Island and had played a key part in bringing Prince Edward Island into Confederation. All the Popes were active and devout monarchists and imperialists, and one of Joseph Pope's earliest memories of his childhood was the visit of the Prince of Wales in 1860.[74] Pope left Prince Edward Island after Confederation and became John A. Macdonald's secretary and eventual biographer, and upon Macdonald's death he became under-secretary at the Department of Secretary of State with special charge of imperial and foreign affairs. Though extremely conservative and a strong imperialist – so strong that he wrote a pamphlet condemning those Canadians who flew the Red Ensign instead of the Union Jack[75] – he admired Laurier. Indeed, it was at Laurier's request that Pope was seconded from the Department of State to work with Maude. Pope's special responsibility was to handle the logistics, particularly the negotiations with the various railway companies, and to oversee federal expenditures. Unofficially his duties were to keep a watchful eye over what was being done in the governor-general's office.

Maude and Pope liked each other and worked well together. They were agreed that the primary function of the tour was to ensure that as many Canadians as possible should have a chance to see their future King and Queen. A train was especially constructed by the Canadian Pacific Railway to take the Duke and his party across Canada. Actually four trains were needed: one for the royal party; one for Lord and Lady Minto and their staff; a third for Laurier, various members of the Canadian government, the press and security officers; and a fourth to carry the royal carriage and horses which had been shipped out from London. Initially the Canadian government set aside $120,000 for the tour, but even though the CPR built the royal train at its own expense the final bill came to $462,881.82.[76] But this did not include all the expenses, some of which were partly hidden within various departmental budgets. The military review in Toronto alone cost $228,000, mainly for the pay and transport of the troops.[77] Moreover, all of the local expenses were absorbed by the municipal or provincial governments, supplemented by private corporations or even individuals. Although the royal tour ended up costing more than the annual budget of some of the smaller provinces, there were remarkably few complaints about the expense of the Duke's visit. In Toronto there was a debate in the City Council in July 1901 over whether to reduce the city's projected expenditure from $10,000 to $5,000, but not only was the vote for $10,000 carried by 18 to 4 but in October, after the tour was over, a vote appropriating an additional $4,000 was carried by 23 to 0, indicating that the dissidents had been persuaded of the tour's value.[78] But the Toronto visit cost far more than $14,000, for the city did not pay for the arches erected by the Foresters and Manufacturers – the latter alone cost $6,500.[79] The city of Ottawa also raised its initial grant for the reception from $2,500 to $10,000, despite the fact that the municipal government was already deeply in debt.[80] Montreal voted $15,000 for the ceremonies but another $17,000 was raised by public subscription. Winnipeg spent $4,687.[81] In Vancouver the city council gave $5,000 and another $1,300 was raised by public subscription.[82] London, Ontario, which had initially been left off the itinerary, spent $2,000 on a one-hour visit.[83] In Hamilton a three-hour visit cost the city $10,000, an amount which did lead to critical letters to the editor of the *Hamilton Spectator*.[84] The Province of New Brunswick spent $22,785 dressing up the exhibition building and the vice-regal residence in Saint John and on a military display, while the city of Saint John spent another $5,000 on the reception.[85] In fact, municipalities and provinces vied with each other to put on impressive displays of fireworks, to erect enormous arches under which the Duke would pass, and to present the Duke and Duchess with elaborate addresses and expensive gifts. It was this latter practice that raised the most criticism. *The Voice*, a weekly newspaper endorsed by the Winnipeg Trades and Labor Council, questioned why the ladies of Ottawa were giving a 'costly gift of furs' to the Duchess, who 'does not need them', when women in Ottawa were 'making pants at 60 cents a dozen, and the combined labor of three women, who work early and late, does not amount to more than four dollars a week'. The resentment against such expenditures, *The Voice* insisted, 'does not arise from any disloyalty, but the demand of the ultra imperialists that something "worthy of the occasion" shall be done is very perplexing to the average civic mind'.[86]

Many more complaints were heard about the itinerary of the tour. The Canadian organisers had to act as arbiters between two conflicting pressures. On the one hand, there was the desire of every community to be included on the route and for the royal visitors to stop for as long as possible. When it was initially announced that the royal tour was not going to include western Ontario there was a wave of protest from all the communities including Guelph, which the Attorney General of Ontario insisted would 'feel slighted' if it did not at least get a 15 or 20 minute visit.[87] In the end, one newspaper reported, 'Guelph got five minutes of the Duke, and is as proud as a dog with seven tails'.[88] Of course, much of this merely reflected civic or regional pride. London was annoyed when it was announced that the Duke was to visit Hamilton but not London. Sherbrooke claimed it merited a stop because it was the unofficial capital of the Eastern Townships. Frederictonians were livid that Fredericton was to be bypassed and that the only major stop in New Brunswick would be in Saint John. Manitobans bitterly complained that the Duke would only spend a few hours in the province. Prince Edward Islanders bitterly noted that theirs was the only province not included on the tour. Much of this anger was directed – unfairly – against the governor-general's office (which perhaps was why Laurier was quite content to let Minto take the primary role in organising the tour). In fact, the real problem was that the organisers were under pressure from the Duke to limit the number of stops and to keep them as brief as possible. By the time he arrived in Canada he had been travelling for nearly six months and he was determined not to extend the time set aside for Canada, even for a day. He wrote to his mother from Canada: 'our tour is most interesting, but it is very tiring and there is no place like dear old England for me'.[89] Minto, who carried the ultimate responsibility, was annoyed with the determination of the Duke to limit his public duties. 'I can't say how strongly I feel', he wrote to Sir George Parkin, 'that the more hail-fellow-well-met he is the better – but I tell you quite privately that I am instructed to cut things down far below what I think advisable.'[90]

When he became King, it was claimed that George had 'in a unique degree personal knowledge of all parts of his dominions',[91] but it is difficult to see how the tour could have given him much insight into Canadian life. There was an incredible sameness about the duties to be performed at each stop on the tour. In the smaller communities where the stop usually lasted for 10–15 minutes there would be a series of presentations, a song or two from a massed choir of children, the rewarding of a few medals, and the royal show was on the road again. In the larger urban centres where the Duke's visit might last from a few hours to three days there was more variety in the programme, but it would still begin with the same formal ceremony at which addresses of welcome would be presented and appropriate responses given, after which the Duke would process around the town in the carriage especially imported from Britain for this purpose. A longer visit might include a stop at the local university, where he would be given yet another honorary degree, or it might involve laying cornerstones or unveiling memorials (usually to the late Queen or to the colonial troops who had died in the South African War). He attended a number of sporting events and made a brief appearance at several industrial or agricultural exhibitions. The Duke had no great interest in art or music. In Toronto the festivities were to include the performance of an opera and some very expensive stars were imported from New York for the occasion, but at the last minute the organisers were told that the Duke would not attend, ostensibly because he was still in mourning for Queen Victoria. In the end the opera was replaced by a concert performance and the Duke – reluctantly – agreed to make a brief appearance. Most evenings there was a private dinner party to attend, usually a display of fireworks, and sometimes a public reception (public dinners and balls were forbidden while the court was still in mourning). It is hardly surprising that the Duke appeared to be bored much of the time. And there were physical limits to the endurance of the Duke and Duchess. At the public reception in Toronto they shook hands with over 2,000 people.

III

Yet there can be no doubt of the enthusiasm of Canadians to meet the royal couple. This enthusiasm was undoubtedly greatest among the social and political elites, and at every stop the list of the party on the official platform reads like a who's who of the community. For a few there was an opportunity to have lunch or dinner with the Duke and for an even smaller number more substantial rewards, since the Duke had been given special authority to confer knighthoods and invest members in various imperial orders. But at the very least an invitation to the formal reception to welcome the Duke was essential to establish one's social credentials. In every community there were volunteers who devoted hours of unpaid labour preparing for the royal visit. In Saint John, New Brunswick, for example, in addition to the General Committee which consisted of the mayor, four aldermen and 12 men, there was an 11-man Firemen and Salvage Corps Committee, a seven-man sub-committee to distribute funds, a seven-man Committee for Decorating Fire Stations and Streets and to Procure Fireworks, a ten-man committee in charge of street decorations, an 11-man civic reception committee (consisting of the mayor and the ten aldermen) and a 14-man Executive of the Citizens Committee (which one assumes had a number of sub-committees of its own).[92] Similar committees – some larger, some smaller, some more and some less representative of the community – existed in every town which the Duke visited, and an examination of their composition tells us a great deal about the structure of political and social power and about who was considered important in these communities. But the enthusiasm was not confined to the elites and occasionally social tensions surfaced. At the major reception in Toronto, where it was decided to have a large public reception, there was a huge crowd and a 'horrible crush, in which many ladies had their gowns torn to pieces'. But when an Ottawa newspaper blamed the problem on the failure to restrict access, the Toronto *Mail-Empire* retorted that, 'If there was any unseemly crush it must have been among the privileged set, and goes to show what an unseemly thing it is to attempt to divide the people into classes at a public event.'[93] Indeed, when it was proposed to charge an entrance fee for the military review in Toronto, there was a public outcry against the charge for barring 'many of the poorer classes from this spectacle'.[94] A number of Canadian newspapers pointed out that in the presence of the monarch all men are equal and demanded that receptions should be 'open to all, regardless of rank and clothing'.[95] Some newspapers also gleefully pointed out that the Duke did not speak with an upper-class English accent like those Canadians who sought to put on airs. In fact, George spoke 'like an educated Canadian'![96] (If true, this was probably because George had never attended a private school or Oxbridge.) If there was resentment against the local arrangements it was usually because they were too exclusive, and it was directed against the local elite for trying to limit access to the monarch, but never against the royal visitors themselves.

In addition to the formal events there were the informal. Pope, who accompanied the tour across the country, was struck by the number of people who hung ribbons or flags beside the track or who stood at a station in the middle of the night to wave at the train as it went by. In Ontario the tour was dogged by bad weather, but in Toronto the 'wind and rain had no appreciable effect upon the throngs that turned out to-day in the welcome and show of loyalty. Wrapped in water-proofs or sheltered under umbrellas the people waited for hours in the sodden streets and warmed themselves with cheers when the prince and princess finally came.'[97] It is the extent of this popular enthusiasm which casts doubt upon those who would interpret the tour as merely an excuse for a holiday. Quite obviously some of the enthusiasm was inspired by the fact that many (but not all) stores and businesses shut for a day in the Duke's honour. Equally obvious there were commercial incentives for some of the enthusiasm. For the newspapers special editions meant extra profits. For the railways large crowds travelling to the events meant more income. There was also an opportunity to promote tourism, even if it meant downplaying some of Canada's less attractive features: 'To a native of Great Britain', a pamphlet issued by the Grand Trunk railway proclaimed, 'a Canadian winter presents many interesting features.' And lest the native of Great Britain associate these interesting features with bitterly cold weather, the pamphlet declared that, 'It is no uncommon thing for the weather to be so warm around Christmas time that even a light overcoat may be dispensed with.'[98] Companies making flags and fireworks were undoubtedly overjoyed by the tour and a host of special commemorative items were produced for the occasion (including something described as 'royal wallpaper'). Pickpockets made windfall profits at the crowded events. Yet all of this activity is also a sign of popular enthusiasm for the tour. The special editions did sell out, the railways were jammed with people determined to see the royal visitors, private homes as well as government buildings and department stores were covered with decorations, and people bought the flags and waved them enthusiastically.

Quite obviously there were degrees of enthusiasm. Mackenzie Wallace noted that the crowds in Quebec were 'not such adepts in the art of vigorous cheering as our Australian and New Zealand cousins', but attributed this coolness to the fact that the French Canadians 'are by nature a more reserved and less demonstrative people'.[99] The *Toronto Daily Star* had a different explanation. It suggested that people in Quebec did not cheer because they did not realise that they were supposed to: 'the whole reception was so entirely in the hands of officials and military authorities, so fixed and formal in all its particulars, that the people felt themselves not to be participants'.[100] Neither explanation rings entirely true. Yet even in Quebec there was no overt opposition to the tour. Although some criticism initially was made of the Duke for his failure to use more French (which George spoke but not fluently), he was applauded by the French-Canadian press when he did make a short speech in French.[101] Virtually every important French-Canadian association, including the Saint Jean Baptiste Society, prepared an address warmly welcoming the Duke, and the major French-Canadian papers carried articles about the Duke and Duchess virtually identical to those found in the English-language press. French-language papers, like their English-language counterparts, printed special editions focusing on the tour and offered for sale portraits of the visitors. And French Canadians did turn out in large numbers to see their future King and Queen. Over 30,000 people – virtually the whole population of Quebec city – watched the military parade on the Plains of Abraham. '*Toute la journée hier, toute la nuit, et depuis le petit jour ce matin, la population de la Vieille Capitale est dans l'attente de Leurs Altesses Royales. – La ville regorge d'étrangers. – Les rues et les places publiques sont littéralement encombrées*', reported *La Presse*.[102] 'Latent French-Canadian enthusiasm', the *Toronto Star* proclaimed, 'so long in germinating, sprouted and blossomed vigorously.'[103] All along the route from Quebec city to Montreal '*le people massait aux différentes gares pour voir les visiteurs royaux et pour les acclamer*'.[104] In Montreal 250,000 people turned out to see the Duke and Duchess, and 'Miles and miles of French Streets were splendidly bedecked'.[105] This showed, according to *La Presse*, that '*ici à Montréal, les deux éléments, qui vivent dans une mutuelle estime, et sous l'empire d'une généreuse réciprocité de sentiments, sont égaux par l'attachment qu'ils portent aux même institutions*'.[106] Similarly, *L'Evénement* declared that the reception given to the Duke proved that '*si l'élément français de ce pays s'est toujours montré réfractaire à toute assimilation anglaise, s'il a gardé envers et contre tous et s'il gardera toujours adèlement ses traditions nationales, sa langue et sa religion, il n'en reste pas moins attaché à la Couronne et aux institutions britanniques*'.[107]

There were a few voices of dissent. *La Nation*, a nationalist journal, showed a marked ambivalence about the tour. It insisted that the ceremonies in Quebec and Montreal had been marked '*par une raideur excessive chez le Prince et par une froideur, une tenue à distance des plus visibles, chez le peuple*'.[108] Several papers suggested that the reason why French-Canadian enthusiasm was muted was the fear that loyalty to the crown might be interpreted as enthusiasm for the policies of Joseph Chamberlain.[109] But most French Canadians in 1901 seem to have had little difficulty in reconciling loyalty to the crown and British institutions with a commitment to the preservation of their own national culture. Most houses in Quebec flew both 'a Union Jack and a tricolor'.[110] And French Canadians sang 'O Canada' with the same gusto with which English Canadians sang 'The Maple Leaf Forever'.[111]

In English Canada the crowds were large and enthusiastic everywhere. In Toronto the crowds of 'Cheering Britishers' were estimated at between 200,000 and a quarter of a million. Since the total population of the city was only around 200,000, a substantial number of the observers – perhaps as many as half – must have come from the surrounding townships and villages.[112] Nearly 8–10,000 gathered at Belleville at 9:15 in the morning for a ten minute stop.[113] In Cornwall 4,000 people waited at the station where the train made a brief stop.[114] In Kingston an estimated 50,000 visitors poured into the city.[115] Over a thousand people gathered at the railway station in Whitby, Ontario, simply to see the train go through. The train left Brockville at 7:45pm and did not reach Belleville until 12:30 in the morning but at every little switchhouse on the line there was 'a crowd of people, cheering and waving whatever piece of cotton linen or bunting they could lay their hands on'. Even the third train, which only carried the mounted escort and did not arrive until 1:30 in the morning, was cheered since the crowds did not know which train was carrying 'the objects of their affection'.[116] In Vancouver and Victoria and throughout the west the size of crowds exceeded all expectations. In Winnipeg the highlight of the visit was a chorus of over 2,000 schoolchildren: 'When they sang "God Save the King" it was with emphasis. When they sang "Rule Britannia" it was with electrifying emphasis on the word "Britannia" that gave meaning to the song.'[117] But the Maritimes was not to be outdone. The biggest crowd in Saint John's history gathered to see the Duke, and in Halifax as many as 10,000 people poured in from the surrounding countryside, the streets were lined with 5,000 soldiers, and a crowd of 25,000 watched as the Duke laid the cornerstone of a memorial to the Nova Scotian volunteers who had fallen in the Boer War.[118] Loyalty to the institution of the monarchy was a national phenomenon, overriding the regional differences that divided Canadians.

The obvious places to look for overt resistance to the tour are in the fledgling labour movement and among Catholics, particularly those of Irish origin. Yet if there were substantial numbers of either group opposed to the tour they largely kept their opinions to themselves. Most of the (relatively few) labour papers did not spend much time on the tour but their coverage was generally positive. The organ of the Winnipeg labour movement, *The Voice*, was the most outspokenly anti-imperial newspaper in Canada. It was critical of British actions in South Africa and believed that, 'British India is worked mainly for the money there is in it for blood-suckers, to provide a field for the swarms of parasitical officials, and to gratify the mere love of conquest'.[119] Yet it concluded that, 'As a holiday and a spectacle Winnipeg enjoyed the day [of the royal visit] to the full (those at work excepted), nothing occurred to mar the pleasantness of the visit, and though there is naturally some criticism of the arrangements and money expended, this will be largely condoned by the success of the visit.'[120] Winnipeg, it declared, had greeted the heir to the throne 'with heartiness and sincerity'. This may have been insincere. But since the labour movement in Canada was very small and its leadership was overwhelmingly British-born, indeed formed of the same kind of men who would lead the Labour Party in Britain, it is more likely that most labour supporters were as royalist as other British Canadians. During the Duke's visit the Trades and Labour Council of Brantford, Ontario, carried a resolution mourning the death of Queen Victoria and expressing their sympathy to Edward VII. Of course, labour saw the Duke's visit as an opportunity not only to parade their loyalty but also to put forward their own political agenda. A number of newspapers carried 'Labour's Loyal Petition', a lengthy poem written by a Marie Joussaye, a labour activist, which declared:

> We know that only the statesman, the soldier, the scribe, the priest,
> The high and rich and mighty may sit at the royal feast,
> But we claim this right for Labour, the right to grasp your hand,
> To look in your eyes and speak to you as man should speak to man.
> The right to tell of the struggle in the land of the Northern Zone,
> Where honest Labour is ground in the dust and Greed usurps the throne.[121]

To the great embarrassment of the Laurier government, the labour movement in British Columbia sought to present an address to the Duke which was 'in reality a petition against the Chinese, and an arraignment of the Govt for having disallowed anti-Mongolian legislation'.[122] Upon Laurier's recommendation, though the blame was generally placed on Minto and Maude, the Duke declined to accept the petition.

The issue of the tour becoming a source of controversy between

Catholics and Protestants was a more serious possibility. That was precisely what had happened in 1860 when the Orange Lodge had used the visit of the Prince of Wales as an occasion for widespread anti-Catholic demonstrations. The Laurier government was determined to prevent similar demonstrations in 1901 and to incorporate Catholics fully into the celebrations. So too was Minto, who warned against the introduction into the programme of any feature 'which might tend to mar the unanimity and heartiness of the welcome' given to the Duke.[123] Thus in Quebec city, in order to balance a visit to a meeting of the synod of the Church of England, a visit to Laval was added to the programme at Laurier's request (over the initial objections of the Duke's advisers who felt the programme was already too heavy).[124] Across the country sincere efforts were made to involve Catholics. In a number of Ontario communities the massed choir of children was expanded to incorporate children from the separate schools. Indeed, in Belleville children from all the city schools gathered to sing the national anthem and 'Rule Britannia', including the pupils from the school for the deaf and dumb who used sign language.[125] In Toronto the editor of the *Catholic Register* reported that the citizens' committee of 500 was 'representative in reality of all classes and creeds' and included 'perhaps half hundred of our leading Catholic citizens'. He correctly predicted that this would ensure 'a loyal and hearty, *and united* welcome'.[126] Even among Irish Catholics there was no opposition to the tour. By 1901, Irish Catholics in Canada had been effectively integrated into the British majority and there was no serious republican movement (certainly no vocal one).[127] Yet though Irish Catholics were as 'emphatic in their declarations of loyalty' as other Canadians, they did point out in their address of welcome 'how much the Empire would be strengthened if those principles of self-government existing in New Zealand, Australia and Canada were applied to Ireland'.[128] The *Catholic Register* felt that it is 'a truth that can never be too often repeated, viz. that Irishmen, in common with all Canadians, are loyal because they have Home Rule'.[129]

Not all cultural minorities were so effectively integrated into the celebrations. In Vancouver, the *World* proclaimed that the Duke will receive a 'cosmopolitan reception ... – Whitemen, Red Indians, Brown Japanese and Yellow Chinese Join in Acclaiming Britain's Heir'.[130] In Halifax Black Canadians and in Vancouver Chinese Canadians were encouraged to present addresses to the Duke and they eagerly sought to show their loyalty. Yet the participation of non-whites in the ceremonies was at best nominal. This was particularly the case with the native peoples. In a number of communities native people were involved in the welcoming ceremonies but they had little control over the nature of that involvement. The image of native peoples carefully cultivated by the Canadian government was of a savage and

uncivilised people who had excelled only in one area of activity – warfare.
Thus native peoples were encouraged to put on war dances in Ottawa and
Calgary and to arrive in war canoes in Victoria and to try to appear as
'savage' as possible. The other image which the Canadian government also
cultivated was its success in bringing civilisation and prosperity to the
native peoples, and so there were visits to industrial schools for native
peoples. The limits placed upon the involvement of native people were most
clearly illustrated in the large native pow-wow arranged to entertain the
King in Calgary. The Department of Indian Affairs organised the event, the
North West Mounted Police (renamed the Royal North West Mounted
Police) provided security, and the access of the native leaders to the Duke
was carefully controlled. The official address from the more than 2,000
Indians who had gathered to welcome the Duke was read by David Wolf
Carrier, a young Sarcee, but it had been written by the Canadian
government's Indian Commissioner and more reflected the views of the
Indian Department than the Indians themselves. When the head chiefs met
individually with the Duke, they did attempt to make clear that they were
far from contented with the status quo.[131] There is no evidence that the Duke
was particularly moved by their grievances. Indeed, he probably shared the
views of his aide-de-camp and friend, Bryan Godfrey-Faussett, who noted
in his diary that although many of the chiefs seemed contented, 'others were
full of growls and dissatisfaction with their lot' and complained not only
that they had been disposed of the vast lands which they had once owned
but that 'white men' continued to encroach upon what was left. Godfrey-
Faussett doubted that these stories were true. Altogether he found the
Indians 'a very contented people' and, while they could not be blamed for
being unhappy with the changes that had taken place in the west, he
predicted that 'The coming generation not having known these good things
will perhaps be more satisfied with its lot; they are I understand slowly but
surely dieing [sic] out – a departing race & perhaps will be a good thing
when they are gone.'[132]

IV

Enthusiasm for the tour was inevitably greatest among English-speaking
Canadians of British ethnic origin. 'Time can weaken the strongest ties',
declared the London *Morning Post*, 'but it has not yet weakened the blood
tie that makes white hands throughout the British Empire clasp each other
as with the knowledge of a hidden secret that will outlive life.'[133] In 1901,
the vast majority of English-speaking Canadians were emigrants from Great
Britain or descendants of British emigrants. In referring to themselves the
term 'English Canadian' was never used; consistently the majority of

Canadians of British origin referred to themselves as Britishers or British Canadians, though those of Scottish and Irish origin also referred to themselves as Scottish or Irish Canadians. In his speech given at the London Guildhall upon his return to England, the Prince of Wales (as he now was) noted how 'touching' it had been to 'hear the invariable references to home, even from the lips of those who never had been or were ever likely to be in these islands'.[134] There has been a continuing debate both in Britain and in Canada over whether there has ever existed a sense of British as opposed to an English, Irish, Scottish, Welsh or even Canadian identity. The problem with this debate is that it tends to see ethnic identities as static and as mutually exclusive. When a sense of being British emerged and how long it survived may be questions open to debate but that it existed both in Britain and in the colonies of Britons overseas in 1901 is clear. Indeed, the monarchy was one of the key institutions promoting a sense of Britishness. In Britain the monarchy had already begun to play down its English roots and to emphasise its British ones by touring Scotland (wearing a tartan, of course) and Ireland. This programme was more successful in Scotland than in Ireland, but in 1901 many Catholics in Ireland (not to mention the majority of Protestants) still had a sense of being British as well as Irish. In the 'little Britains' overseas, which were formed of immigrants from different parts of the British Isles, it was even easier to reconcile the original ethnic identities of the immigrants with a sense of Britishness. When the Duke came to the colonies he consistently stressed his British rather than his English roots. To an extent this was easy to do, since the Hanoverian dynasty had been imported from Germany and for six generations had chosen their spouses from a pool of European – predominantly German – royal families. They had hardly intermarried at all with the local English aristocracy. As the Canadian press was fond of pointing out, the Duchess of Cornwall was the first British-born princess (although even her father had been an impecunious German prince); 'the British people', the Halifax *Herald* noted, 'are now in a fair way to escape fully from a reproachful criticism which used to be made that the British Royal Family was very far from being entirely British'.[135]

The reality that Hanoverians were a bunch of German *parvenus* did not stop Canadian royalists from referring to them as part of a royal house whose roots went back 'for more than a thousand years'.[136] The implication, of course, was that their roots lay in ancient Britain when the whole country had been unified under the mystical King Arthur. In Quebec this emphasis was altered to stress the Norman (i.e. French) roots of the monarchy. In Scottish areas it was the Stuart connection which was stressed. While the Duke was giving a speech in Glengarry, Ontario, where the population was composed largely of descendants of Highland Scots, a piper struck up 'a pronounced Jacobite air', and in his speech the Duke referred to 'his Stuart ancestors', glossing over the fact that the Protestant Hanoverians had been imported to replace the Catholic Stuarts and had only succeeded after crushing the Jacobite rebellion at Culloden.[137] But what was important was that the monarchy was attempting to define itself as a British, not a purely English, institution. This effort struck a responsive chord in the colonies where the Scottish and Irish formed a much larger proportion of the population than they did in the mother country. The Victoria *Daily Times*, for example, noted as evidence of the commitment of the Heir Apparent to imperial unity that he named his eldest son George Andrew Patrick David – 'those of the patron saints of our four nationalities'.[138] In Kingston a special song of welcome proclaimed that the Normans, Saxons and Celts were 'yet Britons'.[139] In 'the representatives of the royal line of the Guelphs', the *Vancouver Province* asserted, 'we have the lineal descendants of three sovereign races whose union into one people have made Britain what she is to-day, the greatest progressive force and the greatest power for good in the known world'.[140]

As Judith Bassett notes, in New Zealand the royal tour of 1901 'drew the whole country together in a celebration of New Zealand as New Zealanders wished it to be seen at that time'.[141] The same might be said of Canadians – certainly of English-speaking Canadians in 1901 – and clearly what they wanted to celebrate was, as Balfour had recognised, their membership in a global empire and their loyalty to the monarchy. Neither distance nor birth in foreign fields made the English-speaking majority feel any less British. Yet this sense of being British did not preclude an equally strong sense of being Canadian. In 1901 Canadians consciously copied British models in organising the royal tour to Canada. They copied what had been done during the 1887 and 1897 jubilee celebrations in Britain, even importing some of the same fireworks specialists. But they also sought to add a distinctively Canadian flavour to the ceremonies. They arranged for the Duke to view Canadian loggers and cattlemen and farmers at work. They organised concerts at which Canadian singers would sing songs about Canada composed by Canadians. They wanted the royal party to view Canadian wildlife (even if George was more interested in shooting it) and to learn about Canadian history, or at least a version of Canadian history which emphasised the sacrifices made by the Loyalists and the efforts of Canadians to preserve the imperial connection during the War of 1812–14. They presented the Duke and Duchess with gifts which were uniquely Canadian or at least embossed with Canadian symbolism. In all these ways they asserted their own identity within the empire as Canadians. 'We are proud to be Canadians[;] God Bless the British Empire' was the wording on one banner welcoming the Duke.[142] There was also a conscious effort to

create the sense of a Canadian monarchical tradition by linking the 1901
tour with the previous 1860 tour. If a university had given the Prince of
Wales an honorary degree, it sought to confer one on his son in 1901. At
Brantford, Ontario, the Duke signed a bible given in 1712 to the Mohawk
Church, the same bible signed by his father in 1860. In Montreal a pause
was made at the Victoria Jubilee Bridge, into which the Prince of Wales had
driven the last rivet in 1860. In Ottawa George viewed a lacrosse game
sitting on a chair built for his father in 1860. Anyone who had been on a
public platform to meet Edward in 1860 was invited back in 1901. In 1860
Laura Secord, heroine of the War of 1812, had been presented to Edward;
in 1901 her daughter was presented to George. In these and in other ways
Canadians – for the initiative came from them – sought to stress the
continuity of the monarchical tradition in Canada.

   The various ceremonies were designed to emphasise that the residents of
Canada were still British and that the monarchy was not an alien institution
but one which belonged as much to those who lived in the 'little Britains'
overseas as to those who lived in the mother country. 'The besetting sin of
the Englishmen of the present generation', noted the Toronto *Globe* (a paper
consistently hostile to any idea of imperial federation), 'is that he has not
come to realize that the British community includes the Britons of Greater
Britain.'[143] But the rituals associated with the royal visit not only enabled the
majority of British Canadians to reaffirm their commitment to the empire
and their sense of being British, they also assisted Canadians in the
construction of their own identity within the empire. The tour was seen as a
symbol of Canada's status as a self-governing nation, taking its place
alongside the other self-governing nations united by loyalty to a common
crown. Supporters of imperial federation hoped that the tour would lead
toward greater integration of the empire, but they represented only a
minority. As the *Manitoba Free Press* pointed out, 'it would be a great
mistake to suppose because of our enthusiastic greeting of Royalty and our
ready acceptance to assist the mother country in South Africa that there is
any disposition to undervalue the constitutional rights of the Canadian
people'.[144] Whatever ambiguity this dual identity of being both British and
Canadian might hold for future generations of Canadians, it clearly held no
such difficulties for most English-speaking Canadians – even native-born
English-speaking Canadians – in 1901. 'Far removed though Vancouver is
from the seat of the empire', noted the Vancouver *World*, 'yet its citizens
feel that they are as true sons of Britain as they among whom royalty
dwells.'[145] The Collingwood *Bulletin* noted that the crowds in Toronto

> cheered as men and women have never cheered in Toronto before;
> [yet] not one in six was born in the old land beyond the seas; not one

in six had heard the lark's mating song and the music of the nightingale, or had scented the hawthorn in the May morning. Yet here they were greeting with passionate acclaim a Prince, who, until that day had been to them but a name.[146]

And when the children broke out in 'Rule Britannia', the paper continued, 'it was with the flutter of several thousand Union Jacks'.[147] At the other end of Canada the Victoria *Daily Times* echoed this feeling: 'Sentiment is one of the most puissant of the forces in human nature. We are bound to the royal family by sentiment; we are joined together as Britishers in England, Scotland and Ireland, in Australia, in India, in the possessions too numerous to mention, and in Canada by sentiment.'[148] There was, of course, another reason for emphasising Canada's commitment to the monarchy. The royal tour, an Ontario paper noted, has been well covered in the United States and 'it has brought home to the minds of the American people the intense loyalty of the Canadians to the British Crown and their invincible attachment to [the] British connection'.[149]

The strength of this sentiment – the desire to build up 'a Canadian nation, yet one thoroughly loyal to the British Throne and devoted to the maintenance of those principles on which British institutions are based'[150] – would be shown in the First World War, when so many Canadians flocked to enlist to fight for a homeland many of them had never seen and others only distantly remembered. One observer noted during a remembrance ceremony in 1935 that many of the youth who sang 'God Save the King' to welcome the Duke to Toronto in 1901 'are now remembered in the cenotaph which now stands [on the spot] where in 1901 the people of Toronto heard the royal duke take pride in the fact that the first title "conferred upon me by my dear grandmother" was that of this city before it became Toronto'.[151] This sense of being British as well as Canadian, and of the royal family as belonging to those who lived in the British Dominions overseas as well as to the British at home, did not quickly dissipate after 1918, a casualty of the First World War. It had not disappeared when George's son, Edward, toured Canada as the Prince of Wales in 1919, or when his other son George VI became the first reigning monarch to visit Canada in 1939. And among many Canadians it had not disappeared in 1951 and 1959 when Elizabeth first as princess and then as queen toured Canada. Royal tours like that of 1901 did not – indeed could not – create this sentiment. It was the product of a peculiar pattern of migration, which meant that (contrary to what is usually believed) Canada was composed of two ethnic cores. In Quebec a substantial majority of the Canadian population defined its roots as French, while outside of Quebec the population of Canada was still overwhelmingly of British origin and most of those who were not were eager to be accepted as part of the British majority. 'Canada is British', proclaimed the Toronto *Globe*, 'because of the desire of its inhabitants to remain British.'[152] For these British Canadians and for several generations of their descendants, the British monarchy was not an alien institution; it was something they could and did imagine as belonging to them, as part of their birthright and as part of their sense of national identity. It would take a major crisis of identity in the period after the Second World War – what José Igartua has called English Canada's 'Quiet Revolution' – to challenge this vision of the monarchy.[153]

NOTES

1. Toronto *Telegram*, 11 Oct. 1901.
2. Toronto *News*, 9 Oct. 1901.
3. See Memorandum of Journalists and Photographers accompanying the Royal Train, Governor General's papers, RG 7 G23, vol.3, no.44, National Archives of Canada [hereafter NAC].
4. E.F. Knight, *With the Royal Tour* (Toronto, 1902); William Maxwell, *With the 'Ophir' Round the Empire* (London, 1902); Joseph Watson, *The Queen's Wish: How it was fulfilled by the Imperial Tour of T.R.H. The Duke and Duchess of Cornwall and York* (Toronto, 1902); Sir Donald Mackenzie Wallace, *The Web of Empire: A Diary of the Imperial Tour of their Royal Highnesses the Duke and Duchess of Cornwall and York in 1901* (London, 1902); Joseph Pope, *The Tour of Their Royal Highnesses the Duke and Duchess of Cornwall and York Through the Dominion of Canada in the year 1901* (Ottawa, 1903). R.A. Loughnan also produced *Royalty in New Zealand* (Wellington, 1902), covering the New Zealand part of the tour.
5. Government of Canada, *Beyond the Printed Word: Newsreel and Broadcasting Reporting in Canada* (Ottawa, 1988), 118.
6. Hector Charlesworth, *Candid Chronicles: Leaves from the Note Book of a Canadian Journalist* (Toronto, 1925), 253.
7. J. Castell Hopkins, *The Life of King Edward VII* (Toronto, 1910), ch.19.
8. Stephen Leacock, *My Discovery of England* (London, 1952), 49.
9. There is a brief discussion of the tour in Carman Miller, *The Canadian Career of the Fourth Earl of Minto: The Education of a Viceroy* (Waterloo, 1980), 183–6.
10. Victoria R. Smith, 'Constructing Victoria: The Representation of Queen Victoria in England, India and Canada, 1879–1914', Ph.D thesis, Rutgers University, 1998, esp. ch.6; Wade A. Henry, 'Royal Representation, Ceremony and Cultural Identity in the Building of the Canadian Nation, 1860–1911', Ph.D thesis, University of British Columbia, 2001.
11. See *Morang's Annual Register for 1901* (Ottawa, 1902), section vi – Canada and the Crown.
12. Robert M. Stamp, *Kings, Queens & Canadians: A Celebration of Canada's Infatuation with the British Royal Family* (Markham, ON, 1987).
13. Jane Connors, 'The 1954 Royal Tour to Australia', *Australian Historical Studies*, 25 (1993), 382.
14. David Cannadine, 'The Context, Performance and Meaning of Ritual: The British Monarchy and the "Invention of Tradition" c.1820–1977', in Eric Hobsbawm and Terence Ranger (eds.), *The Invention of Tradition* (Cambridge, 1983), 101–64; *idem*, 'The Last Hanoverian Sovereign: The Victorian Monarchy in Historical Perspective, 1688–1988', in A.L. Beier, David Cannadine and James M. Rosenheim (eds.), *The First Modern Society* (Cambridge, 1988), 127–65.
15. Walter L. Arnstein, 'Queen Victoria Opens Parliament: The Disinvention of Tradition', *Historical Research*, 63 (1990), 178–94; J.M. Golby and A.W. Purdue, *The Monarchy and*

the British People, 1760 to the Present (London, 1988), 81.

16. See, for example, Edgar Williams, The Myth of the British Monarchy (London, 1989), 45, where he declares that 'the myth of the popularity of the monarchy is straightforwardly the result of incessant, universal and insidious monarchist propaganda'.

17. Raphael Samuel, 'Introduction: The Figures of National Myth', in Patriotism: The Making and Unmaking of British National Identity, vol.3 National Fictions (London, 1989), xxix.

18. See Terence Ranger, 'The Invention of Tradition Revisited: The Case of Colonial Africa', in T. Ranger and O. Vaughan (eds.), Legitimacy and the State in Twentieth-Century Africa (Oxford, 1993), 62–111.

19. The Royal Tour: Official Programme and Souvenir 1901 (Toronto, 1901), unpaginated. See also The Mail-Empire (Toronto), 12 Sept. 1901.

20. Julian Amery, Life of Joseph Chamberlain, vol.4 (London, 1951), 10.

21. There is a lengthier discussion of Chamberlain's motives in Phillip Buckner, 'The Royal Tour of 1901 and the Construction of an Imperial Identity in South Africa', South African Historical Journal, 41 (1999), 326–29.

22. Chamberlain to Minto, 22 Dec. 1900, Sir Joseph Pope papers, MG 30 E86, vol.77, folder 54(1), NAC.

23. Balfour to Edward VII, quoted in Kenneth Rose, King George V (London, 1983), 44.

24. Quoted in the Tasmanian Mail (Hobart), 19 Jan. 1901.

25. HMS Ophir (London, n.d.), 2.

26. Vancouver World, 28 Sept. 1901.

27. Minto to Lord Wenlock, 6 Sept. 1901, RG 7 G23, vol.4, folder 5, NAC.

28. Minto to Laurier, 29 and 31 July 1901, papers of the Fourth Earl of Minto, MS 12557, 337–39 and 343–46, National Library of Scotland [hereafter NLS]; Minto to the King, 25 Oct. 1901, MS 12561, 97–100, NLS.

29. Minto to Laurier, private, 21 July 1901, Minto papers, MS 12557, 343–46, NLS.

30. Toronto World, 8 Oct. 1901.

31. Montreal Star, 9 Oct. 1901.

32. King George V's diary, 29 Sept. 1901, Royal Archives, Windsor Castle [hereafter RA]. I would like to acknowledge the gracious permission of Her Majesty Queen Elizabeth II for permission to make use of material in the Royal Archives.

33. Entry in Pope's diary, 21 Oct. 1901, Pope papers, MG 30 E86, vol.48, folder 21, NAC.

34. Lord Wenlock to Lady Wenlock, 20 July 1901, papers of Lord Wenlock, DDFA (9)/5/1, Brynmor Jones Library, University of Hull.

35. Frank Prochaska, Royal Bounty: The Making of a Welfare Monarchy (London, 1995).

36. Journal of Captain Sir Bryan Godfrey Godfrey-Faussett, 21 Sept. 1901, BGGF 1/50, Churchill Archives Centre, Cambridge University [hereafter CAC].

37. Courier (Brampton), 9 Oct. 1901.

38. Daily British Whig (Kingston), 14 Oct. 1901.

39. Pope, Tour, 2.

40. 'H.M.S. Ophir: Some statistics during her visit to the colonies ...', GV, F&V Ophir Tour, folder 2, RA.

41. Minto to Laurier, private, 2 April 1901, Minto papers, MS 12556, 249–56, NLS.

42. Great Britain, H.C. Deb., 92 (29 March 1901), 257–59; ibid., 93 (9 May 1901), 1210–11, 1245; ibid., 91 (25 March 1901), 1207.

43. The Imperial Institute Catalogue of the Gifts and Addresses Received by Their Royal Highnesses the Duke and Duchess of Cornwall (London, 1902).

44. Chamberlain to the Duke of Cornwall, 11 July 1901, GV/AA51/21, RA.

45. The City of London, the Prince and Princess of Wales, and the Colonies (London, 1902).

46. Rose, George V, 43–44.

47. Anne Edwards, Matriarch: Queen Mary and the House of Windsor (Bury St Edmonds, 1984), 118.

48. Minto to Chamberlain, 11 Dec. 1900, Pope papers, MG 30 E86, vol.75, folder 52(2), NAC.

49. On Canada and the war in South Africa, see Phillip Buckner, 'Canada', in David Omissi and Andrew Thompson (eds.), The Impact of the South African War (Basingstoke, 2002), 235–50.

50. Vancouver *World*, 18 Sept. 1901; *Daily Telegraph* (Berlin, ON), 17 Sept. 1901.
51. *Hamilton Spectator*, 24 Sept. 1901.
52. *Manitoba Free Press* (Winnipeg), 26 Sept. 1901.
53. *Toronto Daily Star*, 14 Oct. 1901.
54. Toronto *Globe*, 10 Oct. 1901.
55. Pope to Laurier, private, 4 Sept. 1901 and Laurier to Pope, 6 Sept. 1901, Pope papers, MG 30 E86, vol.75, NAC.
56. Minto to Queen Victoria, 14 May 1899, Minto papers, MS 12561, 20–25, NLS.
57. Minto to Chamberlain, private, 15 Feb. 1901, Joseph Chamberlain papers, JC 14/1/3/38, University of Birmingham Archives [hereafter UBA].
58. Chamberlain to Minto, 13 Aug. 1901, which incorporates a number of questions submitted to the King and the latter's replies, Pope papers, MG 30 E86, vol.75, folder 2, NAC.
59. Chamberlain to Minto, 21 Feb. 1901, Colonial Office papers, CO 42/881, f.812, Public Record Office, London.
60. Minto to Chamberlain, 5 March 1901, Minto papers, MS 12557, 233–34, NLS.
61. Report of the Committee of the Privy Council, 20 April 1901, Pope papers, MG 30 E86, vol.75, folder 52(2), NAC.
62. Minto to Sir Francis Knollys, private, 8 April 1901, and Minto to Laurier, private, 1 May and 30 May 1901, Minto papers, MS 12557, 233–34, 274–75, NLS.
63. Draft of Minto to Lieutenant Governors, confidential, 5 June 1901, RG 7 G23, folder 5, no.4, NAC.
64. Maude to Minto, 21 July 1901, Minto papers, MS 12570, 72–76, NLS.
65. Minto to Chamberlain, private, 2 Sept. 1901, Chamberlain papers, JC 14/1/3/28, UBA.
66. Laurier to Chamberlain, private, 17 Sept. 1901, with Chamberlain's comments, JC 14/1/3/2, ibid.
67. Sir Arthur Bigge to Edward VII, 28 July 1901, VIC/W6/3A, RA.
68. King George V's diary, 17 Aug. 1901, RA.
69. Wenlock to Minto, 21 Aug. 1901, RG 7 G23, vol.4, folder 5, NAC.
70. See, for example, the *Lindsay Weekly Post*, 18 Oct. 1901.
71. *Courier* (Brantford), 18 Oct. 1901.
72. Pope to Willison, private and confidential, 14 Aug. 1901, RG 7 G23, vol.3, folder 7, NAC.
73. Toronto *Globe*, 17 Aug. 1901.
74. Maurice Pope (ed.), *Public Servant: The Memoirs of Sir Joseph Pope* (Toronto, 1960), 15.
75. Sir Joseph Pope, *The Flag of Canada* (n.p., 1912).
76. 'Auditor General's Account of Expenses of Reception of Duke of York', Pope papers, MG 30 E86, vol.76, folder 53(1), NAC.
77. Deputy Minister of Militia and Defence to Pope, 19 Feb. 1902, ibid.
78. *City Council Minutes Toronto 1901*, 15 July and 28 Oct. 1901.
79. *Morang's Annual Register for 1901*, 264.
80. Toronto *World*, 26 July 1901.
81. *Morang's Annual Register for 1901*, 264.
82. *Vancouver Province*, 18 Sept. 1901.
83. *Toronto Daily Star*, 17 Sept. 1901.
84. *Hamilton Spectator*, 27 July 1901.
85. John R. Hamilton, *Our Royal Guests* (St John, 1902), 55.
86. *The Voice* (Winnipeg), 23 Aug. 1901.
87. Attorney-General of Ontario to Sir Oliver Mowat, 11 Sept. 1901, RG 7 G23, vol.5, folder 9, NAC.
88. *Hamilton Spectator*, 14 Oct. 1901.
89. Quoted in Rose, *George V*, 52.
90. Minto to Parkin, private, 23 Aug. 1901, Minto papers, MS 12557, 379–82, NLS.
91. Sir Charles Lucas, *Greater Rome and Greater Britain* (Oxford, 1912), 143.
92. A list of the committees and their membership is found in a paper marked simply 'St John' in the Pope papers, MG 30 E86, vol.77, folder 54(1), NAC. A list of members of the committees in the other urban centres can be found in *Morang's Annual Register for 1902*, 264–68.

93. Toronto *Mail-Empire*, 19 Oct. 1901.
94. *Manitoba Free Press*, 10 Sept. 1901.
95. Vancouver *World*, 16 Aug. 1901.
96. Toronto *World*, 12 Oct. 1901.
97. Halifax *Herald*, 11 Oct. 1901.
98. *Through the Provinces of Ontario and Quebec, Canada*, an annotated time table of the tour published by the Grand Trunk Railway system (n.p., 1901), unpaginated. A copy made can be found in the Pope papers, MG 30 E86, vol.84, NAC.
99. Wallace, *The Web of Empire*, 362.
100. *Toronto Daily Star*, 17 Sept. 1901.
101. *L'Evénement* (Québec), 21 Sept. 1901.
102. *La Presse* (Montréal), 16 Sept. 1901.
103. Toronto *Globe*, 18 Sept. 1901, and *Toronto Daily Star*, 18 Sept. 1901.
104. *Le Journal* (Montréal), 19 Sept. 1901.
105. Toronto *World*, 19 Sept. 1901.
106. *La Presse*, 19 Sept. 1901.
107. *L'Evénement*, 17 Sept. 1901.
108. *La Nation* (Montréal), 3 Oct. 1901.
109. See, for example, *L'Avenir du Nord*, 23 Sept. 1901.
110. Wallace, *The Web of Empire*, 367.
111. So far as I have been able to discover, 'O Canada' was sung only in Quebec and in French in 1901.
112. Toronto *Telegram*, 9 Oct. 1901; Collingwood *Bulletin*, 17 Oct. 1901.
113. Montreal *Gazette*, 16 Oct. 1901.
114. Ottawa *Citizen*, 17 Oct. 1901.
115. Montreal *Star*, 17 Oct. 1901.
116. Toronto *Globe*, 16 Oct. 1901.
117. *Manitoba Free Press*, 4 Oct. 1901.
118. Unidentified newspaper clipping, dated 21 Oct. 1901, Pope papers, MG 30 E86, vol.83, folder 60(1), NAC.
119. *The Voice*, 28 June and 9 Aug. 1901.
120. Ibid., 27 Sept. 1901.
121. A copy of the poem, published in the Toronto *Telegram*, 11 Oct. 1901, can be found in the Pope papers, MG 30 E86, vol.82, NAC.
122. Pope to Laurier, 31 Aug. 1901, Sir Wilfrid Laurier papers, MG 26 G, microfilm reel 2714, 58477–8, NAC.
123. Maude to P.T. Cronin, 17 July 1901, RG 7 G23, vol.4, folder 5, NAC.
124. Minto to Laurier, 21 Aug. 1901, Minto papers, MS 12557, 371–74, NLS.
125. Montreal *Gazette*, 16 Oct. 1901.
126. Cronin to Minto, 13 July 1901, RG 7 G23, vol.4, folder 5, NAC.
127. Mark G. McGowan, 'The De-greening of the Irish: Toronto's Irish-Catholic Press, Imperialism and the Forging of a New Identity, 1887–1914', *Historical Papers* (1989), 118–45.
128. Quoted in Wallace, *Web of Empire*, 376. The same point was made by the *Catholic Record* (London), 27 July 1901.
129. Toronto *Catholic Register*, 26 Sept. 1901.
130. Vancouver *World*, 28 Sept. 1901.
131. Wade A. Henry, 'Imagining the Great White Mother and the Great King: Aboriginal Tradition and Royal Representation at the "Great Pow-wow" of 1901', *Journal of the Canadian Historical Association*, new series, 11 (2000), 87–108.
132. Godfrey-Faussett's journal, 28 Sept. 1901, BGGF 1/50, CAC.
133. London *Morning Post*, 1 Nov. 1901.
134. Knight, *With the Royal Tour*, 407.
135. Halifax *Herald*, 19 Oct. 1901.
136. The Reverend F.G. Scott quoted in Pope, *The Royal Tour in Canada*, 22.
137. Ibid., 43.

138. Victoria *Daily Times*, 1 Oct. 1901.
139. *Daily British Whig*, 15 Oct. 1901.
140. Vancouver *Province*, 30 Sept. 1901.
141. Judith Bassett, '"A Thousand Miles of Loyalty": The Royal Tour of 1901', *New Zealand Journal of History*, 21 (1987), 139.
142. Printed Ephemera from the Metropolitan Public Library, Canadian Institute for Historical Microreproductions, microfiche no.4329.
143. Toronto *Globe*, 25 Sept. 1901.
144. *Manitoba Free Press*, 9 Oct. 1901.
145. Vancouver *World*, 30 Sept. 1901.
146. Collingwood *Bulletin*, 17 Oct. 1901.
147. Ibid.
148. Victoria *Daily Times*, 30 Sept. 1901.
149. *Daily Sentinel Review* (Woodstock, ON), 16 Oct. 1901.
150. *Daily News-Advertiser* (Vancouver), 3 Oct. 1901.
151. 'Our King's Visits to Canada By Fred Williams', *Mail and Empire* (Toronto), 6 May 1935, MU 2146, Miscellaneous 1901, Provincial Archives of Ontario, Toronto.
152. Toronto *Globe*, 25 Sept. 1901.
153. See José E. Igartua, 'L'Autre Révolution Tranquille. L'Evolution des Représentations de l'Identité Canadienne-Anglaise depuis la Deuxième Guerre Mondiale', in Gérard Bouchard and Yvan Lamonde, *La Nation Dans Tous Ses Etats: Le Québec in Camparaison* (Montréal, 1997), 271–96.

Communication and Integration: The British and Dominions Press and the British World, *c*.1876–1914

SIMON J. POTTER

At the Second Imperial Press Conference, held in Ottawa in 1920, the proprietor of the London *Daily Telegraph*, Lord Burnham, declared that, 'The British world is a world of its own, and it is a world of many homes.'[1] Burnham used the idea of a British world to reconcile the diverse regional, national and imperial perspectives that characterised the early twentieth-century British Empire. As is now being recognised, the concept also offers historians a means of moving beyond the confines of national histories, without returning to an older, equally restrictive imperial historiography.[2] Few contemporaries, however, used the term 'British world' with any precision. Historians who wish to employ the idea are therefore faced with a complex problem of definition and delineation. One of the purposes of the conferences of which this volume is a product is thus to identify and investigate the characteristics of the British world. Another is to explore how far its component parts were effectively integrated into a coherent whole. While this agenda is extremely broad in nature and geographical scope, an examination of the power relationships that bound together Britain and the settler colonies (or Dominions) – military, economic and demographic – provides us with a preliminary view of the nature of the British world, and also of its limits.

In military terms, members of the British world struck an implicit bargain in the mid-Victorian period according to which defence arrangements would be drawn into a coherent, overarching imperial strategy. Each member would contribute to the master plan rather than give priority to local defence.[3] However, by the late nineteenth century, the future of this arrangement was increasingly in doubt. Admiral Sir John Fisher's policy of concentrating the Fleet in 'home' waters brought into question the extent to which Britain would be able to honour its part of the bargain and protect the Dominions from attack and invasion. As the settler colonies thus began to move towards participation in naval defence, a new dilemma became apparent. Would they provide ships for the Royal Navy, or construct their own fleets? Even after the First World War, it remained unclear how far imperial defence concerns would draw the British world together, or, with the outbreak of war in the Pacific, tear it apart.[4]

Financial and demographic patterns also seemed to point to an ambiguous future for the connection between Britain and the settler colonies. During the early twentieth century Britain invested around £1.2 billion in its empire, at least 70 per cent of which went to the Dominions. The bulk of British capital, however, continued to flow to destinations outside the empire, imperial sentiment having little influence over financial decision-making.[5] More worryingly, the impact of two world wars seriously eroded Britain's ability to act as primary lender to the Dominions, gradually allowing direct investment from the United States to fill the vacuum. The history of migration tells a similar story of promise and uncertainty. In contrast with earlier periods, the first decade of the twentieth century saw the majority of British emigrants select empire destinations over 'foreign' countries.[6] British demographic resources would increasingly remain under the flag. Significant levels of return migration, as well as reports in private letters and published pamphlets, also ensured sustained contact between those who left and those who stayed behind.[7] How long such patterns could be sustained was another question, particularly as, by the 1930s and 1940s, Britain no longer seemed able to supply the migrants required by the Dominions – 'demographic competition replaced complementarity'.[8]

However, the relationship between Britain and the Dominions transcended policy decisions about defence and private calculations regarding investment and migration. Individuals and groups in Britain and the settler colonies were also bound into a British world by much more fundamental and less ambiguous networks of contact and communication.[9] Diverse connections bound 'core' to 'periphery', but also forged links between each of the settler colonies, creating more complex webs of communication than has previously been acknowledged.[10] A historical reconstruction of these networks is essential if we wish to improve our understanding of a British world that interacted through friendship, acquaintance, travel, business, correspondence and, crucially, the sharing of news.

Historians are gradually coming to recognise the significance of the press in this regard.[11] Indeed, it could be argued that, for several reasons, the press was *the* single most important institution acting to define the limits for the acceptable integration of the British world in the late nineteenth and early twentieth centuries. First, during this period technological innovation transformed the press into a pioneering medium of imperial mass communication. Advances in printing and distribution methods allowed papers to cater to ever-larger audiences around the empire, while the advent of telegraph cable technology let news flow around the empire more rapidly than ever before. Print journalism did not lose its primacy until the spread of wireless broadcasting during the 1920s. Second, the press brought an unparalleled level of reciprocity to the imperial connection. United Kingdom journalists wrote for Dominion newspapers; colonial journalists provided British papers with the vast majority of their reports from the Dominions; and papers in the settler colonies looked to journalists in the other Dominions to provide news. Third, the press was peculiar in terms of the social inclusiveness of the journalistic profession. Journalism allowed individuals from backgrounds outside of the traditional political elite to enter the arenas of high and low politics, often bringing diverse political perspectives with them. Press migrants travelling and working their way around the British world could find posts on papers wherever they went.[12] A huge variety of voices, representing a diverse range of opinions on issues of common importance to the component parts of the British world, thus found their echo in the pages of the empire's newspapers.

Examining the press also allows us to engage with the questions of identity that are at the heart of any consideration of the idea of a British world. Many theorists have attempted to link the press with the emergence of identity, particularly national identity.[13] Historians in Britain, Canada, Australia, New Zealand and South Africa have also sought to isolate distinctively 'national' press traditions, and in some cases have argued that the press played a major role in stimulating national identity.[14] An examination of the press from a British world perspective, however, demonstrates that the press helped to sustain a variety of identities which, while sometimes competing, also interacted.

I

During the late nineteenth and early twentieth centuries, contemporaries were certainly exercised by the question of how the press functioned in the context of a British world. Perhaps the most celebrated account was provided by the radical Liberal journalist and political and economic thinker, John A. Hobson, whose interest in the imperial role of the press stemmed from a visit to southern Africa during the build-up to the war of 1899–1902. Sent to provide reports for one of Britain's more radical newspapers, the *Manchester Guardian*, at the Cape Hobson picked up the local Liberal argument that Britain was being forced into war against the Boer Republics of the Transvaal and the Orange Free State by the machinations of the region's powerful mining capitalists, who were seeking to establish a regime more favourable to their own interests. Hobson also adopted the Cape Liberal argument that the mining magnates had been able to manipulate public opinion and government policy through the South

African press, which they had purchased over the previous decades.[15] In his published writings, Hobson added to this conspiracy theory by highlighting the close links that existed between newspapers in London, Cape Town and Johannesburg, and by arguing that British papers had become dependent upon South African journalists and newspapers for information. He alleged that these sources were tainted, in the pockets of the capitalists in whose interests he believed the war in South Africa was being fought. For Hobson, the press was allowing sinister interest groups to manipulate public opinion and government policy across the British world.[16]

Hobson's critique reflected a wider contemporary fear about the changing nature of the press. For Liberals, the press was meant to act as a 'fourth estate', a representative institution equal in status to assemblies sitting in parliament that would reflect and also lead public opinion.[17] As James Bryce argued in his classic *American Commonwealth*, the press could help to shape the views of the 'passive' masses in positive ways, if it was controlled by a benevolent, paternalistic 'active class' of statesmen, journalists and other public men.[18] By the later nineteenth century however, it seemed as if this theory no longer matched the reality of an increasingly commercialised press. Across the empire, newspaper offices shifted into larger buildings that housed new machines capable of churning out massively increased print runs. Expanding railway systems brought the products to new breakfast tables, while advertisers seeking to promote their mass-produced, branded goods provided the money to fund press expansion. In Britain and the settler colonies, individual press enterprises thus became larger and more complex than ever before, and newspaper circulation began to reach previously unheard-of levels.[19] By 1899 the *Montreal Star*, the first Canadian mass-circulation penny daily, had 52,600 readers and annual running costs of over £200,000.[20] In Britain, the *Daily Mail* was averaging daily sales of around 750,000.[21] Circulation figures continued to rise across the empire throughout the pre-war period. Between 1903 and 1907, the circulation of the *Cape Times* doubled to reach 22,000.[22] Between 1898 and 1914, the circulation of the Melbourne *Argus* increased from around 47,000 to 108,280.[23] Between 1901 and 1904 the circulation of the Winnipeg *Manitoba Free Press* more than doubled to reach 28,267.[24]

One early casualty of commercialisation was the Liberal belief that the press would help to educate the masses in middle-class standards of morality and political behaviour. Although high circulation papers could reach more readers than ever before, they also had a worrying tendency to cater to the lowest common denominator of public taste in order to capture the large audiences needed to attract advertisers. For Hobson, the press had thus come to accelerate rather than prevent the debasement of the urban working classes, stifling diversity and encouraging single-minded chauvinism. Drawing on contemporary interest in the study of psychology, Hobson and other Liberals came to see the public as a suggestible, nervous mob open to the demagoguery of any passing imperialist – first Cecil Rhodes, then Joseph Chamberlain, Rudyard Kipling and the Harmsworth press.[25] In Australia, the Naval Scare of 1909, which was followed by offers from the New Zealand and Australian governments to contribute Dreadnoughts to the British Navy, seemed to one contemporary to encapsulate the problems that arose from the operation of the new mass circulation press. 'Australia and New Zealand are converted into subjects ideally isolated for psychological experiments on the "crowd mind". By exhibiting to the subject sheets on which are printed in large type "The Race with Germany." "Hastening Construction." "Dreadnoughts Wanted." "New Zealand's Example," some instructive instances of instinctive combativeness are to be obtained.'[26]

Not everyone was convinced, however, that the commercialised, mass-circulation press would act to debase public opinion. Some believed that it offered opportunities for shaping society in new, positive ways. While Hobson was collecting conspiracy theories in southern Africa, a member of the English gentry, Richard Jebb, was travelling around Canada, Australia and New Zealand compiling source material for his own writings. On returning to Britain Jebb published his ideas in the London *Morning Post* and in books such as the ground-breaking *Studies in Colonial Nationalism* (1905). Jebb firmly believed that national identities were becoming increasingly pronounced in the Dominions. He did not argue however that this would necessarily precipitate the disintegration of the empire.[27] Rather, Jebb envisaged that an overarching, inclusive 'colonial nationalism' would develop in Canada, Australia, New Zealand and South Africa, binding diverse peoples together under the umbrella of Britishness. If British policy could be adjusted accordingly, then an empire based on an alliance of equal sister states could be created, allowing new internal and international challenges to be met and overcome.

According to Jebb, the press could play a major role in the realisation of this ideal. He recognised that, by the end of the nineteenth century, the press in the Dominions had come to promote national identities. In Canada, papers such as the Montreal *Witness* and the Toronto *Globe* were helping to build strong settler communities, while in Australia the Melbourne *Age* had prepared the ground for the more pronounced nationalism of the Sydney *Bulletin*.[28] However, paralleling his broader interpretation of the compatibility of national and imperial loyalties, Jebb believed that increased co-operation and inter-communication between the press in Britain and the Dominions was possible, and would promote imperial unity.

Jebb sought to put these ideas into practice. After the publication of

Studies in Colonial Nationalism, he again travelled around the empire, this time to recruit local correspondents for the London *Morning Post*. Together with the editor of the *Post*, Fabian Ware, Jebb sought to further 'a definite policy by which we hoped to make the *Morning Post* as useful as possible in the work of Imperial Union'.[29] Later, in 1914, working in co-operation with a group of Canadian newspaper editors, he began to publish his own periodical, the *Britannic Review*, which aimed to provide a journal written and read by people from across the British world.[30]

   In Britain, and during his travels overseas, Jebb also promoted the idea of a government-controlled imperial telegraph cable system that would provide the press with an expanded imperial news service.[31] Here, he worked closely with Sir Sandford Fleming, the Scottish-born chief engineer of the Canadian Pacific Railroad (CPR). Fleming, who had supervised the erection of the CPR's telegraph line across Canada, wished to establish a cable under the Pacific to allow direct communication between Canada and Australia and New Zealand.[32] In order to combat the entrenched commercial interests of the Eastern and Eastern Extension Telegraph Company, which enjoyed a monopoly over Australian traffic, Fleming came to advocate colonial and imperial state intervention. Stressing that the unity of the British world could be secured only by 'the freest use of the most perfect means of communication known to us', he eventually obtained agreements from the British and Dominion governments to construct and administer the line.[33]

   Fleming had hoped that the press would eagerly seize on the new cable and use it to increase the flow of news around the empire.[34] However, when the line finally opened not only did it receive far less traffic than it was capable of handling but it also failed to win any custom from the press. As a result, Fleming was driven to advocate the establishment of state-run news services.[35] To understand why this was the case requires an examination of the commercial structures that directed the flow of news around the British world in the late nineteenth and early twentieth centuries.

II

By 1876 a network of undersea telegraph cables had been created that linked Britain and the settler colonies. This certainly facilitated communication within the British world. However, the impact of the new technology was by no means as straightforward as some recent writers have suggested. There was no 'Victorian internet', if by that term we mean an infrastructure of information exchange that made large amounts of news available at little or no cost to people separated by vast distances.[36] Telegraphic communication was limited in terms of carrying capacity, as

chronic congestion of the cable network during the South African War and
the First World War indicated. Moreover, for decades after its completion,
the system remained extremely expensive to use, as the private cable
companies set charges at artificially high levels. The Eastern and Eastern
Extension Telegraph Company was in 1886 charging six shillings and seven
pence per word for press messages between Sydney and London.[37] Even at
the turn of the century, the cost of cabling remained prohibitive, preventing
individuals from using the system on a regular basis, and restricting the
amount of cable news that was available to the press. In 1898 *The Times*
spent a quarter of its annual revenue of £200,000 on foreign
correspondence, including £30,000 on telegraphic charges.[38] This brought in
only small amounts of news, including a mere hundred words per week
from Canada.[39]

A niche was thereby created for organisations that could spread
transmission costs between multiple recipients. One of the first companies
to recognise the potential for syndication was Reuters Telegram Company.[40]
Founded in London in 1851, Reuters set up offices overseas throughout
Britain's formal and informal empire as cable connections were established.
By the early 1900s Reuters had built up a network of some 260 agencies and
correspondents. News from these sources was generally compiled at offices
in the major regional centres before being sent to London by cable. There,
services were edited in the head office and then telegraphed to the major
London newspapers and other subscribers and handed over to the United
Kingdom Press Association for distribution to provincial newspapers. The
service was also cabled back to many of the company's overseas agencies,
where reports were re-edited for local consumption.[41]

Reuters' dominance of the British Empire market for news, secured by
a cartel agreement with the other major international news agencies, helped
to turn London into the main centre for the compilation of the British
world's news services. Reuters ensured not only that British papers were
well informed about events across the empire, but also that newspapers in
the colonies received news from a British perspective, gathered and edited
by British and Dominion journalists. Indeed, while it remained a private,
profit-seeking commercial concern throughout this period, Reuters was
keen to identify itself as an imperial organisation, partly in order to cultivate
links with the British and colonial governments.[42]

However, while presenting itself as the empire's news agency, of all the
settler colonies only in South Africa could Reuters sell its news directly to
the press. In Australia and New Zealand, a further layer of intermediary
organisations emerged, established by combinations of newspapers seeking
to restrict domestic press competition. In Australia, the big city dailies that
dominated the major eastern centres agreed to deny the supply of syndicated

news to potential competitors who, due to high cable rates, would not be able to afford to create alternative news services of their own. In 1895 the two main services, controlled by the Melbourne *Argus* and the Melbourne *Age*, merged into a single combination managed by the *Argus*. This would eventually become the Australian Associated Press. After 1886, the New Zealand United Press Association (UPA), formed by a broader alliance of city and country papers, also took its news from the Australian combinations, an arrangement which lasted into the 1920s.[43]

To some extent, the desire of the Australian and New Zealand combinations to keep the cost of news down tied them closely into an imperial network of communication, or what might be called an imperial press system. By the turn of the century almost all of the cable news published in Australia and New Zealand was being filtered through one source, the *Argus* London office. There staff drew directly and exclusively on news gathered by British concerns such as Reuters, the Central News Agency and various London papers – the cheapest means of gathering news.[44] While the *Argus* London staff and the UPA Sydney agent selected items according to their own criteria of newsworthiness, British journalists ultimately determined what news was available from which to choose. As a result, during the South African War for example, coverage throughout the Australian and New Zealand papers was often uniform and heavily dependent on British correspondents. In describing the relief of Ladysmith, subscribers in Australia and New Zealand all drew on the same reports, provided by Winston Churchill of the London *Morning Post* and Bennett Burleigh of the London *Daily Telegraph*.

In Canada the situation was somewhat different. There, the market for news was dominated by the US Associated Press (AP) and other American agencies. Many lamented this state of affairs, alleging that the news distributed to the Canadian press was unreliable and sensationalistic, and that it had been selected for an anti-British American audience (due in part to Irish-American influence).[45] Complaints, however, were muffled. This was partly a result of the cheapness of the arrangement, which provided eastern Canadian papers with between 10,000 and 40,000 words of news per day at a nominal cost.[46] It also reflected the fact that, despite being selected by Americans, a substantial proportion of the news sent by the AP in fact came from Britain. During the South African War, almost a quarter of AP reports printed by the Toronto *Globe* either cited or directly quoted British newspapers or War Office despatches.[47] A much greater proportion of the service must have drawn on unacknowledged British sources. Further news was provided by American correspondents in London such as Isaac N. Ford of the *New York Tribune*, while the London offices of the larger Canadian papers were also able to mail and cable war news or even make arrangements with London papers such as *The Times* and the *Daily Telegraph* to provide material.[48] From 1903, some Canadian papers also received additional news from London through the Canadian Associated Press (CAP), set up by a combination of eastern city dailies, led by John Ross Robertson's Toronto *Telegram* and subsidised by the Canadian government. Like the Australian and New Zealand combinations, the CAP aimed to minimise the cost of providing news. Its London agents even gutted the press for news at their club, rather than pay to subscribe to the papers themselves![49] Like its Australasian counterparts, the CAP also sought to restrict competition and cement the dominance of the newspapers that had founded it.[50]

Given the imperial context in which the press worked in Canada, Australia and New Zealand, it was unsurprising that few papers adopted a 'pro-Boer' tone during the South African War. The source of the news that was published exerted an inevitable influence over how events were reported around the British world. The five British papers most frequently cited by the Montreal *Star* during the South African War were all Conservative and pro-war (*The Times, Daily Telegraph, Daily Mail, Morning Post* and *Standard*).[51] Similarly, in Australia and New Zealand, there was little in the *Argus* service that proved critical of British involvement in the war.[52] To some extent, the Dominion news combinations thus acted to draw the settler press into closer connections with British newspapers and agencies, ensuring a common imperial viewpoint and contributing to a shared imperial identity. The commercial interests of these organisations, in particular their desire to secure supplies of news as cheaply as possible, meant that the vast bulk of the news flowing around the British Empire in this period came via London, selected and processed by British journalists.

However, in attempting to protect the commercial interests of their members, the Dominion combinations could also develop a national tone and help to establish the limits for imperial integration. This became particularly clear in conflicts with Reuters, when it made sense to strike a national pose in the face of an imperial news agency's commercial challenge. When seeking to beat off an attempt by Reuters to take over the work of his CAP, John Ross Robertson adopted a nationalist (although not anti-British) stance, maintaining that, 'The Canadian Associated Press [acts] on the true principle that the news interests of this country differ from the news interests of the United States ... Canadian journals are doing a good, patriotic work when they build up a press service which specialises in a Canadian rather than a continental direction.'[53] Similarly, when seeking to dislodge Reuters from the South African market, a combination called the South African Amalgamated Press Association (SAAPA), founded by the region's main newspaper chains, argued that it could provide a more 'national' service than the imperial agency. The *Transvaal Leader*, likening the new organisation to similar combinations set up elsewhere in the British world, claimed that, 'as South Africa moves towards nationhood it is necessary that the work of supplying overseas news [is taken on by] a news agency owned and operated by our newspapers themselves'.[54]

This relationship between identity and commercial interest also became apparent in the face of attempts to establish improved imperial press communication. For while interested in securing access to news as cheaply as possible for themselves, the Dominion press combinations did not wish the cost of cable news to fall to a level at which potential competitors would be able to establish rival services. Thus while on one level the combinations acted to strengthen the network of imperial communication, on another they became as big an obstacle to the plans of men like Fleming and Jebb as the cable companies themselves.

III

This became particularly clear during the First Imperial Press Conference, held in 1909, when pressmen from around the British world met in London. Much of the proceedings were taken up with political discussions, during which the rhetoric of imperial unity was pervasive. J.W. Kirwan, editor of the *Kalgoorlie Miner*, argued that the growing spirit of 'colonial nationalism' in the Dominions could be reconciled with an increasing sense of imperial unity, creating an empire of 'nations in alliance'. P.D. Ross of the *Ottawa Journal* similarly claimed that he was 'one of those Canadians who joined to a Canadian patriotism, in which they yielded to none ... the hope, the fervent hope, that the future of Canada would be a part of the future of Great Britain'. British speakers, including the leaders of both the Liberal and Conservative parties, meanwhile stressed their respect for Dominion national identities and rights of self-government.[55] Looking back with hindsight, some contemporaries later argued that the Conference had helped to ensure that the British world went into the First World War united.[56]

However, the Conference atmosphere of brotherly love did not extend to discussions of business matters. Here, debate focused on the issue of securing reduced press cable rates, a key aim of the British organisers and newspaper proprietors who supported and funded the Conference.[57] During the meetings a number of British papers (particularly those owned by Lord Northcliffe, honorary treasurer of the Conference organising committee) editorialised on the need for reduced cable rates, while Harry Lawson (later Lord Burnham) of the *Telegraph* pointed out to delegates that cable news represented a large and growing proportion of total costs for British papers.[58] The Dominion representatives, however, were not to be rallied easily to the standard raised by the British proprietors. Crucially, fearing that reduced rates would open the field up to competition, delegates representing the Australian *Argus* combination were determined to disrupt the campaign.[59] While some of the other delegates were more favourable to a reduction in press cable rates, it was only the South African delegation that contained a substantial number in favour of change. This reflected the fact that SAAPA's challenge to Reuters' position in South Africa was by 1909 faring badly. In the run up to the Conference, Geoffrey Robinson, editor of the Johannesburg *Star* (and a constructive imperialist with his own ideological reasons for promoting change), had issued a memorandum proposing the amalgamation of the existing Dominion news agencies into a single imperial organisation which would dispense with Reuters' services.[60] SAAPA thus switched from its nationalist attack on Reuters to advocating the creation of an imperial news agency, with the same ultimate commercial aim in mind.

Given the divisions between the delegates, neither the Conference nor its specially selected cable committee was able to come to an agreement over concrete plans for securing reduced press rates.[61] As a result, the British government refused to intervene, and it was only the bad publicity that they had received during the Conference that led the cable companies themselves to offer reduced rates.[62] The Pacific Cable Board agreed to halve rates if the Australian and New Zealand governments made a similar reduction on their terminal charges, while the Eastern Company offered a special rate for a limited daily service of syndicated government and parliamentary news.[63] The way that the news agencies and combinations reacted to these reductions again reflected commercial imperatives, and shed more light on how these factors influenced the formulation of identity.

The Eastern Company's offer was taken up by Reuters, which instituted a re-branded 'Imperial News Service', subsidised by the British government and giving South African subscribers 77,000 extra words of cable news per annum, free of charge.[64] Although dressed up in the rhetoric of imperial duty, Reuters' actions were clearly intended to reinforce its market position in South Africa. The new expanded 'Imperial' service struck a decisive blow against SAAPA, bringing the South African rebellion to an end.

In Australia, the reduction granted by the Pacific Cable Board meanwhile paved the way for the launch of a new service to rival that administered by the *Argus* combination. During October and November 1909 an Australian Senate Select Committee examined the issue of press cable services, giving country papers an opportunity to express their dissatisfaction with the *Argus* service (to which they had only limited access). Editors and proprietors of country papers echoed the rhetoric of the Imperial Press Conference, and stressed the imperial importance of establishing a second news service for Australia. Robert McMillan, editor of the Sydney *Stock and Station Journal*, argued that the *Argus* service was run for private commercial gain rather than according to imperial interests, and advocated the completion of a state-owned cable system along the lines proposed by Fleming. Thomas Mitchell Shakespeare, secretary of both the Australasian Provincial Press Association and the New South Wales Country Press Association, meanwhile turned to the Canadian Associated Press to provide precedent for government subsidisation of a service of 'Empire news'.[65] The select committee, composed mainly of Labor senators who already believed that the *Argus* combination had prevented the establishment of a pro-Labor daily paper, duly recommended that the country press be subsidised to run its own news service. This led to the foundation of the Independent Cable Association (ICA).[66] Between June 1910 and June 1911, the total amount of press cable traffic between Britain and Australasia increased by two-thirds.[67]

IV

By the eve of the First World War, the press had developed considerably as an effective medium of imperial mass communication. In the wake of the Imperial Press Conference, more news than ever before was travelling within the boundaries of the British Empire, drawing newspapers and news agencies in both Britain and the Dominions into closer co-operation with one another. Many contemporaries recognised that new and better-integrated networks of contact and communication had thus been forged.

At the beginning of the twentieth century Liberals like Hobson worried over the exact form these connections would take. Disagreement focused on how the new imperial press system should be organised. For the radical Liberal *Manchester Guardian*, it was crucial to secure 'such a multiplication of agencies as will ensure that on any question that arises the people will be put into possession of an adequate statement of the case from all the relevant points of view'.[68] For constructive imperialists like Jebb and Fleming, it was more important to increase the total volume of news flowing around the empire, even if this meant establishing a single, state-controlled channel through which that news would flow. Government intervention was an acceptable substitute for private sector plurality. However, beneath these differences lay a broad consensus that the press provided a natural and legitimate arena for the further integration of the British world.

What became clear during the early twentieth century, and was confirmed by the First World War, was that the extent of imperial press integration would be defined, not by public involvement, as constructive imperialists had envisaged, but by private enterprise, as Liberals had always insisted would be the case.[69] To some extent, this involved the emergence of new syndicated news services, such as that provided by the ICA, fulfilling Liberal hopes for diversity. To a large degree however, it meant the continued power of large news agencies such as Reuters, and of the combinations of Dominion papers that already controlled the flow of news.

This had further significance for the integration of the British world. As news agencies, combinations and smaller newspapers jockeyed for position, they frequently came to align themselves with particular identities in order to strengthen and legitimate their commercial interests. In the process, they acted to develop and sustain those identities in ways that proved much more complex than older histories of the press have allowed. Newspapers did not fulfil a simple, nation-building function in this period. Rather, they continued to work within the context of a multiplicity of identities. Ethnic, religious and linguistic identities clearly played a major role here. Moreover, as the above account has sought to demonstrate, press enterprises interacted with at least three *geographical* bases for identity within the British world: regional, national and imperial. Where the emphasis lay for any particular press enterprise in terms of these different bases was, to a significant extent, determined by commercial considerations. In other words, there was a material motivation to the way that the press functioned in terms of promoting and sustaining identities.

Furthermore, commercial imperatives seldom led press enterprises to stress a single base of identity. This may have been unavoidable given the broader context of a British world in which regional, national and imperial identities, while to some extent separate and, indeed, in some cases conflicting, also often overlapped. Two forms of conjunction were particularly common in the case of the press. First, a regional–imperial overlap could occur, bypassing national identity, for example in the Australian case where small country papers sought to challenge larger combinations by mobilising imperial sentiment. Second, a national–imperial overlap could also emerge, as illustrated by the case of the large combinations in Canada or South Africa, which drew on national and imperial identities alternately and sometimes even simultaneously. The picture is thus clearly more complex than historians adopting either a purely national or exclusively imperial perspective might admit. Therein lies the virtue of exploring the concept of a British world.

NOTES

I would like to thank Andrew Thompson for his extremely helpful comments on an earlier draft of this paper.

1. R. Donald, *The Imperial Press Conference in Canada* (London, 1921), 136.
2. On this challenge, see A.G. Hopkins, 'Back to the Future: From National History to Imperial History', *Past & Present*, no.164 (1999), 198–243.
3. P. Burroughs, 'Defence and Imperial Disunity', in A. Porter (ed.), *The Oxford History of the British Empire*, vol.3 *The Nineteenth Century* (Oxford, 1999); A. Clayton, '"Deceptive might": Imperial Defence and Security, 1900–1968', in Judith M. Brown and Wm. Roger Louis (eds.), *The Oxford History of the British Empire*, vol.4 *The Twentieth Century* (Oxford, 1999).
4. David Day, *The Great Betrayal: Britain, Australia and the Onset of the Pacific War 1939–42* (North Ryde, NSW, 1988).
5. L.E. Davis and R.A. Huttenback, *Mammon and the Pursuit of Empire: The Political Economy of British Imperialism, 1860–1912* (Cambridge, 1986).
6. S. Constantine, 'Migrants and Settlers', in Brown and Louis (eds.), *Oxford History of the British Empire*, vol.4, 167.
7. It has been estimated that between 1860 and 1930, up to 40 per cent of emigrants from England and Wales may have returned for some period of time. See A. Thompson, *Imperial Britain: The Empire in British Politics, c.1880–1932* (Harlow, 2000), 19.
8. Constantine, 'Migrants and Settlers', 185.
9. John Darwin has hinted at this in 'A Third British Empire? The Dominion Idea in Imperial Politics', in Brown and Louis (eds.), *Oxford History of the British Empire*, vol.4, 72, 86.
10. For a pioneering discussion of the creation of such links in the early nineteenth century, see A. Lester, 'British Settler Discourse and the Circuits of Empire', *History Workshop Journal*, no.54 (2002), 27–50.
11. See, for example, J.D. Startt, *Journalists for Empire: The Imperial Debate in the Edwardian Stately Press, 1903–1913* (Westport, CT, 1991); and Thompson, *Imperial Britain*, esp.61–80.
12. For a more detailed discussion of these themes, see S. Potter, *News and the British World: The Emergence of an Imperial Press System 1876–1922* (forthcoming), esp. chs.1 and 7. On the fortunes of press migrants, see also E. Morrison, 'Grub Street Inventor: James Harrison's Journalism, Old and New, in Geelong, Melbourne and London', in D. Cryle (ed.), *Disreputable Profession: Journalists and Journalism in Colonial Australia* (Rockhampton, 1997), 55–77; and B. Griffen-Foley, '"The crumbs are better than a feast elsewhere": Australian Journalists on Fleet Street', *Journalism History*, 28 (2002), 26–37.
13. See, for example, M. McLuhan, *The Gutenberg Galaxy: The Making of Typographic Man* (London, 1962); E. Gellner, *Nations and Nationalism* (Oxford, 1983); and B. Anderson, *Imagined Communities: Reflections on the Origin and Spread of Nationalism*, 2nd edn. (London, 1991).
14. In Britain, the idea of a 'national' media tradition, excluding censorship and direct state intervention, but encompassing some public sector institutions, particularly in broadcasting, permeates the literature. See, for example, P.M. Taylor, *The Projection of Britain: British Overseas Publicity and Propaganda, 1919–1939* (Cambridge, 1981), and M.L. Sandars and P.M. Taylor, *British Propaganda during the First World War, 1914–18* (London and Basingstoke, 1982), both of which present propaganda as something inherently 'un-British'; and A. Briggs, *The History of Broadcasting in the United Kingdom*, vol.1 *The Birth of Broadcasting* (London, 1961). For discussions of the nation-building properties of the press in the settler societies, see, for example, R.C. Brown, 'Canadian Nationalism in Western Newspapers', in D. Swainson (ed.), *Historical Essays on the Prairie Provinces* (Toronto, 1970), 89–98; P. Rutherford, *The Making of the Canadian Media* (Toronto, 1978), 38–63; P. Day, *The Making of the New Zealand Press: A Study of the Organizational and Political Concerns of the New Zealand Newspaper Controllers 1840–1880* (Wellington, 1990); K. Sinclair, *A Destiny Apart: New Zealand's Search for National Identity* (Wellington, 1986), 61–64; K.T. Livingston, *The Wired Nation Continent* (Melbourne, 1996); and the essays in

J.D. Vann and R.T. Van Arsdel (eds.), *Periodicals of Queen Victoria's Empire: An Exploration* (Toronto, 1996). The case of South Africa is somewhat different, but a 'national' tradition stressing the impact of mining capital on the press, derived from the Cape Liberal theories discussed below, may be detected. See, for example, W.A. Hachten, *Muffled Drums: The News Media in Africa* (Ames, IA, 1971), 240; R. Ainslie, *The Press in Africa: Communications Past and Present* (London, 1966), 41–4; E. Potter, *The Press as Opposition: The Political Role of South African Newspapers* (London, 1975), 34–43; and S. Marks and S. Trapido, 'Lord Milner and the South African State', *History Workshop Journal*, no.8 (1979), 63–67. A detailed break-down of the various press interests of the mining houses can be found in M. Barlow, 'The Clouded Face of Truth: A Review of the South African Newspaper Press Approaching Union', Ph.D. thesis, University of Bristol, 1988.

15. See P. Lewsen (ed.), *Selections from the Correspondence of J.X. Merriman*, vol.2 *1890–1898* (Cape Town, 1963), 303–06; see also V. Solomon (ed.), *Selections from the Correspondence of Percy Alport Molteno 1892–1914* (Cape Town, 1981), 59, 83–84. From as early as 1896 it was also alleged that Rhodes had purchased a voice in the British press. See Lewsen (ed.), *Selections*, vol.2, 214–16, 110–14.

16. Hobson published his views in articles in the *Guardian* and the *Speaker*, and in *The War in South Africa: Its Causes and Effects* (London, 1900), and *The Psychology of Jingoism* (London, 1901). His famous *Imperialism: A Study* (London, 1902) also incorporated many of the same ideas. For other examples of the Liberal conspiracy theory in Britain, see Bryce to J.A. Spender, 9 Nov. 1899, J.A. Spender papers, Add. Mss. 46391, ff.50–1, British Library, London; G.P. Gooch, 'Imperialism', in C.F.G. Masterman (ed.), *The Heart of Empire: Discussions of Problems of Modern City Life in England* (London, 1901; new edn. Brighton, 1973); 'ILP resolution at Blackburn' and 'Transvaal Committee – report of six month's work', both printed in S. Koss (ed.), *The Pro-Boers: The Anatomy of an Antiwar Movement* (Chicago, 1973), 5, 15.

17. For further discussion of the fourth estate theory see R. Boston, 'W.T. Stead and Democracy by Journalism', in J.H. Wiener (ed.), *Papers for the Millions: The New Journalism in Britain, 1850s to 1914* (Westport, CT, 1988), 91–106; and P. Brendon, *The Life and Death of the Press Barons* (London, 1982), 78–80. Henry Reeve published the classic statement of the fourth estate idea in the *Edinburgh Review*, Oct. 1855.

18. J. Bryce, *The American Commonwealth*, vol.3 (London, 1888), 6–13, 99–106.

19. For good accounts of these changes in Britain and Canada respectively, see L. Brown, *Victorian News and Newspapers* (Oxford, 1985), and M. Sotiron, *From Politics to Profit: The Commercialisation of Canadian Daily Newspapers, 1890–1920* (Montreal and Kingston, 1997).

20. Sotiron, *From Politics to Profit*, 5, 30.

21. S. Constantine, '"Bringing the empire alive": The Empire Marketing Board and Imperial Propaganda, 1926–33', in J.M. MacKenzie (ed.), *Imperialism and Popular Culture* (Manchester, 1986), 200.

22. G. Shaw, *The Cape Times: An Informal History* (Cape Town, 1999), 11.

23. C.P. Smith, 'Historical Records of "The Argus" and "The Australasian"', unpublished typescript MSS (1923), MS 10727, State Library of Victoria, Melbourne.

24. *Manitoba Free Press* advertising rate card, Dec. 1903, Sir Clifford Sifton papers, 145/116026, National Archives of Canada, Ottawa [hereafter NAC], 165/133562, *Manitoba Free Press* advertising rate card, Dec. 1904, ibid.

25. See for example R.A. Scott-James, *The Influence of the Press* (London, 1913), 195.

26. E. Shann, 'The Imperial Cable Service', *Nation*, 5 June 1909.

27. Jebb's views were discussed in the essays collected in J. Eddy and D. Schreuder (eds.), *The Rise of Colonial Nationalism* (Sydney, 1988). However, many of these essays neglected Jebb's argument that colonial nationalism was not incompatible with a stronger imperial bond.

28. R. Jebb, *Studies in Colonial Nationalism* (London, 1905), 190–95.

29. F. Ware to Willison, 26 Sept. 1909, J.S. Willison papers, 47/324/34426–7, NAC.

30. S.J. Potter, 'Nationalism, Imperialism and the Press in Britain and the Dominions, c.1898–1914', D.Phil. thesis, Oxford University, 2000, 289–96.

31. *Morning Post*, 4 and 7 May 1907; see also an article inspired by Jebb – 'Imperial Cables', *Winnipeg Telegram*, 8 Nov. 1905.
32. For detailed treatment of the Pacific Cable campaign see R.W.D. Boyce, 'Imperial Dreams and National Realities: Britain, Canada and the Struggle for a Pacific Telegraph Cable, 1879–1902', *English Historical Review*, 115 (2000), 39–70; and L. Green, *Chief Engineer: Life of a Nation Builder: Sandford Fleming* (Toronto and Oxford, 1993), 146–62.
33. L.J. Burpee, *Sandford Fleming: Empire Builder* (Oxford, 1915), 277; Green, *Chief Engineer*, 145; Fleming to J. Chamberlain, 28 Oct. 1898, S. Fleming papers, 9/59, NAC; Fleming to J.I. Tarte, 1 July 1899, printed in S. Fleming, *Three Letters on the Pacific Cable* (Ottawa, 1899). Fleming to the Earl of Hopetoun, 3 Dec. 1900, printed in S. Fleming, *Letter to his Excellency the Right Hon. the Earl of Hopetoun, Governor General of the Commonwealth of Australia, on a complete system of state-owned cables and telegraphs within the British empire* (Ottawa, 1901). See also S. Fleming, *Open letter to the British people in the Australasian colonies on the Pacific Cable* (1900).
34. S. Fleming, *Cheap telegraph rates – address delivered at the annual meeting of the Canadian Press Association, 28 February 1902* (Ottawa, 1902).
35. See for example S. Fleming, *The establishment of a great imperial intelligence union as a means of promoting the consolidation of the empire – an address delivered by Sir Sandford Fleming before the Eighty Club on July 20 1906* (Ottawa, 1906).
36. This goes against T. Standage, *The Victorian Internet: The Remarkable Story of the Telegraph and the Nineteenth Century's Online Pioneers* (London, 1998).
37. S. Fleming, *Documents in reference to the establishment of direct telegraphic communication between Australia, New Zealand, Canada and Great Britain* (London, 1886).
38. C.F.M. Bell to G. Parkin, 5 March 1898, MLB17/239, Times Newspapers Limited Archive, London [hereafter TNLA]; *The History of the Times*, vol.3 *The Twentieth Century Test* (London, 1947), 447.
39. Bell to Cook, 2 March 1898, MLB17/221, TNLA.
40. On Reuters, see D. Read, *The Power of News: The History of Reuters*, 2nd edn. (Oxford, 1999).
41. R. Jones, *A Life in Reuters* (London, 1951), 19.
42. H. de Reuter to Jones, 20 July and 28 Dec. 1906, Roderick Jones papers, section 1, box 11, Reuters Archive, London [hereafter Reuters]; de Reuter to Jones, 12 Dec. 1906, box 2, ibid.
43. J. Sanders, *Dateline – NZPA: The New Zealand Press Association 1880–1980* (Auckland, 1979), 6–9.
44. 'United Press Association of New Zealand Ltd., Annual Meeting of Shareholders at Rotorua, 23 February 1910, Address by the Chairman – Mr G. Fenwick' (Dunedin, 1910), NZPA Archives, box 70, Alexander Turnbull Library, Wellington.
45. J.W. Dafoe, *The Imperial Press Conference: A Retrospect with Comment* (Winnipeg, 1909), 17.
46. C.P. Hosmer to B. Wilson, 11 March 1897, W.S. Fielding papers, 508/23, Nova Scotia Archives and Records Management, Halifax.
47. See Potter, 'Nationalism, Imperialism and the Press', appendix one.
48. 'The London Times Cables', Toronto *Globe*, 25 Nov. 1899.
49. Extracts from report and financial statement submitted to the annual meeting of the CAP, June 1906, enclosed with R.M. MacLeod to Baron de Reuter, 12 Feb. 1907, Jones papers, section 1, box 1, Reuters.
50. Sotiron, *Politics to Profit*, 70–77; M.E. Nichols, *CP: The Story of the Canadian Press* (Toronto, 1948), 84–87; MacLeod to de Reuter, 4 May 1907, Jones papers, section 1, box 1, Reuters.
51. See Potter, 'Nationalism, Imperialism and the Press', appendix one.
52. On the limited spread of Hobson's ideas in Australia, see B. Penny, 'The Australian Debate on the Boer War', *Historical Studies*, 14 (1971), 526–45; also J. Neal, 'Charters Towers and the Boer War', BA Hons thesis, James Cook University of North Queensland, 1980. For comments on the character of the *Argus* service during the war, see K.S. Inglis, 'The Imperial Connection: Telegraphic Communication between England and Australia, 1872–1902', in A.F. Madden and W.H. Morris-Jones (eds.), *Australia and Britain* (London, 1980), 36–37;

also *Launceston Examiner*, 20 Jan. 1901 (I am grateful to Craig Wilcox for bringing the latter reference to my attention).

53. 'A good service to Canada', *Toronto Telegram*, 28 Feb. 1907.
54. 'The nation and the press', *Transvaal Leader*, 1 Oct. 1908.
55. T.H. Hardman (ed.), *A Parliament of the Press: The First Imperial Press Conference* (London, 1909), 44, 58, 66, 103. See also speeches by Brierley, Fenwick, Macdonald, Nichols and E.S. Cunningham, 67, 171–72, 175, 183.
56. Viscount Burnham, 'Foreword', in J.S. Mills, *The Press and Communications of the Empire* (London, 1924); J.A. Spender, *Life, Journalism and Politics*, vol.1 (London, 1927), 226; L.S. Amery, *My Political Life*, vol.1 *England Before the Storm 1896–1914* (London, 1953), 339.
57. Lord Northcliffe to Garvin, 3 March 1909, J.L. Garvin papers, Harry Ransom Centre, Austin, Texas; 'Foundation of the Imperial Press Conference and the Empire Press Union', undated typescript by Harry Brittain, Harry Brittain papers, M1581, British Library of Political and Economic Sciences, London.
58. 'The opinion-making power', *Observer*, 6 June 1909; 'The reduction of cable rates', *The Times*, 26 June 1909; 'The imperial press', *Westminster Gazette*, 5 June 1909; 'Nerves of the empire', *Daily Chronicle*, 8 June 1909; Hardman (ed.), *Parliament of the Press*, 144.
59. M. Cohen to Fleming, 27 May 1909 and 3 June 1909, Fleming papers, 10/69, NAC; J.H. Heaton to Garvin, 5 June 1909, Garvin papers; cables from Jose to *The Times*, 23 Feb. and 1 March 1909, A.W. Jose papers, 266/2, Mitchell Library, Sydney. The following account goes against the argument proposed by Denis Cryle, who argues that the Australian and New Zealand delegates were united in their quest for reduced cable rates, in the face of British indifference. See D. Cryle, 'The Empire Press Union and Antipodean Communications: Australian–New Zealand involvement 1909–1950', *Media History*, 8 (2002), 49–62.
60. Memo by G. Robinson, 3 March 1909, A17, G. Fowlds papers, 20/2/91, University of Auckland Archives and Manuscripts, Auckland.
61. Hardman, *Parliament of the Press*, 13–14 and 135–48; 'Proceedings of the Imperial Press Conference Cable Rates Committee', 13 and 25 June 1909, J.W. Dafoe fonds, box 1, Provincial Archives of Manitoba, Winnipeg [hereafter PAM].
62. Hardman (ed.), *Parliament of the Press*, 116–21.
63. Cohen to Fleming, 3 June 1909, Fleming papers, 10/69, NAC; 'Proceedings of the Imperial Press Conference Cable Rates Committee', Dafoe fonds, box 1, PAM.
64. Read, *Power of News*, 93; Jones to de Reuter, 23 and 30 March 1910, Jones papers, section 1, box 6, Reuters.
65. *Senate report of the select committee on press cable service* (Melbourne, 1909), 46–59.
66. Press cable subsidy, copy of agreement between Minister of State for External Affairs and the Independent Cable Association of Australia Limited, 24 Sept. 1912, CRS A1, item 1916/24780 cables, National Archives of Australia, Canberra.
67. Department of External Affairs prepared answers for Postmaster General, c.July 1912, ibid.; 'Weekly international returns, Pacific Cable Board', records of the Post Office Department, RG 3, vol.681, file 112159, NAC.
68. 'The need of cheaper cable rates', *Manchester Guardian*, 8 June 1909.
69. See Potter, *News and the British World*, ch.8.

'Brushing Up Your Empire': Dominion and Colonial Propaganda on the BBC's Home Services, 1939–45

SIÂN NICHOLAS

The impact of empire on British popular culture continues to fascinate and divide historians. Recent research in particular has sought to demonstrate how heavily the empire featured in British popular culture even beyond the Second World War. However, Robert Colls, for instance, in his recent study of English identity, affirms that beliefs about empire 'had never been anything but confused', and popular impressions of empire essentially 'pictoral and exhibition-gauge'.[1] The outbreak of the Second World War itself, while on one level appearing to confirm imperial loyalties, also called into question many of the perceptions on which they were based. The practical realities of war – Allied war aims that threatened to undermine the very legitimacy of imperial rule, and domestic wartime propaganda that promoted alternative conceptions of Britain as both great world power and plucky little island – challenged the British people's ideas of the world around them and their place in that world.

The British Broadcasting Corporation (BBC), with its celebrated remit to 'inform, educate and entertain', had been a leading player in pro-imperial propaganda in the inter-war years. During the war empire was again a persistent theme in British domestic as well as overseas broadcasting.[2] The BBC thus found itself playing an essential mediating role between the needs of empire publicists and the attitudes to empire of ordinary listeners in Britain (and indeed beyond) throughout the whole course of the war. This role was both complex and significant. In order to provide successful broadcast propaganda BBC programme-makers needed to understand and reflect, first, what government wished to get across to listeners, second, what they, the programme-makers themselves, felt was important – and practicable – to broadcast, and third, what they believed, and their listener research indicated, would appeal most to the British general public. The BBC's record in 'broadcasting the Empire' thus offers a unique insight into the attitudes of the British domestic audience itself, one of the least ambiguous measures of popular interest in things imperial, and how listeners thought of themselves, their empire and their world. For topics that corresponded to listeners' preoccupations and interests attracted high audiences; uninterested listeners literally switched off.

This article therefore considers the projection of the British Empire by the domestic services of the BBC during the Second World War. It investigates how BBC policy and programming regarding the empire developed during the war, what problems BBC staff faced, and how successfully they overcame them. Particular attention is given to coverage of the Dominions, which tended to take a central role in any broadcasts on empire,[3] and to the terminology of the debate. For in wartime propaganda and discussion, what it meant to be 'British' – that is, the distinctions between British, Imperial and United Kingdom, between the Empire and the Overseas Empire – had a precise significance, though it was, arguably, recognised more by broadcasters than by listeners.[4]

I

In inter-war Britain, wireless meant the BBC. By 1939 in a population of just under 48 million, some nine million households held radio licences. The BBC itself estimated a potential national audience of 33 million adult listeners, and to all intents and purposes everyone who wanted it had access to a radio.[5] In fact much of the listening was to the light entertainment of Radio Luxembourg, and the BBC's much-vaunted status as the nation's most authoritative source of news and information was compromised by its peculiar status (nominally independent of government yet dependent on it for its very existence) and by its shrinking from political controversy. That notwithstanding, within barely ten years of its creation the BBC under its first and most celebrated Director-General, Sir John Reith, had succeeded in establishing itself as a national institution in its own right.

As John MacKenzie has outlined, Reith's powerful belief in the British Empire ideal made the BBC a willing, even evangelical, propagandist of empire in the inter-war years, whether in schools talks, the increasingly elaborate annual celebrations of Empire Day (broadcast in close association with the Empire Day Movement), or the BBC's famous Christmas Day 'Empire greetings' features that linked over the air the whole of the British Empire and culminated in the King's Christmas address to his people.[6] Indeed, the inter-war BBC's projection of empire went further. From its earliest years, talks about the Dominions and colonies peppered BBC schedules. The Prince of Wales's tour of southern Africa in 1925 was widely reported on the BBC, particularly in 'Schools Talks'. Sunday afternoons on the National Programme often featured 'Missionary Talks'. Advances in wireless technology encouraged the exploitation of imperial ties: for instance, for Dominion Day (1 July) 1934, the 67th anniversary of Canada's creation as a United Dominion was celebrated by the BBC's first full-length broadcast direct from Canada.[7] With 'controversy' largely taboo on the inter-war BBC (particularly regarding international affairs, where opinions expressed on the BBC were often assumed to be the British government's own), such broadcasts tended to emphasise the safely picturesque. However, BBC talks staff, several of whom had backgrounds in imperial service, also made a concerted attempt to promote a view of the empire as a modern living phenomenon in series like *The Empire At Work* (1935), which set out, through tales of personal experience in Dominion and colonial occupations, to 'show the Empire, not as an achievement in the past, but as a day-to-day reality'.[8] In 1936 the BBC launched a new series of topical talks from the Dominions and India as part of its established talks series *World Affairs* (itself modelled on the success of their *Transatlantic Bulletins* from the United States), with the aim of fostering mutual understanding with the wider 'British world'.[9] Indeed, from 1934 to 1937 the BBC's annual Empire Day features were produced, not by the BBC at all, but in turn by the domestic broadcasting services of Australia, Canada, South Africa and (jointly) India and Ceylon. The inherent 'Britishness' of the Dominion connection was even invoked to enliven the commemoration of British saints' days: thus, for instance, in 1936, 1937 and 1938 St David's Day was marked by special broadcasts from Welsh communities in Canada, Australia and South Africa respectively.[10]

But these broadcasts were not an unambiguous success. For all its good intentions, *The Empire at Work* tended to deal in stereotypes: fur-trapping in Canada, police work in Malaya, and cocoa cultivation in West Africa. After a startlingly hostile response from the Government of India, the *World Affairs* talks deliberately avoided politically sensitive topics.[11] Although the number of international relay broadcasts from the Dominions steadily increased, from 11 between 1929 and 1932 to 26 in 1937, the number from the United States was always substantially higher (over 80 in 1937) as well as on a grander scale (notably the relay broadcast of the inauguration of President Franklin D. Roosevelt in 1933).[12] Meanwhile, as Scannell and Cardiff point out, Empire Day and associated topics were a 'constant source of embarrassment' to BBC talks and features producers all too well aware of the ambiguities of empire.[13] In the late 1930s the BBC's big Christmas Day features did not in fact highlight the empire at all, featuring instead a dramatisation of the nativity in 1936, traditional Christmases in Europe and the Mediterranean in 1937, and Christmas over Europe in 1938. However the greatest problem in assessing the BBC's role in fostering imperial sentiment is the lack of any reliable audience research until the founding of the BBC's Listener Research Department in 1936. Although the proportion of the population with some imperial link (whether through employment, service or emigration) must have been significant, it is impossible to be sure how many people listened to these programmes, or what they thought of them. But their educative value at least might be questioned: in what became regarded as a touchstone of empire awareness, a BBC Listener Research survey in January 1943 found that most people in Britain did not know the difference between a colony and a Dominion and believed that the term 'British Commonwealth of Nations' was simply a more democratic-sounding euphemism for 'British Empire'.[14]

II

When war broke out in 1939 the nation turned to the BBC. The BBC, convinced of the importance of broadcasting to home front morale (as well as of the danger of losing audiences to overseas – including enemy – broadcasters), adopted a more populist tone in response. Over the next six years two wartime services, the Home Service and Forces Programme, became the principal provider of news, entertainment and debate in Britain; its overseas services projected British aims and ideals to the overseas empire and the wider world.[15] One of the first home propaganda themes was empire unity: in the immediate term, the ambiguities of empire could be bypassed, and the BBC set out, without government prompting, to mark the empire's own contribution to the war effort, celebrating a fellowship of nations and territories united in common purpose against the enemy.

Thus for instance *The Empire's Answer*, a 'radio chronicle of the entry into the war of the Nations of the British Commonwealth' broadcast in the Home and Overseas services on 6 October 1939, featured descriptions of their country's response to the declaration of war hurriedly provided by the broadcasting authorities of every Dominion and major colony, plus speeches by the four Dominion prime ministers and an epilogue by the Dominions Secretary, Anthony Eden. Intended as a 'most resounding and heartening' contribution to the war effort, it dealt mainly in colourful platitudes that clearly went down better at home than overseas.[16] Meanwhile, from November 1939 a new series, *Dominion Commentary*, alternating fortnightly on Saturday nights with *American Commentary* (the popular successor to *Transatlantic Bulletins*) brought topical dispatches from the Dominion capitals into British homes.

The arrival of the Dominions expeditionary forces in Britain was also reflected in domestic broadcast schedules. The Canadian forces (an estimated 200,000 by the end of 1940) came accompanied by a programme unit from the Canadian Broadcasting Corporation (CBC). One of the first actions of the BBC Forces Programme was to collaborate with CBC to produce dedicated programmes for the Canadian troops, including a half-hour of ice-hockey highlights on Sunday evenings, a half-hour of variety, a weekly *Canadian Newsletter*, and, once the ice-hockey season came to an end, a weekly forces magazine programme. Later additions to the schedules included *Johnny Canuck's Revue*, and a series of weekly camp concerts, *The Canadians Entertain*, which CBC also rebroadcast in Canada. By the end of 1942 the Forces Programme was broadcasting over two hours a week of material for the Canadians (aside from sports specials), including for the first time a five-minute summary of Canadian news in French. Such programmes served a dual function: to provide morale-boosting entertainment for Dominion troops stationed in Britain, and to encourage home identification with these troops as an integral part of the British Empire's war effort. Provision for the other Dominion forces inevitably followed: a sporting magazine, *Calling the Australians*, and an *Australian Newsletter* were introduced in the summer of 1940 (as well as programmes for Anzac troops stationed in the Middle East), and a *New Zealand Newsletter* and *Calling the New Zealanders* shortly after. Since no South African Expeditionary Force was stationed in Britain, provision for the South Africans was slower in coming, though a newsletter was broadcast to South African troops in the Middle East. However, in April 1942, after approaches to the BBC by the South African High Commissioner, a *South African Newsletter*, aimed as much at civilian expatriates as servicemen, was added to the home schedules.[17] The BBC found it difficult always to broadcast these programmes at times when servicemen could tune in, and there was some embarrassment when it was discovered that the Canadian message series *Greetings From Home* was scheduled at a time when few could listen. But a questionnaire circulated among Canadian servicemen in January 1944 confirmed their general popularity, with ice hockey and *Johnny Canuck's Revue* in particular heard regularly by 80 per cent of Canadian servicemen with access to a radio.[18]

Meanwhile, to engage British servicemen's interest directly in their fellow empire troops, in October 1940 the Forces Programme introduced *Meet the Empire: Bill and Bob at the BBC*. 'Bill and Bob' had previously appeared in *Parlez-vous Français*, an attempt to teach rudimentary French to the British Expeditionary Force. With the BEF now back home, the new programme saw Bill, an ignorant but keen cockney serviceman, and Bob, better informed and more serious, question representatives of the overseas empire forces about their homelands, history, traditions and lifestyles. The series came to an end in January 1941 having covered in unexceptional fashion Canada, the Gold Coast, Nigeria and British East Africa.[19]

The most direct engagement that British listeners had with the empire in the early years of the war was probably with the children evacuated under the Children's Overseas Reception Board scheme. In 1940 the BBC began broadcasting *Children Calling Home*, a two-way transatlantic link-up programme, in which parents in a radio studio in Britain spoke directly to their children in a studio in the United States or Canada. An Australian *Children Calling Home* was instituted in early 1941 and a South African edition from July 1941, each broadcasting every eight weeks and featuring between five and ten families. These programmes, though often traumatic for parents and children alike, were a popular endorsement of Dominions hospitality in time of crisis, and were enlivened by cannily arranged link-ups (for instance, one edition featured parents in South Wales and Newcastle, and their children in Newcastle, New South Wales). After a suggestion by the Australian Broadcasting Commission (ABC), a monthly series, *Hello Parents*, that broadcast messages from children to parents only, commenced from Australia in April 1942 and from South Africa in August 1942. New Zealand messages (pre-recorded and then shipped to Sydney) were included in the Australia edition from October 1942. Well over half the 800 evacuees in Australia and New Zealand, and almost all the 350 evacuees in South Africa, must have sent messages home via the BBC over the course of the war.[20]

Yet even at this relatively early stage in the war, imperial considerations were found to raise all manner of unexpected policy problems. For instance, a BBC talk by Lord Halifax in July 1940, which described the war as 'this crusade for Christianity ... four-square against the forces of Evil', was widely criticised as an insult to the non-Christian members of the empire. In August 1940, Professor Vincent Harlow, Rhodes Professor of Imperial History at London University and co-ordinator of the Ministry of Information's (MOI) 'Empire Campaign', warned the BBC *not* to propound the idea that the Dominions had come to help the Motherland, since this was an attitude much resented in the Dominions ('they look on the war as their concern as much as ours').[21] Meanwhile, home listener responses were discouraging. Audiences for *Dominion Commentary* were considered 'very disappointing' (averaging at around 14.5 per cent, that is, 4–5 million listeners). Reasons subsequently adduced by the BBC included a lack of interesting material, contributors who were weak broadcasters, very bad reception quality – the South Africa and New Zealand commentaries had to be re-read by Dominion nationals in London – and lack of continuity, with each Dominion featuring only once every eight weeks. Two reasons above all stood out. First, since these programmes were closely monitored by Dominion nationals themselves, in particular the High Commissioners in London who notoriously 'resented frankness', BBC producers did their best to avoid anything remotely controversial; in consequence the South African commentary in particular came to be regarded as a political embarrassment.

Second, the BBC found itself confronted with the listening public's 'usual indifference to broadcasts about Dominion affairs'.[22] In December 1940 *Dominion Commentary* was replaced by *Palm and Pine* ('men from distant lands of the Dominions and Colonies come to the microphone ... to tell of the trade they followed and the homes they left to join the fight for freedom'), which was even less successful (10 per cent audience figures); it was in turn replaced in April 1941 by *The Week in Westminster*. Even *Children Calling Home* caused problems (namely, unreliable atmospherics, under-rehearsed children, and incoherent or even hysterical parents), and there was some intemperate criticism in London of the 'particularly un-educated and illiterate' parents of evacuees to Australia.[23] Ironically, at the same time that the BBC was seeking further ways to publicise the British–Dominion bond, expatriates in Britain were complaining that the BBC Home Services were ignoring the empire altogether.[24]

III

In mid-1941, with the British Empire the target of widespread criticism, in particular in the United States, its positive projection both at home and overseas became seen as a vital part of the British domestic and international propaganda effort. Such exercises as the Nuffield College Conference on Colonial Policy of July 1941 marked a renewed initiative in the projection of the Empire and Commonwealth, a need highlighted that August when the Atlantic Charter proclaimed every nation's right to 'sovereign rights and self-government'. The BBC found itself drawn in immediately by the Colonial Office, the Dominions Office and the MOI as a key publicist of empire.

However, BBC personnel were quick to note the weaknesses of their propaganda position. An internal report of September 1941, 'The Colonies as "News"', bleakly identified the principal problem, viz. how to show 'that our democratic professions are not a hypocritical pretence.' This, the paper went on, would be no small feat given that the Colonial Office was so reluctant to publicise its new policy initiatives (such as the 1940 Colonial Development and Welfare Act); that the colonies had traditionally had news value only when things went wrong; and that even the terminology of discussion – notably the terms 'trusteeship' and 'native' – tended to cause offence overseas.[25] A meeting of representatives of all the BBC's home and overseas services, called by Director of Talks George Barnes in late October, concluded that the subject must be approached indirectly ('infiltration'), since 'Talks on Overseas questions in the Home Service often seem to induce listeners to switch off'. Thus, for instance, the BBC should use Dominions speakers more frequently in talks that were *not* specifically empire-related (for instance, for a talk about the wool industry the BBC might approach an Australian).[26] A programme of flashes of war news from around the world should be 89–90 per cent but *not* 100 per cent empire, to project a 'world' rather than 'imperial' perspective. Meanwhile, in order to counteract the vagueness of such terms as 'Empire', 'Colonies' and 'Dominions', they should be avoided where possible in preference for the more specific 'Australian', 'African', 'West Indian'.[27] The last quarter of 1941 thus saw a sharp increase in talks either about or given by speakers from the colonies and in particular the Dominions, and the BBC began sending regular lists of relevant Home Service talks to the Dominions Office for information. Nevertheless, caution was still paramount: after a well-received *Postscript to the News* in August 1941 by Australian Eric Baume led to a South African follow-up, the BBC reassured the Dominions Office that the speaker, Major Jooste of South Africa House, 'would not touch on South African politics at all'.[28]

The profound shock of the fall of Singapore on 15 February 1942 put the broadcasters even more on the defensive. With long-standing assumptions about colonial loyalties seemingly in tatters, it became essential to distance the empire from accusations of exploitation and native subjection, while actively promoting its positive attributes. This again was more difficult than it first appeared. In March 1942 a proposal for a features series based on the theme that 'the British Commonwealth of Nations has become part of a greater Commonwealth – the Commonwealth of Freedom', that 'together with its three great allies, the USA, the USSR and China', subscribed to the idea that man has certain inalienable rights 'irrespective of race or colour', was thwarted by the difficulty of fitting South Africa into such a scheme. The plan was withdrawn in a 'strategic retreat' in favour of a half-hour literary feature.[29] A series of meetings the following month (involving, among others, the reluctant convert to the British Empire, Arthur Koestler) concluded that a successful approach must admit frankly the black spots in Britain's colonial history before emphasising the positive momentum behind the contemporary empire. In a colourful metaphor, the discussants suggested envisaging the empire as an 'incubator ... hatching the eggs of independent nationhood. How the eggs got in the incubator it doesn't matter now so much, the important thing is "are they being given the quickest possible development and what are we going to do about providing a decent poultry run in which so many independent chickens can scratch in the future?"'[30] Most tellingly perhaps, in late April the BBC Features department decided to abandon a proposed programme of Kipling for that year's Empire Day celebrations after consultation with the High Commission for India elicited the opinion that such a plan was 'most undesirable ... – in fact, mad'; this following a controversial *Postscript* by

Captain L.D. Gammans MP in which he had declared that 'the old Kipling idea of Empire is dead'.[31] Empire Day talks for 1942 were instead arranged around the theme of the responsibilities of empire (for home audiences) and of 'the real stocktaking which is now going on in Britain' (for overseas empire audiences).[32]

In May 1942 Roosevelt's chief foreign policy adviser Sumner Welles announced that 'The age of imperialism is ended'. With the international legitimacy of colonial administration arguably at its lowest ebb, in July 1942 the BBC's joint Directors-General, Robert Foot and Sir Cecil Graves, personally requested that Home Controllers devise their autumn programme plans with the empire in mind, to reflect not simply the empire's war effort, but the life and history of the Dominions and Colonies.[33] But again, after consultation with the Dominions Office, Colonial Office and MOI, the BBC Talks Department recommended *no* special provision for empire talks: rather, (in their words) to 'pepperpot' Dominions and Colonial talks and speakers through the schedules in programmes like *Westminster and Beyond* and *Postscripts*. Schools programmes, already reflecting the empire in such programmes as *Travel Talks* and *Current Affairs*, undertook to give it more prominence in youth programmes such as *Youth Magazine* and *Senior History*. A new feature series, *Empire Scrapbook*, for Home and Empire listeners, began in the autumn. In other examples of infiltration at work, an Australian discussed 'What is an Englishman?' in *Living Opinion*, and a Canadian 'Should Men Help in the House?' in the women's series *This is My Home*.[34]

IV

In an important policy document drawn up during September 1942, R.A. Rendall, BBC Assistant Controller (Overseas Services) and chair of the interdivisional Committee on Anglo-American relations, admitted that projecting the empire on the home services was 'more intractable' than almost any other campaign with which the BBC had had to deal. If the main objective was to stimulate interest, dispel ignorance and prejudice, and foster a responsible and intelligent attitude to imperial problems among the general public – and by so doing to encourage friendly relations with Dominions and Colonial subjects 'of whatever colour' in Britain – the main problem was the 'ignorance, indifference and prejudice' of the ordinary British listener. To combat the 'very widespread view' that the British Empire was an embarrassing anachronism and had no place in the post-war world, Rendall recommended an end to propaganda that was 'merely informative, non-controversial and backward-looking' (travellers' tales, official recollections, idealised portraits of empire builders), and instead make the appeal as wide as possible: to the audience's materialism, idealism, patriotic pride, love of adventure (particularly with respect to post-war opportunities overseas), sentiment and curiosity, through talks (particularly again from Dominion speakers on general subjects), news (why not a worldwide Dominions newsgathering organisation?), dramatic features and documentaries, and entertainment – though 'the "pukka sahib" type of joke in its most harmful aspects should be discouraged'. Above all, the BBC should take an altogether bolder approach. With censorship constraining so many aspects of British life, listener attention was always engaged by controversy; government departments must be persuaded that 'controversy is a sine qua non if broadcasting is to do its job'. For '[t]oday no picture which neglects the warts will carry any conviction'.[35]

In October Rendall began chairing a new interdivisional committee 'to keep Empire ideas in front of producers', and again stressed to Colonial Office representatives (including the parliamentary under-secretary at the Colonial Office, Harold Macmillan) that 'controversy was essential to interest'. However, neither any high-level definition of Corporation policy nor any authoritative government pronouncement of a constructive policy for the future emerged, and the BBC's propaganda effort continued to lack a consistent focus. Although a proposed *Empire Round-Up*, a weekly news programme of short reports from the Dominions, India and a colony from time to time, on the lines of the existing *American Round-Up*, might 'help the British public to become conscious of the need for understanding what is happening to the Dominions',[36] a revival of *Dominion Commentary* was ruled out in favour again of 'infiltration' of items in popular programmes, and general treatments in series like *Travellers' Tales*.

The policy, such as it was, certainly had an impact on schedules. In the last half of 1942 three times as many Dominions speakers appeared in general talks as in the comparable period in 1940, and on the Forces Programme weekly newsletters now supplied nationals from each Dominion – and any interested British listeners – with news from home. Between June 1942 and June 1943 the amount of empire material in the Home Service alone went up some 25 per cent (from 19½ hours to 24½ hours), and from 14 programmes to 37.[37] Meanwhile, the BBC began far closer monitoring of empire terminology, to promote the correct use of the words 'British Empire', 'United Kingdom', 'Overseas Empire'. Significantly, however, the warning went out, 'Don't use the adjective "IMPERIAL" at all. It is commonly used to mean three quite different things and in addition is disliked in certain parts of the British Empire. Thus its use is undesirable because it creates both confusion and prejudice.' The BBC may in fact have added to listener confusion by its ruling that the term 'British troops' was 'the phrase which covers troops from *all* parts of the

Empire'.[38] The recommended term for servicemen from the islands of Britain was 'United Kingdom troops', but there is no evidence that this ever really caught on or that listeners understood the distinction.

Over the winter of 1942 and early 1943 a new confidence seems to have coloured the discussion of imperial propaganda. The Allied war effort was at last progressing. Further imperial losses had not materialised as feared. The revelation of segregation and racism among American GIs in Britain had gone some way towards shaking the United States from its moral pedestal in the eyes of the British public. In November 1942 the BBC's acting Empire Intelligence Director, W.M. Macmillan (former Professor of History at Witwatersrand University), recommended linking the future of the empire with world stability after the war, and casting the 'Colonial problem' as a problem of modernity: 'man's belated attempt, with the help of modern science, to conquer at last the Tropics'.[39] The MOI's appointment in December of Gervas Huxley, formerly a colleague of Sir Stephen Tallents at the Empire Marketing Board, to co-ordinate colonial publicity in Britain, exemplified this new mood. Huxley argued that just as the war itself was now renewing British self-confidence, so it should be seen as a new opportunity to embrace the colonial challenge. The watchword should no longer be 'trusteeship' but 'partnership'; the empire should be presented as opening a world of opportunity for adventurous young men of all classes returning from the armed services after the war. A specially commissioned Listener Research report about British public attitudes to the empire (see page 210 above) had found that although a high degree of misapprehension still existed about the correct terminology of empire and substantial reservations were held about how the empire had been acquired, there was a strong sense that, 'Our colonial record is mixed, but the good exceeds the bad' and that the ultimate aim of colonial policy should be 'the admission of all Colonial territories into equal partnership with Great Britain and the self-governing Dominions.'[40]

Emboldened by these findings, the Talks Department renewed plans to introduce more hard-hitting topical discussion programmes addressing 'the nature, scope and influence of the British empire today', and in the autumn of 1943 Barnes at last agreed to reinstate a modified form of *Dominion Commentary*. For while '[n]o one would now question, I think, the importance of making the British public aware of what is happening and what people are thinking about in the Dominions', clearly so little was being reported in Britain about current affairs in the Dominions that a political commentary as such would have little meaning or interest to listeners. A more picturesque approach, telling listeners 'what the ordinary man or woman in the Dominions is thinking and feeling and doing' would work better.[41] A key point was, of course, how such a programme cast the relationship between Britain and the Dominions themselves, and a proposal to include commentaries from all four Dominions in one weekly programme (as had briefly been attempted with the Dominion forces newsletters) was rejected since the Dominions themselves clearly resented such lumping together. In fact, as Talks producer Isa Benzie strongly urged, 'to be realistic ... we should avoid acting as if the United Kingdom were the centre of a sort of spider's web ... We shall have to think increasingly of the UK as *one of His Majesty's Dominions*.' Another difficulty was with controversy: here Benzie suggested the BBC should lobby for full microphone independence for their Dominion commentators (such as was enjoyed by the BBC's American commentators) in return for reciprocal privileges for Dominions broadcasters reporting from London. To bypass expected interference by Dominion High Commissions, she suggested running four or five editions from Canada (the least problematic) to begin with, on the grounds that once the programme was a success the other Dominions would feel left out and lobby to come in on the BBC's terms.[42] Unfortunately, events overtook the relaunch. By January 1944, the anticipated effect on Forces Programme schedules of the imminent invasion of Europe had thrown programme planning into turmoil, and Talks Department was advised there was no chance at all of re-establishing *Dominion Commentary*. Despite continued discussions and periodic representations from Dominions representatives in London, the series did not reappear until October 1946 (fortnightly, each edition featuring one Dominion in rotation – just as in December 1939).[43]

In 1943, alongside the regular programme strands, the BBC tried a different approach: something 'on cheaper and "brighter" lines', 'less exacting to the listener', that would spark among listeners a curiosity on which a deeper interest might hopefully be built, viz. an empire quiz, that would take the Dominions, India and the Colonies in turn 'and elicit startling information regarding each of them – not disdaining to appeal frankly to the "believe it or not" sort of interest'.[44] This became *Brush Up Your Empire* (the title based on a series of inter-war self-help books), two series of six weekly programmes broadcast on the Forces Programme over the winter of 1943 and summer of 1944.[45] Questions were collected through BBC listener research or compiled within the Talks Department, for use as the basis for discussion between compère and guest. The Colonial Office offered its help in finding speakers. Talks Department even tried to secure the BBC's highest-profile compère, Leslie Mitchell – unfortunately they could not afford him, but managed to secure Lionel Gamelin instead, after begging leave of absence from his Home Guard unit. The first series included programmes on Australia, West Africa, Canada, India, South Africa and Malaya.[46] The omission of New Zealand was regretted – its absence from other empire propaganda (for example the film *Desert Victory*) had already led to bad feeling among New Zealanders – but it was deemed to be 'worse than nothing' to tack New Zealand onto Australia. The omission of Eire was deliberate, since the subject was 'dynamite'.[47] The speakers might be thought not to have quite tallied with the programme's declared aim of gently informative entertainment, including as they did Sir Louis Bussau, Agent General for Victoria, Lady Ranganadhan, wife of the Indian High Commissioner in London (the choice of a woman speaker considered to have cleverly avoided the dilemma of choosing a Hindu or Muslim representative), and Stoffel Coetzie, Public Relations Officer at South Africa House. However, the second series (East Africa, New Zealand, the West Indies, the Pacific Islands, Burma and lastly the United Kingdom itself – with questions from Colonial and Dominions servicemen) managed to secure a more populist range of speakers, notably the West Indian cricket star Learie Constantine.[48]

By the end of 1943 the provision of Empire and Commonwealth-related programmes in the Home Service included the weekly *Travellers' Tales* and *Brush Up Your Empire*, and the monthly *Red on the Map* ('a series of discussions on the meaning and obligations of Empire'), plus a considerable number of one-off talks, regular features on empire themes, and an exchange series with CBC. Programmes at the planning stage included the revamped *Dominion Commentary* and an exchange series with ABC. But in early 1944 there was a sudden drop in the amount of programme space for empire subjects as the Forces Programme was relaunched as the new 'General Forces Programme' with primary responsibility to the advancing Allied forces; in consequence, many popular Forces Programme series moved wholesale to the Home Service, and less popular programmes were squeezed out. *Red on the Map* came to an end with nothing planned to replace it, a new series of *Travellers' Tales* could find no space in the schedules, several talks spaces were curtailed altogether, and plans for *Dominion Commentary* and the ABC exchange were abandoned. BBC producers seem to have declined to fight for space for the 'Empire project', though they deplored the loss of the reciprocal and exchange programmes ('vital to the future developments of radio in the service of the Commonwealth') for broadcasting rather than propaganda reasons. With American criticism of the British Empire now rather more muted, the Dominion and Colonial Offices also seem to have accepted this reduction in empire-oriented programmes. One thing, however, seems not to have changed: 'If Listener Research reports in the past have been even approximately correct there is a deplorable apathy in the adult Home audience regarding the Empire.'[49]

V

The wartime BBC's empire campaign therefore can hardly be judged an unequivocal success. But this can be attributed to a number of factors, technical, administrative, ideological and practical, mostly outside the BBC's control. For instance, the physical connection between the Dominions and London was always dependent on the vagaries of wireless technology. Relays from the Dominions were often difficult to arrange and reception was unreliable. The time of day, and the season of the year, all affected transmission quality, particularly from South Africa and Australia (which had in addition a prohibitive time difference). Transmission from New Zealand relied on a double short-wave link via Australia so unpredictable that the BBC recommended instead pre-recording broadcasts on disc and shipping them to Sydney for transmission. One edition of *Hello Parents* from Australia for Easter 1943 was beamed 11 times to London without success; sent at last by sea mail, it arrived just in time for Easter 1944.[50]

The BBC's relationship with the Colonial and Dominions Offices was not always smooth, though the BBC maintained a comparative independence (especially compared with some other government ministries) when it came to the selection of topics or speakers. The Colonial Office, Professor Macmillan concluded in November 1942, 'hates publicity in any form'; just six months in office had seen even Harold Macmillan retreat from his previously expressed belief that a successful broadcast policy must embrace controversy. According to one BBC producer, the principal obstacle to free broadcast discussion of the 'colonial question' was the 'definite reluctance on the part of the official mind to cooperate with us', though the excessive workload of the Colonial Office Public Relations Officer, Noel Sabine, and the lack of good Colonial Office publicists with adequate colonial background also contributed.[51] During 1942 alone, BBC requests for talks by, for instance, Sir Arthur Dawe on his tour of West Africa, and Clement Attlee on his appointment to the Dominions Office, had been turned down; the Colonial Office had vetoed a proposed talk by the first African to be appointed to the administration in Gold Coast (on the grounds that it would seriously embarrass the Governor of Nigeria, who had opposed such a step in his own territory); and in a planned talk about the new Governor of Hong Kong, Sir Mark Young, the young and progressive Colonial Office official F.J. Pedler had been replaced by retired former Attorney-General Sir Graeme Tyrrell. A further problem in finding speakers is demonstrated by the example of Dr Harold Moody, Chairman of the London Missionary Society and leading figure in the League of Coloured People, who told the BBC his time was too valuable to be wasted at the rate of reimbursement they generally offered.[52]

The fear of political controversy blighted Dominions and colonial coverage throughout the war, as it had in the inter-war years. South Africa was particularly problematic in this respect, although Field Marshal Smuts was regularly called on as a popular and uncontroversial speaker. India was of course the most difficult of all, and the Government of India the most unhelpful; in the earlier part of the war Indian politics were mostly dealt with by nervous avoidance, although the BBC's series of *Round Table* discussions on the future of India were widely publicised as proof of Britain's commitment to the spirit of the Atlantic Charter. By contrast, New Zealand was regarded as too *un*controversial to attract listener interest. Any attempt to make such programmes as *Dominion Commentary* as critically objective as, for instance, *American Commentary*, were further hamstrung by the sensitivities of expatriate Dominions listeners, servicemen and High Commissions – and through them their press back home, who angrily publicised even the mildest critical comment from London.[53]

There was, however, a more immediate problem for broadcasters: that is, the 'ignorance, indifference and prejudice' among listeners that Rendall had noted in 1942. As Sabine had admitted in September 1941, 'I am afraid that the depressing truth is that when quite a large number of home listeners hear the magic word "Empire" their automatic reaction is to switch off.' Huxley himself believed that the British public's interest in empire had collapsed after the First World War, though he saw the Second World War as a chance to restore it. In November 1942, Rooney Pelletier, CBC liaison with the Canadian forces, put the BBC's task most bluntly: 'it is a battle to "sell" the Dominions to the UK public'.[54] BBC programme-makers' adoption of 'infiltration' as the main agent of policy was an implied acknowledgment of this fact: if one wanted to promote the empire on air, one had to do it surreptitiously, or – as with *Brush Up Your Empire* – by turning it into entertainment. But by doing so, the policy message itself was inevitably blunted.

Unfortunately, this was not a problem that the BBC alone could easily resolve. The wartime reduction in newspaper size had reduced still further the negligible amount of news about the empire that generally appeared in the British press. What news was printed tended to be the 'black spots and difficulties' (for example India, Malaya and Burma) that often served only to further suspicion and prejudice.[55] In the BBC's opinion, generous newspaper coverage of American affairs had stimulated listener interest in *American Commentary*, while perfunctory press coverage of the empire had made it additionally difficult to find any listener interest in a *Dominion Commentary*. In October 1943, Barnes noted that any revival of *Dominion Commentary* 'must depend ... on the inclusion of more news about the Dominions in the newspapers and in our own bulletins'; currently 'there is not enough news about the Dominions for a weekly commentary on it to be worth listening to'.[56]

But if the problem, never satisfactorily resolved, was how to persuade British audiences that the empire was indeed relevant to them, the wider broadcasting context highlights how difficult that task really was. For the British public – and therefore the BBC – had other more immediately pressing interests, in comparison with which the Empire/Commonwealth faded into the background. For one thing, the BBC's promotion of the empire during the war was clearly subsidiary to its promotion of the island of Britain. Throughout the war years, the BBC not only utilised every available cliché of British national identity for propaganda purposes ('those inevitable speeches of Queen Elizabeth linked by those inevitable bits of Elgar to those inevitable sonnets of Rupert Brooke', as one impatient radio critic put it),[57] but for the first time made a concerted effort to bring the nation of Britain in all its diversity of region, occupation and accent to the microphone, 'democratising the airwaves' in talks, features and even light entertainment (where series like *Merry-Go-Round* or *Works Wonders* gave ordinary members of, respectively, the fighting forces and war factories, a showcase for their variety talents). The audience response was very positive: listeners liked to hear about *themselves*; they liked particularly to hear other nationalities talking about how well *they* (the British) were doing.[58] When in the last years of the war 'reconstruction' became the watchword, it was programmes about housing, health provision and 'jobs for all' which attracted vast audiences, not the post-war international settlement.

The British public's failure to engage with empire during the war cannot, however, be attributed simply to a turning inwards. If during the war British listeners became less interested in empire, in the 'British world' as such, they certainly became more interested in the wider world than ever before. The Soviet Union's entry into the war in June 1941, in particular its resistance to the German army which provided for so long the only positive Allied war news, prompted a remarkable interest in all things Russian which the MOI encouraged the BBC to meet at every opportunity. From July 1942 the BBC instituted a fortnightly *Russian Commentary* in which despatches from Alexander Werth, the *Sunday Times* Moscow correspondent, gave the 'Russian point of view' (the term 'Soviet' tended to be downplayed for policy reasons) to a regular audience of over four million listeners. Roughly comparable in audience size to *Dominion Commentary*, it was by contrast considered a great success. The BBC broadcast annual celebrations of Red Army Day, Stalin's birthday and the anniversary of the Russian Revolution that became if anything even more elaborate than its inter-war Empire Day features. The Russian war effort was praised by speakers as diverse as Sir

Stafford Cripps and the Archbishop of York, and the victories at Leningrad and Stalingrad were lavishly celebrated. An all-star serialisation of *War and Peace* was a drama highlight of 1943.[59] Studiously avoiding politics in favour of an all-purpose high-heroic tone, wartime pro-Russianism on the BBC was mirrored in the cinema, in the press and in the political arena – where Lord Beaverbrook, the former architect of Empire Free Trade, was perhaps the most unlikely of evangelists for the USSR. The British people were encouraged at every opportunity to love the Russians, according to wartime opinion polls with considerable success.[60] The contrast with empire coverage was not lost on contemporary critics, who noted that the BBC was in danger of devoting more attention to Russia than to the Commonwealth.[61]

But it is British popular interest in the United States that provides the most dramatic contrast to their engagement with empire, and the American example that haunted the BBC's wartime discussions of pro-empire propaganda. There had of course been a revolution in interest in the United States in inter-war Britain, fostered by the invasion of popular American music into the British market and by the phenomenal impact of the Hollywood film industry. *American Commentary*, with its warts-and-all coverage of American life, culture and politics, had been a popular fortnightly BBC fixture since 1930. In the early years of the war it led the way in explaining American isolationism to its five million regular listeners; from April 1941, scheduled weekly, its audience figures peaked at six million. During the blitz, broadcasts of sympathy and support by Americans were hugely popular items in the BBC schedules, as was *Hi Gang!*, starring American expatriates Bebe Daniels, Vic Oliver and Ben Lyon. It was axiomatic within the BBC that a key reason for the comparative failure of *Dominion Commentary* in 1940 was 'that the Dominions are neither so important nor so interesting to the British public as is the United States of America'.[62]

During the second half of 1941, when adverse comparisons between the Soviet and American war efforts became widespread among the British public, the MOI launched a concerted propaganda effort to encourage pro-American understanding and fellow-feeling among the British public, to which the BBC contributed with such series as *It's Different in the USA* and *America Decides*. Once the United States had entered the war, and especially once American troops began arriving in Britain, the BBC became part of an official propaganda blitz aimed at transatlantic understanding that quite overshadowed its pro-empire broadcasting. Pro-American broadcasts ranged from the feature series *Let's Get Acquainted*, to Brer Rabbit stories in *Children's Hour* (read by a black GI), and culminated in 1943 in *Transatlantic Call – People to People*, a technically ambitious simultaneous broadcast on the BBC and the Columbia Broadcasting System (CBS) that

portrayed on alternate weeks true stories of British and American people at
war. Such publicity was not always positive in its impact (many listeners
professed themselves appalled at the loud, brash and self-centred picture
that some of these programmes seemed to paint of Americans), and it
certainly misled some (the disillusionment of many 'GI brides' after the war
has been well documented). But although the USSR remained the British
people's favourite ally until the end of the war, the United States had the
highest public profile.[63]

Significantly, the BBC's policy initiatives in pro-imperial broadcasting
in the war years tended to a remarkable degree to follow, and take their
inspiration from, their *American*-oriented broadcasts. *Dominion
Commentary* itself began as an attempt to ape the success of *American
Commentary*. *Children Calling Home* began as a programme linking
parents with their children evacuated to the United States. This was
mirrored in government: the Nuffield Conference on Colonial Policy was in
part aimed at American political and public opinion, while it was the
increased British interest in things American after Pearl Harbor that
prompted a renewed propaganda effort to stimulate comparable interest in
the empire. The BBC's interdivisional committee to project the empire was
an offshoot of, and modelled itself on, its Committee on Radio in Anglo-
American Relations. Technical considerations played to American
advantage: the BBC's New York office had a highly-developed
infrastructure, excellent relay contacts with London, and a productive
working relationship with CBS, while BBC relations with ABC in
Australia, for instance, tended to be more strained (internal BBC
memoranda were not always complimentary about Australian broadcasting
standards), and technical links with all the Dominions except Canada were
highly vulnerable. American special treatment continued in one particularly
significant area for Dominions broadcasters. Whereas Dominion troops
stationed in Britain (and cast as part of the wider 'British' war effort) had to
make do with a few hours of dedicated programmes on the BBC Forces
Programme, the American Expeditionary Force (though originally
outnumbered by Canadian forces by nearly 2–1) was immediately given the
right to broadcast its own radio service, the American Forces Network,
within Britain.[64]

VI

During the inter-war years the BBC had maintained a firm commitment to
publicising the empire on its home services. But this commitment had
steered clear of critical engagement and arguably did little to consolidate
factual knowledge as opposed to vague, if pervasive, impressions of empire

in the public mind. During the war the BBC was again a principal medium for the projection of empire, both under official direction and on its own account. Yet during the war the British people turned their attentions away from the empire, as propaganda and the practical realities of war turned them both further inwards (to 'island Britain') and outwards in new directions (to Europe, and especially to the United States).

In general, the British public lacked sufficient background knowledge, particularly political knowledge, about the empire to take a constructive interest in the political future of the Empire/Commonwealth. But how could audiences be persuaded to address their own ignorance? To maintain a topical news interest in the Dominions, for instance, proved almost impossible: while the BBC's *Russian Commentary*, heavily censored at source, sought not much more than to give a positive, morale-boosting view of the USSR, and *American Commentary* prided itself on its freedom to offer friendly criticism of its host nation, Dominion commentaries fell between two stools, neither fully controlled nor fully independent, but fatally hamstrung by the political sensitivities of the imperial relationship. Attempts simply to engage listener curiosity risked stereotyping and trivialisation. Indirect publicity ('infiltration') by its very nature generally failed to hit home. It may have been in any case an impossible task, trying to accommodate radically diverging perceptions of empire. BBC attempts to meet Dominion and colonial dislike of the conventional British terminology for empire arguably only confused British listeners, particularly in the inconsistent use of the term 'British' and the avoidance of the very term 'imperial'. In the spirit of the modern Commonwealth, the BBC endeavoured to meet (and even anticipate) Dominion demands for separate coverage that identified them as independent nations rather than an undifferentiated bloc – yet this separate treatment arguably weakened in the public mind the very imperial link that such coverage was supposed to be celebrating.

During the war the British public simply preferred to hear about brash Americans, heroic Russians, or – especially – their plucky selves, rather than about their imperial relations. Perhaps this should not be surprising. Despite the much-vaunted centrality of empire in inter-war British popular culture, the cultural watchword of the period had always been Americanisation. Moreover, whereas America represented dynamism and modernity in the public mind, the most popular cultural manifestations of empire in inter-war Britain had always been rooted firmly in a vanished *past*. Imperialist juvenile literature, cigarette card heroes, above all those 'imperial epics' (often American-made) so popular among inter-war cinema-goers, inhabited an escapist Kiplingesque never-land that was increasingly far from contemporary imperial realities. During the war people looked to the present, not the past, and close to home rather than across the world. British interest in the war in the Far East was negligible compared to interest in the D-Day landings and the advance on Berlin, and even if the will to challenge this existed, the technical wherewithal certainly did not. The future was the reconstruction of Britain first and Europe after, rather than devolved government in India and the reshaping of the Commonwealth of nations.

Although the wartime BBC's pro-empire propaganda sought seriously to address current and future imperial concerns and developments, it had to accommodate British audiences who only really expressed interest in imperial broadcasts when they had a general audience appeal (for instance, sport or variety) or involved their own lives (for instance, *Children Calling Home*), and British-based Dominions audiences all too eager to complain at being patronised, stereotyped or insufficiently differentiated from their other imperial relations. During the war, for the first time in its history the BBC had as a matter of national urgency to give its listeners programmes they wanted to hear as much as those they 'ought' to hear. Its decision therefore to 'infiltrate' most of its pro-empire propaganda into its home schedules could not be more telling. Such propaganda, while at least maintaining the empire as that former vague and imprecise presence in the British outlook, could do nothing in practice to strengthen – or in fact to slow the decline of – positive imperial feeling for the post-war world.

NOTES

I would like to acknowledge the help provided by the Arts and Humanities Research Board's Research Leave scheme in enabling me to carry out the original research for this article. Many thanks are also due to Aled Jones, Nicholas Owen, and especially Andrew Thompson, for their comments on earlier drafts.

1. For a concise introduction to the debate surrounding the cultural impact of imperialism, see Stuart Ward, 'Introduction', in Stuart Ward (ed.), *British Culture and the End of Empire* (Manchester, 2000), 1–20; see also Robert Colls, *Identity of England* (Oxford, 2002), 138, 106.

2. The standard history of the BBC is still Asa Briggs' monumental five-volume *History of Broadcasting in the United Kingdom* (1961–95). The second and third volumes, *The Golden Age of Wireless* (London, 1965), and *The War of Words* (London, 1970), discuss in some depth the origins and development of broadcasting *to* the Empire in, respectively, the inter-war years and the Second World War, but say little about home broadcasts *about* the Empire. For further discussion of inter-war and wartime broadcasting in Britain (though again with only incidental discussion of Empire as a broadcasting topic), see Mark Pegg, *Broadcasting and Society, 1918–1939* (London, 1983); Paddy Scannell and David Cardiff, *A Social History of British Broadcasting*, vol.1 *Serving the Nation, 1922–39* (London, 1991); and Siân Nicholas, *The Echo of War: Home Front Propaganda and the Wartime BBC 1939–45* (Manchester, 1996). The principal account of the BBC as propagandist of empire is John M. MacKenzie, '"In touch with the Infinite": The BBC and the Empire, 1923–53', in John M. MacKenzie (ed.), *Imperialism and Popular Culture* (Manchester, 1986), 165–91; and see

also his 'The Popular Culture of Empire in Britain', in Judith M. Brown and Wm. Roger Louis (eds.), *The Oxford History of the British Empire*, vol.4 *The Twentieth Century* (Oxford, 1999), 212–31. For a recent discussion of empire coverage on the wartime BBC home services, see Thomas Hajkowski, 'The BBC, the Empire and the Second World War, 1939–1945', *Historical Journal of Film, Radio and Television*, 22 (2002), 135–55, which covers some of the same ground as this article. For the Colonial Office perspective on the problem of propaganda and empire, see, for instance, Rosaleen Smyth, 'Britain's African Colonies and British Propaganda during the Second World War', *Journal of Imperial and Commonwealth History*, 23 (1985), 65–82. I am indebted to Carl Bridge for this reference.
3. Thus India, a special case for a number of reasons, is not addressed specifically in this discussion.
4. That being said, although in this period the term 'British' might refer in different contexts to either the British Empire or the British isles, in the following discussion (except where otherwise indicated) it will be used to mean the latter.
5. See George Orwell, *The Road to Wigan Pier* (London, 1937), 83.
6. MacKenzie, 'In touch with the Infinite', *passim*.
7. See 'From Canada' programme outline, File R47/212/1: Relays: Dominion Day, and BBC Programmes Records Index (from 1922), BBC Written Archive Centre, Caversham [hereafter BBC WAC].
8. John Green to Mr James, 28 Jan. 1935, BBC WAC R51/133: Talks: Empire at Work, 1934–35. For details of the imperial backgrounds of leading wartime BBC personnel see Hajkowski, 'BBC and Empire', 136–37.
9. See J.B. Clark, Empire Service Director (ESD), to representatives of Dominions broadcasting services, 27 Oct. 1936, BBC WAC R47/853/1: Relays: Talks from Dominions. In BBC internal correspondence, personnel were sometimes identified by name, sometimes by position. Where possible, I have identified both name and position on first reference in footnotes, and thereafter cited them as they appear on each occasion.
10. See BBC WAC R34/213/1: Policy: Anniversaries: Empire Day, File 1, 1928–38, and R47/784/1: Relays: St David's Day: From South Africa, 1937–38, *passim*.
11. See Sir Frank Noyce, Deputy Secretary, Government of India, Department of Industries and Labour, to Lionel Fielden, Controller of Broadcasting, Government of India, 25 June 1936 ('we are ... committed to the exclusion of current politics from the microphone'), and subsequent correspondence, BBC WAC R47/853/1: Relays: Talks from Dominions.
12. See BBC WAC BBC Programme Records index, 1929–37.
13. Scannell and Cardiff, *Serving the Nation*, 289. See Lindsay Wellington to J.C. Stobart, 10 Feb. 1931 ('We none of us regard [Empire Day] as a highly important festival nowadays'), BBC WAC R34/213/1.
14. BBC Listener Research report LR/1558, 'The British Empire: Some aspects of public opinion on the British Empire, and in particular, the Colonial Empire (January 1943)', 22 Feb. 1943, BBC WAC Audience Research, Special Reports.
15. The BBC Home Service was inaugurated on 1 Sept. 1939, replacing the two pre-war National and Regional Programmes; it provided a 'mixed' schedule of news, talks, classical and light music, drama and variety. The Forces Programme was launched in Jan. 1940 as a 'light' alternative for the many thousands of servicemen now based in Britain; its preponderance of dance music and variety soon made it the most popular service with civilians as well. It was converted into the General Forces Programme (incorporating the General Overseas Service) in Feb. 1944, aimed at all servicemen overseas as well as home listeners; in 1946 it was relaunched as the new BBC Light Programme. The BBC's Empire Service had been created in 1932, broadcasting in English across five time zones across the globe. In Nov. 1939 it was incorporated into a general comprehensive Overseas Service, including North American, African, Pacific and Eastern Services. See Briggs, *Golden Age*, 369–410, and *War of Words*, 176–78.
16. In one account of listener reaction in Montreal, most of the programme was apparently received with hilarity, and the Canadian extract ('Farmers stood looking over the fields with quiet gaze ...') 'in blushing silence'. C.A.L. Cliffe, Overseas Programme Director (OPD) to Laurence Gilliam, Assistant Director of Features (ADF), 29 Oct. 1939, BBC WAC

R19/302/1–2: Entertainment: The Empire's Answer. The programme's title appears to have caused some confusion, often appearing in correspondence as *The Empire Answers*.

17. Despite regular representations calling for equal recognition of the 'oldest Dominion', the BBC refused to institute a *Calling the Newfoundlanders*. Director of Programme Planning (DPP) to Programme Organiser, 11 June 1940, BBC WAC R34/270/1: Policy: Broadcasts for the Fighting Forces: Dominion Troops 1940–45.

18. See R.G. Wilmot (CBC) to Gladstone Murray (BBC), 7 Aug. 1941, BBC WAC R34/270/1, and Captain Brian Meredith, Broadcasting liaison officer, Canadian Military Headquarters, London, to Godfrey Adams (DPP), 28 Jan. 1944, R34/270/2. For the development of programmes for Dominions forces based in Britain, see files R34/270/1–2, and R51/352: Talks: Newsletters, South Africa, 1942–46.

19. See BBC WAC R19/719: Entertainment: Meet the Empire (Bill and Bob at the BBC), 1940–41, *passim*.

20. See Miss Maxwell (Children's Hour) to Home Presentation, Langham Place, 31 March 1942, BBC WAC R11/43: Children's Hour (Overseas): Hello Parents: Australia, 1942–44. See also R11/12: Children's Hour: Children Calling Home, Australia 1941–43; R11/13 (New Zealand, 1941–50); R11/15 (South Africa, 1941–44). Under the auspices of the Children's Overseas Reception Board around 3,500 children were evacuated overseas: 836 to the USA, 1,532 to Canada, 576 to Australia, 203 to New Zealand, and 353 to South Africa. Only invitations from English-speaking countries were considered. Figures taken from Ruth Inglis, *The Children's War: Evacuation, 1939–1945* (Glasgow, 1990), 105.

21. *The Listener*, 25 July 1940, 115; Imlay Watts to various BBC staff, 16 Aug. 1940, BBC WAC R34/350/1: Policy: Empire, File 1a, 1940–46.

22. See George Barnes, Director of Talks (DT) to Sir Richard Maconachie, Controller (Home) (C(H)), 8 Dec. 1943, and Barnes to Tritton (BBC representative in Australia) and S.J. de Lotbinière, Director of Empire Service (DES) (then in Canada), 15 Oct. 1943, BBC WAC R47/210/1: Relays: Dominion Commentary, File 1, 1943–46.

23. The South African evacuees' parents were apparently 'of a better type altogether'. Miss Maxwell to Ivan Smith, Pacific Service Director (PSD), 12 April 1943, BBC WAC R11/12.

24. Professor W.M. Macmillan to DES, 13 Aug. 1940, BBC WAC R34/350/1. Apparently the second-in-command at South Africa House had been particularly vociferous.

25. BBC Empire Service Papers, No.2, 'The Colonies as "News"', 15 Sept. 1941, BBC WAC R51/91/1: Talks: Colonies and Dominions, File 1a, 1940–42.

26. C.L.F. Rushbrook-Williams, Eastern Service Director, to Assistant Eastern Service Director, 4 Nov. 1941, BBC WAC R34/350/1. Of course, any talk about wool would also have to go through the Ministry of Agriculture (Barnes to Lord Dufferin (MOI), 9 Dec. 1941).

27. Norman Collins, Empire Talks Manager, to J. Grenfell-Williams, African Service Director (ASD), 4 Nov. 1941, BBC WAC R34/350/1; Barnes to Miss Bucknell (Talks Dept.), 19 Oct. 1941, R51/91/1.

28. Barnes to R.B. Pugh (Dominions Office), 4 Oct. 1941, BBC WAC R51/91/1.

29. Nesta Pain (Features and Drama Dept.) to ASD, 30 March 1942; Lotbinière note to ASD, 9 April 1942, BBC WAC R34/350/1.

30. Ivan Smith to R.A. Rendall, Assistant Controller (Overseas Service) (AC(OS)), 3 April 1942, BBC WAC R34/350/1.

31. See Cecil McGivern (Features) to Val Gielgud, Director of Features and Drama, 30 April 1942, BBC WAC R34/213/2, and attached memorandum, 'Kipling', n.d. The quotation is from Lionel Fielden. As the Indian High Commissioner himself pointed out, 'Indians … regard Kipling as the apostle of an Empire founded on the dominance of the white race and the subjection of coloured races' (also quoted in memorandum).

32. AC(OS) to C(OS), 14 May 1942, BBC WAC R34/213/2.

33. Programme Planners Minutes, no.188, 10 July 1942, BBC WAC R51/91/1.

34. DT to C(H), 29 July 1942, BBC WAC R51/91/1. Proposed topics for features (subject to the Department obtaining a clearly defined policy) included a radio portrait of Sir Walter Raleigh ('the first imperialist') by Louis MacNeice, a radio biography of Field Marshal Smuts, a Salute to the Maoris, and 'Flynn of the Flying Doctor Service'. Other themes included 'the unadvertised and positive achievements of Great Britain as a trustee for the subject peoples'

(the Aswan Dam, the fight against malaria, the working of a typical district magistrates court in Africa or Asia), and empire builders (explorers, administrators, missionaries, 'friends of the native'). See ADF to DEP, 5 Aug. 1942, BBC WAC R34/350/1.

35. Rendall, 'Broadcasts about the British Empire', P38/42, 6 Oct. 1942, BBC WAC R51/91/1.
36. 'When that need is felt we shall be only too happy to satisfy it.' Barnes to Rooney Pelletier (CBC liaison), 2 Nov. 1942, BBC WAC R51/91/1.
37. Elspeth Huxley (BBC Colonial Liaison Officer) to Grenfell-Williams, 21 July 1943, BBC WAC R34/350/1.
38. Memo, n.d., (late 1942), BBC WAC R34/350/1, my italics.
39. Macmillan to AC(OS), 10 Nov. 1942, BBC WAC R34/350/1.
40. Gervas Huxley, 'Colonial Publicity in the United Kingdom', n.d. (Dec. 1942), BBC WAC R51/91/1. See also Smyth, 'Britain's African Colonies', 67–71; S. Wolton, *Lord Hailey, the Colonial Office and the Politics of Race and Empire in the Second World War* (Basingstoke, 2000), 123.
41. Barnes to Tritton and Lotbinière, 15 Oct. 1943; Barnes to C(H) 8 Dec. 1943, BBC WAC R47/210/1.
42. Isa Benzie to DT through C.V. Salmon, Assistant Director of Talks (ADT), 18 Nov. 1943 (her emphasis), BBC WAC R47/210/1. She had the South African High Commissioner especially in mind.
43. See Barnes to Lotbinière, 12 Jan. 1944 and *passim*, BBC WAC R47/210/1. The tension between the political and the picturesque was not fully resolved. For instance, the first South African edition, 3 Nov. 1946, by Dr T.W.B. Osborn of Witwatersrand University, received favourable notices, partly for daring to mention South Africa's racial problems, but mostly for its colourful description of gold mining (T.B. Radley memo, 3 Nov. 1946, BBC WAC R47/210/2).
44. Ursula Eason, Northern Ireland Programme Director, to DT, 27 Oct. 1943, BBC WAC R51/60: Talks: Brush Up Your Empire, 1943–44.
45. Another suggested title for the series was George V's reputed last words, 'How is the Empire' – flatly rejected by talks producer Guy Burgess. Addendum to Hilton Brown circular, 21 Oct. 1943, BBC WAC R51/60.
46. Hilton Brown to DT, 2 Nov. 1943, BBC WAC R51/60.
47. Eason to DT, 27 Oct. 1943, and reply 30 Oct., BBC WAC R51/60 – and see Hilton Brown addendum: 'Curious how one *does* forget about Eire being in the Empire'.
48. Hilton Brown to Kenneth Adam (Director of Publicity), 17 Nov. 1943, BBC WAC R51/60. Lady Ranganadhan was in fact an Indian Christian. For more on *Brush Up Your Empire*, see Hajkowski, 'The BBC and Empire', 147–50.
49. See AC(OS) to William Haley, BBC Director-General (DG), 28 Feb. 1944; C(H) to DG, 5 March 1944, BBC WAC R34/350/1.
50. See Miss Maxwell to Presentation Director, 14 March 1944, and DPP to Miss Maxwell, 28 March 1944, BBC WAC R11/43.
51. Macmillan to DT, 26 Nov. 1942, BBC WAC R34/350/1.
52. H.V.L. Swanzey to Peter Pooley, Empire News Talks Editor, 28 Oct. 1942, BBC WAC R34/350/1.
53. Particularly the Australians. See Tritton to Barnes, 14 June 1944, BBC WAC R47/210/1
54. Sabine to Gilliam, 13 Sept. 1941; Huxley, 'Colonial Publicity'; Pelletier to Barnes, 6 Nov. 1942, BBC WAC R51/91/1.
55. Rendall, 'Broadcasts about the British Empire', BBC WAC R51/91/1.
56. Barnes to Tritton and Lotbinière, 15 Oct. 1943, BBC WAC R47/210/1.
57. Grace Wyndham Goldie, *The Listener*, 8 Feb. 1940, 287.
58. See Nicholas, *The Echo of War*, ch.8, *passim*.
59. See S. Nicholas, '"Partners now": Problems in the Portrayal by the BBC of the Soviet Union and USA 1939–45', *Diplomacy and Statecraft*, 3 (1992), 243–71, and *Echo of War*, 163–71; also Ian McLaine, *Ministry of Morale: Home Front Morale and the Ministry of Information in World War II* (London, 1979), ch.7. Special broadcasts included Geoffrey Bridson's, *Stalingrad* (25th anniversary of the Russian Revolution, 1942), 'Ode to the Red Army' by Poet Laureate John Masefield (Red Army Day 1944), and the première of Prokofiev's, *Toast*

to Stalin (Stalin's birthday, Dec. 1944). The first anniversary of the Soviet entry into the war was marked by the première of Shostakovich's, *Leningrad Symphony*. Sunday 7 Nov. 1943 was officially celebrated throughout Britain as the 'Soviet National Day', with the entire following evening on the BBC devoted to broadcasts *In Honour of Russia*.

60. See P.M.H. Bell, *John Bull and the Bear: British Public Opinion, Foreign Policy and the Soviet Union, 1941–45* (London, 1990), esp. ch.3.
61. Briggs, *War of Words*, 410.
62. Barnes to Pelletier, 2 Nov. 1942, BBC WAC R51/91/1.
63. For further discussion see Nicholas, '"Partners now"', and *Echo of War*, 172–79.
64. The BBC made a point of breaking this news to their CBC liaison personally rather than letting them read it first in the press. DPP to Basil Nicolls, Controller (Progammes) 20 March 1943, BBC WAC R34/270/2.

Notes on Contributors

Vivian Bickford-Smith has written extensively on Cape, and especially Cape Town, history. He is the author of *Ethnic Pride and Racial Prejudice in Victorian Cape Town* (1995), and co-author of *Cape Town: The Making of a City* (1998) and *Cape Town in the Twentieth Century* (1999). He teaches at the University of Cape Town.

Carl Bridge is Professor of Australian Studies and Head of the Menzies Centre for Australian Studies, King's College London. His publications include *Holding India to the Empire* (1986), (ed.), *Munich to Vietnam: Australia's Relations with Britain and the United States since the 1930s* (1991), (ed.), *Manning Clark: Essays on his Place in History*, and (ed. with Bernard Attard), *Between Empire and Nation: Australia's External Relations from Federation to the Second World War* (2001).

Phillip Buckner is a Professor Emeritus of the University of New Brunswick and a Senior Research Fellow at the Institute of Commonwealth Studies, University of London.

Lisa Chilton teaches in the History Department at the University of Prince Edward Island.

Stephen Constantine is Senior Lecturer and Head of the History Department at Lancaster University. His current research concerns migration and settlement in the British Empire-Commonwealth and the history of child migration.

Kent Fedorowich is a Senior Lecturer in British Imperial History at the University of the West of England, Bristol. Books include *Unfit for Heroes* (1995), and with Bob Moore, *The British Empire and its Italian Prisoners of War, 1940–47* (2002). He has also edited two collections of essays: one with Bob Moore, *Prisoners of War and their Captors during World War II* (1996); and with Martin Thomas, *International Diplomacy and Colonial Retreat* (2000).

Aled Jones is Sir John Williams Professor of Welsh History at University of Wales, Aberystwyth, and **Bill Jones** is Senior Lecturer in Modern Welsh History at Cardiff University. They are writing histories, respectively, of the Welsh in India and Australia, and co-authored *Welsh Reflections: Y Drych and America, 1851–2001* (2001).

Donal Lowry is Senior Lecturer in History at Oxford Brookes University, and Tutorial Fellow in Modern History, Greyfriars Hall, University of Oxford. He has published articles and essays on various aspects of southern African, British imperial and Irish history, and has edited, and contributed to, *The South African War Reappraised* (2000).

Neville Meaney is an Associate Professor in History at the University of Sydney. His publications include *The Search for Security in the Pacific, 1901–14* (1976), *Australia and the World* (1985), *Fears and Phobias: E.L. Piesse and the Problem of Japan* (1996), and *Japan and Australia's Foreign Policy, 1945–1952* (2000).

Siân Nicholas is lecturer in modern British history at the University of Wales Aberystwyth. Her recent publications include 'Being British: Creeds and Cultures', in K. Robbins (ed.), *The British Isles, 1901–1951* (2002). Her research interests are in media history and wartime national culture.

Simon J. Potter lectures in Imperial History at the National University of Ireland, Galway. His monograph, *News and the British World: The Emergence of an Imperial Press System 1876–1922*, will shortly be published by Oxford University Press.

Ian van der Waag teaches military history in the Faculty of Military Science, University of Stellenbosch (South African Military Academy). While he has published widely on various aspects of Southern African military history, his major research interests fall within the fields of war and societal studies and Anglo-South African relations.

Index